CONTRIBUTIONS FROM THE
MUSEUM OF THE AMERICAN INDIAN
HEYE FOUNDATION
VOL. XXI, PART 1

AMERICAN INDIAN PAINTERS

A Biographical Directory

Compiled by

JEANNE O. SNODGRASS

NEW YORK
MUSEUM OF THE AMERICAN INDIAN
HEYE FOUNDATION
1968

Library of Congress catalog card number 67–27949

Printed in Germany at J. J. Augustin, Glückstadt

Price $ 7.50

71B 614

Dedicated to

Dad and Mother,
and
our Cherokee ancestors

CONTENTS

FOREWORD

A LTHOUGH conventional interest in the American Indian and his cultural activities has tended to revolve around "artifacts"— the familiar objects of stone, wood, hide, clay and shell — a small but enthusiastic group of patrons has long realized the values inherent in the graphic arts of these people. That painting did not enjoy an equal stature in earlier collecting was due in large part to the relative rarity of this art expression as compared with the more numerous productions in the other media, plus the inescapable fact that most of the selective judgment followed European standards and taste. With greater maturity, the art world has increasingly accorded the ethnic artist a status such that today an exhibition of Indian art which does not include painting is rare indeed.

Accompanying this interest in painting has been a growing demand for information relating to the lives of the artists. However, modesty, indifference to these details, and inability to communicate have resulted in a situation in which the most difficult Amerindian research data to obtain today are those facts concerning the careers of artists and craftsmen. It is the purpose of this book to help overcome some of that deficiency.

This volume had its inception in an early meeting with the compiler, then Curator of Indian Art at Philbrook Art Center. During her career at that institution she became acquainted with a large number of artists who regularly participated in the Philbrook Indian Art Annual; as part of her responsibilities she collected a large file of biographical data. When the existence of this rich resource was brought to my attention, we examined the possibility of organizing it for publication. In view of the long-time interest of this Museum, and its own extensive collection of Indian paintings, Mrs. Snodgrass was invited to submit a manuscript for inclusion in our *Contributions* series.

Details of more than 1,100 Indian artists' careers have been located and compiled for this work, making it by far the largest single body of such data. All available information to the time of publication has been included, but it is readily acknowledged that many individuals and facts are missing. Since it is planned to bring this work up-to-date in subsequent revisions, it is the earnest hope of the compiler and this institution that any additional informat ionor corrections of existing data will be forwarded to the undersigned for inclusion.

One of the primary problems in listing these individuals has been that of spelling Indian names. Since all transliterations are basically recorded in a foreign tongue, *i.e.*, that of the White man, the net result has been a variety of forms in which these names have appeared over the years; in many instances the same name appears in several spellings. Even the Indian himself has been guilty of inconsistencies in signing his name to his work, making the task of the student even more difficult. Equally perplexing is the matter of hyphenation — that childish adoption of the 19th Century scribe — which is in itself equally inconsistent. At best, this is an awkward form; at worst, completely erroneous in meaning. As an example, the term *Lóloma* in the Hopi tongue is a one-word concept as well as a proper noun; to spell it *Lo-lo-ma* is just as artificial as to transcribe the common English name *Wil-ker-son*; both lose grace by such rendering. Furthermore, incorrect hyphenation can change meanings, unless the language is well known to the transcriber. It has, therefore, seemed most practical to use the least amount of hyphenation possible; the attempt has been to render Indian words in their meaningful context, rather than to break them into ambiguous fragments. In those instances where the artist *consistently* includes hyphens, the form is retained. This practice has also been followed with regard to the use of separated syllables.

It is clearly recognized that the format will present some problems to the reader. Unfortunately, with so much necessary duplication, printing costs alone made such abbreviation imperative; the forebearance of the reader is solicited.

We join with the compiler of this directory in expressing our most sincere appreciation to those many individuals who have been so helpful in verifying information and supplying many of the facts included herein. It is sincerely hoped that this volume will serve as a further contribution to the establishment of Indian art and the Indian artist in their proper perspectives in the contemporary art world.

October 1968   FREDERICK J. DOCKSTADER
                                                Director

PREFACE

DURING the past ten years, as curator of American Indian art at Philbrook Art Center, I received an increasing number of inquiries for information about Indian artists and it became apparent that a single biographical reference volume would be useful. Since the time that Philbrook had inaugurated the first annual exhibition of Indian art in 1946, elementary biographical files had been established. The need had become so acute that out of a discussion with the Director of the Museum of the American Indian, the possibility arose of publishing a comprehensive volume for use by all those interested in the subject. It was from the records of the artists who submitted their work to this national competition that this compilation was initially organized.

I have attempted to include all Indian painters of whom I had knowledge during the research period from January 1963 through December 1966. Inasmuch as this work records data obtained during this three-year period, it cannot hope to include all worthy individuals nor supply the complete range of achievement for all those who are included.

A total of 1,187 artists are included herein, approximately one-third of whom, or their descendants, have been contacted personally. In addition, 157 public museum holdings and 973 private collections have been indexed. For the most part, sources for collections were derived from the records of artists, collectors, institutions, publications, and sales personnel. Exhibition catalogs aided substantially in verifying tribal affiliations and providing leads for personal contacts. Some addresses may now be outdated, but they have been included to establish the residence of last contact. Failure to locate all the living artists and the unavailability of registrar records from the Indian schools account for most omissions and incompleteness in names and addresses. Any reader who can supply missing or incomplete information concerning the artists listed, is cordially requested to write to The Museum of the American Indian in New York City.

No effort has been made to segregate artists by style. However, it may be of interest to note that of the total number represented, approximately 70 per cent execute a flat, two-dimensional painting style on paper and their preferred medium is a water-base paint or casein. These styles can be defined as traditional, primitive, pictographic (or hide type), European-derived representational, abstract, and symbolic. Inasmuch as the term "traditional" has been affixed to a particular style employed by the larger majority of Indian artists, I also have used this, solely as a convenient frame of reference. A more definitive analysis might also determine the media each artist prefers. This compilation does not do so, simply because it was impossible to examine the work of all artists included. My inquiries were primarily confined to work in paint, crayon, chalk, pencil and ink, executed on paper, canvas, and hide, plus a small sampling of graphic media.

Each artist appears under the name by which he is best known, and cross-filed by any other name he may use. All such secondary names appear in the individual résumés as well. Indian names have been spelled in the manner most often recorded.

The extreme importance of artists, collectors, institutions and exhibitors maintaining adequate art history records cannot be overstressed. It is an all-too-common practice to overlook or ignore completely the value of good, basic record keeping, which should include the artists' tribe, address, schooling, history of participation in exhibits, and sales records. Since many artists have contacted me over the years for record of their own accomplishments, it is an obvious indication that they also maintain few, if any, personal files. It may be of added interest to many artists to note that, unknown to them, their works have been widely exhibited and purchased by institutions and individuals.

It is the hope of the writer that the material included in this volume will provide resources for future research, as well as result in an increased appreciation for and recognition of the important place American Indian painting occupies in our heritage.

Tulsa, Oklahoma   JEANNE O. SNODGRASS
October, 1967

ACKNOWLEDGMENTS

Grateful acknowledgment is extended to the following for their help during the three and one-half years this compilation was being prepared.

To the artists themselves and private collectors, whose patience and generosity with their time made this detailed study possible; to the directors and curators of many museums and historical societies who provided basic lists of acquisitions and often expressed their enthusiasm by volunteering more detailed data; to the literally hundreds of individuals who provided a date, or an address, or even pages of pertinent material for consideration.

Special acknowledgment and thanks go to Dr. Frederick J. Dockstader, Director, Museum of the American Indian, for recognizing the need of this undertaking, extending guidance and constructive criticism, and for assistance and enthusiasm beyond my expectations.

To Dr. Victor C. Hurt, President, Southwestern Art Association; to Dr. Donald G. Humphrey, Director, Philbrook Art Center, for their interest and for giving me access to Philbrook's records; and to the Philbrook staff for their courtesies.

To the late Dr. Oscar B. Jacobson, Professor Emeritus of Art, University of Oklahoma, and his wife, Mrs. Jeanne D'Ucel Jacobson, for compiling lists and granting numerous interviews that provided invaluable data; to Miss Edith Mahier, former professor under Dr. Jacobson at the University, for detailed recordings of her recollections in connection with her work at Oklahoma University; to Mr. Byron Harvey III, Phoenix, Arizona, who provided extensive material on many new-to-the-scene Hopi artists; to Mr. Joe H. Herrera, Santa Fe, New Mexico, who helped me obtain further information on Pueblo and Navaho artists.

To Mr. Maurice DeVinna, Fine Arts Editor, *Tulsa World*, for his files from the Tulsa Art Association's WPA art center, as well as catalogs of early local exhibitions; to Miss Anne Forbes, Cambridge, Massachusetts, Mrs. Dorothy Dunn Kramer, Los Altos, California, Mrs. Karen D. Petersen, St. Paul, Minnesota, and Mrs. Clara Lee Tanner, Tucson, Arizona, for providing research material I could not have obtained without their knowledge and cooperation.

To Mrs. Margaret C. Blaker, Archivist, Office of Anthropology, Smithsonnian Institution; Mr. John C. Ewers, Smithsonian Institution; The Indian Arts and Crafts Board, U.S. Dept. of the Interior; and the Bureau of Indian Affairs, Washington, D.C., for making files available and giving assistance in numerous ways.

To Mrs. Jacques Johnet, Novato, California, for editorial assistance and personal encouragement in the project, and to Mrs. Mary Jane Rutsch, who did the final editing.

To Mr. Charles Stewart, Taos, New Mexico, for courtesies, assistance, and encouragement during an extended research period in that state; Mrs. Bettye Burley, and Miss Mary Leonard, Tulsa, Oklahoma, for assistance in typing and indexing; and to my parents Mr. and Mrs. Chester A. Owens, Muskogee, Oklahoma, for stenographic aid and for their encouragement, particularly during the nearly five months my typewriter was pounding away in their home.

To my husband Tom and son Pat, for their aid in so many ways, and for understanding and encouraging me in this project.

JEANNE O. SNODGRASS

ARTISTS

Aanote (*see* Tohausen)

Abeita, Tom Diego   *Isleta*
  COLLECTIONS: *Private*: Denman.

Abeyta, Augustine   *Tesuque*
  BORN: 1917, Tesuque Pueblo. Son of Julio Abeyta, onetime governor of his
  pueblo and an excellent silversmith, and brother of Crucita, a well-known
  potter.
  EXHIBITIONS: AIEC.
  COLLECTIONS: *Private*: Balph.

Abeyta, Emiliano   *San Juan*
  Sa Pa
  EXHIBITIONS: OU/ET.
  COLLECTIONS: *Public*: MAI, OU/MA. *Private*: Wyman.

Abeyta, Narciso Platero   *Navaho*
  Ha So Deh, Ascending; *Hoskiel*, Forceful.
  BORN: December 15, 1918, Cañoncito, N.M. Son of Narciso Ortize (*sic*)
  Abeyta and Pablita.
  MARRIED: Sylvia Ann, 1953. Three children: Pablita, 1953; Elizabeth, 1954;
  Rosemary, 1960.
  > It is recorded that Abeyta drew his first creations in charcoal on canyon walls.
  > Approximately 32 years later, in 1961, his work was published in *Art in America*.
  > An excellent painter with a unique style, his production has suffered because of
  > shellshock in WWII.
  EDUCATION: Graduated Santa Fe Indian School, 1939; attended Somerset
  Art School near Williamsburg, Pa., summer 1940; attended Ranger Combat
  School, Hawaii, 1943; B.A., New Mexico U., 1953.
  SERVICE: WWII, U.S. Army, four years; participated in invasion of Okinawa
  and Iwo Jima.
  CAREER: Job placement interviewer and workman recruiter in the field,
  New Mexico State Employment Commission, Gallup, N.M., 1953–.
  HONORS: While a student at Santa Fe, he was chosen as one of a small group
  of Indian artists to demonstrate painting at the SFWF; scholarship to
  Stanford U. (army induction prevented acceptance).
  BOOKS ILLUSTRATED: Birney (1935).
  WORK PUBLISHED: Jacobson and D'Ucel (1950), Tanner (1957). *Art in Amer-
  ica* (No. 3, 1961).
  EXHIBITIONS: AIEC, AIM, AIW, BAA, CAI, ITIC, JGS, MAI, MNM, NGA,
  NJSM, OU/ET, OU/MA, PAC, SFWF, SMM, SN.
  AWARDS: Fourteen, including ITIC Grand Award, MNM, SFWF poster
  contest.

COLLECTIONS: *Public*: AU/ASM, MAI, MNM, OU/MA, PAC; Scottsdale (Ariz.) Chamber of Commerce. *Private*: Dietrich, Elkus, Frazier, Lockett, Thoeny.
ADDRESS: 102 Viro Circle, Gallup, N.M.

Able To Stand Up Again (*see* Eckiwaudah, Tennyson)

Acenemah (*see* Zotigh, Barbara Tallamonts)

Acque, Philbert   *Zuni*
EXHIBITIONS: MNM, 1965.
ADDRESS: Box 312, Zuni, N.M.

Adakai, Pat   *Navaho*
BORN: July 7, 1946, Blackrock, N.M.
EDUCATION: Graduated Gallup, 1966.
EXHIBITIONS: NACG; Gallup Public Schools, N.M.
AWARDS: Two from NACG during 1964.
COLLECTIONS: *Private*: Berg.
ADDRESS: Blackrock, N.M.

Adol Beak Ka (*see* Rowell, Charles Emery)

Aguilar, Alfred   *San Ildefonso*
EXHIBITIONS: MNM, 1959; SN, 1963.
ADDRESS: Route 1, Box 318-A, Santa Fe, N.M.

Aguilar, José Angela   *San Ildefonso*
MARRIED: Rosalie Simbola (Picurís). One child: José Vicente Aguilar (*q.v.*).
EXHIBITIONS: JGS, 1955.
COLLECTIONS: *Public*: CU/LMA, DAM, MAI.
ADDRESS: Route 1, Box 317, Santa Fe, N.M.

Aguilar, José Vicente   *San Ildefonso*
Sua Peen, Warm Mountain
BORN: January 8, 1924, San Ildefonso Pueblo, N.M. Son of José Angela Aguilar, *q.v.* (San Ildefonso) and Rosalie Simbola (Picurís). Both parents have exhibited pottery nationally, and his father has exhibited paintings.
MARRIED: Darlene Rose Cordier, 1954. Two daughters: Virginia Susan, 1955; Arlene Joyce, 1957.
  The artist has been actively engaged in art and related subjects since 1944. In 1949, he began his painting experiments in new directions.
EDUCATION: San Ildefonso, 1929–33; Montezuma Boys' School, Los Altos, Calif., 1933–35; Santa Fe, 1935–40; Monson (Mass.) High School, 1941–43; Hollywood High School, Hollywood, Calif., 1943–44; Otis, 1947–49; New Mexico U. and Hill, 1949–50; Los Angeles Trade Technical Junior College, Calif., 1951; Los Angeles County Art Institute, Calif., 1954; Los Angeles Art Center School, 1958–59.
SERVICE: WWII, U.S. Army, two years; European Theater.
CAREER: Technical artist, 1951–. Lockheed Aircraft Corp., Burbank, Calif.; Douglas Aircraft Co., Santa Monica, Calif., 1951–53; North American Aviation, Inc., Los Angeles, Calif., 1954–.

EXHIBITIONS: 1949–64: 31 group exhibitions in museums, art centers, libraries, universities, and Indian ceremonials, including DAM, FAIEAIP, FWG, HM, ITIC, MNM, PAC. *One-man shows*: San Gabriel, Calif. Women's Club, 1952.

AWARDS: 1949–64: 11 from DAM, MNM, PAC; ITIC Grand Award, 1952.

COLLECTIONS: *Public*: DAM, MAI, MNM, PAC, SFRR. *Private*: Adlerblum, H. Cushman, W. Cushman, Denman, Elkus, V. Price, Sheets, Thoeny, Wyman.

ADDRESS: 9682 Mount Barnard Drive, Buena Park, Calif.

Ahgupuk, George Aden *Eskimo*

The artist began to draw while in the hospital recovering from a broken leg (before 1946). His favorite medium is ink and he generally sketches on walrus skin, caribou hide or paper.

EXHIBITIONS: PAC, USDS.

COLLECTIONS: *Public*: IACB, MAI. *Private*: Elkus.

ADDRESS: Box 134, Anchorage, Alaska.

Ahhajumba (*see* Anderson, Jimmy)

Ahmehate (*see* Goodbear, Paul J.)

Ah Quade (*see* Alberty, Dewey)

Ahsey Sututut (*see* Jake, Albin Roy)

Ahsit (Also known as White Man and Whiteman.) *Southern Cheyenne*

BORN: *ca.* 1851.

The artist was among the 72 Plains Indians taken as prisoners from Fort Sill, Okla., to Fort Marion, St. Augustine, Fla., in 1875. After prison and government schooling, he returned to Oklahoma in 1880.

CAREER: Earned money by executing pictographic drawings on fans during years in prison and school.

COLLECTIONS: *Public*: AMNH, HI, YU/BRBML.

Akima, Calvin *Hopi*

COLLECTIONS: *Public*: SM.

Alberty, Dewey *Cherokee*

Ah Quade, Limping

BORN: March 17, 1926, Sand Springs, Okla.

MARRIED: Maggie Proctor. Four children: Sue Ann, Ann Sue, James, David.

EDUCATION: Graduated Chilocco, 1947; Bacone College, 1949; University of Oklahoma, 1953.

SERVICE: WWII and Korean War, U.S. Navy, five years.

CAREER: Employed by American Airlines, Tulsa, Okla., and paints intermittently, 1950–.

ADDRESS: 1632 South Cincinnati, Tulsa, Okla.

Allen, Mary *Navaho*

EDUCATION: Santa Fe, *ca.* 1938.

EXHIBITIONS: AIW.

Al Qua Kou (*see* Toppah, Herman)

Aluh Hochi (*see* Toledo, José Rey)

Always Prepared (*see* Zotigh, Barbara Tallamonts)

1*

American Horse   *Oglala Sioux*
Wasechun Tashunka

BORN: Date unknown. From Pine Ridge area. Killed at Slim Buttes, S. Dak.,
1875. His father was Sitting Bear and his father-in-law, Red Cloud (Cheyenne).
There were two men by the name of American Horse. *See* Hyde (1937).

American Horse asserted that the Oglala Winter Count in his possession was
started by his grandfather and continued by his father and himself. It contained
104 pictographic drawings and covered the period from 1775 to 1879. Cloud Shield
(*q.v.*) made copies of this Count.

HONORS: Appointed chief of the Smoke People by Indian Agent McGillicuddy; later became chief of the True Oglala Band; signed the land agreement of 1889.

WORK PUBLISHED: Ewers (1939), Jacobson and D'Ucel (1950). *BAE, 4th AR.*
COLLECTIONS: *Public*: AMNH, OAA/SI, OU/SM. (The last is a buffalo robe
illustrating the artist's personal combats during the period *circa* 1870–80;
this work is variously attributed to American Horse and to his nephew.)

Amiotte, Arthur Douglas   *Oglala Sioux*
Warpa Tanka Kuciyela, Low Black Bird

BORN: March 25, 1942, Pine Ridge, S. Dak. Son of Walter Douglas Amiotte
(Oglala Sioux) and Olive Louise Mesteth (Oglala Sioux). M/GGF: Standing
Bear (*q.v.*) (Miniconjou Sioux). M/GGM: Louise Renick, the nurse whom
Standing Bear married in 1886 during a tour of Europe with Buffalo Bill's
Wild West Show. P/GGGF: Antoine Janis, one of the first fur traders in
the upper Missouri River area. P/GGF: Steven Amiotte, an Indian trader.
P/GGM: Zohy Labuff, daughter of an Indian trader.

MARRIED: Amelia Sue Wohlers, August 8, 1964.

With his mother and stepfather, George A. Erring (Hunkpapa Sioux), the
artist moved to Custer, S. Dak., in 1946. While a sophomore at Northern State,
he became acquainted with Oscar Howe (*q.v.*), who introduced him to Indian
art. Although he paints in the flat manner, he has developed a style bordering
on cubism.

EDUCATION: Graduated Custer (S. Dak.) High School, 1960; attended
Institute; studied under Oscar Howe at University of South Dakota, summer,
1961; B.S., Northern State, 1964.

CAREER: Painter, lecturer, and teacher. Art instructor, Woodrow Wilson
High School, Sioux City, Iowa, September 1964–. His current lectures are
"Awareness Sioux Indian" and "Contemporary Indian Art," each having
the purpose of revealing Sioux history, legends, lore, and religious beliefs.

HONORS: Four-year South Dakota Indian Scholarship; four-year BIA
Scholarship Grant; C.A. Schwarz Art Education Scholarship; Σ T Δ, National
Honor English Fraternity; K Δ Π, National Honor Education Society;
Φ Δ K, International Men's Professional Educators Fraternity; represented
in *Who's Who in American Universities and Colleges*, 1963–64.

EXHIBITIONS BIA/A, BNIAS, FNAIC, PAC, USDI; Northern State Teachers College, Dakota Hall Gallery; University of South Dakota, William
H. Over Gallery; Sioux City (Iowa) Art Center. *One-man shows*: BIA/A;
Dakota Hall Gallery, Presentation Junior College, Aberdeen Civic Auditorium, S. Dak.

AWARDS: Five during 1963–64.

COLLECTIONS: *Public*: BIA/A, IACB; Northern State Teachers College; William H. Over Gallery; Office of Senator George McGovern, Washington, D.C. *Private*: O. Anderson, Burgess, P. Corwin, Hanson, Jasinsky, Lee, Pederson, Schwarz, O. Scott.

ADDRESS: 504 38th Street Place, Sioux City, Iowa.

Anasteen   *Navaho*
COLLECTIONS: *Public*: MAI.

Anderson, Jimmy   *Creek*
Ahhajumba, Sweet Potato (clan name)
BORN: August 14, 1932, Kansas City, Mo.
EDUCATION: Haskell; Bacone College; Central State College; University of Oklahoma.
CAREER: One-time singer with the Indian quartet, "Osceola Four"; recording artist with Spike Jones Band. Currently active in Christian religious work.
EXHIBITIONS: AIE, JGS, PAC.
AWARDS: 1954–57: six from AIE, PAC.
COLLECTIONS: *Public*: PAC. *Private*: Birchmore.
ADDRESS: Navaho Baptist Mission, Fruitland, N.M.

Andrews, William A.   ?
EXHIBITIONS: MNM, 1965.
AWARDS: MNM, 1965.
ADDRESS: Box 299, Mesilla, N.M.

Anko   *Kiowa*
Ankopaaingyadete, In The Middle Of Many Tracks (Also known as Aunko.)
BORN: Date unknown; died "early in the 20th century."
MARRIED: Bainmi, GA of Charles E. Rowell (*q.v.*).

Anko kept a Kiowa pictographic calendar, originally on brown wrapping paper and representing the years from 1863–64 to 1884–85. One copy was made for Gen. Hugh L. Scott before 1900 and is recorded as being at the Smithsonian Institution, although it cannot be located. Another calendar for the same years, executed in black pencil and kept in a notebook, is attributed to the artist. A copy was reportedly made on buckskin in the 1890's for James Mooney, and Charles E. Rowell has also reproduced it.

WORK PUBLISHED: La Farge (1956). Mayhall (1962). *BAE, 17th AR*.
COLLECTIONS: *Public*: OA/USNM (?). *Private*: R. Hall. (As a young child, Mrs. Hall watched her grandfather, Anko, work on the canvas calendar now in her possession.)

Ankopaaingyadete (*see* Anko)

Annnanooruk (*see* Immana, Annie Weokluk)

Anquoe, Evans   *Kiowa*
COLLECTIONS:: *Private*: Deupree.

Antelope, Louis   *Flathead*
COLLECTIONS: *Public*: CCHM.

Antelope, W.   *Cheyenne*
COLLECTIONS: *Public*: ACM.

Apache Man (*see* Williams, David Emmett)

Apie Begay (*see* Begay, Apie)

Apomonu   *San Ildefonso*
COLLECTIONS: *Public*: SM.

Apowmuckcon (*see* Racine, Albert Batiste)

Aquino, Frank   *San Juan*
EDUCATION: Albuquerque, 1962–63.
EXHIBITIONS: School-sponsored exhibitions and local Indian functions.
ADDRESS: c/o Albuquerque Indian School, Albuquerque, N.M.

Aquino, Juan B.   *San Juan*
Shaking Eagle Tail
EDUCATION: Bacone College.
EXHIBITIONS: MNM, PAC.
AWARDS: PAC.
COLLECTIONS: *Public*: MNM.
ADDRESS: Box 861, San Juan Pueblo, N.M.

Aquino, Robert   *San Juan*
EDUCATION: Santa Fe, *ca.* 1960.
EXHIBITIONS: MNM, PAC.
AWARDS: MNM, 1958.
COLLECTIONS: *Public*: MNM. *Private*: Long.
ADDRESS: San Juan Pueblo, N.M.

Aragon, Ralph   *San Felipe*
BORN: 1944, Algadones, N.M.
EDUCATION: Institute, 1965–66.
EXHIBITIONS: SAIEAIP, YAIA.

Archilta, Clara   *Kiowa-Apache*
BORN: September 26, 1912, Tonkawa, Okla. Daughter of David Williams
(Tonkawa) and Helen Sunrise (Kiowa-Apache).
MARRIED: Widowed, 1956. Six children: Roger P. Williams, 1930; Maxie
Williams, 1939; Leatrice J. Archilta, 1941; Arliss F. Archilta, 1943; Walsie
B. Archilta, 1946; Roselene Archilta, 1949.
> Although handicapped by a severely injured arm, Mrs. Archilta began to paint
> in 1957 and was selling her work shortly afterward. She has had no formal art
> training but received encouragement from Mrs. Susie Peters and Mrs. Catherine
> Cochran, Indian Welfare Service workers.

EDUCATION: Boone School, Apache, Okla.; Chilocco, two years; schooling
through the eighth grade.
CAREER: Part-time guide, Indian City U.S.A., Anadarko, Okla.
WORK PUBLISHED: Program cover, Oklahoma Health and Welfare Admin-
istration, November, 1959.
EXHIBITIONS: AIE, PAC.
AWARDS: Four from AIE, 1961.
COLLECTIONS: *Public*: BIA/D (Department of Welfare); Department of
Public Welfare, Anadarko, Okla.
ADDRESS: Route 2, Apache, Okla.

Archuleta, Antonio   *Taos*
BORN: Date unknown; deceased.
COLLECTIONS: *Public*: MNM

Archuleta, Betty Keener   *Cherokee*
Qued
BORN: May 22, 1928, Pawhuska, Olka. M/GGF: George Butler (Cherokee), active in tribal affairs.
MARRIED: Marcos Lawrance Archuleta, 1953.
  Although Mrs. Archuleta first showed an interest in drawing at the age of five, she did not start painting until 1961.
EDUCATION: Dord Fitz School of Art, Woodward, Okla., 1961–.
CAREER: Housewife. Active in local art club.
EXHIBITIONS: ITIC, MNM; Lil-Red School, Shattuck, Okla.; Enid, Okla.; Spearman, Tex.; Amarillo, Tex.; Liberal, Kan.; New York, N.Y.; Woodward County Fair, Woodward, Okla.
AWARDS: 1962–63: eight ribbons from Woodward County Fair.
COLLECTIONS: *Private*: Killebrew, Marken, Mercado, H. Roberts, Stiglets.
ADDRESS: 1207 Sixth Street, Woodward, Okla.

Archuleta, Trinidad   *Taos*
COLLECTIONS: *Public*: MNM.

Arkeketa, Benjamin   *Oto-Missouri*
Ark Kaketa, Waiting Up
BORN: February 27, 1928, Red Rock, Okla. Son of George B. Arkeketa (Oto-Missouri) and Edna Jones (Oto-Missouri). P/GF: Benjamin Arkeketa. P/GGF: George (Bushy Tail) Arkeketa, Oto chief of the Buffalo Clan and medicine man. P/GA: Mary Arkeketa Thompson, daughter of Arkeketa, the last Oto chief.
MARRIED: Mary Freeman (Creek), 1953. Five daughters: Susan, 1955; Janice, 1956; Kim, 1957; Annette, 1959, Ginger, 1960.
  Inspired by Brummett Echohawk and Acee Blue Eagle (*qq.v.*), the artist has received several award ribbons. His paintings often reflect his strong interest in Indian archaeology and ethnology, and in Christian philosophy.
EDUCATION: Oklahoma Public Schools; X-Ray Technician Certificate, 1954, from St. John's Hospital, Tulsa, Okla.
SERVICE: Korean War, U.S. Marine Corps, four years.
CAREER: X-Ray Technician, Clinton (Okla.) State Hospital, 1955–1965; Tulsa (Okla.) Hospital, 1965–.
EXHIBITIONS: SN; Ponca Indian Free Fair, Ponca City, Okla.; Public Library, Clinton, Okla.; Henson Gallery, Yukon, Okla.
COLLECTIONS: *Private*: Curlechief, Fisher, Sukman.
ADDRESS: 11608 West 32nd St., Sand Springs, Okla.

Ark Kaketa (*see* Arkeketa, Benjamin)

Armstrong, Tirador   *Cheyenne-Caddo*
BORN: May 8, 1935, Clinton, Okla.
MARRIED: Dola Jean Tartsah (Kiowa), 1961.
  Encouraged, as many Plains Indian artists, by Mrs. Susie Peters, Mr. Armstrong has been interested in art since elementary school.

EDUCATION: Attended Concho.
SERVICE: WWII, U.S. Marine Corps, three years.
EXHIBITIONS: AAIE; Baltimore, Md.
AWARDS: Several honorable mentions.
COLLECTIONS: *Public*: OHSM. *Private*: Beebe, Peters, C. West, E. Wilson.
ADDRESS: 820 North 20th St., Clinton, Okla.

Arqurero, Avelino   *Cochiti*
EDUCATION: Santa Fe, *ca.* 1938.
EXHIBITIONS: AIW.

Asah, Spencer   *Kiowa*
Lallo, Little Boy
BORN: *ca.* 1905–10, near Carnegie, Okla. Died in 1954, Norman, Okla. Son
of a Buffalo medicine man.
MARRIED: Ida (Comanche). Three children: Ola Mae, Ida L., and Kay, a son
killed in 1953.
   Asah grew up in an atmosphere of tribal legends and rituals, the influence of
   which is evident in his paintings. Asah is one of the original Five Kiowas (*q.v.*).
EDUCATION: Government Indian schools through the sixth grade; St.
Patrick's Mission School, Anadarko, Okla.; University of Oklahoma, special
non-credit classes, 1926–27.
CAREER: Artist and farmer.
HONORS: Represented in *Indians of Today*.
COMMISSIONS: *Murals*: OHSM, OU; St. Patrick's Mission School; Federal
Building, Anadarko, Okla.; Fort Sill Indian School.
WORK PUBLISHED: Jacobson (1929), Jacobson and D'Ucel (1950), Blue
Eagle (1959). *Introduction to American Indian Art* (1931), *The American
Magazine of Art* (August 1932).
EXHIBITIONS: AIE, AIEC, EITA, OU/MA, PAC.
COLLECTIONS: *Public*: ACM, DAM, GM, MAI, MKMcNAI, MNA/KHC,
MNM, OSAF/GC, OU/MA, SPL. *Private*: Denman, O. Jacobson.

Asaute (*see* Keahbone, George Campbell)

Asawoya (*see* Davis, Jesse Edwin, II)

Ascending (*see* Abeyta, Narciso Platero)

Atencio, Gilbert Benjamin   *San Ildefonso*
Wah Peen, Mountain of the Sacred Wind
BORN: 1930, Greeley, Colo. Son of Isabel M. Montoya (San Ildefonso) (*q.v.*).
M/GA: María Martínez, San Ildefonso potter. M/U: Alfred Montoya (*q.v.*).
   Atencio's strong sense of family and tribal responsibility has resulted in his
   seldom venturing from his native pueblo. He has recently experimented with
   adaptations of his flat-style paintings.
EDUCATION: San Ildefonso; graduated Santa Fe, 1947.
CAREER: Artist.
HONORS: Governor of San Ildefonso Pueblo, 1966.
WORK PUBLISHED: Jacobson and D'Ucel (1950), Tanner (1957). *Arizona
Highways* (August 1952), *Smoke Signals*, IACB (No. 42, 1964), *Southwest
Indian Arts II*, CPLH (1965).

EXHIBITIONS: AU/ASM, CPLH, FAIEAIP, FWG, HM, ITIC, JGS, NGA, OU, OU/ET, PAC, PAC/T. SN, USDS, WRNGA; 26 other leading museums and galleries in North America.

AWARDS: Seventeen top awards by 1949, including ITIC Grand Award; 12 during 1950–64, including PAC Grand Award.

COLLECTIONS: *Public*: AF, BIA, GM, IACB, LNBTC, MAI, MNM, PAC. *Private*: E. Adkins, Denman, Dietrich, Elkus, A. Forbes, Lockett, D. Maxwell, Mullan, W. S. Price, Schonwald, Thoeny.

ADDRESS: Rural Route 1, Box 306, Santa Fe, N.M.

Atencio, John   *San Juan*

EDUCATION: Institute, 1965–66.

EXHIBITIONS: YAIA.

Atencio, Lorencita   *San Juan*

T'o Pove

Until 1950, Lorencita Atencio was an active artist. Since she has become the mother of several children, she has seldom painted.

EDUCATION: Santa Fe, under Dorothy Dunn.

CAREER:: Crafts instructor at Santa Fe and Albuquerque.

WORK PUBLISHED: La Farge (1960).

EXHIBITIONS: AIW, NGA, 1953; OU/ET.

COLLECTIONS: *Private*: Dietrich.

Atencio, Pat   *San Ildefonso*

Koo Peen, Mountain Rock

BORN: January 22, 1932. Son of Isabel M. Montoya (San Ildefonso), and brother of Gilbert and Tony Atencio *(qq. v.)*.

Pat has painted infrequently in recent years. He lives at the pueblo with his six children.

EDUCATION: Santa Fe.

COLLECTIONS: *Public*: MAI, MNM.

ADDRESS: Rural Route 1, Box 306, Santa Fe, N.M.

Atencio, Tony   *San Ildefonso*

Su Ta, Painted Arrow

BORN: January 24, 1928. Son of Isabel M. Montoya (San Ildefonso), and brother of Gilbert and Pat Atencio *(qq.v.)*.

Tony painted only animals while he was in school. Since then, he has painted very little. Most of his adult life has been spent in the Navy. Now out of the service, he hopes to attend a vocational training school.

EDUCATION: Santa Fe through the eleventh grade, *ca.* 1945.

SERVICE: U.S. Navy, 1945–61.

EXHIBITIONS: ITIC, MNM, NMSF.

ADDRESS: Rural Route 1, Box 306, Santa Fe, N.M.

Auchiah, James   *Kiowa*

BORN: 1906, near Medicine Park, Okla. GF: Chief Satanta (Kiowa). GF: Red Tipi (Kiowa), a medicine man and tribal artist.

Although not officially one of the Five Kiowas *(q.v.)*, he joined the group in their special classes at the University of Oklahoma in the fall of 1927.

SERVICE: WWII, U.S. Coast Guard.

CAREER: Part-time employee, U.S. Army Artillery and Missile Center Museum, Fort Sill, Okla.; civilian employee in Fort Sill painting shop.
HONORS: Certificate of Appreciation, IACB, 1966.
COMMISSIONS: *Murals*: OHSM, USDI; Fort Sill Indian School; Northeastern State College; St. Patrick's Mission School; Muskogee Federal Building, Muskogee, Okla.
WORK PUBLISHED: Jacobson (1929), Jacobson and D'Ucel (1950). *The Art Digest* (September 1, 1931), *The American Magazine of Art* (August 1932), *American Indian Exposition and Congress* (Tulsa: Chamber of Commerce, 1937), cover.
EXHIBITIONS: Throughout the U.S. in the 1930's; AIW, EITA, OU/ET, PAC/T.
AWARDS: Southwest States Indian Art Show, Santa Fe, N.M., 1930; ITIC.
COLLECTIONS: *Public*: ACM, FSM, GM, MAI, MKMcNAI, MNM, OHSM, OSAF/GC, OU/MA, PAC, SI; Castillo de San Marcos National Monument, St. Augustine, Fla. *Private*: Cone, Denman, Elkus, Field, O. Jacobson, D. Maxwell.
ADDRESS: Carnegie, Okla.

Augustine, Jimmie   *Navaho*
EXHIBITIONS: SN.
AWARDS: SN, 1964.

Aukemah (*see* García, María)

Aukemah (*see* Terasaz, Marian)

Aunko (*see* Anko)

Aun So Te (*see* Belindo, Dennis)

Austin, Frank   *Navaho*
Bahah Zhonie, Happy Boy
BORN: April 10, 1938, Tsegi Canyon, near Tonalea, Ariz. Son of Buck Austin (Navaho) and Martha (Navaho).
MARRIED: Rose L. Adajie, 1960. Two children: Camellia Rose, 1961; Dwayne, 1964.
  Although he has been interested in art for as long as he can recall, it was in 1954 that Austin, encouraged by Lloyd H. New, began to express himself as a creative artist.
EDUCATION: Elementary school, Tuba City, Ariz.; graduated Phoenix, 1958. Attended Arizona S.C./T.; four summers of special classes, University of Arizona, Tucson, Ariz.
CAREER: Silk screen designer and textile painter, 1956–.
HONORS: International Design Award, American Institute of Interior Designers, 1962; scholarship to University of Arizona, "Southwest Indian Art Project."
EXHIBITIONS: 1961–65: AIAE/WSU, ASF, ITIC, SN, regional galleries and fairs.
AWARDS: Seven during 1961–65, including SN Grand Award.
COLLECTIONS: *Public*: IACB, MAI. *Private*: Bimson, Elkus, Thoeny.
ADDRESS: 1729½ East Second Street, Santa Fe, N.M.

Au Tup Ta (*see* Hood, Rance)

Awa Tsireh   *San Ildefonso*
  Awa Tsireh, Cattail Bird (Also known as Roybal, Alfonso.)
  BORN: *ca.* 1895; died *ca.* 1955. Nephew of Crescencio Martinez (*q.v.*).
    By 1917, Alice Corbin Henderson had commissioned the artist to execute paint-
    ings for her. Later, although without formal education beyond the primary
    grades, Awa Tsireh painted daily with Fred Kabotie (*q.v.*) and Velino Shije
    Herrera (*q.v.*) at the School of American Research, without outside influences.
    On September 6, 1925, the following appeared in the *New York Times:* "Awa
    Tsireh's drawings are, in their own field, as precise and sophisticated as a Persian
    miniature. The technique that has produced pottery designs as perfect as those
    of an Etruscan vase has gone into his training."
    The *St. Louis Post Dispatch* of November 5, 1933, quoting John Sloan, said:
    "...when Awa Tsireh sits down to paint a leaping deer he remembers not only
    the way a deer looks when leaping over a log but he feels himself leaping in the
    dance, with antlers swaying on his forehead and two sticks braced in hands for
    forelegs."
    Later, he turned, for a time, to silversmithing and various jobs unrelated to art.
    "Because of his poor eyesight, shaky hands, and other personal reasons, this
    famous artist abandoned painting almost completely although there continued
    to be a demand for his work" (*El Palacio*, August 1950).
  EDUCATION: San Ildefonso.
  HONORS: Palmes d'Académiques, 1954.
  WORK PUBLISHED: Alexander (1932), Jacobson and D'Ucel (1950), Josephy
  (1961). *International Studio* (March 1922), *American Magazine of Art* (Sep-
  tember 1928; August 1932), *Travel* (1931), *Exposition of Inter-Tribal Arts,
  Inc.* (December 1931), cover, *Theatre Arts Monthly* (August 1933), *Cincin-
  nati Art Museum, Bulletin* (January, 1938), *Arizona Highways* (August
  1952), *El Palacio* (1956), *Paintings by American Indians*, CPLH (1962).
  EXHIBITIONS: ACC, EITA, JGS, NGA, OU/ET, PAC, SI; Newberry Library,
  Chicago, Ill., 1925; Society of Independent Artists, New York, N.Y., *ca.*
  1918, entered by John Sloan.
  AWARDS: AIM; AIW; EITA, first award and his painting reproduced on
  cover of exhibit's publication.
  COLLECTIONS: *Public*: AF, AMNH, BM/B, CAM, CGA, CGFA, CIS, DAM
  (42 works), DCC, MAI, MAM, MMA, MNA/KHC, MNM, MRFM, OU/MA,
  PAC, RM, SHSW, SI, SM, WRNGA. *Private*: H. Adams, Adlerblum, Den-
  man, Dietrich, Dockstader, Elkus, Hogue, Lockett, Thoeny, Walch, Waters,
  Wyman.

Ayawat, William   *Comanche*
    The artist was among the 72 Plains Indians taken as prisoners from Fort Sill,
    Okla., to Fort Marion, St. Augustine, Fla., in 1875.
  COLLECTIONS: *Public*: Castillo de San Marcos National Monument, St. Augustine, Fla.

Baby (*see* Collins, Martha Adele)

Baca, Henry   *Santa Clara*
  Okuwasta
  BORN: Date unknown; deceased.
  COLLECTIONS: *Public*: MNM (dated 1936).

Backford, Alexandra   *Aleut*
BORN: Alaska.
EDUCATION: Institute, *ca.* 1954.
EXHIBITIONS: FAIEAIP.
AWARDS: MNM, 1965.
COLLECTIONS: *Public*: IACB.

Back Track (*see* Geionety, George)
Bad Hand Boy (*see* Claymore, Thomas William)
Bad Heart Buffalo (*see* Bad Heart Buffalo, Amos)

Bad Heart Buffalo, Amos (Also known as Bad Heart Bull)   *Oglala Sioux*
Tatanka Cante Sice, Bad Heart Buffalo
BORN: *ca.* 1869; died, 1913. Son of Tatanka Cante Sice (Bad Heart Buffalo),
Oglala warrior and participant in the Battle of Little Big Horn. Nephew of
He Dog, a Sioux chief.
> From the stories told him by his father and uncle, the artist filled three army
> ledgers with detailed pictographic drawings of the Battle of the Little Big Horn.
> (At the time of the battle, he was seven.) Alexander (1938) wrote that this artist
> was the "most notable northern Indian artist whose work is known."
CAREER: Cowboy, Indian policeman.
WORK PUBLISHED: Alexander (1938), Jacobson and D'Ucel (1950), Josephy
(1961a), Sandoz (1961), Blish (1967).
COLLECTIONS: *Public*: The University of Nebraska Press, Lincoln, Neb.

Bad Heart Bull, Amos (*see* Bad Heart Buffalo, Amos)

Badonie, Thomas   *Navaho*
EDUCATION: Received scholarship to Arizona, "Southwestern Indian Art
Project," summer, 1961.

Bahah Zhonie (*see* Austin, Frank)

Bahe, Stanley K.   *Navaho*
EDUCATION: Attended Phoenix.
EXHIBITIONS: PAC.

Ball, Lois Harjo   *Creek*
BORN: Okmulgee, Okla. Her mother was related to the Paddy Carr family,
well known in Creek history. GF: Menawa, Creek chief and warrior.
EDUCATION: Graduated from Okmulgee High School, Okmulgee, Okla.,
1926; attended Oklahoma C.U.; A.A., Stephens College, Columbia, Mo.;
private study under Minta B. Walker.
COLLECTIONS: *Public*: CCHM.

Ballard, Louis Wayne   *Quapaw-Cherokee*
Honganozhe, Grand Eagle
BORN: July 8, 1931, Quapaw, Okla. Son of Charles G. Ballard (Cherokee)
and Leona Quapaw (Quapaw). Reared by M/GM, Newakis Quapaw, interpreter for the Quapaw Indian Agency. P/GGF: Joel B. Mayes, a Cherokee
chief. M/GGF: Pius Quapaw, Quapaw medicine chief.
MARRIED: Delores Lookout (Osage), 1954. Divorced January, 1964. Three
children: Louis Anthony, 1954; Anne Marie, 1956; Charles Christopher,
1957. Married Ruth Dorè, 1965.

Although active in the visual arts early in his career, Mr. Ballard's primary interest now is confined to music.

EDUCATION: Graduated Bacone College High School, 1949; A.A., Northeastern A.M., 1951; Oklahoma, 1950; B.A. and B. Mus. Ed., 1954, and M.M., 1962, Tulsa; Darius Milhaud School of Music, Aspen, Colo., 1963.

CAREER: Music teacher, Tulsa Public Schools, 1956–58; draftsman and illustrator, Tulsa, 1958–61; Chairman, Music and Drama Dept., Institute of American Indian Arts, 1962–.

HONORS: F. B. Parriott Graduate Fellowship, 1961; Φ Γ Κ; presented a lecture tour of Switzerland, sponsored by USDS and Jelmoli, Inc., 1964.

EXHIBITIONS: AIE, BC, NAMC, PAC.

COLLECTIONS: *Public*: EOC, KM, OU, PAC.

ADDRESS: c/o Institute of American Indian Arts, Santa Fe, N.M.

Bark Dye (*see* Moses, James Kivetoruk)

Battese, Stanley   *Navaho*
Kehdoyah, Follower

BORN: January 29, 1936, Fort Defiance, Ariz. Son of Charlie Smith (Navaho) and Gee Eh Bah (Navaho), who live on the reservation near Pine Springs, Ariz. The artist was adopted by Anthony Battese (Potawatomi) and Josephine Bruner Battese (Creek-Shawnee).

Battese began painting at an early age and made remarkable progress during his school years. Since his university graduation, however, he appears to have lost interest in painting and exhibiting.

EDUCATION: Flagstaff Public School, Wondow Rock School, Ariz.; graduated from St. Michaels Catholic High School, St. Michaels, Ariz., 1956; B.A., Arizona S.C./T., 1961.

CAREER: Arts and crafts teacher, Shiprock Junior High School, Shiprock, N.M., 1962; teacher in adult education program, White Cone Day School, White Cone, Ariz., 1962; warehouse employee, Navaho Tribal Sawmill, 1962–63; carpenter, Ciniza Refinery, Gallup, N.M., 1963; welder, Steel Tank Construction Co. of Houston, 1963; gas department, Navaho Tribal Utilities Authority, Window Rock, Ariz., 1964.

COMMISSIONS: *Murals*: Hayden Hall, T K E Fraternity House, Arizona S.C./T.

WORK PUBLISHED: Tanner (1957). *Arizona Highways* (July 1956).

EXHIBITIONS: GCIC, ITIC, MNM/T, NTF, PAC; Concord Art Association, Concord, Mass.; DAR Exhibit, Greenwich, Conn.; Riverside Art Center, Riverside, Calif.; Charles Reynolds Gallery, Taos, N.M.; Valley National Bank, Phoenix, Ariz.; National High School Art Exhibit, Carnegie.

AWARDS: Nineteen during 1952–57.

COLLECTIONS: *Private*: R. Moore, Mullan, Thoeny.

ADDRESS: 1611 Red Rock Drive, Gallup, N.M.

Bear (*see* Robinson, John)

Bear, J. Michael (*see* Byrnes, James Michael)

Bear, James (*see* Byrnes, James Michael)

Bear, Jobie (*see* Byrnes, James Michael)

Bear Claw (*see* Byrnes, James Michael)

Bear Feathers (*see* Bushyhead, Allan)

Beard, Lorenzo   *Cheyenne-Arapaho*
Horse Chief
BORN: 1914.
EDUCATION: Concho; graduated Santa Fe.
WORK PUBLISHED: La Farge (1956).
EXHIBITIONS: AIEC, NGA, OU/ET.
COLLECTIONS: *Public*: OU/MA, SM. *Private*: Denman, Dietrich.
ADDRESS: Box 232, Watonga, Okla.

Bear's Arm, Martin   *Mandan*
Bear's Arm, considered a tribal historian, executed a pictographic chart on heavy
canvas long before the late 1890's. The drawings represent the Like-a-Fish-Hook
Village on the Ft. Berthold Reservation in central North Dakota.
COLLECTIONS: *Public*: SHSND.

Bear's Face   *Sioux*
COLLECTIONS: *Public*: MPM (pictograph on paper).

Bear's Heart, James   *Cheyenne* or *Kiowa*
The artist was among the 72 Plains Indians taken as prisoners from Fort Sill,
Okla., to Fort Marion, St. Augustine, Fla., in 1875.
WORK PUBLISHED: National Museum of Canada, *Bulletin No. 163* (Ottawa).
COLLECTIONS: *Public*: HI, MAI, MHS/B, OA/USNM, YU/BRBML.
Private: R. Robinson, Rodee.

Beatien Yazz (Also known as Jimmy Toddy.)   *Navaho*
Beatien Yazz (*Bea Etin Yazz*), Little No Shirt
BORN: March 5, 1928, near Wide Ruins, Ariz.
MARRIED: Elizabeth Roan (Navaho). Divorced. Five children: Irvin, 1951;
Marvin, 1952; Calvin, 1959; Velma, 1955; Jan, 1957.
The artist was drawing with crayons at eight years of age. Sallie and Bill Lipin-
cott, operators of the Wide Ruins Trading Post, influenced him most by recognizing and encouraging his talents. While still a student, he sometimes worked in
oils from a model. Today, Jimmy prefers to paint "animals and people, not landscapes" in the casein medium. *Spin a Silver Dollar* and *Paint the Wind* together
provide an insight into the young artist's struggles and pleasures and the particular situations and individuals that have helped to shape his career.
EDUCATION: Wide Ruins Day School; Santa Fe, two years; Fort Wingate,
three years; Sherman, one year; schools in Stewart, Nev., two years; Mills,
1949, under Yasuo Kuniyoshi.
SERVICE: WWII, U.S. Marine Corps, two years; South Pacific and China
Theaters (Navaho code unit).
CAREER: Navaho Police Dept., Fort Defiance, Ariz.; art teacher, Carson
Indian School; full-time artist.
HONORS: Received scholarship to Mills; two books by Alberta Hannum are
based on his life and career.
COMMISSIONS: *Murals*: Navaho Tribal Court Room, Navaho Police Head-
quarters Building, Fort Defiance, Ariz. *Tiles*: Gila Pottery, designs. *Fabric*:
Tumble-weed Prints, designs. *Greeting Cards*: Reproduction of the artist's
designs by several companies.

BOOKS ILLUSTRATED: Hannum (1945; 1958), Steiner (1961).
WORK PUBLISHED: Hannum (1945; 1958), Jacobson and D'Ucel (1950).
The Gallup Independent (May 14, 1953), *Arizona Highways* (July 1956; December 1958; July 1959), *New Mexico* (December 1960), *The Amerindian* (May–June 1961).
EXHIBITIONS: AAIE, AIAE/WSU, BG, CAI, DAM, DMFA, FAIEAIP, FWG, HM, ITIC, JGS, MAI, MHDYMM, MNM, NGA, PAC, PAC/T, SAIEAIP, SN; Mandell Brothers Gallery, Chicago, Ill.; Riverside Museum of Art, Riverside, Calif.; Cleveland Museum of Art, Cleveland, Ohio; Santa Barbara Museum of Art, Santa Barbara, Calif.; Illinois State Museum, Springfield, Illinois; represented in five permanent sales galleries. *One-man shows*: BG, HM, SM; La Jolla Gallery of Art, La Jolla, Calif.
COLLECTIONS: *Public*: BM, GM, LMA/BC, MAI, MNA/KHC, PAC, SMNAI, SM. *Private*: Berg, Bialac, Canavan, Denman, Dietrich, Dockstader, Elkus, C. Fenton, A. Forbes, Goff, Kemm, Lockett, D. Maxwell, R. Moore, Morris, Mullan, Schreiber, Sewell, Thoeny, M. Vann, Wyman.
ADDRESS: Box 607, Chambers, Ariz.

Beautiful (*see* Susunkewa, Manfred)

Beaver (*see* Scott, Johnson Lee)

Beaver, Fred   *Creek*
Eka La Nee, Brown Head
BORN: July 2, 1911, Eufaula, Okla. Son of Willie Beaver (Creek) and Annie Johnson (Creek). P/GF: Itshaus Micco, subchief of Okfuskee town group in Alabama, who moved his people to Oklahoma where the town of Eufaula now stands.
MARRIED: Juanita D. Brown, 1945.
  At first interested in music and athletics, Beaver began to paint as a hobby in 1945. Since then, he has achieved a distinguished record.
EDUCATION: Graduated Eufaula (Okla.) High School, 1931; attended Bacone College, 1931; graduated Haskell, Business College, 1935; private instruction in art and voice, Italy, 1944.
SERVICE: WWII, U.S. Air Corps, three years; European Theater.
CAREER: Entered BIA Field Service, Okmulgee, Okla., July 1, 1935, as clerk and interpreter under Five Civilized Tribes Agency; remained with BIA until 1942, when he was inducted into the armed services; returned and resigned July 8, 1960, to devote himself to his art and music interests.
HONORS: Oklahoma All-State, football and basketball, 1930–31; Waite Phillips Outstanding Indian Artist Trophy, PAC, 1963.
COMMISSIONS: *Murals*: Thunderbird Restaurant and Motel, Oklahoma City, Okla.; Seminole Arts and Crafts Center, West Hollywood, Fla.
WORK PUBLISHED: Pierson and Davidson (1960). *Newsweek* (September 4, 1950), *American Indian Exposition Program Booklet* (1956), cover, Anadarko, Okla., *Museum News* (June 1962), *Sunday Oklahoman, Orbit Magazine* (May 10, 1964; January 23, 1966).
EXHIBITIONS: 1946–65: 103, in 34 states and District of Columbia: AIE, BNIAS, DAM, FAIEAIP, ITIC, JAM, MNM, OHSM, PAC, PAC/T, SPIM,

USDS; Agra Gallery, Washington, D.C. *One-man shows*: Nineteen, including DAM, JAM, PAC, SPIM.
AWARDS: Thirty-two during 1951–65, including PAC Grand Award.
COLLECTIONS: *Public*: BIA, GM, IACB, KM, MAI, PAC; YMCA, Hotel Lawtonka, Carnegie Library, Ardmore Sanitorium, Ardmore, Okla.; Stephen A. Foster Memorial, White Springs, Fla. *Private*: G. Alexander, Alford, Austin, John Brown, Callaway, Clay, Coke, Cone, Cox, DeLong, Edwards, Eisenhower, Field, Fields, Fleishman, Franks, Hodges, D. Maxwell, McCracken, R. McPherson, Medina, Merrick, R. Moore, Phillips II, B. Sanders, W. Schofield, Schonwald, J. Snodgrass, Steed, Sutton, Wearin.
ADDRESS: 437 Locust Street, NW., Ardmore, Okla.

Beck, Clifford, Jr. *Navaho*

BORN: January 11, 1946, Keams Canyon, Ariz. Son of Clifford Beck (Navaho), tribal councilman in 1965, and Ester Yellowhair (Navaho).
EDUCATION: Piñón Boarding School, Holbrook Elementary School, Holbrook, Ariz.; graduated Flagstaff, 1963; California C., 1964–.
CAREER: Probation and Parole Department, Navaho Tribe, Window Rock, Ariz., summer 1965; illustrator, *Navajo Times*.
HONORS: Scholarship to California C.
WORK PUBLISHED: *Navajo Times* (September 9, 1965).
EXHIBITIONS: 1964–65: NACG, NTF; United Bay Area Art Festival, Oakland, Calif., 1964; Morwear Art Gallery, Berkeley, Calif. *Two-man shows*: With Patrick Swazo Hinds (*q.v.*), Berkeley, Calif., 1965.
AWARDS: Six from NTF, 1965.
COLLECTIONS: *Private*: Reagan, Tikker.
ADDRESS: 2133 Harrison Street, Oakland, Calif., *or*, c/o Clifford Beck, Sr., General Delivery, Piñón, Ariz.

Bedah, Timothy *Navaho*

BORN: October 4, 1945, Tohatchi, N.M.
Listed as a promising student by Duane O. Berg, his art instructor, Bedah has been painting since 1960.
EDUCATION: Graduated Gallup public schools, Gallup, N.M., 1965.
EXHIBITIONS: ITIC; Gallup Community Indian Center, Gallup, N.M.
AWARDS: Three as of 1962 from ITIC.
ADDRESS: Tohatchi, N.M.

Bedonni Quid (*see* Maulson, Gerald)

Beeler, Joe *Cherokee*

BORN: December 25, 1931, Joplin, Mo. Son of Jack Beeler (Cherokee) and Lena Setser. P/GGM: Cherokee, known for her knowledge of native medicines, who traveled the Tennessee hill country on horseback ministering to the sick.
MARRIED: Sharon. Two children: Tracy, 1958; Jody, 1964.
"I am goin' (*sic*) full steam ahead now with sculpturing and casting bronzes, and the paintings I do are done on commission only," said the artist in 1965. Beeler's early paintings were inspired by the "old Devil's Promenade Pow Wow at Quapaw, Okla." Today he paints the West as a westerner sees it.

EDUCATION: Graduated Joplin High School, Joplin, Mo.; attended Los Angeles and Tulsa; graduated Kansas S.

SERVICE: Korean War, U.S. Army (while overseas he did art work for *Stars and Stripes*).

CAREER: Worked in "Fats" Jones' Stables, North Hollywood, Calif., painting signs and decorating "old-time" wagons, stagecoaches, and other props used in motion pictures, *ca.* 1957; full-time painter, sculptor, and writer, *ca.* 1958–.

COMMISSIONS: *Baptistry*: Spring River Indian Baptist Church, Quapaw, Okla.

BOOKS ILLUSTRATED: "About 15 for University of Oklahoma Press, six for Grosset and Dunlap," according to a letter from Beeler.

WORK PUBLISHED: *Montana* (Summer 1961; April 1964); "An Artist Looks at the American Indian," author and illustrator; *Western Horseman* (September 1961), cover.

EXHIBITIONS: Represented in four permanent sales galleries. *One-man shows*: BG, GM, MHS/H, NCHF.

COLLECTIONS: *Public*: GM, MHS/H, NCHF. *Private*: R. Anderson, Bimson, Britt Brown, Justin, Kidd, Light, Pabst, Phillips, Schonwald, W. Smith, S. Stewart, J. Woodard, Woodruff.

ADDRESS: Sedona, Ariz.

Begay Apie (*see* Begay, Apie)

Begay, Apie   *Navaho*
Begay Apie, Son of Milk
(Also known as Apie Be Gay.)

BORN: Date unknown; died "many years before 1936."

In 1902, Dr. Kenneth Chapman found the artist sitting on the floor of his hogan attempting to reproduce sandpainting designs in the only two colors he had: red and black. When Dr. Chapman gave Begay a full box of crayons, he immediately set out to execute detailed replicas of sandpaintings. Three of these first crayon drawings are now in the Indian Arts Fund Collection at the MNM.

WORK PUBLISHED: *El Palacio* (December 1948).

COLLECTIONS: *Public*: MNM.

Begay, Arthur C.   *Navaho*
BORN: December 15, 1932, Newcomb, N.M.
EDUCATION: Correspondence school, Westport, Conn.
CAREER: Electrician and artist.
EXHIBITIONS: ITIC, NTF, PAC.
COLLECTIONS: *Public*: AF.
ADDRESS: Box 412, Shiprock, N.M.

Begay, Fred   *Navaho*
EXHIBITIONS: AIAE/WSU.

Begay, Harrison   *Navaho*
Haskay Yah Ne Yah, Warrior Who Walked Up To His Enemy

BORN: November 15, 1917, White Cone, Ariz. Son of Black-Rock Begay (Navaho) and Zonnie Tachinie (Navaho), and stepson of Katherine Begay.

2

MARRIED: Ramona Espinosa, 1940. Divorced, 1945.
Begay's paintings have exerted greater influence on Navaho artists than any others. His work is internationally known.

EDUCATION: Fort Wingate, 1927; Fort Defiance Indian School, Fort Defiance, N.M.; Tohatchi Indian School, Tohatchi, N.M.; graduated Santa Fe, 1939; attended Black Mt., 1940–41; Phoenix J.C., 1941.

SERVICE: WWII, U.S. Army, three years; European Theater and Iceland.

CAREER: Full-time artist; co-founder of Tewa Enterprises.

HONORS: High school salutatorian; Palmes d'Académiques, 1945; listed in *Indians of Today.*

COMMISSIONS: *Murals*: Maisel's Trading Post, Albuquerque, N.M.

BOOKS ILLUSTRATED: Clark (1957).

WORK PUBLISHED: Jacobson and D'Ucel (1950), Tanner (1957), LaFarge (1956; 1960), Dockstader (1961), Bahti (1964). *Arizona Highways* (February, 1950; December 1958).

EXHIBITIONS: 1946–65: AIAE/WSU, AIHA, AIW, ASF, CPLH, DAM, FAIEAIP, FNAIC, FWG, HM, ITIC, JGS, MNM, NGA, NJSM, OU/ET, PAC, PAC/T, SAIEAIP, SI, WRNGA.

AWARDS: Thirteen, including ITIC, PAC, state and tribal fairs; two ITIC Grand Awards.

COLLECTIONS: *Public*: AF, AU/ASM, BIA, DAM, GM, IACB, JAM, MAI, MAM, MKMcNAI, MNA/KHC, MNM, MRFM, OU/MA, PAC, SM, SMNAI. *Private*: Denman, Dietrich, Dockstader, Elkus, Finley, A. Forbes, O. Jacobson, Lockett, R. Moore, Mullan, Newmann, Pace, Pritzlaff, Schonwald, Thoeny, Wyman.

ADDRESS: Greasewood Trading Post, Ganado, Ariz.

Begay, Harry B.   *Navaho*
EDUCATION: Santa Fe, *ca.* 1959.
EXHIBITIONS: MNM.
AWARDS: MNM.

Begay, Jerome   *Navaho*
BORN: 1953.
EDUCATION: Scholarship to Arizona, "Southwestern Indian Art Project," summers, 1960–61 (sculpture major).

Begay, Jimmy   *Navaho*
EDUCATION: Scholarship to Arizona, "Southwestern Indian Art Project," summer, 1961 (textile major).

Begay, Keats   *Navaho*
EXHIBITIONS: AIW; NGA, 1953.
COLLECTIONS: *Public*: MNA/KHC, MNM. *Private*: Denman, Dietrich.

Begay, Paul Lee   *Navaho*
COLLECTIONS: *Public*: JAM.

Begay, Raymond   *Navaho*
BORN: December 9, 1945, Crownpoint, N.M.
The artist began painting in 1959. Duane O. Berg, his art instructor, listed him as a promising student.

EDUCATION: Gallup and McKinley County, N.M.; graduated Gallup, 1964.
EXHIBITIONS: ITIC, NACG.
AWARDS: Four during 1963–64.
ADDRESS: General Delivery, Crownpoint, N.M.

Begay, Richard *Navaho*
EDUCATION: Fort Sill.
EXHIBITIONS: PAC.

Begay, Timothy *Navaho*
BORN: Chinle, Ariz.
EDUCATION: Graduated Santa Fe, 1942.
SERVICE: WWII; European Theater.
EXHIBITIONS: ITIC, MNM, PAC; Los Angeles Public School Exhibit.

Belindo, Dennis *Kiowa-Navaho*
Aun So Te, Foot
BORN: December 12, 1938, Phoenix, Ariz. Son of Damon Belindo (Navaho) and Ruby Goomda (Kiowa). His family's Kiowa ancestry seems to have originated when the Sioux captured a Kiowa woman, and, consequently, he can trace his lineage to Red Cloud (Sioux) and Lone Wolf (Kiowa). M/GF: Devoted his life as Keeper of the Tiame (Sun Dance God). P/GF: Red Whiskers, Navaho medicine man.
MARRIED: Julia Marie Bayhylle (Pawnee-Choctaw), 1960. One child.
EDUCATION: Public schools in Oklahoma City, Okla.; Fort Wingate; graduated Bacone College, 1958; B.F.A., Oklahoma, 1962.
CAREER: Artist, Times Journal Publishing Co., Oklahoma City, Okla., 1962–66.
EXHIBITIONS: ITIC, MNM, PAC, SAIEAIP. *One-man show*: OU.
AWARDS: PAC, 1961.
COLLECTIONS: *Public*: LNBTC, OHSM. *Private*: Deupree, Hollon, Humphrey, R. Moore, Payne, Schonwald.
ADDRESS: 902 East Campbell, Edmond, Okla.

Bellrock, Buster *Crow*
COLLECTIONS: *Public:* GM.

Benally, Chee B. *Navaho*
BORN: June 6, 1947, Blackrock, N.M.
EDUCATION: Thoreau Boarding School, N.M.; Gallup public schools, Gallup, N.M., since fourth grade; graduated Gallup, 1966. Engineering Drafting School, Denver, Colo., 1966–.
EXHIBITIONS: 1963: ITIC, NACG.
COLLECTIONS: *Private*: Berg, Newell, Shippy, L. Williams.
ADDRESS: Box 312, Vanderwagen, N.M.

Bercier, Mary *Navaho*
EXHIBITIONS: 1967: Heard.
COLLECTIONS: Harvey.

Bernal, Eloisa *Taos*
EXHIBITIONS: AIEC.

2*

Bernal, Pauline *Taos*
The artist's father, Paul Bernal, is a native of Taos Pueblo; her mother is non-Indian.
EDUCATION: Attended Taos.

Big Back *Cheyenne*
BORN: Date unknown; deceased.
Richard Irving Dodge's *Our Wild Indians* (1883) has "reproduced in exact facsimile from the original drawings, expressly for this work, drawings done with colored pencil by Big Back...."
WORK PUBLISHED: Dodge (1883), Hamilton (1950).

Big Black (*see* Hollowbreast, Donald)

Big Bow (*see* Big Bow, Woody)

Big Bow (Chief) *Kiowa*
Zepko Ettee, Big Bow Man
(Also known as Bow Big Man.)
BORN: *ca.* 1845; died 1901, Hobart, Okla. Brother of White Horse (*q.v.*).
SERVICE: U.S. Army; sergeant in charge of a detachment of Kiowa scouts stationed on Sweetwater Creek; served under Lt. Richard H. Pratt and Gen. Hugh L. Scott; honorably discharged a few years before his death.
CAREER: Chief, warrior, and artist; active with Kicking Bird and Satanta (*q.v.*) in Texas and Oklahoma raids during the mid-1800's.
COLLECTIONS: *Public*: MAI. *Private*: Deupree, Wiesendanger (pictographic drawings in ledger books).

Big Bow, Abel *Kiowa*
COLLECTIONS: *Public*: GM (pictographic style on paper).

Big Bow, "Old Man" *Kiowa*
BORN: Date unknown; died 1934.
Manuscript notes at Gilcrease Museum refer to a Kiowa calendar in book form by "Old Man" Big Bow in the collection of Woody Big Bow (*q.v.*).

Big Bow, Woodrow Wilson (*see* Big Bow, Woody)

Big Bow, Woody *Kiowa*
Tse Ko Yate, Big Bow
(Also known as Big Bow, Woodrow Wilson.)
BORN: January 29, 1914, Carnegie, Okla. GF: Chief Big Bow (*q.v.*). Three children: Larry, Steven, Vivian.
Woody designed the red and yellow thunderbird insignia of the Oklahoma 45th Infantry Division.
EDUCATION: Oklahoma, 1939.
CAREER: Set painter for western movies; contractor and builder.
WORK PUBLISHED: Jacobson and D'Ucel (1950).
EXHIBITIONS: PAC, PSC; Tulsa County Libraries, Tulsa, Okla.
COLLECTIONS: *Public*: GM, KM, MAI, OAC, OHSM, OU/L, PAC, SM; Utica Square National Bank and the YMCA, Tulsa, Okla. *Private*: Andelman, Deupree, Feemster III, Germundson, R. Moore, Obermire, Owens, Schonwald, W. S. Price.

Big Brave *Piegan Blackfoot*
The artist assisted in the execution of a 61-year count (*see* Elk Horn).

Big Lefthanded   *Navaho*
Klah Tso, Lefthanded Big
(also known as Old Hostin Claw; *see also* Choh.)
BORN: Date unknown. "Lived either near Indian Wells or near Tuba City,
Ariz., probably the former."
> The artist "made paintings between 1905 and 1912 ... on dark tan-colored
> cotton cloth. The pigments employed were native pigments in some native ad-
> hesive, opaque commercial watercolors, and some commercial oils." One painting
> (USNM) of "galloping horses and the dust thrown up by their flying hooves, and
> the attitudes of the riders make this one of the loveliest known early American
> Indian paintings." Wyman (1965).

WORK PUBLISHED: Wyman (1965).
COLLECTIONS: *Public*: MNA/KHC, USNM (five secular paintings).

Big Little (*see* Kahn, Chester)

Big Man, Max   *Crow*
BORN: Crow Agency, Mont. Deceased.
> Painting was Big Man's hobby. He was active in tribal functions, promoted the
> Custer Battlefield Association, and conducted an educational program about
> Indians for CBS radio and New York schools. His paintings reflect his own
> activities and tribal life.

HONORS: Represented in *Indians of Today*; made an honorary chief by
Chief Plenty Coups; received Commercial Club Medal of Service, Rapid
City, S. Dak.

Big Missouri   *Teton Sioux*
> Big Missouri is known to have executed a Dakota Winter Count for the years
> 1796 to 1926 (*see* BAE Bull. 173).

COLLECTIONS: *Private*: J. A. Anderson.

Big Road, Chief   *Sioux*
WORK PUBLISHED: BAE, *4th AR*.
COLLECTIONS: *Public*: OAA/SI.

Big Springs, William, Sr.   *Blackfoot*
BORN: 1919, East Glacier Park, Mont.
CAREER: He operates an 18,000-acre ranch near Glacier Park, Mont., with
his son, Bill, Jr.
HONORS: Chairman, First Annual Western Art Show, Glacier Park, Mont.
EXHIBITIONS: BNIAS, FAIEAIP.
ADDRESS: Box 531, East Glacier Park, Mont.

Bill Nix (*see* Red Corn)

Bilokila (*see* Luján, Lorenzo A.)

A Bird (*see* Herrera, Justino)

Bird, Larry   *Santo Domingo-Laguna*
Little Bird
BORN: 1941.
EDUCATION: Institute.
CAREER: Employed by MNM, *ca.* 1965.
AWARDS: *Interior Design Magazine* Award for Painting.
EXHIBITIONS: FAIEAIP, MNM, SN, YAIA.
COLLECTIONS: *Private*: McGrath.

Biss, Earl   *Crow*
BORN: 1947, Renton, Wash.
EDUCATION: Institute, 1965–66.
EXHIBITIONS: MNM, YAIA.
AWARDS: MNM, 1965.

Biter (*see* Zotom)

Black (*see* Sweezy, Carl)

Black Bear   *Miniconjou Sioux*
Mato Sapo, Bear Black
BORN: Date unknown; in 1868–69, lived on the Cheyenne Agency Reserva-
tion on the Missouri River near the mouth of the Cheyenne River, near Fort
Sully, Dakota Territory.
  The artist executed a Winter Count chart (1800–01 to 1868–69), referred to as a
  "History of the Miniconjous," which covers almost the same period as that
  recorded by The Flame, The Swan, and Lone Dog (*qq.v.*).
WORK PUBLISHED: BAE, *4th AR.*

Black Cloud (*see* Levings, Martin)

Black Crow   *Sioux*
  Black Crow, chief of the Milk River Band, painted a buffalo hide record of
  exploits occuring in the 1870's.
WORK PUBLISHED: BAE, *4th* and *10th AR.*
COLLECTIONS: *Public*: OAA/SI.

Black Heart   *Oglala Sioux*
  At the Pine Ridge Agency, S. Dak., 12 men drew their autographs in a book.
  Among them is the signature of Black Heart — a figure with a triangular black
  heart.
COLLECTIONS: *Public*: MAI.

Black Horse   *Sioux*
Shunka Sapa, Black Horse
  One of the five artists whose works, now referred to as the Cronau Album (*see*
  Sinte), were commissioned and collected by Rudolf Cronau during 1880–83.
COLLECTIONS: *Public*: AMNH.

Black Moon (*see* Riddles, Leonard)

Black Thunder   *Teton Sioux*
WORK PUBLISHED: BAE, *Bull. 61.*

Blackbear (*see* Bosin, Blackbear)

Blackbear, Levi   *Plains*
COLLECTIONS: *Public*: MAI.

Blackmore, Bill   *Athabascan*
Nazia, Great Hunter
(Also known as Blackmore, William Arvin.)
BORN: July 3, 1940, Whitehorse, Yukon Territory, Canada. Son of Mickey
Alvin Blackmore and Bessie Johnson (Athabascan).
  Interested more in textile and fashion design than in painting, the artist received
  encouragement from Lloyd H. New and Carl Heinmiller.

EDUCATION: Elementary school, Dawson City, Y.T.; high school, Clesta and Salmon Arm, British Columbia, Canada; Institute.

SERVICE: U.S. Army, December, 1963–.

CAREER: Construction worker; hunting guide.

EXHIBITIONS: MNM; British Columbia, Canada; Juneau, Alaska.

ADDRESS: c/o Mr. and Mrs. Berry Germans, Salmon Arm, B.C., Canada.

Blackmore, William Arvin (*see* Blackmore, Bill)

Blackowl, Archie *Cheyenne*
Mis Ta Moo To Va, Flying Hawk

BORN: November 23, 1911, in Custer County, Okla. M/GGF: Crow Necklace, chief of the Cheyennes. The artist is a descendant of Roman Nose (Cheyenne).

MARRIED: Mollie Curtis. Seven children: George, Jasper, Daniel, Joseph, Bryon, Richard, Archie, Jr.

> Blackowl became aware of art at the age of six when he saw old Red Tooth painting a skin tipi. Encouraged by Woodrow Wilson Crumbo (*q.v.*), he began to paint seriously in the early 1930's.

EDUCATION: Fort Sill; Haskell; Kansas; Chicago; studied various painting techniques under muralist Olaf Nordmark.

CAREER: Civil Service employee in the 1940's, Fort Sill, Okla.; industrial painter during WWII, Douglas Airplane Co., Tulsa, Okla.; with Convair Aircraft Corp., San Francisco, Calif., during the 1940's.

COMMISSIONS: *Murals*: PAC; The Palmer House, Chicago, Ill.; Cafeteria and gymnasium, Fort Sill Officer's Club, Fort Sill, Okla.; Riverside Indian School; Kiowa Hospital, Lawton, Okla.

WORK PUBLISHED: Jacobson and D'Ucel (1950), Jacobson (1964).

EXHIBITIONS: 1946–65: AIAE/WSU, ITIC, MNM, OHSM, PAC, PAC/T, USDS; Agra Gallery, Washington, D.C.

AWARDS: AIAE/WSU, ITIC, PAC; state and tribal fairs.

COLLECTIONS: *Public*: ACM, GM, IACB, KM, MAI, MNA/KHC, MRFM, OHSM, OU/SM, PAC, SPIM. *Private*: Callaway, Choteau, Deupree, Dockstader, C. Fenton, Fields, Haddock, Hogue, O. Jacobson, D. Maxwell, B. McCormick, R. Moore, Owens, W. S. Price, Schonwald, Thoeny, Walch.

ADDRESS: 911 North 17th, Clinton, Okla.

The Blaze (*see* The Flame)

Bloody Knife *Sioux*

COLLECTIONS: *Public*: OAA/SI (photographs of a pictographic robe).

Blue Bird (*see* Herrera, Joe Hilario)

Blue Eagle, Acee *Creek-Pawnee*
Che Bon Ah Bu La, Laughing Boy; *Lumhee Holattee*.
(Also known as McIntosh, Alex C.)

BORN: August 17, 1907, on the Wichita Reservation, north of Anadarko, Okla. Died, June 18, 1959. Son of Solomon McIntosh (Creek) and Mattie Odom (Pawnee). P/GF: William McIntosh, Creek chief. Blue Eagle's parents died before he was five and shortly afterward he was adopted by his grandparents. After their deaths, W. R. Thompson of Henryetta, Okla., was appointed his guardian. Although he never used it professionally, the artist's given name was Alex C. McIntosh; rather, he adopted the name Blue Eagle from his paternal grandfather. His desire to paint the various tribes authentically took him to museum archives throughout North America and Europe. Blue Eagle is buried in the U.S. National Cemetery at Fort Gibson, Okla.

MARRIED: Loretto Thornton Kendrick (Cherokee), 1937. Divorced 1937. Later married and divorced Devi Dja (Javanese), *ca.* 1946.

EDUCATION: Indian Schools at Anadarko, Nuyaka, and Euchee, Okla.; Haskell; graduated Chilocco, 1928; Oxford University, Oxford, England, non-credit classes, 1935; Bacone College; Oklahoma; Oklahoma S.U./S.T., commercial art classes, 1951–52.

SERVICE: WWII, U.S. Air Force, three years.

CAREER: Painter, craftsman, writer, lecturer, teacher, and dancer. Toured U.S. and Europe giving lecture-exhibition program, "Life and Character of the American Indian," 1935; established and headed Art Department at Bacone College, 1935–38; toured U.S. West Coast exhibiting and lecturing on ways to improve TV programs for children; conducted TV program, Muskogee, Okla., *ca.* 1954; free-lance artist.

HONORS: Invited to lecture on Indian art, "International Education Conference," Oxford University, England, 1935; represented Oklahoma Boy Scouts on Europe tour, 1929; listed in *Who's Who in Oklahoma, Who's Who in American Artists, Who's Who in American Art, Indians of Today*; honored as one of nine "Colorful Personalities" and "foremost living Indian artist," by *American Magazine* (April 1937); named "Outstanding Indian in the United States," Anadarko, Okla., 1958; memorial biography, *Indian Life,* Inter-Tribal Indian Ceremonials (1960); resolution honoring him posthumously for service to the state, Oklahoma Legislature, 1959; building on Haskell campus named for him.

COMMISSIONS: *Murals*: Edmond Teachers College; Oklahoma College for Women, Chickasha; Muskogee Public Library; Federal Building, Colgate and Seminole, Black Hawk Club, Oklahoma City, Okla.; U.S.S. Oklahoma. Blue Eagle spent the greater part of 1934 painting murals in Oklahoma as part of a Public Works of Art Project (WPA).

BOOKS ILLUSTRATED: Blue Eagle (1959).

WORK PUBLISHED: Jacobson and D'Ucel (1950); Pierson and Davidson (1960); Jacobson (1964). *Dancing Moccasins*, Indian Pageant, Tulsa, Okla. (1957), cover; *Blue Eagle—A Retrospective Exhibition*, PAC (1959); *Indians of Oklahoma*, BIA (1966). His work has been silk screened commercially.

EXHIBITIONS: 1932–65: AAIE, AIE, AIEC, AIW, CCP, CWC/I, DAM, EITA, FANEA, FCTM, GCG, GM, IAESS, JGS, PAC, PAC/T, USDS. *One-man shows*: PAC; Young Gallery, Chicago, Ill.; Muskogee Public Library, Muskogee, Okla. *Retrospective*: PAC. *Memorial*: GM.

AWARDS: Forty: AIE, DAM, IAESS, ITIC, PAC. Fairs and Indian ceremonials.

COLLECTIONS: *Public*: BC, BIA, CCHM, DAM, GM, KM, MNM, MRFM, OHSM, OU/MA, OU/SM, PAC, SPL. *Private*: Abbott, Alfonso, Billingslea,

Bishop, Bruner, Bush, Callaway, Corkille, Covelle, Curnow, Deupree, Fite, Foreman, W. Hunt, O. Jacobson, Jamell, Kinkade, Leathers, D. Maxwell, Maytubby, McMahan, Mileham, Obermire, I. Oldham, Powhatan, W. S. Price, Roosevelt, Schonwald, Selassie, Thoeny, Toller, Vernon, Walch, Weaver, N. Wheeler, Woodring, Wyman.

Blue Flower (*see* Pop Chalee)

Blue Horse (*see* Keith, C. Hobart)

Blue Jay (*see* De Groat, Jay)

Bluehorse, George   *Navaho*
EDUCATION: Albuquerque, 1960.
EXHIBITIONS: MNM, 1960.

Bobb, Henrietta   *Navaho*
EDUCATION: Scholarship to Arizona, "Southwest Indian Art Project," 1962.
ADDRESS: 28 Res Road, Reno, Nev.

Boide (*see* The Flame)

Bolin, Floyd   *Cherokee*
EDUCATION: Institute, 1965–66.
EXHIBITIONS: YAIA.

Bosin, Blackbear   *Kiowa-Comanche*
Tsate Kongia, Blackbear
(Also known as Bosin, Francis Blackbear.)
BORN: June 5, 1921, near Anadarko, Okla. Son of Frank Blackbear Bosin (Kiowa) and Ada Tivis (Comanche). P/GGF: Tsate Kongia, Kiowa sub-chief. P/GM: Mahnkee. M/GM: Kahchatscha, Comanche Awl Band medicine woman.
MARRIED: Nola Davidson Simmonds, November 26, 1953. Four children by previous marriage: Rowena Marie, 1939; Patricia, 1940; Francis Blackbear, Jr., 1942; Niles Raymond, 1944. Stepson: David Wayne Simmonds, 1945.
The artist was the eldest of four children. At 17, he helped maintain the family farm, painting in spare moments. Although unable to accept two university art scholarships because of family obligations, he achieved success with little formal training and became the only American Indian artist to be represented in the 1965 White House Festival of the Arts.
EDUCATION: St. Patrick's; public schools in Anadarko, Okla.; graduated Cyril High School, Cyril, Okla., 1940.
SERVICE: WWII, U.S. Marine Corps, two years; Pacific Theater.
CAREER: Color separator and platemaker, Western Lithograph Co., Wichita, Kan.; illustrator, Boeing Aircraft Co., Wichita, Kan.; Graphic Arts Section of Training Aids Division, McConnell Air Force Base, Wichita, Kan.; co-owner, Great Plains Studio and Gallery, 1960–64, and owner, 1964–.
HONORS: 1959 Civil Servant Award, U.S. Chamber of Commerce; member, Board of Directors, Wichita Art Guild, Wichita, Kan.; Certificate of Appreciation, IACB, 1966; listed in *Who's Who in American Art, Who's Who in Greater Wichita*, and *Indians of Today*.
COMMISSIONS: *Murals*: McConnell Air Force Base, North High School, and Broadview Hotel, all in Wichita, Kan.

WORK PUBLISHED: Stirling (1955), LaFarge (1956; 1960), Pierson and Davidson (1960), Dockstader (1961). *National Geographic Magazine* (March 1955), *Oklahoma Today* (Summer 1958), *Life International* (March 16, 1959), *American Indian Paintings from the Collection of Philbrook Art Center* (1964), cover; *Sunday Bonanza, San Francisco Chronicle* (August 22, 1965), *Oklahoma Today* (Winter 1965).

EXHIBITIONS: 1945–65: 58 museums, galleries, and art centers, including AAID, CAI, CPLH, JGS, NGA, PAC, PAC/T, SI, TAI, WRNGA; White House Festival of the Arts, Washington, D.C. *One-man shows*: AHNHG, HM, PAC, WAAG, WMWA.

AWARDS: During 1946–65: 33 from AAID, CPLH, DAM, ITIC, MNM, PAC, and SN, including four grand awards.

COLLECTIONS: *Public*: BIA, DAM, GM, HM, IACB, PAC, WAAG, WAM. *Private*: Beach, Britt Brown, Dickinson, Dowell, Fry, Goff, Harvey, Humphries, J. McPherson, Melville, G. Milburn, Mullan, Pritzloff, Schonwald, Thoeny, N. Thorne, Vickery, Whitridge, Zavatsky.

ADDRESS: 1032 West 13th, Wichita, Kan.

Bosin, Francis Blackbear (*see* Bosin, Blackbear)

Boswell, Helen *Cherokee-Chippewa*
BORN: 1906, Chicago, Ill.
MARRIED: Richard F. Howard.
EXHIBITIONS: BMA, FAIEAIP, ITIC, JGS, PAC. *One-man shows*: HM. *Two-man shows*: PAC.
ADDRESS: 4183 Cliff Road, Birmingham, Ala.

Botella, Emmett *Mescalero Apache*
EXHIBITIONS: MNM, 1957.
ADDRESS: Mescalero, N.M.

Boudetah (*see* Smoky, Lois)
Bougeta (*see* Smoky, Lois)
Bougetah (*see* Smoky, Lois)
Bow-Arrow (*see* Waano-Gano, Joe T.N.)
Bow Big Man (*see* Big Bow [Chief])
Boy (*see* Gorman, Alfred Kee)
Boy Of The Woods (*see* Des Jarlait, Patrick Robert)

Boyd, George, Jr. *Sioux-Assiniboin*
BORN: January 20, 1910, Blare, Mont.
MARRIED: Helen R. Sparks, 1933. Seven children: Roberta, 1932; Winona, 1934; Pattsy, 1939; Lionel, 1944; Doyle, 1947; Judith, 1950; Terry, 1952.
   Mr. Boyd has worked with livestock nearly all his life, an interest reflected in his representational paintings.
EDUCATION: Brockton Public Schools, Brockton, Mont.
CAREER: Rancher for 25 years; board member, Sioux Tribal Credit Program Committee.
AWARDS: First award, Montana State Fair, 1934.
COLLECTIONS: *Private*: Feiock.
ADDRESS: Brockton, Mont.

Boyiddle, Parker, Jr. *Kiowa-Wichita-Delaware-Chickasaw*
BORN: 1948. His father was a Kiowa and his mother was Wichita, Delaware, and Chickasaw.
EDUCATION: Graduated Classen High School, Oklahoma City, Okla., 1965.
HONORS: Art scholarship, Oklahoma Science and Art Foundation, Oklahoma City, Okla.
EXHIBITIONS: YAIA.
ADDRESS: 1730 North West 13th, Oklahoma City, Okla.

Bradley, Roberta C. (*see* Weckeah)

Branded Corn (*see* Sánchez, Ramos)

Brando, Stephen *Chippewa-Ottawa*
BORN: July 27, 1949. Son of Vincent Brando and Marian (Chippewa-Ottawa).
This young artist is interested in many art forms and has received considerable local recognition.
EDUCATION: Crestwood High School, Crestwood, Pa.
EXHIBITIONS: Local.
ADDRESS: 722 Church Road, Mountain Top, Pa.

Brave, Franklin P. *Osage-Cherokee*
Wa Shun Keh, Thorn (or Sand Burr)
BORN: December 21, 1932, Pawhuska, Okla.
EDUCATION: Haskell; Kansas City.
SERVICE: U.S. Army Airborne Paratroopers, 18 months.
CAREER: Advertising artist, Western Auto Supply Co., Kansas City, Mo.
EXHIBITIONS: PAC.
COLLECTIONS: *Private*: Nordling.

Brave Bull *Sioux*
COLLECTIONS: *Public*: MPM (pictograph on paper).

Bright Wing (*see* Fox, Guy)

Brim, Mary *Cherokee*
EXHIBITIONS: AAIE, 1959.

Broken Leg (*see* Cohoe, William).

Brown Hat (*see* Good, Baptiste)

Brown Head (*see* Beaver, Fred)

Brunette, J. M.
COLLECTIONS: *Public*: AU/SM.

Buffalo Meat *Apache* or *Cheyenne*
The artist was among the 72 Plains Indians taken as prisoners from Fort Sill, Okla., to Fort Marion, St. Augustine, Fla., in 1875.
COLLECTIONS: *Public*: MHS/B, OAA/SI, OHSM ("Apache" drawings thought to be the artist's), YU/BRBML.

Buniyuk (*see* Smart, Clara Mary)

Burdeau, George Henry *Blackfoot*
BORN: November 16, 1944, Great Falls, Mont. Son of George Burdeau (Blackfoot) and Ada C. Burbridge (Winnebago).
EDUCATION: Loma Linda Elementary School, Phoenix, Ariz.; Wasatch

Academy, Mount Pleasant, Utah; Arizona, "Southwest Indian Art Project,"
1961–62; Institute, *ca.* 1963.
CAREER: Gallery assistant, BIA, 1965–.
HONORS: Scholarships to attend: Utah S.; Utah; Arizona, summers, 1961–62.
WORK PUBLISHED: *Smoke Signals*, IACB (Autumn 1965).
EXHIBITIONS: BNIAS, FAIEAIP, YAIA; Utah State High School Art Ex-
hibition; National Scholastic Art Contest; University of Arizona Museum
of Art.
AWARDS: BNIAS; best painting in show, first award, and gold medallion
for sculpture, Utah State High School Exhibition.
ADDRESS: 2212 East Whitton, Phoenix, Ariz., *and* 1925 Calvert Street,
Washington, D.C.

Burton, Jimalee   *Creek-Cherokee*
Ho Chee Nee, Leader
BORN: January 23, 1906, El Reno, Indian Territory (now Okla.). Daughter
of James A. Chitwood (Cherokee) and Mary Beck (Creek-Cherokee). Her
father operated his first of four stores in Oklahoma City, Okla., shortly
after taking part in the "Cherokee Run" of 1889.
MARRIED: Dan A. Burton, 1933; widowed, 1954.
    Shortly after her husband's death, Mrs. Burton moved from Tulsa to Florida
    and began to concentrate on writing and painting Indian legends. In her exten-
    sive research in the field of Indian lore, she has traveled throughout the
    Western Hemisphere.
EDUCATION: Indian schools in Colony, Geary, and Weatherford, Okla.; South-
western Teachers College; Tulsa. Studied sculpture under H. Q. Edwards
at Tulsa, 1938, and painting under Carlos Mérida at Mexico.
CAREER: Supervisor of a radio program featuring her poetry for nearly ten
years in the 1930's; recorder of original songs and publisher of her poetry;
associate editor, *The Native Voice*; artist.
HONORS: National Penwomen Association award for short story, "Indian
Legend of Creation."
COMMISSIONS: *Movie: Indian Legends of Ho Chee Nee*, documentary, 1963.
EXHIBITIONS: DAM, FAIEAIP, MHDYMM, PAC, RM; Glenbow Foundation,
Calgary, Alberta, Canada; Lowe Gallery, Miami, Fla.; Brown University,
Ringling Museum; Galveston (Texas) Art Center, Oklahoma Art Center,
Oklahoma City, Okla. *One-man shows*: El Centro Gallery, Miami, Fla.; Uni-
versity of Florida; University of Georgia.
AWARDS: PAC Purchase Award, 1947; honorable mentions.
COLLECTIONS: *Public*: PAC.
ADDRESS: 700 John Ringling Blvd., Sarasota, Fla.

Bush   *Sioux*
    This artist was known to have executed a Dakota Winter Count for the years
    1800–01 to 1869–70 (see BAE, *Bull. 173*).

Bushotter, George   *Teton Sioux*
BORN: December 24, 1860, at the forks of Owl Creek, Dakota Territory (now
Butte County, S. Dak.). Died, February 2, 1892, Hedgesville, W. Va. Son

of Amos Bushotter (Yankton) and Gray Goodroad (Miniconjou). Bush-otter's stepfather belonged to the Society of Those Who Have Revelations From the Buffalo, whose mysteries the artist often illustrated.

MARRIED: Evalina Hull, March 8, 1888.

> The artist's collection (known as the Bushotter Collection) was described as "the most extensive that had been gained from among the tribes of the Siouan family, and it is the first contribution by an Indian" (BAE, *8th AR*, 1886–87).

EDUCATION: Hampton; Virginia Theological Seminary.

CAREER: March, 1887, began work for Bureau of American Ethnology assisting James Owen Dorsey with Teton dialect of the Dakota Indians; marriage license, 1888, states his occupation as teacher (taught school one year in Dakota Territory).

WORK PUBLISHED: BAE, *11th AR*.

COLLECTIONS: *Public*: OAA/SI.

Bushyhead, Allan   *Cheyenne-Arapaho*
Nakowhoadoniulzi, Bear Feathers
BORN: 1917; childhood spent in Oklahoma.
EDUCATION: Santa Fe.
SERVICE: WWII, U.S. Army; Pacific Theater.
WORK PUBLISHED: Jacobson and D'Ucel (1950), LaFarge (1960).
EXHIBITIONS: AIEC, AIW, OU/ET.
COLLECTIONS: *Public*: OU/MA. *Private*: Dietrich.

Butterfly   *Mandan*
> The artist executed a Winter Count covering the period 1833–76 (see Howard, 1960).

Buzzard   *Cheyenne*
COLLECTIONS: OHSM, YU/BRBML (probably executed while a prisoner at Fort Marion).

Byrnes, James (*see* Byrnes, James Michael)

Byrnes, James Michael   *Acoma-Laguna-Sioux*
Kyash Petrach; *Hofyee*; *Hotyee*.
(Also known as Bear, J.; Bear, J. Michael; Bear, James; Bear Claw; Byrnes, James; Jobie Bear; Standing Bear; Sunrise.)
BORN: 1938, N.M. His father was Sioux and his mother Acoma-Laguna.
EDUCATION: Graduated from Albuquerque, *ca.* 1956.
CAREER: Hospital orderly.
COMMISSIONS: *Murals*: Barelos Community Center, with Charles Vicenti and Dixon Shebola (*qq.v.*).
EXHIBITIONS: MNM, NMSF. *One-man shows*: HM, 1964 (Byron Harvey III Collection).
COLLECTIONS: *Public*: MAI, MNM. *Private*: Harvey.
ADDRESS: 1718 Gold SE, Albuquerque, N.M.; Genl. Del., Denver, Colo.

C.D.T.   *Zuni*
(Last name possibly Tullma.)
COLLECTIONS: *Public*: DAM (dated 1905).

Caje, Richard   *Apache*
BORN: 1941.
EDUCATION: Albuquerque, 1960; Arizona, "Southwest Indian Art Project."
EXHIBITIONS: 1958–60: ITIC, MNM.
AWARDS: Four: ITIC, MNM.
ADDRESS: Mescalero, N.M.

Calvert, John   *San Juan*
EDUCATION: Santa Fe, *ca.* 1958.
EXHIBITIONS: MNM, 1959.

Candelario, James   *San Felipe*
EXHIBITIONS: MNM, 1963 (student division).
ADDRESS: San Felipe Pueblo, Algodones, N.M.

Cannon, Tommy   *Caddo*
BORN: 1946, Lawton, Okla.
EDUCATION: Institute, 1965–66.
EXHIBITIONS: 1964–66: AIE, SAIEAIP.
AWARDS: AIE, 1964.

Cante Wani Ca (*see* No Heart)

Cariz, Santiago   *Pueblo* (?)
COLLECTIONS: *Public*: RM.

Carraher, Ronald G.   *Colville*
BORN: 1935, Colville Indian Reservation, Omak, Wash.
EDUCATION: B.A., Washington, 1956; M.A., San Jose, 1961; studied photography under Ansel Adams, 1962.
SERVICE: U.S. Army, 1956–58; Germany.
CAREER: Assistant, Henry Art Gallery, University of Washington, 1954–56; adult education teacher, San Jose Unified School District, San Jose, Calif., 1960–61; part-time teacher, San Jose City (junior) College, 1962; part-time instructor, San Jose State College, 1961–62; art instructor, Central Washington State College, 1961, 1962–63; Assistant Professor of Design, Rhode Island School of Design, 1964–65; art instructor, San Jose State College, 1965–.
HONORS: Scholarship to University of Washington, 1956; graduate assistantship, Central Washington State College, 1959; Art Editor, *Columns* (University of Washington magazine), 1954–55; Chairman of catalogs and brochures, Central Washington State College, 1964.
COMMISSIONS: *Educational Films*: Assisted in production, "Print with a Brayer" (16 mm color, eight-minute, sound), "Mosaics for Schools" (19 mm color, ten-minute, sound); graphic artist-photographer, National Defense Education Title VII Project, San Jose State College, 1959–61.
BOOKS ILLUSTRATED: Kemp (1962).
EXHIBITIONS: PAC; Washington State Fair Art Exhibit; Kingsley Art Annual, Crocker Gallery, Sacramento, Calif.; San Jose City College Arts Festival Invitational; Pacific Northwest Arts and Crafts Fair, Bellevue, Wash.; San Jose Art Center Invitational; 81st San Francisco Art Institute

Painting Annual; 48th Northwest Painting Annual, Seattle Art Museum; 20th American Drawing Annual, Norfolk, Va.; Stone Court Gallery, Yakima, Wash.; Northwest Watercolor Society Annual, Seattle Art Museum; Palace of the Legion of Honor, Winter Invitational, San Francisco; Pacific Arts Associations Invitational; represented in an exchange exhibit with Fukuoka, Japan. *One-man shows*: Central Washington State College. *Tours*: Western Association of Art Museums Traveling Exhibit.
AWARDS: 1954–64: six, including two purchase awards and a PAC Grand Award; Washington State Fair Art Exhibit; Pacific Northwest Arts and Crafts National Fair; San Jose Spring Arts Festival.
COLLECTIONS: *Public*: IACB. *Private*: D. Foster, Lincoln.
ADDRESS: RFD 1, Ellensburg, Wash.

Casias, Johnny Gabriel   *San Juan-Navaho*
Cea Shoe Pin, Pine Mountain
BORN: December 26, 1934, San Juan Pueblo, N.M. Son of Miguel L. Casias (San Juan) and Aurelia H. Casias (Navaho).
MARRIED: Elicia M. One child: Jonna Marie, 1964.
EDUCATION: San Juan, 1944–52; Santa Cruz, 1953–54; graduated Española, 1956.
SERVICE: U.S. Navy, 1956–60; New Mexico National Guard, 1953–56.
CAREER: Artist, 1953–; storekeeper, Casias Cash Store, San Juan, N.M., 1960–; editor, *Voice of Youth*, San Juan Youth Club Bulletin (active in promotion of the Pueblo art program); art instructor, San Juan Day School, summer, 1952.
WORK PUBLISHED: *Tah-Weh*, Española High School yearbook cover, 1956; *USS Hooper-Wespac*, U.S. Navy Cruise publication, cover, 1960.
EXHIBITIONS: BNIAS; Española High School.
COLLECTIONS: *Private*: Forkner.
ADDRESS: Box 813, San Juan Pueblo, N.M.

Casiquito, Lucy   *Jémez*
EDUCATION: Jémez, 1961.
EXHIBITIONS: MNM, 1961.

Casiquito, Vidal, Jr.   *Jémez*
BORN: Jémez Pueblo, N.M.
EDUCATION: Jémez, *ca.* 1954.
CAREER: Education department, United Pueblo Agency, Albuquerque, N.M.
EXHIBITIONS: MNM, PAC.
AWARDS: At age 14, while attending Jémez Day School under Al Momaday (*q.v.*), Casiquito was one of 12 winners in a national poster contest sponsored by the National Cartoonists' Society and the Savings Bond Division of the U.S. Treasury Dept. His poster, based on "the dream you save for," received national recognition, and he was granted a personal interview with President Harry S. Truman.
COLLECTIONS: *Public*: MNM.

Cassady, Ann Virginia   *Cherokee*
Dhealdh Yazzie Bitsi, Little Mustache's Daughter
BORN: July 12, 1909, Durango, Colo. Her parents left Oklahoma for the
Navaho Reservation where they operated a trading post at Red Rock, N.M.
MARRIED: Harvey Cassady, 1934. Five children.
EDUCATION: Public schools in Reno and Carson City, Nev., in Vallejo and
San Francisco, Calif., and in Tulsa, Okla. Instruction in art under Doris
Robertson, Hilda Reake, Dorothy Herger, and Elizabeth Polly in Vallejo,
under Warren Brandon in San Francisco, and under Virginia Harsh in
Carson City.
CAREER: Commercial artist and professional painter; active in Vallejo
Potter's Guild and Art League.
HONORS: Nevada Art Gallery, coordinator for exhibition, "Indian Heritage
'62"; accepted by National League of American Penwomen, rating of Art,
Design, and Mosaic.
EXHIBITIONS: FAIEAIP, PAC; extensively in Nevada and California. *One-
man shows*: Three.
AWARDS: Seven, in pottery, mosaic, watercolor, and collage.
ADDRESS: 200 Dwight Way, Vallejo, Calif.

Cattail Bird (*see* Awa Tsireh)

Cawastuma   *Laguna*
EXHIBITIONS: AIEC.

Cehu'pa (*see* Jaw)

Ce Komo Pyn (*see* Naranjo, José Dolores)

Cetaniyatake (?) (*see* Sitting Hawk)

Cetan Luta (*see* Red Hawk)

Chamon, John A.   *Jémez*
(Also known as Chamon, Juan.)
COLLECTIONS: *Public*: MNM.

Chamon, Juan (*see* Chamon, John A.)

Chapita, Dempsey   *Zuni*
BORN: 1922, Zuni Pueblo, N.M.
During his schooling, the artist painted for pleasure. He has not painted since
he left school, *ca.* 1939.
SERVICE: Discharged from armed services, 1945.
CAREER: Laborer near Zuni, N.M.
WORK PUBLISHED: Jacobson and D'Ucel (1950).
COLLECTIONS: *Private*: Denman.

Chapito, Tony   *Zuni*
EDUCATION: Santa Fe, 1937.
EXHIBITIONS: AIEC.

Charges Strong   *Crow*
WORK PUBLISHED: *Anthrolopogical Papers* (AMNH, Vol. 21, Pt. 4., autobiographical pictographic style painting on a buffalo robe).

Charging Bear (*see* Grass, John)

Charging Man (*see* Whitehorse, Roland N.)

Charlie Boy   *Zuni*
COLLECTIONS: *Public*: MAI.

Chauncey, Florence Nupok   *Eskimo*
Nupok, Upright Post
(Also known as Nupok, Florence.)
BORN: March 4, 1906, Gambell, Alaska.
MARRIED: Malegotkuk (or Malegoohtik) Chauncey. One adopted son, 1933.
Florence started drawing at home at the age of eight. Her uncle purchased old
drawing tablets for her use. Later, she executed drawings on sealskin for the
Gambell Weather Bureau. In 1947, she wrote, "...looking for good sealskins,
but hard to get, but I will make pictures in February, it wait 2 months to dry in
very coldest weather—make very white." The artist draws by the light of an
Eskimo lamp.
EXHIBITIONS: MNM, PAC, PAC/T; Alaska U.; Philander Smith College.
COLLECTIONS: *Public*: MAI, PAC. *Private*: Elkus, J. Snodgrass.
ADDRESS: Gambell, St. Lawrence Island, Alaska.

Chavarria, Elmer   *Pueblo* (?)
EDUCATION: Scholarship to Arizona, "Southwest Indian Art Project," 1962.
COLLECTIONS: *Public*: AU/ASM.
ADDRESS: Española, N.M.

Chávez, Calvin Fenley   *San Felipe-Laguna*
BORN: December 27, 1924, Winslow, Ariz. Son of Lazaro B. Chávez (San
Felipe) and Amy Bell (Laguna).
The artist often exhibited his oil portraits at the Annual Indian Market, Santa
Fe, N.M. He is also known as a carver of plaques with Kachina motifs. In 1964,
he underwent brain surgery which, for a time, threatened his career in art.
EDUCATION: Public schools, Winslow, 1938–47; Arizona S.C./F.; Art In-
struction, Inc., Minneapolis, Minn., 1948–50.
CAREER: Sign painter and commercial artist, Navaho Ordnance Depot,
1952; full-time artist.
COMMISSIONS: *Murals*: Chamber of Commerce, Flagstaff, Ariz. *Portraits*:
J. Howard Pyle, Governor of Arizona, 1954.
HONORS: Outstanding Jaycee in State of Arizona, 1954.
EXHIBITIONS: AIM, ASC, ASF, ITIC, MNM, PAC. *One-man shows*: ASC,
MNM.
AWARDS: 1946–48: ASF, ITIC.
COLLECTIONS: *Private*: Harvey.
ADDRESS: Box 8036, Cubero, N.M.

Chávez, Manuel "Bob"   *Cochití*
Owu Tewa
BORN: 1915, Cochití Pueblo, N.M.
EDUCATION: Santa Fe; graduated St. Catherine's; B.A., Loyola.
CAREER: Artist; employed at Santa Fe Statuary Mart.
WORK PUBLISHED: *La Turista* (June 7, 1957).
EXHIBITIONS: AIM, SAIEAIP.
COLLECTIONS: *Public*: MKMcNAI; Cornwall Heights, Philadelphia, Pa.;

Oklahoma State University. *Private*: Denman, R. Moore.
ADDRESS: 130 Spruce Street, Santa Fe, N.M.

Chea Sequah (*see* Hill, Joan)

Che Bon Ah Bu La (*see* Blue Eagle, Acee)

Che Chilly Tsosie (*see* Mitchell, Stanley C.)

Chee, Robert *Navaho*
BORN: 1938.
EDUCATION: Attended school in Bellemont, Ariz.; Inter-Mt.
SERVICE: 1958–61; nine months in Germany.
CAREER: Full-time artist.
WORK PUBLISHED: *New Mexico Magazine* (December 1960), *Inter-Tribal Indian Ceremonial Annual Magazine* (1961; 1962).
EXHIBITIONS: 1957–65: AIAE/WSU, FAIEAIP, MNM, PAC, PAC/T, SN; Philander Smith College.
AWARDS: 1960–64: nine, from AIAE/WSU, ITIC, MNM, PAC, SN.
COLLECTIONS: *Public*: AU/ASM, BIA, IACB, KM, MAI, MNA, MNM, PAC, SMNAI. *Private*: Berg, Bush, Dockstader, Elkus, C. Fenton, A. Forbes, R. Moore, Silberman, J. Snodgrass, Thoeny, Wyman.
ADDRESS: Box 71, Saint Michaels, Ariz.

Chenenaete (*see* Shave Head)

Chester, Eddie *Navaho*
EDUCATION: Albuquerque, 1959.
EXHIBITIONS: MNM, 1959.

Chester, Richard *Apache*
EXHIBITIONS: ITIC, 1958.
AWARDS: ITIC, 1958.

Chetlahe *Navaho* (?)
EXHIBITIONS: 1962–63: ITIC, SN.
AWARDS: 1962: SN, special award for non-traditional style painting.

Chet-toint, Charles (*see* Ohet Toint)

Chevarillo, Dario *San Felipe*
COLLECTIONS: *Public*: MNM (dated 1926).

Cheyatie, Patone *Zuni*
COLLECTIONS: *Public*: MNM (dated 1928). *Private*: Denman.

Chief Bull (*see* Sanderville, Richard)

Chief Charging Skunk (*see* Newton, Ranzy Alison)

Chief Killer *Cheyenne*
The artist was among the 72 Plains Indians taken as prisoners from Fort Sill, Okla., to Fort Marion, St. Augustine, Fla., in 1875.
COLLECTIONS: *Public*: YU/BRBML.

Chief Of Humor (*see* Wagoshe, Russell William)

Chinana, Christina *Jémez*
EDUCATION: Jémez, 1962.
EXHIBITIONS: MNM, 1962 (student show); SN, 1963.
AWARDS: MNM, honorable mention, 1962.

Chinana, Felipe   *Jémez*
  BORN: 1944.
  EDUCATION: Jémez.
  EXHIBITIONS: 1957–60: AAIE, AIE, PAC.
  AWARDS: AIE, 1957.

Chinana, Lawrence   *Jémez*
  COLLECTIONS: *Private*: Adlerblum.

Chinana, Paul   *Jémez*
  BORN: 1946.
  EDUCATION: Jémez, 1958.
  EXHIBITIONS: 1958–60: AAIE, MNM.
  AWARDS: MNM, 1958.
  COLLECTIONS: *Public*: MAI, MNM.

Chinana, Ricky   *Jémez*
  EDUCATION: Jémez, 1962.
  EXHIBITIONS: MNM, 1962.
  AWARDS: MNM, 1962.

Chinosa (*see* Lone Dog)

Chisholm, Calvin   *Cherokee-Shawnee*
  BORN: 1924, Sperry, Okla.
  EXHIBITIONS: AIEC.

Chiu Tah (*see* Mirabel, Vicente)

Choh   *Navaho*
  "In 1886, a Navaho by the name of Choh was making colored drawings of native
  men and women, birds and animals, a 'gaudily dressed chief riding at full tilt
  upon his Indian steed,' and occasional other subjects." Tanner (1950). (*See also*
  Big Lefthanded.)
  WORK PUBLISHED: Shufeldt (1889).

Chulundit (*see* Jones, Ruthe Blalock)

Chuokaichi, Linland   ?
  COLLECTIONS: *Private*: Elkus.

Chuyate, Charles   *Zuni*
  COLLECTIONS: *Private*: Harvey.

Clah, Alfred   *Navaho*
  EDUCATION: Institute, *ca.* 1962–64.
  EXHIBITIONS: PAC, YAIA.
  COLLECTIONS: *Public*: BIA. *Private*: McGrath.

Clarke, John Louis   *Blackfoot*
  Man Who Speaks Not
  BORN: Highwood, Mont.
    Scarlet fever in childhood left the artist unable to hear or speak. Well-known as
    a painter and sculptor, he is now blind.
  EDUCATION: Fort Shaw Indian School, Fort Shaw, Mont.; after illness,
  attended a school for the deaf in Milwaukee, Wisc.
  HONORS: Represented in *Indians of Today*.

EXHIBITIONS: CAI; Philadelphia Academy of Fine Arts, Pa.
AWARDS: Gold medal, Philadelphia Academy of Fine Arts, 1919; silver
medal, Spokane Art Association, 1928.
ADDRESS: East Glacier Park, Mont.

Claymore, Thomas William   *Sioux*
Nape Sica Hoksila, Bad Hand Boy
BORN: March 30, 1909. Cheyenne Agency, Cheyenne River, S. Dak. Son of
John Claymore (Sioux) and Katherine Carter (Sioux).
MARRIED: Idita M. Three children: Paul T., 1935; Gayle, 1940; Tommie
Cheryl, 1941.
> "Albert Yardley, Carlisle graduate, gave me my first small tips on drawing and a
> definite understanding of depth perception. Later, a cousin, George Claymore,
> showed me about shading."

EDUCATION: Elementary school in La Plant, S. Dak.; Haskell, 1927–30;
Bacone College, 1936–38; Redlands, 1949–51; Northern, 1963; B.F.A.,
N. Dak., 1965; oil painting instruction under William Dietz at Haskell, 1929.
CAREER: Artist; art instructor "in various schools over the years;" com-
pleted Office of Economic Opportunity program with youth, 1965.
EXHIBITIONS: 1954–65: Bismarck, N. Dak.; Aberdeen, S. Dak.; Charlotte,
N.C.; Washington, D.C.; Phoenix, Ariz.; Rapid City, S. Dak.
AWARDS: 1965: Territorial Art Show, Range Days; Wahpiya Luta Club
Art Show, Rapid City, S. Dak.
COLLECTIONS: *Public*: BIA, IACB.
ADDRESS: 1734 Beverly Glen Boulevard, Los Angeles, Calif.

Cleveland, Frederick   ?
EDUCATION: Albuquerque.
EXHIBITIONS: MNM, 1962.

Cloud Shield   *Oglala Sioux*
BORN: Date unknown; from the Pine Ridge Agency area, S. Dak.
WORK PUBLISHED: BAE, *4th AR*.
COLLECTIONS: *Public*: OAA/SI (a 34-page book containing 102 sketches
copied by Cloud Shield from the original Winter Count of 1777–1879 in his
possession; 104 sketches copied by Cloud Shield from the original Winter
Count of 1775–1879 in the possession of American Horse, *q.v.*).

Clutesi, George Charles   *Nootka*
BORN: January 1, 1905, Alberni, B.C., Canada
MARRIED: Name unknown. Five children.
> The artist has said it is his desire to depict on canvas the "past culture of my
> own race on the west coast of Vancouver Island, B.C., Canada."

EDUCATION: Alberni Boarding School through the eighth grade.
CAREER: British Columbia Packers, Ltd., B. Gregory Branch, Port Alberni,
B.C., 13 years; piledriver, bridge and dockworker, 20 years.
HONORS: Canadian Council Grant, 1961–62; named one of the "Indians of
North America," 1961.
BOOKS ILLUSTRATED: Street (1963).

EXHIBITIONS: 1945–64: throughout Canada and the U.S., including Seattle World's Fair. *One-man shows*: Victoria, Port Alberni, Ogama, Edmonton, Toronto, and Seattle.

COLLECTIONS: *Public*: UBC. *Private*: Frost.

ADDRESS: Rural Route # 3, Alberni, B.C., Canada.

Cochran, George McKee   *Cherokee*
Man Alone

BORN: October 5, 1908, Stilwell, Okla. Son of Oscar Cochran (Cherokee) and Ada Redbird (Cherokee).

MARRIED: Avanell Hooks. Seven children: Joan, Betty, William, Thomas, Oscar, Sue Nell, James.

  After WWII, the artist traveled around the country sketching various tribes.
  He later organized the Northwest Cartoonists' and Gagwriters' Association.

EDUCATION: Wyandotte; Chilocco; Hominy High School, Hominy, Okla.; Haskell, 1927.

HONORS: American Indian Festival of Arts, member of board of directors; represented in *Who's Who in the West, Who's Who in American Art,* and the *World Almanac of Art.*

COMMISSIONS: *Murals*: Church of Latter Day Saints, Eugene, Oreg.

BOOKS ILLUSTRATED: Cochran (1939).

EXHIBITIONS: AAID; Oregon State Fair; Hollywood (Calif.) Park Gallery, University of Oregon; American Indian Festival of Arts, La Grande, Oreg.

AWARDS: 1952–61: AAID Grand Award; Oregon State Fair.

COLLECTIONS: *Public*: BIA; Haskell Institute; Truman Library, Independence, Mo.; Seattle Public Library; *Oregonian*, Portland, Oreg.; Warm Springs Tribal Council, Oreg.

ADDRESS: 681 Chase Street, Eugene, Oreg.

Cochran, J. Woody   *Cherokee*
BORN: September 28, 1919, Tahlequah, Okla. Son of George W. Cochran (Cherokee) and Nellie Ann Ballard.

MARRIED: Geraldine Ione Berg, 1943. Two children: Melanie Jo, 1943; Woody Kim, 1951.

EDUCATION: Oklahoma S.U., 1937–41; Chicago, 1946–47; B.A., Tulsa, 1950; M.A., Tulsa, 1956.

SERVICE: WWII, U.S. Air Force, four years; Southwest Pacific Theater (Distinguished Flying Cross, Silver Star, Purple Heart, Air Medal, four Presidential Citations for combat action).

CAREER: Associate Professor of Art, University of Tulsa, 1950–.

HONORS: Selected by the U.S. War Department as "An Indian American" to represent minority Americans at the *New York Herald Tribune Forum,* "Pioneering for a Civilized World," Waldorf-Astoria, New York, N.Y., November, 1943.

EXHIBITIONS: BM/B, CAI, DMFA, NYWF, OAC, PAC, SAM/S, SN, TAI, WAM; Mid-America Exhibition, WRNGA; Invitational Print Show, Philadelphia Art Alliance, Philadelphia, Pa.; 18th Annual International Exhibition, The National Serigraph Society, 1957, Meltzer Gallery, New

York, N.Y. *One-man shows*: PAC; University of Tulsa; East Branch Library, Tulsa, Okla.; Northeastern State Teachers College.
AWARDS: 1948–65: Six from DMFA, OAC, PAC, SN.
COLLECTIONS: *Public*: DMFA. *Private*: Bruestle, Cadenhead, Enlows, Grubb, Ch. Harris, Hayden, Henneke, Humphrey, E. Johnson, Kaho, Livingston, McMorris, Patman, Place, W. S. Price, Randolph, Underwood.
ADDRESS: 1553 East 46th Place, Tulsa, Okla.

Coffee   *Cheyenne* (?)
There was a Coffee, formerly a Southern Cheyenne but living with the Northern Cheyenne, who was a helper to the chief medicine man of the tribal medicine lodge. The artist Coffee may be the same man.
> With the aid of an old man, he painted a war record of mounted men on deerskin. The skin was heavily damaged when a torrential rain flooded a portion of the Lowe Gallery.

WORK PUBLISHED: Alexander (1938).
COLLECTIONS: *Public*: UM/LG.

Coho, Vernon   *Navaho*
EDUCATION: Riverside, *ca.* 1961; scholarship to Arizona, "Southwest Indian Art Project," 1962.
EXHIBITIONS: PAC.
COLLECTIONS: *Private*: Frazier.
ADDRESS: Box 21, Ramah, N.M., and 2515 Reagon Street, Apt. 202, Dallas, Tex.

Cohoe, William   *Southern Cheyenne*
Mohe, Elk; *Mapera Mohe*, Water Elk (or Moose); *Nohnicas*, Lame Man.
(Also known as Broken Leg, Cojo, and Cripple.)
BORN: *ca.* 1854, in Colo.; died, March 18, 1924, in Blaine Co., near Bickford, Okla. Son of Sleeping Bear and Plain Looking. The artist's father was killed in the massacre of Black Kettle's camp, Sand Creek, 1864.
MARRIED: Small Woman (Cheyenne), who married him before he was sent to prison and remained his wife until his death. One child: Walking Coyote (Charles Cohoe), 1882. After his return from prison and school, Cohoe was given his wife's sister, Pelican (or Surprise) Woman (also known as Vister) as a second wife. They had one son, Black Bird (Bruce Cohoe), *ca.* 1885.
> Cohoe was one of 72 Plains Indians taken as prisoners from Fort Sill, Okla., to Fort Marion, St. Augustine, Fla., in 1875. During his three years there, he drew pictures of his relatives and of the events in his life. He apparently drew little, if at all, after leaving prison.

EDUCATION: After imprisonment, one of the first Indian students admitted to Hampton, April 1878; among the first students enrolled at Carlisle, 1879.
SERVICE: U.S. Army, scout at Fort Supply, 1887–88.
CAREER: Apprentice tailor, 1879; laborer, millhand, teamster (transported supplies), farmer, and butcher, Cheyenne-Arapaho Agency (present site of Darlington), Okla., 1880; appointed baker of bread, Cheyenne-Arapaho Agency School, December 1, 1881; later worked as a clerk in a local trading post for about six years. By 1891, he was farming his own land.

HONORS: Head chief of the Onihanotria (War Dancers Society) in his last years.

WORK PUBLISHED: Cohoe (1964).

COLLECTIONS: *Public*: MHS/B, YU/BRBML. *Private*: Petersen.

Cojo (*see* Cohoe, William)

Colbert, Frank Overton   *Chickasaw*

Red Feather

(Also known as Colbert, Chief F. Overton.)

BORN: August 10, 1896, Riverside, Okla. Died March 20, 1935, Fort Lyon, Colo. Son of Holmes Colbert (Chickasaw), who with Sampson Folsom drafted a constitution for the Chickasaw Nation in 1856. Holmes Colbert was elected first national secretary of the bicameral legislature of his tribe. P/GF: B. F. Colbert, who built and operated the first ferry across the Red River near Colbert, Okla. The artist was a descendant of Dougherty "Winchester" Colbert, governor of the Chickasaws from 1858 to 1860.

MARRIED: Kate London; divorced, 1933. One son: Robert Holmes, 1926.

The artist is descended from a long line of distinguished and prosperous Chickasaws (see *Oklahoma Almanac*, 1959). He lived in Paris from 1923 to 1926 and in Greenwich Village, New York City, after WWI. A member of the Whitney Club, he was a well-known "Village" personality in the 1920's. He later moved to Santa Fe, N.M., traveled extensively, and studied the arts and crafts of many Indian tribes.

EDUCATION: Calera (Okla.) Public School, Murray State Agricultural College, Tishomingo, Okla.; attended art classes in New York City and Paris, 1918–25.

SERVICE: WWI, U.S. Navy, two years.

CAREER: Artist.

EXHIBITIONS: Before 1923, Architectural League, New York; The Independents, Groupe de Parnasse, Paris; with sculptress Renée Prahar. *One-man shows*: Three, including Montrose Gallery, New York, and a retrospective show of 100 paintings and drawings, Galerie Paula Insel, New York, 1963.

COLLECTIONS: *Public*: OHSM. *Private*: Colbert, Garland, Taylor.

Collins, Howard Rufus (*see* Ducee Blue Buzzard)

Collins, Martha Adele   *Chickasaw-Choctaw*

Pucunubbi, Baby

BORN: January 14, 1908, Blanchard, Okla. Daughter of Emmett L. Victor (Chickasaw) and Lee Desmond. P/GU: Douglas Johnston, governor of the Chickasaws. P/GM: Lucy Moncrief, half sister of Johnston.

MARRIED: Patrick Collins, 1934.

EDUCATION: Criner (Okla.) Rural School, 1914; Lindsay (Okla.) Elementary Schools, Mt. Mary's Academy, Oklahoma City, Okla., *ca.* 1912–26: St. Elizabeth's Indian School, Purcell, Okla., *ca.* 1927; private art instruction under Emalita Newton Terry, 1960–.

CAREER: Housewife; active in community art affairs; member of Las Vegas (Nev.) Art League, 1951–.

EXHIBITIONS: MNM, OAC, PAC, SAIEAIP; Art Fair, Community Fair, Art Roundup, Art Show, Mobile Home Show, Art League Exhibition, and

Sierra Vista Ranchos Exhibition (all in Las Vegas, Nev.). *One-man shows*: HM.

AWARDS: 1957–64: 18 from ITIC, MNM, and various Las Vegas competitions; two trophies, Sierra Vista Ranchos Exhibition.

COLLECTIONS: *Public*: IACB. *Private*: L. Allen, Greenberg, R. Maxwell, Noble, Ried, H. Roberts, H. Snodgrass, Stalcup, Zellehofer.

ADDRESS: 1631 Curtis Drive, Las Vegas, Nev.

Coloque, Mary Nancy   *Jémez*
EDUCATION: Jémez, 1960.
EXHIBITIONS: MNM, 1960.
AWARDS: MNM, 1960.

Colville, Clyde   *Navaho*
COLLECTIONS: *Public*: PU/M.

Comanche Enemy (*see* Geionety, George)

Coma Pesva (*see* Lomayesva, Louis)

Concha, John   *Taos*
The artist was still painting in 1950, although his work was not readily available to the general public.
COLLECTIONS: *Public*: MNM.

Connery, Stanley   ?
EXHIBITIONS: MNM, 1965.
AWARDS: MNM, 1965.
ADDRESS: 2749 West 33 Avenue, Denver, Colo.

Conte Feri (*see* Hard Heart)

Coochwatewa, Victor H.   *Hopi*
COLLECTIONS: *Public*: MAI.

Cooke, Connie   *Hopi*
EXHIBITIONS: PAC.

Cooyama, Homer   *Hopi*
(Also known as Coyama.)
The artist began his art career at 12. He has painted church fonts throughout the U.S. In 1927, he executed a painting on a curtain for the stage of the Western Navaho Indian School. He operated a painting shop in Flagstaff for several years.
EDUCATION: Government Indian school, Keams Canyon, Ariz.; Sherman; Kansas City; School of Applied Arts, Bear Creek, Mich.
CAREER: Artist, cabinetmaker, sign-painter.
EXHIBITIONS: FWG, HM.
COLLECTIONS: *Public*: AF (signed H. S. Cooyama).

Cordova, Louis   *Santa Clara*
(Also known as Cordova, Luis.)
EDUCATION: Santa Fe.
COLLECTIONS: *Public*: MAI (painting dated *ca.* 1920's).

Coriz, Fidel   *Santo Domingo*
EDUCATION: Santa Fe, 1953.
COLLECTIONS: *Private*: Wyman.

Coriz, Nat   *Tesuque*
COLLECTIONS: *Public*: CU/LMA.

Cornine, Barbara   *Cherokee*
EDUCATION: Bacone College.
EXHIBITIONS: PAC, 1958.
AWARDS: PAC.

Cornplanter, Carrie   *Seneca*
COLLECTIONS: *Public*: MAI.

Cornplanter, Jesse   *Seneca*
BORN: Cattaraugus Reservation, N.Y. Died *ca.* 1961. Last living descendant
of the well-known Cornplanter of George Washington's era.
MARRIED: Elsina Billy (Seneca).
  The artist held many distinguished tribal positions, including: ritual chief of the
  Long House; chief of New Town, Indian village of Snipe Clan; singer for the
  Great Feather Dance; head singer for many tribal ceremonies.
SERVICE: WWI, 20 months.
CAREER: Instructor of False Face mask carving, WPA Indian Arts and
Crafts Project; master carver of ceremonial False Face masks; author,
singer, and painter.
HONORS: Represented in *Indians of Today*.
COMMISSIONS: *Illustrations*: At the age of nine, he executed sketches relating
to the life of the Long House people (commissioned by the State of New
York).
BOOKS ILLUSTRATED: Cornplanter| (*ca.* |1903; 1938), Parker (1910; 1913;
1923), Hamilton (1950).
COLLECTIONS: *Public*: MAI, RMAS; New York State Library.

Cosen, Gilbert   *Apache*
EDUCATION: Bacone College, 1960–61; scholarship to Arizona, "Southwest
Indian Art Project," 1962.
EXHIBITIONS: PAC.
ADDRESS: Box 182, Whiteriver, Ariz.

Cosen, Lydia M.   *Apache*
BORN: 1935.
EDUCATION: Scholarship to Arizona, "Southwest Indian Art Project."
ADDRESS: Whiteriver, Ariz.

Costilow, Eunice   *Cherokee*
EXHIBITIONS: PAC, 1965.
ADDRESS: Lake Euchee, Jay, Okla.

Coyama (*see* Cooyama, Homer)

Cree   *Crow*
BORN: Date unknown; from Fort Benton, Mont.
  A medallion of strouding outlined with a band of black and white beads, quilled
  horizontal strips, and painted drawings of horses and men, was given by the
  artist to W. M. Cary. In 1861, this gift was acquired by M. H. Schiefflin and is
  now in MAI collections.
COLLECTIONS: *Public*: MAI.

Cripple (*see* Cohoe, William)

Crispin, Santiago   ?
   EDUCATION: Santa Fe, 1924.
   COLLECTIONS: *Public*: MNM (dated 1924).

Crispin, Sutero   *Navaho*
   EDUCATION: Santa Fe, 1958; Albuquerque, 1959.
   EXHIBITIONS: MNM, 1958–59.

The Crow (Chief)   *Sioux*
   Kanribeloka, The Crow
   One of five artists whose works, commissioned and collected by Rudolf Cronau,
   1880–83, are now referred to as the Cronau Album (*see* Sinte).
   COLLECTIONS: *Public*: AMNH.

Crow Indian (*see* Yellow Nose)

Crow Nose (*see* Roman Nose)

Crumbo, Woodrow Wilson   *Creek-Potawatomi*
   (Also known as Crumbo, Woody.)
   BORN: January 31, 1912, Lexington, Okla. Son of Alex Crumbo and Mary.
   MARRIED: Lillian Faye Hogue, 1941. Two children: Minisa, 1942; Woody
   Max, 1946.
   > At the end of the third grade, Crumbo's schooling was interrupted for nearly
   > ten years. During this period he, and other young Indian boys of Anadarko,
   > Okla., were encouraged by Mrs. Susie Peters (*see* Five Kiowas), who worked
   > with them, finding them materials with which to paint and a market for their
   > work. "Some of us were so small," Crumbo said, "that we sat on gallon buckets
   > and used the backs of chairs for easels". The artist returned to school at 17 to
   > study art, anthropology, and history and to pursue his many talents. In 1952, he
   > said, "Half of my life passed in striving to complete the pictorial record of Indian
   > history, religion, rituals, customs, way of life, and philosophies. It is now ac-
   > complished—a graphic record that a million words could not begin to tell." In
   > 1939, Philbrook Art Center was given the first Indian painting in its collection,
   > Crumbo's "Deer and Birds."
   EDUCATION: Fort Sill; Chilocco; scholarship to American, 1931–33; Wichita,
   1933–36; Oklahoma, 1936–38; studied mural technique under Olaf Nordmark, watercolor under Clayton Henri Staples and painting and drawing
   under O. B. Jacobson.
   CAREER: Conducted a dance group in a government-sponsored tour of re-
   servations throughout the U.S., 1933; camp director of arts and crafts,
   Estes Park, Colo., summer, 1934; instructor of hobbies, Wichita Public
   Schools, 1934–35; director of arts and crafts, Kit Carson Summer Camp
   for Boys, Colo., summer, 1935; director of arts and crafts, Rancho Verde
   Camp for Boys, Colo., summer, 1936; silversmithing instructor, University
   of Oklahoma, 1936–37; director of art, Bacone College, 1938–41; aircraft
   designer in Tool and Die Dept., Cessna Aircraft, Wichita, Kan., 1941–42;
   designer in Tool and Die Dept., Douglas Aircraft, Tulsa, Okla., *ca.* 1942;
   freelance artist, Taos, N.M.; artist in residence, Gilcrease Museum, Tulsa,
   Okla.; assistant director, El Paso (Tex.) Museum of Art, *ca.* 1962–.
   HONORS: High school valedictorian; scholarship to American Indian
   Institute; won National Dance Contest (with partner), ITIC, 1935; Julius

Rosenwald Fellowship, 1945–46; represented in *Indians of Today*; member Δ Φ Δ (National Collegiate Art Fraternity.)

COMMISSIONS: *Murals*: OU, PAC, USDI; Fort Sill Indian School; Nowata Federal Building; Home of Sequoyah, Sallisaw, Okla.; home of G. A. Hoult, Wichita, Kan. *Stained Glass Window*: Rose Chapel, Bacone College.

WORK PUBLISHED: La Farge (1956). *3rd Annual American Indian Week Brochure*, Tulsa (October 18–22, 1938), *Tulsa Sunday World Magazine* (December 7, 1952), *Sooner Magazine* (November 1954); *Oklahoma Today* (Summer 1958); *Life International* (March 16, 1959).

EXHIBITIONS: 1936–65: Over 200 exhibitions in Europe and North and South America: AAUW, AIEC, AIW, AMNH, CGA, DAR (Washington, D.C.), FWG, HM, ITIC, KM, MNM, OAC, OU, PAC, PAC/T, SFMA, SN; Yale University; Texas State; City Library, Bartlesville, Okla.; Junior League of Tulsa Building, City Library, Fayetteville, Ark.; Enid (Okla.) Art Association, *One-man shows*: AMNH, MNM, OAC, OU, PAC, USDI, WAM, WU.

AWARDS: Sixteen during 1938–60.

COLLECTIONS: *Public*: BIA, CCHM, GM, IACB, KM, MAI, MNA/KHC, OU/L, OU/SM, PAC, SMNAI. *Private*: Callaway, Denman, Elkus, Field, Schonwald, Thoeny, Walch, Wurlitzer, Wyman.

ADDRESS: 1516 Murchison Street, El Paso, Tex.

Crumbo, Woody (*see* Crumbo, Woodrow Wilson)

Cruz, Ramoncita *San Juan*
EDUCATION: Santa Fe, 1938.
EXHIBITIONS: AIW.

Crying Wind (*see* Doonkeen, Eulamae Narcomey)

Cusick, David *Tuscarora*
Although his education was not extensive, the artist was "thought to be a good doctor by both whites and Indians."
BOOKS ILLUSTRATED: Cusick (1828).
COLLECTIONS: *Public*: OAA/SI (watercolor and ink sketches credited to Cusick).

Cut Ear *Apache*
COLLECTIONS: *Public*: OHSM (the artist was one of the 72 prisoners taken from Fort Sill, Okla., to Fort Marion, St. Augustine, Fla., in 1875).

Da, Anthony *San Ildefonso*
The artist, the son of Popovi Da (*q.v.*), has attended schools of higher learning and recently served in the armed services.
EXHIBITIONS: 1959–60: ITIC, MNM, PAC; Tulsa (Okla.) Central Library.
AWARDS: ITIC, MNM.
COLLECTIONS: *Public*: MAI. *Private*: A. Forbes.

Da, Popovi *San Ildefonso*
BORN: In New Mexico. Son of Julián Martínez (*q.v.*) and María Montoya, the internationally known potter (both San Ildefonso). The artist has legally changed his name from Tony Martínez to Popovi Da.
MARRIED: Anita Cata (Santa Clara).

Like his father, the artist has done his best work with symbolic designs and geometric figures. After his father's death in 1943, he did most of the designing and decorating of his mother's pottery.

SERVICE: WWII.

HONORS: Governor of his pueblo, *ca.* 1952.

CAREER: Owner and operator of an arts and crafts shop in San Ildefonso Pueblo, *ca.* 1948–.

EXHIBITIONS: NGA, 1953.

COLLECTIONS: *Private*: Denman, D. Kramer, Thoeny.

ADDRESS:: Route 1, Box 160, Santa Fe, N.M.

Da, Tony (*see* Da, Anthony)

Dagadahga (*see* Dick, Cecil)

Dage, Lynn   *Choctaw*

EXHIBITIONS: MNM, 1965.

AWARDS: MNM, 1965.

ADDRESS: 1835 Cruse, Las Cruces, N.M.

Dahadid, Posey   *Navaho*

COLLECTIONS: *Public*: MNM.

Damrow, Charles   *Cherokee*

COLLECTIONS: *Private*: Thoeny.

Dancing Boy (*see* Mirabel, Vicente)

Darby, Raymond Lee   *Kiowa*

Thayhaiya (and Hunting Horse)

BORN: August 1, 1938, Carnegie, Okla. Son of Ethelene Darby (Kiowa).

MARRIED: Karen Ann. Three children.

EDUCATION: Cache Elementary and High Schools; Cameron Junior College, Lawton, Okla.

CAREER: Night club entertainer, Nashville, Tenn.; artist.

COLLECTIONS: *Private*: Deupree, R. Moore, Thoeny.

ADDRESS: 2113 Arlington, Lawton, Okla.

Darling, Marcell J.   *Potawatomi*

Wasconadie, Prairie Flower

BORN: 1911, Mayetta, Kan.

EDUCATION: Haskell.

CAREER: House painter, artist.

EXHIBITIONS: PAC.

ADDRESS: 1808 North Atlanta Court, Tulsa, Okla.

Davenport, Julia Chisholm   *Chickasaw-Cherokee*

COLLECTIONS: *Public*: OHSM.

David, Neal   *Hopi*

COLLECTIONS: *Public*: MAI.

Davis, Jesse Edwin, II   *Comanche*

Asawoya, Running Wolf

BORN: July 9, 1921, Anadarko, Okla. Son of William G. Davis (Creek-Seminole) and Richenda E. Merrick (Comanche-Cheyenne). P/GGM: Alice

Brown Davis, only woman chief of the Seminoles (appointed by the President) and postmistress of Okemah, Okla., she and her Scottish husband owned and operated the Arbeka Trading Post in Oklahoma Territory. P/GF: Jesse Edwin Davis, who inherited and operated the Arbeka Trading Post, later U.S. Marshal in Indian Territory. M/GGF: Comanche Jack, a scout for the U.S. Army at Fort Sill, Okla. M/GF: Eustace Merrick (Comanche), a leader in resettling the Indians of the area. M/GA: Mary Inkanish (Cheyenne), a noted beadworker at Anadarko, Okla
MARRIED: Vivian Saunkeah (Boiled Man) (Kiowa), 1944. One son: Jesse Edwin, III, 1944.

> The artist has never been a prolific painter, and each year he paints less as he becomes more active in photography and music. At the peak of his painting career, about 1957, he showed promise of becoming one of the outstanding Plains Indian painters.

EDUCATION: B.F.A., Oklahoma, 1949.
SERVICE: WWII, U.S. Navy, three years; South Pacific Theater.
CAREER: Production planner, Tinker Air Force Base, Oklahoma City, Okla., 1951–.
WORK PUBLISHED: Jacobson and D'Ucel (1950). *Oklahoma Today* (Winter 1961–62; Spring 1962); *Hughesnews* (March 12, 1965).
EXHIBITIONS: AAID, AIE, BNIAS, MNM, MNM/T, MPI, PAC; Frontier City, U.S.A. *One-man shows*: PAC.
AWARDS: 1948–59: Six from PAC (Grand Award, 1957); AAID, Best in Show, 1957.
COLLECTIONS: *Public*: PAC. *Private*: Field, Holway, Marriott, Schonwald.
ADDRESS: 517 Wildewood Terrace, Oklahoma City, Okla.

Davis, Ralph U.   *Navaho*
COLLECTIONS: *Public*: IACB (silk screened cards).

Davis, Truman   *Navaho*
EDUCATION: Santa Fe.
EXHIBITIONS: FWG, 1943.
COLLECTIONS: *Private*: Hogue.

Dawes, Ermaleen   *Cheyenne*
EDUCATION: Chilocco.
EXHIBITIONS: PAC.

Dawn Walker (*see* Pushetonequa, Charles)

Day After Day (*see* Kabotie, Fred)

De Cinq-Mars, Tahcawin Rosebud Josephine Marie Louise (*see* Tahcawin)

Decker, Vernon Edward   *Shoshoni*
Little Bear
BORN: 1943, Schurz, Nev. Son of Evlyne Pete Decker.
EDUCATION: Graduated Stewart. Attended Institute, 1963.
EXHIBITIONS: SAIEAIP, 1965.
ADDRESS: 852½ Wisconsin Street, Chico, Calif.

De Cora, Angel   *Winnebago*
MARRIED: William H. (Lone Star) Dietz (listed in *Indians of Today*).

EDUCATION: Art school, Boston, Mass.; Hampton.
CAREER: Instructor, Carlisle Indian School.
COMMISSIONS: *Murals*: Carlisle Indian School.
WORK PUBLISHED: La Flesche (1900).

Deere, Eli   *Creek*
BORN: *ca.* 1914. Orphaned and reared by his grandfather, Mose Bird, who lived on Honey Creek, near Okmulgee, Okla.
EDUCATION: Chilocco.
COLLECTIONS: *Public*: CCHM.

Deere, Noah   *Creek*
BORN: August 23, 1929, Eufaula, Okla.
EDUCATION: Bacone College; Benedictine.
SERVICE: U.S. Army, two and one-half years; Japan and Korea.
CAREER: Commercial artist and illustrator in 1958.
WORK PUBLISHED: Stirling (1955). *National Geographic Magazine* (March, 1955).
EXHIBITIONS: JGS, NGA, PAC, PAC/T, SFWF.
AWARDS: PAC, 1949–50.
COLLECTIONS: *Public*: MHDYMM, PAC.

De Groat, Jay   *Navaho*
Joogii, Blue Jay
BORN: May 16, 1947.
EDUCATION: Graduated Gallup, 1965.
EXHIBITIONS: Window Rock, Ariz.; Crownpoint and Gallup, N.M.
AWARDS: Three during 1962–63.
COLLECTIONS: *Private*: Berg.
ADDRESS: Box 222, Window Rock, Ariz.

Delena, Sam   *Zuni*
COLLECTIONS: *Public*: MNM.

De Mott, Helen   *Seneca*
BORN: 1923, New York, N.Y.
EDUCATION: National Academy of Design; Art Students League, N.Y.
EXHIBITIONS: RM; Seligman Gallery, Ashby Gallery, and Queens College, N.Y.; Research Institute, Maitland, Fla.
ADDRESS: 43–30 48th Street, Long Island City, N.Y.

Denetdale, Myron   *Navaho*
EXHIBITIONS: HM, 1951.

Denetsosie, Hoke   *Navaho*
Kiya Ahnii, Slim Navaho (or *Kiyaa Nii*, House Standing Upright)
BORN: *Ca.* 1919, near Cameron, Ariz., on the Navaho Reservation.
    Toward the end of his studies at Phoenix Indian School, the artist met Lloyd H. New, then art director, whose encouragement was his major influence during this period. The artist's most productive years were between 1930 and 1940.
EDUCATION: Schools in Leupp and Tuba City, Ariz.; graduated Phoenix.
CAREER: Visual Aid Division, BIA, Window Rock, Ariz., 14 years; formerly a logger and commercial artist.

COMMISSIONS: *Murals*: Arizona Craftsmen Building, Scottsdale, Ariz., ten panels.
BOOKS ILLUSTRATED: Clark (1939).
WORK PUBLISHED: Jacobson and D'Ucel (1950).
EXHIBITIONS: FWG, HM.
COLLECTIONS: *Public*: MNM.

Denton, Coye Elizabeth   *Cherokee*
BORN: October 14, 1914, Romulus, Okla. Daughter of Lester Jerome Hathcock (Cherokee) and Izetta Robins (Cherokee).
MARRIED: Booth Dewey Denton, 1938. Two sons: E. Q. Denton (stepson), 1933; Ernest Dewey Denton (deceased, 1946).
  Mrs. Denton is a nontraditionalist. She is a charter member of the Ada Artists' Association and was instrumental in establishing an art center in Ada, Okla. From 1950 to 1964, she toured numerous countries to study art.
EDUCATION: Hays Elementary School, Ada, Okla.; graduated Ada High School, 1933; B.S., East, 1941; graduate studies, East, 1946. Private art studies under Ida Hoover, Kenneth F. Campbell, Lunda Gill, Glenn Swenlund, Richard Van Wagoner, and with the Ada Artists' Association.
CAREER: Housewife; active in civic and church affairs; arts and crafts teacher in the Salvation Army Bible School, *ca.* 1954–60; member of the Salvation Army Advisory Board.
EXHIBITIONS: 1947–63: FAIEAIP, ITIC, PAC; Oklahoma Federated Women's Clubs; East Central State College, Linschied Gallery; Ada Public Library (all in Ada, Okla.).
AWARDS: Four during 1947–48.
COLLECTIONS: *Private*: Cravens, Downs, F. Fleet, M. Fleet, J. Harris, Hauger, R. Hoover, Love, Mayhue, Pherigo, R. Thomas, Welborn, Wray, Yagol.
ADDRESS: Box 444, Ada, Okla.

Desautel, Ernie   *Colville*
BORN: March 14, 1944.
EDUCATION: Santa Fe.
EXHIBITIONS: MNM, PAC.
AWARDS: MNM, 1962.
ADDRESS: Box 1006, Elmer City, Wash.

Des Jarlait, Patrick Robert   *Chippewa*
Nagawbo, Boy Of The Woods
BORN: March 1, 1921, Red Lake, Minn., on the Chippewa Reservation. Son of Solomon Des Jarlait and Elizabeth Blake.
MARRIED: Ramona Needham, August 24, 1945. Five children: Robert, 1946; Patrick, 1952; Charmaine, 1953; Delmar, 1956,; Ronald, 1962.
  Before WWII, the artist organized an art department in an Arizona War Relocation Center. Although he was interested in both painting and music, he chose art as a more satisfying means of self-expression.
EDUCATION: Graduated from Pipestone (Minn.) Indian Training School, 1935; Red Lake (Minn.) High School, 1939; Phoenix J.C., 1940–41.
SERVICE: WWII, U.S. Navy, four years; Visual Training.

CAREER: Japanese War Relocation Center, Poston, Ariz., 1941; commercial artist specializing in film animation for TV, training and industrial films, and general commercial art, 1948–.

HONORS: Represented in *Who's Who in American Art*.

EXHIBITIONS: 1946–64: ITIC, PAC, PAC/T, SN. *One-man shows*: San Diego Fine Arts Gallery, St. Paul (Minn.) Art Gallery.

AWARDS: Nine during 1946–64, including SN Grand Award.

COLLECTIONS: *Public*: PAC; Campbell Mitcun Advertising Agency, Minneapolis, Minn. *Private*: Bimson, Needham.

ADDRESS: 7641 62nd Avenue North, New Hope, Minn.

Dewa, R. B. *Zuni*

COLLECTIONS: *Public*: OU/SM.

Dewayesva (*see* Talahytewa, Gibson)

Dewey, Wilson *San Carlos Apache*

Sundust

BORN: June 25, 1915, on the San Carlos Reservation, Ariz.

EDUCATION: Attended San Carlos, *ca.* 1923, 1927, 1931–33; St. John's Mission School, Komatke, Ariz., 1928; Santa Fe, *ca.* 1938.

SERVICE: WWII, U.S. Army.

CAREER: Football and basketball player; rodeo calf roper.

WORK PUBLISHED: Jacobson and D'Ucel (1950). *Paintings by American Indians*, CPLH (1962).

EXHIBITIONS: AIW, CPLH, FWG, HM, MNM, OU/ET, PAC, PAC/T; Paul Elder Co., San Francisco, Calif.

COLLECTIONS: *Public*: GM, MNM, MRFM, PAC. *Private*: Denman, Dietrich, Elkus, Hogue, Schonwald.

Dhealdh Yazzie Bitsi (*see* Cassady, Ann Virginia)

Dick, Cecil *Cherokee*

Dagadahga, Standing Alone

BORN: 1915, Rose, Okla. Since deceased.

Although orphaned at 12 and reared in Indian boarding schools, the artist became an authority on Cherokee mythology and the Cherokee written language.

EDUCATION: Seneca; Sequoyah; Bacone College; Santa Fe; graduated Bagley High School, Tahlequah, Okla.

CAREER: Art instructor, Chilocco Indian School, 1939–42; illustrator in aircraft plant during WWII.

COMMISSIONS: *Murals*: Bagley High School; Sequoyah; Rocky Ford Indian Day School, Jay, Okla.; Chilocco; U.S. Indian Hospital, Claremore, Okla.; Oak Hill School, Valliant, Okla.; Santa Fe. *Displays*: John Wanamaker (International Sports Show), New York, N.Y., 1936; Sequoyah Weavers Exhibit, New York, N.Y., 1946.

WORK PUBLISHED: Jacobson and D'Ucel (1950). *Oklahoma Today* (Summer 1958), *Life International* (March, 16, 1959); *Sunday Bonanza, San Francisco Chronicle* (August 22, 1965).

EXHIBITIONS: AIEC, AIW, NGA, PAC, PAC/T.

COLLECTIONS: *Public*: GM, MAI, PAC. *Private*: Deupree, Field, D. Maxwell, Middleton.

Dickson, Larry   *Zuni*
EDUCATION: Albuquerque, 1962–63.
EXHIBITIONS: MNM, 1963.

Dineh Ligaai (*see* Mitchell, George Charlie)

Dishta, Duane   *Zuni*
EXHIBITIONS: AAIEAE.
COLLECTIONS: *Private*: Adlerblum.

Dishta, Virgil, Jr.   *Zuni*
EXHIBITIONS: MNM, 1965.
AWARDS: MNM, 1965, special award.
ADDRESS: Box 223, Zuni, N.M.

Dodge, Adee (*see* Dodge, Aydee)

Dodge, Aydee   *Navaho*
WORK PUBLISHED: *Arizona Highways* (December 1958; July 1959; August 1965).
EXHIBITIONS: ITIC, 1958.
COLLECTIONS: *Public*: ASU. *Private*: Denman, Mullan, Thoeny.

Doha (*see* Tohausen)

Dohasan (*see* Tohausen)

Dohate (*see* Tohausen)

Dohausen (*see* Tohausen)

Dolwiftema (*see* Nahsohnhoya, Thomas Dolwiftema)

Donations (*see* Paukei, George)

Don't Braid His Hair   *Sioux*
COLLECTIONS: *Public*: MAI (pictographic painting on paper).

Doonkeen, Eulamae Narcomey   *Seminole*
Hah Gay Kee Hooduh Lee, Crying Wind
BORN: December 12, 1931, Oklahoma City, Okla. Daughter of John Osceola Narcomey (Seminole-Creek) and Maggie Coker (Seminole-Creek). P/GGGF: Narkome, killed in the Civil War serving under Gen. Stand Watie in the Confederate Home Brigade. M/GGGU: Ispahitcher, a circuit judge at Okmulgee, Okla., previously chief of the Creeks during the Green Peach War and a Confederate officer during the Civil War. M/GM: Jennie Lasley, whose ancestors were Hitchiti and Cheyaha. M/GF: Dave Coker. M/GGGF: London Coker, a lighthorseman.
MARRIED: Al Doonkeen, March 15, 1953. Five children: Kotcha, 1957; Alfreda Margaret, 1958; Dana Charles, 1960; Conchattee, 1962.
EDUCATION: Attended Northeast Senior High School, Oklahoma City; Chilocco; graduated Bacone College High School, 1950; Central, 1963–.
SERVICE: WAF, Continental Air Command, 1951–54.
CAREER: Stenographer; art student, with minor in education.
HONORS: Princess of Seminole Tribe of Oklahoma, 1946–56; model for artist Pierre Tarteau, three years.

EXHIBITIONS: Conservative Artists' Sidewalk Show, Oklahoma City, Okla., 1961.
COLLECTIONS: *Private*: W. Brown, S. Carter, Laughlin.
ADDRESS: 1608 North West 35th, Oklahoma City, Okla.

Dorsey, Tom (*see* Two-Arrows, Tom)

Dorsey, Tom, Jr.   *Onondaga*
BORN: 1943. Son of Tom Two-Arrows (*q.v.*).
EXHIBITIONS: PAC.

Double Runner   *Blackfoot*
The artist assisted in the execution of a 61-year count (*see* Elk Horn).

Double Shields (*see* Pepion, Victor)

Doyce, Clarence   *Jémez*
EDUCATION: Jémez, 1961.
EXHIBITIONS: MNM, 1961.

Draper, Robert D.   *Navaho-Laguna*
BORN: November 20, 1938, Chinle, Ariz. Son of Frank Draper (Laguna) and Janet Descheeny (Navaho).
MARRIED: Ruby S. Three children.
EDUCATION: Chinle, 1947–51; Inter-Mt., 1951–56.
CAREER: Art instructor, Chinle Boarding School; instructional aid, child guidance, BIA, Chinle Boarding School.
EXHIBITIONS: AIAE/WSU, ITIC, NTF, PAC, SAIEAIP.
AWARDS: Five during 1964–65 from ITIC, NTF.
COLLECTIONS: *Private*: Leonard, Ruedin.

Draper, Teddy, Sr.   *Navaho*
Keeti Bahi, Grey Boy
BORN: April 2, 1923, Chinle, Ariz. Son of Elsitty Draper (Navaho) and Margaret (Navaho).
MARRIED: Lucy (Navaho). Seven children.
EDUCATION: Fort Wingate; Box High School, Brigham City, Utah; Utah S.; graduated Arizona S.C./T., 1962.
SERVICE: WWII, three and one-half years; Pacific Theater.
CAREER: Supervisory instructional aid, child guidance, Nazlini Boarding School, Ganado, Ariz.
EXHIBITIONS: HM.
COLLECTIONS: *Public*: Inter-Mountain Indian School.
ADDRESS: c/o Nazlini Boarding School, Ganado, Ariz.

Duahkapoo, Anthony   *Hopi*
COLLECTIONS: *Public*: MNM.

Ducee Blue Buzzard   *Creek*
(Also known as Collins, Howard Rufus.)
BORN: July 8, 1894, Checotah, Okla. (formerly Indian Territory). Son of Henry R. Collins and Aurora (Creek). Related to the Creek chiefs, William F. McIntosh and W. E. McIntosh.
MARRIED: Margery McBee, 1939. One son: Gene, 1918.

EDUCATION: Eufaula and Wetumka (Okla.) Creek Mission, *ca.* 1905; Oktaha (Okla.) High School, 1909; St. Joseph College, Muskogee, Okla., 1910–12.
CAREER: Commercial artist.
EXHIBITIONS: MNM; local.
ADDRESS: 2003 Columbus, Muskogee, Okla.

Duncan, Clifford *Northern Ute*
EXHIBITIONS: MNM, Senior High-College Division, 1962; PAC, 1959.
ADDRESS: Box 19, White Rocks, Utah.

Duncan, Dallas *Sauk-Fox*
BORN: June 19, 1944.
EDUCATION: Institute.
EXHIBITIONS: PAC, SN.
ADDRESS: Tama, Iowa.

Duncan, Marcellus *Sauk-Fox*
BORN: 1904.
EDUCATION: Chilocco; Haskell.
EXHIBITIONS: AIEC.

Dupree, William *Sioux*
EDUCATION: Santa Fe.
EXHIBITIONS: NGA, 1953.
COLLECTIONS: *Private*: Dietrich, M. Kramer.

Duran, George *Picurís*
George is the son of Roland Duran (*q.v.*). In 1950 the artist was no longer paint-ing.
EDUCATION: Santa Fe, 1946–47.
COLLECTIONS: *Public*: MAI.

Duran, Joe Evan *Tesuque*
Pove Peen
His instructors encouraged him to develop his own style. Duran received advanc-ed training in the fields of art history, design, theory, and philosophy, as well as modern art.
EDUCATION: Hiler; Hill.
COMMISSIONS: *Murals*: DAM; SFWF (with Charles Loloma and Ignacio Moquino, *qq.v.*).
EXHIBITIONS: OU/ET.
COLLECTIONS: *Public*: OU/MA.

Duran, Roland *Picurís*
Tolene
BORN: Date unknown. Died *ca.* 1961.
Roland Duran and his son, George (*q.v.*), were reportedly living in California in 1950, and had stopped painting. Roland's most productive period was between 1930 and 1940.
COLLECTIONS: *Public*: MNM.

Duvayestewa (*see* Polelonema, Tyler)
Duwenie, Dick *Hopi*
EDUCATION: Hopi.
EXHIBITIONS: ITIC, 1959.
AWARDS: ITIC (student exhibit), 1959.

Eagle, Thomas, Jr.   *Arikara*
EXHIBITIONS: BNIAS.
ADDRESS: Emmet, N. Dak.

Eagle Crow   *Sioux*
COLLECTIONS: *Public*: MPM.

Eagle Elk (*see* Red Elk, Herman)

Eagle Feather, Eli (*see* Eagle Feather, Elijah)

Eagle Feather, Elijah   *Sioux*
Hehon Womblee, Owl Eagle
(Also known as Eagle Feather, Eli.)
BORN: June 15, 1926, Hamill, S. Dak., on the Rosebud Reservation. GF:
Owl Eagle, and Felix Crazy Bull, a tribal officer and advisor, 1929–.
MARRIED: Teresa Stands.
SERVICE: WWII, U.S. Army, 11th Airborne Division, two years.
CAREER: Artist and farm laborer, 1951– .
EXHIBITIONS: BNIAS, PAC.
ADDRESS: c/o James Dvorak, Winner, S. Dak.

Eagle Shield   *Teton Sioux*
BORN: Date unknown; a medicine man.
WORK PUBLISHED: BAE, *Bull. 61* (pictographic style).

Eagle's Tail (*see* Tsabetsaye, Roger)

Eah Ha Wa (*see* Mirabel, Eva)

Echohawk, Brummett   *Pawnee*
Mr. Echohawk is a commercial artist and illustrator whose work is generally
available through special commission and contract. His comic strip, "Little
Chief," appearing in the *Tulsa World*, is familiar to many Oklahomans.
ADDRESS: Box 1922, Tulsa, Okla.

Eckiwaudah, Tennyson   *Comanche*
Yutsuwuna, Able To Stand Up Again
BORN: September 26, 1912, Cyril, Okla. Son of Bernice Looking Glass.
M/GF: Big Looking Glass (Pianaronit), chief of the Comanches during the
early settlement of Oklahoma.
MARRIED: Eva Geimausaddle, 1936. Four children: Colleen, 1937; Dennis,
1939; Arnold, 1941; Donald, 1946.
Although the artist has been painting since 1935, he has not exhibited often.
His greatest encouragement came from Susie Peters and James Auchiah (*q.v.*).
CAREER: Artist.
EXHIBITIONS: 1953–64: AIE, DAM, PAC.
AWARDS: AIE, 1961–62.
COLLECTIONS: *Public*: Cyril State Bank, Cyril, Okla. *Private*: Schonwald.
ADDRESS: Box 115, Cyril, Okla.

Edaakie, Anthony P.   *Zuni*
Eedeeahkai
(Also known as Edaakie, Tony; Tomahawk, A. E.)
CAREER: Painter, Wallace Trading Post and Maisel's Trading Post, N.M.
EXHIBITIONS: AAIE, 1959.
COLLECTIONS: *Public*: MAI, MNA/KHC. *Private*: Harvey.

Edaakie, Tony (*see* Edaakie, Anthony P.)

Eder, Earl   *Sioux*

BORN: 1944, Poplar, Mont.

EDUCATION: Institute, 1965–66.

HONORS: Gallery assistant, American Indian Performing Arts Exhibition, Washington, D.C., 1965.

WORK PUBLISHED: *Smoke Signals*, IACB (Autumn, 1965).

EXHIBITIONS: FAIEAIP, SAIEAIP, YAIA.

COLLECTIONS: *Public*: BIA, IACB.

ADDRESS: Poplar, Mont.

Edwards, Bronson Wilbur   *Ottawa*

BORN: May 22, 1913, Miami, Okla. Son of Marvin E. Edwards and Elizabeth Jones (Ottawa). M/GM: Skash. M/GF: Mon Ton Kee, Ottawa chief, 1880–88, and veteran of the Union Army. M/GGF: John W. Early (Was Kas), Ottawa chief, born near Sandusky, Ohio, and removed from there to Indian Territory by the U.S. Government, *ca.* 1836.

MARRIED: Katherene Daisy Bonner, 1938. Three children: Larry Duane, 1939; Karen Louana, 1942; Nina Jean, 1944.

> Mr. Edwards has been interested in art since childhood but did not begin to paint seriously until 1947. His work is similar to the European wash style, but, on close examination, it contains a degree of the flat technique so common to Indian painting. The artist says, "I have had an undying ambition to improve my art work and to continue to paint for many years yet."

EDUCATION: Graduated Miami (Okla.) High School, 1932; correspondence course in commercial art, Art Instruction, Inc., Minneapolis, Minn., 1958–62.

CAREER: Freelance artist; commercial artist, Video Theaters, 1954–62; Crane Co., Miami, Okla., 1962–.

HONORS: Secretary-treasurer, Ottawa Tribal Council, 1947–.

COMMISSIONS: *Murals*: National Boy Scout Jamboree, Colorado Springs, Colo.

EXHIBITIONS: AAID, AIEC, AIW, BNIAS, DAM, FAIEAIP, ITIC, LAIC, MHDYMM, MNM, PAC, SN, SPIM; Greenville (S.C. Arts Festival); Miami County Historical Society, Ottawa County Fair, and Northeastern Oklahoma A & M. *One-man shows*: HM, SPIM.

AWARDS: 1938–65: 39, from PAC and county fairs.

COLLECTIONS: *Public*: MAI. *Private*: Bartlett, Burks, Caldwell, Dobson, Gilmore, Gunn, Hollis, Holt, Jordahm, R. Kennedy, D. Maxwell, J. Snodgrass, R. M. Thomas, S. Ward.

ADDRESS: 1022 A Street, NW, Miami, Okla.

Eedeeahkai (*see* Edaakie, Anthony P.)

Eileohi, Antonio   *Zuni*

EXHIBITIONS: FWG, 1951.

Eka La Nee (*see* Beaver, Fred)

Elk (*see* Cohoe, William)

Elk (*see* Tyndall, Calvin T.)

Elk Horn *Piegan Blackfoot*
BORN: 1845. Died 1901.
Along with Big Brave and Double Runner (*qq.v.*), the artist executed a 61-year count (*see* Wissler 1911).

Ellen, Mary *Navaho*
EDUCATION: Santa Fe.
One of the few women of her tribe to attempt watercolor painting. By 1950, she had apparently ceased to paint.
EXHIBITIONS: AIEC, NGA, OU/ET.
COLLECTIONS: *Public*: OU/MA, MNM, SM. *Private*: Denman, Dietrich, M. Kramer.

Ember Of Fire (*see* Saul, C. Terry)

Emerson, Roberta Joan Boyd *Sioux-Assiniboin*
BORN: June 18, 1931, Brockton, Mont. Daughter of George A. Boyd and Helen Roberta Sparks.
MARRIED: Emory Elwood Emerson, 1953. Four children: Roxanne, 1956; Roy, 1958; Eugene, 1959; Robert, 1960.
EDUCATION: Public schools, Brockton, Mont.; graduated high school, 1951; Montana State College, Bozeman, Mont.
HONORS: Outstanding Young Indian Artist Award (in high school).
EXHIBITIONS: Several first awards in local school shows.
COLLECTIONS: *Private*: Larson.
ADDRESS: Box 6, New Cuyama, Calif.

Enjady, Errol *Mescalero Apache*
EDUCATION: Albuquerque, 1962–63.
EXHIBITIONS: MNM, 1963.

Este Songah (*see* Wolfe, Edmond Richard)

Etahdleuh *Kiowa*
The artist was among the 72 Plains Indians taken as prisoners from Fort Sill, Okla., to Fort Marion, St. Augustine, Fla., in 1875.
COLLECTIONS: *Public*: HI, MHS/B, OAA/SI, YU/BRBML.
Private: R. Robinson.

Eustace, Lebeck *Zuni*
COLLECTIONS: *Public*: MNM.

Evarts, Mark *Pawnee*
The artist was among the 72 Plains Indians taken as prisoners from Fort Sill, Okla., to Fort Marion, St. Augustine, Fla., in 1875.
COLLECTIONS: *Public*: Castillo de San Marcos National Monument, St. Augustine, Fla.

Eya (*see* Johnson, Alfred)

Falling In Winter (*see* Vigil, Romando)

A Fan (*see* Patkotak, Paul)

Farmer, Ernie *Bannock-Shoshoni*
EDUCATION: Bacone College.
EXHIBITIONS: PAC, 1950–51.

Fast Deer   *Sioux*
  Hechaka Lucahan, Fast Deer
    One of five artists whose works, commissioned and collected from 1880 to 1883
    by Rudolf Cronau, are now referred to as the Cronau Album (*see* Sinte).
  COLLECTIONS: *Public*: AMNH.

Fast Eagle   *Oglala Sioux*
  Wanble Orko
  BORN: Date unknown; from Pine Ridge Agency, S. Dak. One of 12 auto-
  graphs (*see* Black Heart).
  COLLECTIONS: *Public*: MAI.

Fawn (*see* Tahcawin)

Feather, Buddy   *Sioux*
  EXHIBITIONS: FWG, 1943.

Feathers, Gerald T.   *Blackfoot*
  Tail Feathers
  MARRIED: Irene Good-Striker (Blood). Two children: Sherry Lynn, Pamela.
    The artist has been showing his paintings since he was about 16. He works in a
    variety of media and specializes in portraying the days of buffalo hunting.
  EDUCATION: Banff School of Fine Arts, Canada; Provincial School of Tech-
  nology and Art, Banff.
  CAREER: Draftsman for a petroleum company in Canada.
  HONORS: Received an art scholarship while in his teens; scholarship from
  Anglican Church to complete art training.
  ADDRESS: Box 734, Calgary, Alberta, Canada.

Feathers, Kirby   *Ponca-Sioux*
  EDUCATION: Institute, 1965–66.
  EXHIBITIONS: YAIA.

Fife, Phyllis   *Creek*
  EDUCATION: Institute, 1965–66.
  EXHIBITIONS: YAIA.

Fire Bear (*see* Standing, William)

Fireshaker, Franklin   *Ponca*
  Ti Ookeah Bahze
  BORN: August 12, 1918; Greyhorse, Okla. Son of Joseph Four Eyes (Ponca)
  and Anna Black Cloud (Ponca). At the age of 11, after his mother's death,
  he was adopted by McKinley Horse Chief Eagle and reared by his aunt,
  Mrs. Albert Four Eyes Roy.
  MARRIED: Jerry Ann Marshall (Creek), 1942. Two children: Alona Robin,
  1950; Quannah Eagle, 1956.
    Mr. Fireshaker is a dedicated student of Ponca history and customs. He and his
    family have traveled "throughout the world and have learned to speak several
    languages." The artist is an authority on Indian dances and is a frequent judge
    at tribal dance contests. His paintings and murals are done as special commis-
    sions.
  EDUCATION: Pawnee (Okla.) Indian School; Chilocco; Bacone College.
  CAREER: House painter and artist.
  HONORS: Listed in *Who's Who in Oklahoma.*

EXHIBITIONS: GM, ITIC, MPI, PAC; Tulsa County Libraries, Okla.
AWARDS: AIE, ITIC, PAC.
COLLECTIONS: *Public*: GM, PAC.
ADDRESS: c/o 205 North Junction, Muskogee, Okla.

Fireshaker, Quannah Eagle   *Ponca*
BORN: 1956. Daughter of Franklin Fireshaker (*q.v.*) and Jerry Ann Marshall (Creek).
EXHIBITIONS: ITIC.
AWARDS: ITIC (student classification), 1964.
ADDRESS: c/o 205 North Junction, Muskogee, Okla.

Fish In Water (*see* Poodry, C. Earl)

Five Kiowas
  In 1926, at Anadarko, Oklahoma, the late Mrs. Susie C. Peters, then a government field matron, "organized a 'Fine Arts Club' for Indian girls and boys who showed talent in drawing and painting pictures, bead work, and other native work. Mrs. Willie Baze Lane gave them a few lessons and great encouragement."
  In 1936, Mrs. Peters recalled, "about this time I sent some of the fifteen or more boys' and girls' work to Mr. Ralph Mores, artist and dealer of Taos, N.M. He bought some of the drawings and asked for more to be sent to him. He wrote that these boys had something fine to give to the world. So we were encouraged. Mrs. Lane told me that if I could interest O.B. Jacobson at the University he could make them famous."
  Edith Mahier, member of the teaching staff at the art school of the University of Oklahoma, said, "Mrs. Peters brought Asah and Hokeah (*qq.v.*) to Norman one Sunday afternoon. Dr. Jacobson was out of town. She brought the boys' paintings of Indian dancers done on brown paper bags and the covers of shoe boxes. They looked like Leon Bakst and I felt that I was seeing for the first time an Oklahoma art expression, true and fresh, and deserving of interest from educators."
  In the fall of 1926, Asah, Hokeah, Mopope, and Tsatoke (*qq.v.*) were taken to the University for an interview. In 1965, Dr. Jacobson recalled, "the boys had none of the necessary entrance requirements to be enrolled as students in the University and it was just as well since I did not wish for them to attend regular art classes and absorb the usual things deemed essential in white art."
  Jacobson, then head of the University art school, enlisted the understanding help of Miss Mahier, whose office was used as a studio for the boys since at "no time did they attend regular University art classes." Miss Mahier did a "splendid job, giving them instruction in technique, criticisms at the proper time and steady encouragement." And, as Asah said, "she understands us."
  Dr. Jacobson assumed the responsibility of more or less supporting the students financially during the first four or five months they remained at Norman in 1926–27. He did so by persuading friends and the University to purchase the boys' paintings. He lectured to clubs and eventually arranged for the group to give programs as further means of providing interest and income for them. "Tsatoke was the singer and drummer, Hokeah and Mopope performed the Eagle Dance. Asah, too, was a dancer...rhythmic, methodical, ritualistic. Martha, Tsatoke's wife, sang a lullaby." Miss Mahier also recalls, "it was never necessary to discuss design and composition or drawing or colors with these boys because they were dancers, singers, and drummers and rhythm was a natural living thing" for them.
  There were several prominent people who did not look with favor on Jacobson's work with the Indians. They "growled at [his] bringing troupes of Indians to give dances in Oklahoma, Texas, and at the noted National Folk Festival in St.

Louis, where the performers received further acclaim. They claimed that [he] was wasting valuable time on something that 'we must get away from.'"

In January, 1927, Lois Smoky joined the four boys at the University, and, in the late spring, the boys "returned to the Reservation to plant their crops. In the fall of 1927, the five returned with Auchiah. Lois later became the first to drop from the office-studio classes."

The group required more financial aid than Dr. Jacobson or the programs could provide if they were to remain at the University. Dr. Jacobson said: "With the help of Lewis Ware, a Caddo-Kiowa member of the Oklahoma Legislature, we turned to Lew H. Wentz, an oil multimillionaire at Ponca City, Oklahoma. Mr. Wentz was agreeable to help, provided I gave my word that it was a worthwhile project. I gave my word of honor that if he assisted, I would make the boys famous in a few years. Quite an order; one I fear he didn't believe. His support, while far from lavish, was enough to make it possible for the group to devote full time to painting with less financial worries. When the Kiowas were ready for shows I began to secure them a national hearing. I was able to book shows of their works at leading museums and universities throughout the country. At the First International Art Exposition, held in Prague, Czechoslovakia, in 1928, they created a sensation. The outcome of this exhibit was *Kiowa Indian Art*, published in France in 1929, and later in 1950, *American Indian Painters*. Then after the world had acclaimed it, Oklahoma finally discovered Indian art as a living phenomenon, giving considerable attention to it in the press after such magazines as *American Magazine of Art, International Studio, Creative Arts, Western Arts, Connoisseur of London*, had acclaimed it much earlier.

"During the great depression of the 1930's, I was a supervisor of artists on relief in Oklahoma. Among others, I placed all my competent Indian artists to work decorating public, state and federal buildings with murals. When two of the Kiowas were selected to execute murals at the Department of Interior Building in Washington, D.C., I sent a newspaper clipping and a note to Mr. Wentz saying, 'I hereby redeem my promise to you that I'd make these Indians famous.'"

Mrs. Peters had recognized the Kiowa's ability when they were ten years old and "gave them watercolors and encouraged them to paint what they knew." In 1936, however, she said that it was "through Mr. Jacobson that the small group of Kiowas gained fame."

"All of our Indian artists, by remaining Indian, have made a magnificent contribution to American culture," said Jacobson, and continued, "I am happy to have had a small part in encouraging and coaxing many towards this goal. I fear that I am even guilty of 'Indianizing' some who had lost their heritage."

(Auchiah, Hokeah, Mopope and Smoky still reside in Oklahoma. Asah and Tsatoke are deceased. See listing for individual artists.)

The Flame   *Teton Sioux*
Boide
(Also known as The Blaze.)

In 1877, the artist lived at Peoria Bottom, 18 miles south of Fort Sully, Dakota Territory. He generally lived with the Sans Arcs, although by birth he was of the Two Kettle group. His Winter Count chart covered a longer period than that of Lone Dog and The Swan (*qq.v.*)

WORK PUBLISHED: BAE, *4th AR*.
COLLECTIONS: *Public*: OAA/SI.

Flaming Arrow (*see* Paytiamo, James P.)

Fleetfoot (*see* Ladd, Edmund J.)

Flores, William Vann *Cherokee-Papago*
Laughing Bull
BORN: October 2, 1927, Appleton, Wisc. Son of Alonzo Flores (Papago) and Jesse E. Vann (Cherokee).
MARRIED: Marilyn P. Wells, 1950. One son: William Vann, Jr., 1958.
Mr. Flores is best known as a cartoonist of Indian subjects. He says he feels certain "they know I'm not laughing at them, but rather laughing with them." Interested in drawing for fun and practice since schooldays, the artist has been called a "Master of Indian Humor" because of his spare time caricaturing.
EDUCATION: Public schools in Anadarko, Okla.; graduated Chilocco, 1947; Kansas City, 1950–52; Los Angeles, 1956–57; Oklahoma C.U.
SERVICE: Korean War, U.S. Army, two years.
CAREER: Printer, *ca.* 1942–52; medical illustrator, Civil Aero-Medical Research Institute, Federal Aviation Agency, Oklahoma City, Okla., 1958–; presents color film-lectures on painting and care of art supplies.
WORK PUBLISHED: *FAA Horizons* (July 1963), *The Oklahoma Journal* (February 20, 1965).
EXHIBITIONS: AAIE, BNIAS, FAIEAIP, PAC, SN; New York, N.Y.; Los Angeles, Calif.; Washington, D.C.; Kansas City, Mo.; Art Originals, Inc., Oklahoma City, Okla. *One-man shows*: University of Arkansas.
COLLECTIONS: *Private*: Marriott, Rachlin.
ADDRESS: Box 84, Concho, Okla.

Flying Eagle (*see* Goodbear, Paul J.)
Flying Hawk (*see* Blackowl, Archie)
Follower (*see* Battese, Stanley)
Foot (*see* Belindo, Dennis)
Footprints Of A Buffalo (*see* Odle Pah)
Forceful (*see* Abeyta, Narciso Platero)

Four Bears *Mandan*
Mato Tope (and *Mah To Toh Pa*)
BORN: Date unknown; near Fort Clark, N. Dak., 1833–34.
Prince Maximilian's collection contains examples of paintings by Four Bears, collected during the winter sojourn of Karl Bodmer and the Prince at Fort Clark, 1833–34 (*see* Yellow Feather). It is quite possible that Four Bear's interest in painting was spurred by sitting for portraits for Bodmer and George Catlin, the latter having said, "There is no man amongst the Mandans so generally loved."
CAREER: Second chief and the most prominent warrior of the tribe.
WORK PUBLISHED: Catlin (1841), Ewers (1939; 1965), Jacobson and D'Ucel (1950). *Catlin, Bodmer, Miller, JAM* (1963).
COLLECTIONS: *Public*: AMNH, BM (latter not confirmed), NNGCC.

Four Hills (*see* Pahsetopah, Paul)

Fox, Elaine *Arikara-Sioux*
EXHIBITIONS: BNIAS.
ADDRESS: Emmet, N. Dak.

Fox, Guy *Hidatsa Sioux*
Bright Wing
BORN: March 4, 1902, on the Fort Berthold Reservation, N. Dak.

MARRIED: Grace Parshall, 1931. Seven children: Maynard, 1945; Belinda, 1947; Catherine, 1948; Gerald, 1949; Arline, 1953; Dean, 1954; Theola, 1957. Mr. Fox is a self-taught nontraditionalist painter, who has been active since 1948. His hobby, hunting, is often reflected in his paintings.
EDUCATION: Attended Pipestone Indian School, Pipestone, Minn., through the seventh grade.
EXHIBITIONS: BNIAS.
COLLECTIONS: *Private*: Conroth, Leno, R. McAlpin, M. Peterson, R. Ward.
ADDRESS: New Town, N. Dak.

Fragua, Augustine *Jémez*
BORN: 1945.
EDUCATION: Jémez; graduated Albuquerque.
EXHIBITIONS: 1958–63: MNM, PAC.

Franco, D. *Papago*
COLLECTIONS: *Public*: AF.

Franklin, Ernest *Navaho*
BORN: 1942.
EDUCATION: Albuquerque, 1960; scholarship to Arizona, "Southwest Indian Art Project."
EXHIBITIONS: MNM, 1960.
AWARDS: MNM, 1960.

Franklin, Herman *Sauk-Fox*
BORN: 1912.
EDUCATION: Chilocco; Haskell.
EXHIBITIONS: AIEC.

Frazier, Carol Lee *Paiute*
EDUCATION: Institute, 1965–66.
EXHIBITIONS: YAIA.
ADDRESS: 1609 Franklin Street, Apt. No. 2, San Francisco, Calif.

Fredericks, Oswald (*see* White Bear)

Freeman, Brenda *Cherokee*
BORN: Muskogee, Okla. Daughter of Glen Freeman and Opal.
MARRIED: Jimmy Kilgore. Two children.
EDUCATION: Bacone College.
COLLECTIONS: *Private*: W. Fenton, Johnet.
ADDRESS: Muskogee, Okla.

Freeman, Robert Lee *Yankton Sioux*
BORN: January 14, 1939, on the Rincón Indian Reservation, Calif. Son of Herman Edward Freeman (Mission) and Louise Pratt (Sioux).
MARRIED: Edwina Ophelia Alvarado, November 25, 1960. Three children: Robert Lee, Jr. (by previous marriage), 1958; Robert Florentino, 1961; Tina Louise, 1966.
SERVICE: U.S. Army, 1957–60; Korea.
CAREER: Laborer; artist, 1960–.
EXHIBITIONS: SAIEAIP, SN; San Diego County Fair, Calif. *One-man shows*:

Oceanside, Calif., 1962.
AWARDS: 1964–65: Three from SN.
COLLECTIONS: *Private*: Attridge, Binnici, Blackley, Britton, Chávez, D. Hill, L. Hill, F. Jones, Morrison, Pratt, Prieto, Ruggles, H. Smith, Thoeny, Williamson.
ADDRESS: 3838 Linda Vista, Vista, Calif.

Freimark, Robert M.   *Chippewa*
EXHIBITIONS: PAC, 1954–55.
ADDRESS: 223 Michigan Street, Toledo, Ohio.

Froman, Robert   *Peoria-Miami*
EDUCATION: Bacone College.
EXHIBITIONS: PAC, 1954.

From The Middle Of The Sky (*see* Smith, Ernest)

Frost On The Mountain (*see* Peña, Josè Encarnación)

Gachupin, Juan   *Jémez*
COLLECTIONS: *Public*: MAI, MNM, SM.

Gachupin, Manuelino   *Zia*
BORN: 1934.
COLLECTIONS: *Public*: MNM.

Gachupin, Maxine   *Jémez*
BORN: 1948.
EDUCATION: Jémez, St. Catherine's.
EXHIBITIONS: 1959–64: AAIE, MNM, PAC, SN.
AWARDS: MNM, PAC, SN.
COLLECTIONS: *Public*: MAI.
ADDRESS: Jémez Pueblo, N.M.

Gachupin, Paul   *Jémez*
BORN: 1947.
EDUCATION: Jémez.
EXHIBITIONS: AAIE, ITIC.
AWARDS: ITIC (student division), 1958.

Gachupin, Rose M.   *Jémez*
EDUCATION: Jémez.
EXHIBITIONS: 1962–63: MNM, SN.
AWARDS: MNM, 1962.
COLLECTIONS: *Public*: MNM.

Gachupin, Wald   *Zia*
COLLECTIONS: *Public*: SM.

Gaco, Philip   *Laguna*
EDUCATION: St. Catherine's, 1965.
EXHIBITIONS: MNM; PAC, 1965.
COLLECTIONS: *Private*: Bush.
ADDRESS: Paguate Pueblo, N.M.

Ga Hes Ka (*see* Two-Arrows, Tom)

Galvan, Andreas *Zia*
Henate
EXHIBITIONS: NGA, 1953.
COLLECTIONS: *Private*: Denman.

Gamble, Thomas J. *Navaho*
EDUCATION: Albuquerque, 1961.
EXHIBITIONS: MNM, 1961.

Gaon Yah (*see* Smith, Ernest)

García, Alexander *San Juan*
BORN: N.M.
EDUCATION: Institute.
EXHIBITIONS: FAIEAIP, YAIA.

García, Carlos *San Juan*
Nanatside
BORN: Date unknown; once lived at Chamita, N.M.
EXHIBITIONS: AIEC, 1937.

García, Ernest P. *Isleta*
Oysla
BORN: January 25, 1944, Los Angeles, Calif. Son of Climoca D. García
(Isleta) and Ignacita B. Córdova.
EDUCATION: Santa Fe; graduated Sierra High School, Whittier, Calif., 1962;
Rio Hondo Junior College, Whittier, Calif., instruction under Yoshio Naka-
mura (drawing and painting), classes in ceramics; Cerritos Junior College,
Norwalk, Calif.
CAREER: Commercial screen printer, Dyer Specialty Co., Inc., 1964–.
EXHIBITIONS: FAIEAIP, PAC.
AWARDS: SN (creative writing category), 1965.
COLLECTIONS: *Private*: Silberman.
ADDRESS: 1163 Tilley Avenue, Whittier, Calif.

García, José J. *Santo Domingo*
EDUCATION: Santa Fe, *ca.* 1937.
EXHIBITIONS: AIEC, 1937.
COLLECTIONS: *Public*: SM. *Private*: Denman, Dietrich, Elkus.
ADDRESS: Santo Domingo Pueblo, Peña Blanca, N.M.

García, Lorenzo *Santo Domingo*
EDUCATION: Santa Fe, under Dorothy Dunn.
SERVICE: WWII.
EXHIBITIONS: AIW, 1938; NGA, 1953.
COLLECTIONS: *Public*: GM. *Private*: D. Kramer.
ADDRESS: Santo Domingo Pueblo, Peña Blanca, N.M.

García, Marcelino *San Juan*
BORN: 1932.
COLLECTIONS: *Public*: MNM.

García, María   *Comanche*
Aukemah
EDUCATION: Studied under Acee Blue Eagle (*q.v.*).
EXHIBITIONS: PAC.
COLLECTIONS: *Public*: MAI.

García, Peter   *San Juan*
EDUCATION: Santa Fe.
EXHIBITIONS: N.M.
COLLECTIONS: *Public*: SPL.
ADDRESS: San Juan Pueblo, N.M.

García, Ruth Bussey   *Cherokee*
BORN: August 24, 1916, Claremore, Okla. M/GGF: Chief Lewis Downing
(Cherokee). Her M/GF, Willie Vann, and M/GM, Eliza Downing, arrived in
Oklahoma on the "Trail of Tears."
MARRIED: Florencio García, 1937. Two children: Donald, 1933; Martha,
1941.
EDUCATION: Whitaker Orphanage, Pryor, Okla.; Hominy (Okla.) Public
Schools, Oaks Indian Mission, Okla.
CAREER: Art instructor, Oaks Indian Mission: hospital occupational therapist,
arts and crafts instructor; portrait artist.
EXHIBITIONS: YWCA; New Mexico Health Building, Bacas Restaurant,
and New Mexico State Fair, in Albuquerque, N.M.; Cedars Supper Club,
Cedar Crest, N.M.
COLLECTIONS: *Private*: C. Bussey, J. Bussey, W. Bussey, W. W. Bussey,
Coffey, C. Dennis, A. García, P. García, Gonzales, A. Gutiérrez, J. Gutiérrez,
N. Jaramillo, R. Jaramillo, Johnston, Salazar, Weller, E. West, H. Wister.
ADDRESS: 1101 Granite, NW, Albuquerque, N.M.

Gaseoma, Lee Roy   *Hopi*
COLLECTIONS: *Public*: MAI.

Gashwytewa, Ivan S.   *Hopi*
  In addition to his paintings, the artist has been considered an outstanding
  carver of Kachina dolls.
COLLECTIONS: *Public*: MNM (painting).

Gasper, Pete   *Zuni*
EDUCATION: Graduated Santa Fe, 1958.
EXHIBITIONS: 1958–60: AAIE, ITIC, MNM.
AWARDS: MNM, 1958; ITIC.
COLLECTIONS: *Public*: MNM, SMNAI. *Private*: Waters.

Geionety, George   *Comanche*
Geionety, Comanche Enemy (or Back Track); *Oyebi*, Side of a Mountain.
BORN: 1913, Lawton, Okla. P/GF: "Old Man" Silverhorn. M/GF: *Oyebi*
(Side of a Mountain).
COLLECTIONS: *Private*: R. Moore.

Ghahatt, Barton   *Zuni*
EDUCATION: Fort Lewis A & M. College, Durango, Colo.; scholarship to
Arizona, "Southwest Indian Art Project," summer, 1962.
ADDRESS: Box 104, Zuni Pueblo, N.M.

Ghost Bear, Theodore   *Sioux*
COLLECTIONS: *Public*: WRNGA.

Ghost Wind   *Navaho*
COLLECTIONS: *Private*: Thoeny.

Gifts (*see* Paukei, George)

Gobin, Henry   *Snohomish*
BORN: May 19, 1941, in Washington.
EDUCATION: Santa Fe, 1960–61; Institute, 1962–63.
EXHIBITIONS: FAIEAIP, MNM, PAC, YAIA.
AWARDS: MNM, SN.
COLLECTIONS: *Public*: BIA. *Private*: L. Stewart.
ADDRESS: 1413 Second Street, Marysville, Wash.

Golden Dawn (*see* Velarde, Pablita)

Gone Man (*see* Wolfe, Edmond Richard)

Gonzales, Louis   *San Ildefonso*
Wo Peen, Medicine Mountain
(Also known as Gonzales, Luis.)
BORN: September 10, 1907. Son of Juan Gonzales.
MARRIED: Juanita (San Ildefonso). Two children: Adelphia, 1937; Edmund,
1949.
   Known as a pioneer Pueblo muralist, Wo Peen painted actively in the early
   1920's. A hunting accident caused the loss of his right hand; however, he still
   paints occasionally.
EDUCATION: Graduated Santa Fe.
CAREER: Model for sculptor Philip S. Sears, 1932; gave pottery demonstra-
tions, exhibited paintings, and presented native songs and dances with his
family, Rochester Museum of Arts and Sciences and Buffalo Museum of
Art, N.Y.; traveled extensively for four years throughout the U.S., assisting
W. Allen Cushman, lecturing, exhibiting his paintings, and demonstrating
songs and dances.
HONORS: Governor of his pueblo, 1944–45.
COMMISSIONS: *Murals*: YMCA's Lodge of 7 Fires, Springfield, Mass. (seven
murals).
WORK PUBLISHED: Alexander (1932), Jacobson and D'Ucel (1950). *The
Art Digest* (September 1, 1931).
EXHIBITIONS: 1932–: AIEC, BAC, CCP, EITA, ITIC, JGS, MNM, NGA.
COLLECTIONS: *Public*: CU/LMA, DAM, KM, MAI, MNA/KHC, MNM,
MRFM, OU, PAC. *Private*: H. Adams, Dietrich, A. Forbes, Thoeny, Woffard.
ADDRESS: Route 1, Box 158, Santa Fe, N.M.

Gonzales, Luis (*see* Gonzales, Louis)

Good, Baptiste   *Brulé Sioux*
Wapostangi; Brown Hat; High Hawk; Good, John.
(*See also* High Hawk.)
BORN: *Ca.* 1822; was at Rosebud Agency, Dak., 1879–80. Died 1894. Son of
Afraid Of Horse. His son, Joseph Good, continued his father's Winter
Count and added the years 1894–1922 (BAE, *10th AR*).

MARRIED: Susie, whom the Indians called Old Lady Good.

HONORS: Sub-chief for a time after 1865; his Winter Count was the only one among the Sioux that recorded events prior to 1775. *See* Hyde (1961).

WORK PUBLISHED: BAE, *4th* and *10th AR*.

COLLECTIONS: *Public*: DAM, OAA/SI (a copy of his Winter Count), SIECC (original Winter Count).

Good, John   *Sioux*
   May be grandson of Baptiste Good (*q.v.*), who was also named John.

COLLECTIONS: *Public*: MNM.

Good Rain   *Taos*

EXHIBITIONS: FWG.

Goodbear, Paul J.   *Northern Cheyenne*
   Ahmehate, Flying Eagle

BORN: 1913, on the Cheyenne Reservation, Mont. Deceased. GF: Chief Turkey Legs. GGF: Chief Star and Chief (Old) Whirlwind (*q.v.*).
   Mr. Goodbear spent his childhood in Oklahoma where he attended public elementary and high schools. Many of his illustrations and paintings have been "reproduced in school books."

EDUCATION: Wichita; New Mexico U.; Chicago.

SERVICE: WWII; Okinawa.

CAREER: Artist, dancer, singer, teacher, professional boxer; clerk, department store, Washington, D.C.

COMMISSIONS: *Murals*: Coronado Monument, Bernalillo, N.M.; Ranch Bar, Chicago, Ill.; Osceola Bar, Miami, Fla.

WORK PUBLISHED: Jacobson and D'Ucel (1950).

COLLECTIONS: *Public*: GM, MNA/KHC, MNM, OU.

Goodenough, James

Gorman, Alfred Kee   *Navaho*
   Kee, Boy

BORN: April 12, 1957, Encino, Calif. Died July, 1966. Son of Carl Nelson Gorman (*q.v.*) (Navaho) and Mary Excie Wilson, and brother of R. C. Gorman (*q.v.*).

EDUCATION: Napa Street School, Northridge, Calif., kindergarten and first grade; Window Rock Public School, Ariz.

EXHIBITIONS: ITIC, MNM, NTF, SN; Manchester Gallery, Taos, N.M.; first paintings were shown at Krogh Tile, Northridge, Calif.

AWARDS: ITIC, MNM, NTF.

COLLECTIONS: *Public*: MNM. *Private*: R. Corwin, Krogh.

Gorman, Carl Nelson   *Navaho*
   Kinyeonny Beyeh, Son Of The Towering House People

BORN: October 5, 1907, Chinle, Ariz. Son of Nelson Gorman (Navaho) and Alice Peshlakai (Navaho). The artist's parents founded the Presbyterian Mission at Chinle, Ariz. His father was well known as a cattleman and Indian trader, and his mother taught weaving to women in the Chinle area and translated many hymns into Navaho. M/GF: Beshlagai Ithline, a silversmith and leader in the Crystal area. M/U: Fred Peshlakai (*q.v.*) and Frank Peshlakai.

MARRIED: Adella Katherine Brown (Navaho), 1930; divorced, November 1945. One son: Rudolph Carl Gorman (*q.v.*), 1931. Married Mary Excie Wilson, March 24, 1956. Two children: Alfred Kee Gorman (*q.v.*), 1957; Zonnie Marie, 1963.

> As a boy, Carl liked to draw horses, but his stockman father warned him there was "no money in that kind of horses." Despite the passing years and the extensive action he saw at Guadalcanal, Tarawa, and Saipan, he never relinquished his desire to become an artist. The GI Bill made possible his dream of a formal education. He believes "not only in the traditional but in the adaptation of the traditional to the modern, whether in painting, silver, or music." He, with his good friend, the late Ralph Roanhorse, was one of the first to lead Navaho artists in art directions other than the traditional.

EDUCATION: Chinle; Rehoboth Mission, Gallup, N.M.; graduated Albuquerque, 1928; Otis, 1951; extension classes, Santa Monica Technical School, Santa Monica, Calif.; South Bay Adult School, Manhattan Beach, Calif.; Radio School, USMC.

SERVICE: WWII, U.S. Marine Corps; Pacific Theater (code talker).

CAREER: Co-owner, with his brother, Wallace, of a trucking business, Chinle, Ariz., until 1936; clerk, timekeeper, and rangerider, USDI, Land Management, 1936–42; clerk, Southwest Indian Jewelry Shop, Los Angeles, Calif.; technical illustrator, Douglas Aircraft, Santa Monica, Torrance, and Lawndale, Calif., 1951–63; co-owner, Desert Designs (silk screening), 1963–64; manager, Navaho Arts and Crafts Guild, 1964–67.

HONORS: Los Angeles Indian Center Art Committee; member, Board of Directors, Treasurer, Vice-Chairman, Chairman of Exhibit Committee; Navaho Club of Los Angeles; Arts and Crafts Guild Exhibit Committee. Chairman, NTF; member, Exhibit Committee, ITIC.

WORK PUBLISHED: *Westways Magazine* (August 1956; August 1962), cover. Numerous ceremonial designs for Los Angeles Indian Center and Los Angeles Navaho Club.

EXHIBITIONS: 1947–65: ASF, FAIEAIP, ITIC, MNM, MYDYMM, NMSF, NTF, PAC; SN; Pacific Coast Club Gallery, Ceramic Spectacular Show, Long Beach, Calif.; Los Angeles County Aboretum, Arcadia, Calif.; Otis Art Institute Alumni Association, Descanso Gardens, La Cañada, Calif.; Douglas Annual Art Exhibits, Santa Monica, Calif.; The Art Wagon, Phoenix, Ariz.; Manchester Gallery, Taos, N.M.; The Little Gallery, Northridge, Calif.; American Friends Service Committee Indian Art Exhibit, Seattle, Wash.; Lynda Kay Gift Shop, Ganado, Ariz.; Gallup Chamber of Commerce, Gallup, N.M.; Management and Procedures Office, Navaho Tribe, Window Rock, Ariz.; BIA, Chinle, Ariz.; Duncan Vail Gallery, Shambrey Gardens-International Art Festival, Los Angeles, Calif. *One-man shows*: Gallup Public Library, Gallup, N.M.; Open Gallery, Playa Del Rey, Calif.; Pow Wow Indian Trading Post, Woodland Hills, Calif.; United Nations Delegation Dinner, Window Rock, Ariz.; Los Angeles YMCA and Women's University Club, Los Angeles, Calif. *Two-man shows*: HM, PAC.

AWARDS: ITIC, NMSF, NTF, SN; Hobby Recreation Show, Los Angeles, Calif.; Indian Center Art Show, Douglas Aircraft Annual Art Show, Santa Monica, Calif.; Compton Gem and Mineral Club Show, Long Beach, Calif.

COLLECTIONS: *Public*: SM; Trinity Presbyterian Church, Chinle, Ariz.; *Westways Magazine*, Los Angeles, Calif.; Ganado Mission, Ganado, Ariz. *Private*: P. Allen, Balcomb, Bimson, D. Brock, Bryant, Butler, Carroll, Dalton, Dentzel, Dorfman, Farwell, J. Forbes, Gorman, Hunter, Krogh, Lauritzen, McCabe, McDonald, McLarens, Plummer, Russell, Tatgenhorst, Thoeny, Tso, E. Vance, D. Vann, A. Williams.
ADDRESS: Box 8, Window Rock, Ariz.

Gorman, R. C. *Navaho*

(Also known as Gorman, Rudolph Carl.)
BORN: July 26, 1932, Chinle, Ariz. Son of Carl Nelson Gorman (*q.v.*) (Navaho) and Adella Katherine Brown (Navaho).

> Although R.C. majored in literature at Arizona State College and is a gifted writer, he has chosen painting, his first love, as a career. The artist has said: "The reservation is my source of inspiration for what I paint; but yet I never come to realize this until I find myself in some far-flung place like the tip of Yucatan or where-have-you. Perhaps when I stay on the reservation I take too much for granted. While there, it is my inspiration and I paint very little, and off the reservation it is my realization."
>
> In addition to the encouragement he has received from his father, the artist says that Miss Jenny Louis Lind, his high school art teacher, "made art important" to him and that too often art teachers neglect to do so.

EDUCATION: Chinle; St. Michaels; graduated Ganado (Ariz.) High School, 1950; attended Guam Territorial College, Marianas Islands; Mexico C.C.; San Francisco; Arizona S. C./F.
SERVICE: U.S. Navy, *ca.* 1952–56.
CAREER: Artist.
HONORS: Recipient of the first scholarship for study outside the U.S. given by the Navaho Tribe to a student of outstanding merit; Chairman, Painting Committee, American Indian Artists, San Francisco.
WORK PUBLISHED: Bahti (1964). *Western Review*, (Winter 1965).
EXHIBITIONS: AIAE/WSU, FAIEAIP, ITIC, NACG, PAC, SAIEAIP, SN, USDI, USDS; Madonna Festival, All-City Outdoor Art Festival, Los Angeles, Calif.; Poorman's Gallery, Coffee Gallery, Zieniewicz Gallery, San Francisco, Calif.; The Harlequin Gallery, Vallejo, Calif.; Jack London Square Art Show, Oakland, Calif.; El Cerrito (Calif.) Art Festival. *One-man shows*: Student Union, University of California; The Bridgeway, Sausalito, Calif.; Friendship House, Oakland, Calif.; The Arizona State Bank, Phoenix, Ariz.; Manchester Gallery, Taos, N.M. *Two-man shows*: HM, PAC.
AWARDS: AIAE/WSU, ITIC, NTF, PAC, SN.
COLLECTIONS: *Public*: BIA, IACB, MAI, PAC; Mexico City College; Ganado High School, Ganado, Ariz.; Zieniewicz Gallery, San Francisco, Calif.; Gibbs Art Gallery, Charleston, S.C. *Private*: E. Adkins, R. Anderson, C. Baker, Basehart, Browgh, Burdick, Dalton, Deaner, DiRe, Dodds, Dutton, Elkus, R. Evans, Fontaine, Gerash, Hamilton, Hammond, Henry, Huckstein, Huldermann, Humphrey, E. Jacobson, Kael, Klotz, Lipelt, Lohr, Loweiro, Manchester, Perlman, O. Perry, R. Perry, Pettinger, Poland, R. Potter, W. Price, Roundtree, L. Scott, Shackelford, Silva, Sneider, Snell, J. Snod-

grass, Stephenson, Tsosy, VanVoorhuysen, Ventura, A. Williams, Wixman.
ADDRESS: 4135 Army Street, No. 10, San Francisco, Calif.

Gorman, Rudolph Carl (*see* Gorman, R. C.)

Gorospe, Josephine   *Laguna*
EDUCATION: St. Catherine's, 1965.
EXHIBITIONS: MNM, PAC.
AWARDS: MNM, 1965.
ADDRESS: Laguna Pueblo, N.M.

Gough, Agnes   *Eskimo*
EXHIBITIONS: PAC, PAC/T.
AWARDS: PAC.
COLLECTIONS: *Public*: DAM, PAC.
ADDRESS: Box 922, Anchorage, Alaska.

Gould, Jay   *Navaho*
COLLECTIONS: *Public*: MNM.

Grand Eagle (*see* Ballard, Louis Wayne)

Grass (*see* Grass, John)

Grass, John (Chief)   *Blackfoot(?)-Hunkpapa Sioux*
Pezi, Grass; *Mato Wantakpe*, Charging Bear; *Wahacanka Yapi*, Used As
A Shield.
(Also known as Jumping Bear.)
    Chief Grass was one of four Sioux chiefs who relinquished all claims to the Black
    Hills and Powder River Country to the government at Standing Rock Agency,
    ca. 1883. [*See* Hyde (1956), Vestal (1933) and BAE *Bull. 61.*]
CAREER: Army scout; presiding judge for more than 30 years, Court of Indian
Offenses, Standing Rock Reservation, N. Dak.
COLLECTIONS: *Public*: MAI (autograph sketch; *see* Black Heart).

Grass, John, Jr.   *Hunkpapa-Teton Sioux*
BORN: Date unknown; in 1902 was on the Standing Rock Reservation in
N. Dak. Son of John Grass (*q.v.*).
WORK PUBLISHED: *News Letter*, CIS (November 1945).
COLLECTIONS: *Public*: CIS.

The Greatest (*see* Speck, Henry)

Great Hunter (*see* Blackmore, Bill)

Green, Homer   *Peoria-Cherokee*
BORN: 1938, Fort Defiance, Ariz.
EDUCATION: Bacone College.
EXHIBITIONS: AAIE, FAIEAIP, PAC, USDS.
ADDRESS: 1811 Kanawha Street, Hyattsville, Md.; Adelphi, Md.

Green Corn (*see* Mirabel, Eva)

Green Rainbow (*see* Mofsie, Louis Billingsly)

Gregg, Wilkie   *White Mountain Apache*
BORN: 1942.
EDUCATION: Scholarship to Arizona, "Southwest Indian Art Project," 1960.

Grey Boy (*see* Draper, Teddy, Sr.)

Grey Squirrel (*see* Hinds, Patrick Swazo)

Gritts, Franklin   *Cherokee-Potawatomi*
Oau Nah Jusah, They Have Returned; *Oon Nah Susah*, They Have Gone
Back.
BORN: August 8, 1914.
MARRIED: Non-Indian, former librarian at Haskell Institute.
   Gritts received his first art lessons from his father; he recalls liking to draw
   from the very first time he held a pencil. The artist prefers to paint only what
   he has seen.
EDUCATION: Fort Sill; Riverside; Haskell; B.F.A., Oklahoma, *ca.* 1939.
Studied mural technique under Olaf Nordmark and painting under Acee
Blue Eagle (*q.v.*). Summer classes in anthropology, New Mexico U.
SERVICE: WWII, U.S. Navy (aerial photographer); Pacific Theater. Medical
discharge after two years hospitalization for combat injuries.
CAREER: Formerly an art instructor, Haskell Institute.
COMMISSIONS: *Murals*: Haskell Institute. Assisted in the preparation of a
series of exhibits shown at the Progressive Education Convention, Chicago,
Ill., 1940.
WORK PUBLISHED: Jacobson and D'Ucel (1950).
EXHIBITIONS: 1938–58: AIW, DAM, ITIC, PAC, PAC/T; Palmer House,
Mandel Bros., Chicago, Ill.; St. Louis, Mo.
AWARDS: ITIC, 1938.
COLLECTIONS: *Public*: GM, JAM, MNA/KHC, OU/MA. *Private*: O. Jacobson.
ADDRESS: 12552 Pepperwood, St. Louis, Mo.

Growing Plant (*see* Hunt, Wolf Robe)

Gruber, Raymond   *Navaho*
COLLECTIONS: *Private*: R. Moore.

Guatogue, Leo   *Zuni*
EXHIBITIONS: EITA.
COLLECTIONS: *Private*: A. White.

Gutiérrez, Clarence   *Santa Clara*
EDUCATION: Santa Fe, *ca.* 1937.
EXHIBITIONS: AIEC, 1937.

Gutiérrez, José la Cruz   *Santa Clara*
EDUCATION: Santa Fe.
CAREER: Employed at U.S. Naval Station, Salt Lake City, Utah, in 1963.
COLLECTIONS: *Public*: SM.

Gutiérrez, José Leandro   *Santa Clara*
Kgoo Ya
(also known as Leandro, José)
EXHIBITIONS: OU/ET.
COLLECTIONS: *Public*: OU. *Private*: Denman, Dietrich.

Gutiérrez, Juan B.   *Santa Clara*
EDUCATION: Santa Fe, *ca.* 1937.
EXHIBITIONS: AIEC, 1937.
COLLECTIONS: *Public*: OU/SM.

Ha A Tee (*see* Quintana, Ben)

Hadaɔütse (*see* Red Corn)

Hadley, Wade *Navaho*
 EDUCATION: Santa Fe.
 EXHIBITIONS: FWG, 1943; NGS.
 COLLECTIONS: *Private*: Dietrich.

Hah Gay Kee Hooduh Lee (*see* Doonkeen, Eulamae Narcomey)

Hanemi Da (*see* Whitehorse, Roland N.)

Haney, Kelly Enoch *Seminole*
 BORN: 1940, Seminole, Okla.
 EDUCATION: Bacone College; scholarship to Arizona, "Southwest Indian Art Project," summer, 1962.
 EXHIBITIONS: FAIEAIP, PAC, SN.
 AWARDS: PAC.
 COLLECTIONS: *Private*: Gridley, G. Maxwell.
 ADDRESS: 909 North East 28th Street, Oklahoma City, Okla.

Hanna, R. W. *Kiowa*
 COLLECTIONS: *Public*: AF.

Hanson, Joan Stone *Cherokee*
 BORN: 1945, New Orleans, La.
 EXHIBITIONS: PAC, FAIEAIP, 1965.
 ADDRESS: 2310 East Broadway, Muskogee, Okla.

Haozous (*see* Houser, Allan)

Hapaha, L. *Navaho*
 EXHIBITIONS: EITA.
 COLLECTIONS: *Private*: Newcomb.

Happy Boy (*see* Austin, Frank)

Hard Heart *Oglala Sioux*
 Conte Feri
 BORN: Date unknown; from Pine Ridge Agency, S. Dak.
 COLLECTIONS: *Public*: MAI (*see* Black Heart).

Hardin, Helen *Santa Clara*
 Tsa Sah Wee Eh
 (Also known as Terrazas, Helen Hardin.)
 BORN: 1946. Daughter of Herbert O. Hardin and Pablita Velarde (*q.v.*) (Santa Clara).
 MARRIED: (?) Terrazas.
  Miss Hardin is a regular co-exhibitor with her famous mother, and has rightly achieved her own success as a painter.
 EDUCATION: Graduated from Pius X High School, Albuquerque, N.M.; scholarship to Arizona, "Southwest Indian Art Project," summer, 1960.
 WORK PUBLISHED: *American Artist* (April 1965).
 EXHIBITIONS: AIAE/WSU, AIM, ITIC, MNM, SN. *One-man shows*: Enchanted Mesa Trading Post, Albuquerque, N.M., 1964.

AWARDS: 1959–64: ITIC, MNM.
COLLECTIONS: *Private*: Elkus, Schonwald.
ADDRESS: Box 778, Española, N.M.

Harris, Ed　　　　　　　　　　　　　　　　　　　*Paiute*
COLLECTIONS: *Public*: SM.

Harry Hand (*see* Sitting Eagle)

Harvey, Pete, Jr.　　　　　　　　　　　　　　　*Navaho*
EDUCATION: Fort Sill.
EXHIBITIONS: PAC.

Harvier, Michael　　　　　　　　　　　　　　　　*Taos*
Quameomah
BORN: Date unknown. Son of Tonita Harvier, who lives and works in Taos.
EDUCATION: Bacone College.
CAREER: Employed by USDI; BIA.
EXHIBITIONS: 1952–56: DAM, FWG, MNM, PAC.
COLLECTIONS: *Public*: MNM. *Private*: A. Forbes.

Haskay Yah Ne Yah (*see* Begay, Harrison)

Ha So Deh (*see* Abeyta, Narciso Platero)

Hastings, Cain　　　　　　　　　　　　　　　　　*Navaho*
EXHIBITIONS: ITIC, 1963.
ADDRESS: Box 232, Whiteriver, Ariz.

Hatch, Glenn　　　　　　　　　　　　　　　　　　*Ute*
COLLECTIONS: *Public:* SMNAI.

Haungooah (*see* Silverhorn)

Haungoonpau (*see* Silverhorn)

Hawelana (*see* Herrera, Marcelina)

Hawgone (*see* Silverhorn)

Hawk　　　　　　　　　　　　　　　　　　　*Gros Ventres*
COLLECTIONS: *Public*: HSP/L (three sheets, 1858–60).

Hawk Man　　　　　　　　　　　　　　　　　　　*Sioux*
BORN: Date unknown; from Standing Rock Reservation, Dakota Territory.
Died 1890 (?).
CAREER: Hawk Man is thought to have been among the Indian police from
the Fort when the 1890 skirmish at Sitting Bull's camp took place and the
chief was killed. *See* Vestal (1933).
COLLECTIONS: *Public*: MAI (dated *ca.* 1884).

Haydah, William D.　　　　　　　　　　　　　　　*Hopi*
COLLECTIONS: *Public*: MNM.

Hayokah (*see* Mana)

Hehaka Wambdi (*see* Red Elk, Herman)

Hehon Womblee (*see* Eagle Feather, Elijah)

Helele (*see* Ladd, Edmund J.)

Henry, Fred *Hopi*
BORN: Date unknown. The artist is from Shungopovi, Second Mesa, Ariz.
COLLECTIONS: *Public*: MAI.

Henry, Gary ?
EDUCATION: Phoenix, 1964.
EXHIBITIONS: FAIEAIP.

Henry, Woodworth V. *Snohomish*
BORN: May 8, 1931, Oso, Wash.
EDUCATION: The Burnley School of Art and Design, Seattle, Wash.
SERVICE: U.S. Air Force, three years.
CAREER: Cartoonist and commercial artist, D.S. Wood and Associates, Tacoma, Wash.
EXHIBITIONS: PAC; Pacific Gallery Artist's Annual; College of Puget Sound Annual Exhibition, Tacoma, Wash.; Lakewood Artist's Annual.
AWARDS: FAIEAIP, PAC; Pacific Gallery Artist's Annual.
ADDRESS: 421 Perkins Building, Tacoma, Wash.

Herman, Jake *Oglala Sioux*
CAREER: Writer of the column, *Wa Ho Si*, in *The Shannon County News*, Pine Ridge, S. Dak.
EXHIBITIONS: PAC, 1962.
ADDRESS: Pine Ridge, S. Dak.

Herrera, Delphino *Cochití*
EDUCATION: Albuquerque.
EXHIBITIONS: MNM, 1962–63.

Herrera, Diego *Tesuque*
CAREER: Farmer.
EXHIBITIONS: AIW; FWG, 1943.
COLLECTIONS: *Public*: CU/LMA, OU/MA.
ADDRESS: Tesuque Pueblo, N.M.

Herrera, Elroy *Tesuque*
EDUCATION: Tesuque, *ca.* 1959.
EXHIBITIONS: MNM, 1959.

Herrera, Ernest *Tesuque*
EDUCATION: Tesuque, *ca.* 1959.
EXHIBITIONS: MNM, 1959–61.
AWARDS: MNM, two.
ADDRESS: Route 1, Box 59, Tesuque Pueblo, N.M.

Herrera, Joe Hilario *Cochití*
See Ru, Blue Bird
(Also known as Herrera, Joe H.)
BORN: May 17, 1923, Cochití Pueblo, N.M. Son of Felipe Herrera (Cochití) and Tonita Peña, *q.v.* (San Ildefonso).
MARRIED: Julia Paisano, 1944 (Laguna). Two children: Joseph, Yvonne.
Mr. Herrera is closely associated with tribal and state affairs. He conducts a radio program from Santa Fe that serves as an information center to the Pueblos. In recent years his many-faceted interests unfortunately have taken him away from painting his well-known symbolic expressions.

EDUCATION: Albuquerque; graduated Santa Fe, 1940; B.A., New Mexico U., 1953; M.A., Ed., New Mexico U., 1962; studied under Raymond Johnson, and, for a short while, at the University of Puerto Rico.

SERVICE: WWII, U.S. Air Force; Caribbean Theater.

CAREER: Instructor, Highland High School, Albuquerque, N.M., 1953–56; instructor, University of Arizona, "Southwest Indian Art Project," summer, 1960; placement officer and Assistant Director of Indian Education, New Mexico State Department of Education, 1956–.

HONORS: Palmes d'Académiques, 1954; Executive Secretary, All-Pueblo Council; area consultant, Save the Children Federation, Inc.; subject of an educational movie, *Joe Herrera—Pueblo Artist*; listed in *Indians of Today*; Chairman, Annual Governors' Inter-State Indian Council, 1964–65.

COMMISSIONS: *Murals*: Santa Fe Indian School; Maisel's Trading Post, Albuquerque, N.M.

WORK PUBLISHED: Jacobson and D'Ucel (1950), Tanner (1957). *Arizona Highways* (February 1950); *El Palacio* (August 1950; December 1952); *New Mexico Magazine* (January 1960); *America Illustrated*, USDS, Office of International Information (No. 33).

EXHIBITIONS: AIEC, AIW, DAM, FWG, HM, ITIC, MNA, MNM, MNM/T, OU/ET, PAC, PAC/T.

AWARDS: 1947–63: Eight top awards including ITIC Grand Awards; American Youth Forum Contest, when he was very young.

COLLECTIONS: *Public*: AF, DAM, MAI, MNA/KHC, MRFM, OU/MA, TM. *Private*: Denman, Dietrich, Elkus, A. Forbes, Lockett, Patania, Sewell, Thoeny, Wyman.

ADDRESS: 576 Camino del Monte Sol, Santa Fe, N.M.

Herrera, José   *Tesuque*
COLLECTIONS: *Private*: Hogue.

Herrera, Justino   *Cochití*
Stimone, A Bird
BORN: 1920.

> In the 1940's the artist wrote: "I figured a plan to do while I was in the army when I come home. I'd marry my sweetheart and have our own home on my farm, raise stock and I could keep painting, too. Well, it happened. We got married and we had a little girl. Couple months later my wife took sick... it took her strong and she left me and my little baby daughter to raise. I am employed as a farmer here at St. Michael's Indian School."

EDUCATION: Santa Fe, *ca*. 1937–40.

SERVICE: WWII, U.S. Army, three years; North African, Italian, and European Theaters.

EXHIBITIONS: AIM, MNM, PAC.

AWARDS: AIM.

COLLECTIONS: *Public*: CAMSL, GM, MAI, MNM, PAC. *Private*: Adlerblum, Elkus, Wyman.

Herrera, Marcelina   *Zia*
Hawelana
MARRIED: B. Trujillo.

EDUCATION: Santa Fe, under Dorothy Dunn; New Mexico U.
EXHIBITIONS: NGA, 1953.
COLLECTIONS: *Private*: D. Kramer.
ADDRESS: San Juan Pueblo, N.M.

Herrera, Martin   *Santo Domingo*
COLLECTIONS: *Public*: SM.

Herrera, Senefore (*see* Herrera, Senofre)

Herrera, Senofre   *Tesuque*
Oye Gi
(Also known as Herrera, Senefore.)
EDUCATION: Santa Fe.
EXHIBITIONS: AIE; FWG, 1943.
COLLECTIONS: *Public*: CU/LMA.

Herrera, Velino Shije   *Zia*
Ma Pe Wi, Oriole (or Red Bird)
(Also known as Velino Shije.)
BORN: October 22, 1902, Zia Pueblo, N.M. Son of Pedro Herrera and Reyes
Ancero.
MARRIED: A Nambé girl, *ca.* 1925; later married Mary Simbola (Picurís).
Five children: Ola, 1930; Calvin, 1938; Velino, Jr., 1933; Harold, 1937;
Clifford, 1944.

> The artist adopted his childhood nickname *Ma Pe Wi* as a nom-de-plume. The
> name has a punning significance, meaning either "oriole" or "bad egg." He has
> credited Dr. Edgar L. Hewett for getting him started in the field of art. When
> the State of New Mexico adopted the sun symbol of the Pueblo Indians as its
> official insignia, he was accused by his own people of betraying them by giving
> the design to the whites. José Rey Toledo (*q.v.*) describes Herrera as a "singing
> artist"—one would know which ceremony he was painting by the song he sang
> at the drawing board. A tragic auto accident in the 1950's killed his wife Mary
> and injured him for life. He no longer paints.

EDUCATION: Zia; Santa Fe.
CAREER: Began painting *ca.* 1917; had a successful studio in Santa Fe,
1932; painted briefly for School of American Research; painting instructor,
Albuquerque Indian School, 1936; rancher.
HONORS: Palmes d'Académiques, 1954.
COMMISSIONS: *Murals*: KM, USDI; Abuquerque Indian School; Rancho
San Ignacio, Sapello, N.M.; Tecoletenos Ranch, near Las Vegas, N.M.;
reproduced (in fresco) the kiva drawings at Kuaua, near Bernalillo, N.M.
BOOKS ILLUSTRATED: Clark (1941; 1943), Underhill (1938; 1941; 1945;
1946; 1951).
WORK PUBLISHED: Alexander (1932), Jacobson and D'Ucel (1950), La Farge
(1956; 1960), Pierson and Davidson (1960), Dockstader (1961). *School Arts
Magazine* (March 1931); *Introduction to American Indian Art, Part I* (1931);
American Magazine of Art (September 1928; August 1932); *Arizona High-
ways* (February 1950), *Compton's Pictured Encyclopedia* (1957).
EXHIBITIONS: AIEC, AIM, AIW, EITA, HM, ITIC, JGS, MNM, OU/ET,
PAC, PAC/T, SM.

AWARDS: AIM; ITIC Grand Award, 1948; PAC.
COLLECTIONS: *Public*: AMNH, CAM, CAMSL, CGA, CGFA, DAM, GM, KM, MAI, MKMcNAI, MNA/KHC, MNM, MRFM, PAC, PU/M, W/JSC. *Private*: H. Adams, Bates, Denman, Dietrich, Dockstader, Elkus, A. Forbes, Hewett, Lockett, Mullan, Pritzlaff, Rockefeller, Thoeny, Wheelright, Woffard, Wyman.
ADDRESS: 142 Bob Street, Santa Fe, N.M.

Herrera, Victor   *Cochiti*
EDUCATION: Santa Fe.
COLLECTIONS: *Public*: MAI.

Hessing, Valjean McCarty   *Choctaw*
BORN: August 30, 1934, Tulsa, Okla. Daughter of Vernon Clay McCarty (honorary chief of the Choctaws) and Madelyn Helen Beck. Sister of Carol Jane McCarty Mauldin (*q.v.*). The artist was reared by her mother's parents, the F.L. Becks. P/GM: Etta Regina Davis (Choctaw). P/GF: Carl McCarty (Choctaw).
MARRIED: Robert C. Hessing, 1954. Four children: Robert Bart, 1947; Jane Ann, 1958; Lauri Lynn, 1959; Bradly Lewis, 1962.
   The artist's interest in painting began in grade school. After high school, and
   until 1964, she had devoted most of her time to rearing a family. Now she is
   painting again and giving more time to exhibiting regularly.
EDUCATION: Public schools in Tulsa, Okla.; graduated Tulsa Central High School, 1942; attended Mary Hardin-Baylor College, Belton, Tex., 1952–54; Tulsa, 1954–55.
HONORS: Received scholarship, PAC art classes, 1945; scholarship to Mary Hardin-Baylor College, 1952; yearbook artist, Tulsa Central High School, 1949–52; yearbook art editor, cover artist for journalism magazine, and Student Union staff artist, Mary Hardin-Baylor College; member of Alpha Epsilon Chapter of K Π Fraternity; Secretary, Art Unlimited (Tulsa artists' association), 1965.
COMMISSIONS: Ad for Triangle Blue Print and Supply Co., Tulsa, which also appeared in *Today's Art* (April 1956).
EXHIBITIONS: 1945–65: PAC, SAIEAIP, SN, USDI; Art Unlimited Exhibitions; Tulsa Council of Indians 1965 Exhibition.
AWARDS: 1948–65: 17 from local, state, and national high school Scholastic Art Exhibits; Paint and Palette Award, Mary Hardin-Baylor College; Art Unlimited Exhibits; first place in writing, designing, producing, and directing a short musical in college, 1954.
COLLECTIONS: *Public*: PAC. *Private*: Combs, Cook, Ewing, Hammett, J. Mauldin, Rexroth, Rhodd, Woolley.
ADDRESS: Box 169 R.C., Route 1, Owasso, Okla.

Hevovitastamiutsts (*see* Whirlwind)

Hicks, Al   ?
COLLECTIONS: *Private*: Elkus.

Hicks, Bobby   *Navaho*
BORN: 1934.
EDUCATION: Scholarship to Arizona, "Southwest Indian Art Project," 1960.

CAREER: Art instructor, Fort Defiance Public School, Fort Defiance, Ariz.
EXHIBITIONS: 1957–63: ITIC, MNM, PAC, SN.
AWARDS: Four during 1958, from ITIC, PAC.
COLLECTIONS: *Public*: RM. *Private*: C. Fenton.
ADDRESS: Box 382, Window Rock, Ariz.

Hide Away (*see* Watchetaker, George Smith)

High Dog *Sioux*

BORN: Date unknown; from Standing Rock Reservation.
High Dog's Winter Count on unbleached muslin covers 114 years (at SHSND).
COLLECTIONS: *Public*: SHSND.

High Hawk *Teton Sioux*

Baptiste Good (*q.v.*) was also called High Hawk and executed a Winter Count.
These names apparently refer to the same man.
WORK PUBLISHED: Curtis (1907–30), a Winter Count illustrating 221 events.

Hill, Bobby *Kiowa*

White Buffalo
EXHIBITIONS: PAC.
COLLECTIONS: *Public*: IACB; Carnegie High School, Carnegie, Okla. *Private*:
Deupree, R. Moore, Walch.
ADDRESS: Box 571, Carnegie, Okla.

Hill, Joan *Creek-Cherokee*

Chea Sequah, Red Bird
BORN: December 19, 1930, Muskogee, Okla. Daughter of William McKinley
Hill (Creek-Cherokee) and Winnie Davis Harris (Creek-Cherokee). P/GF:
George Washington Hill (Creek). Operated Amanda Trading Post near
Hoffman, Okla. and was formerly President of the Creek Board of Educa-
tion; a member of the House of Kings and the House of Warriors; Chief
of the Creeks, 1923, re-elected by the tribe until 1928. P/GM: Lucy Grayson
Hill (Creek-Cherokee). P/GGF: William Grayson (Creek), Union soldier
who fought in Battle of Honey Springs, Indian Territory. M/GF: Chea Sequah
B. Harris (Creek-Cherokee), who, with two others, established Harris School
(now Harris-Jobe School), Muskogee County, Okla. M/GM: Nellie Carter
(Cherokee). M/GGM: Ellen Rogers Harris (Creek-Cherokee). M/GGF: Col.
Red Bird Harris (Cherokee). M/GGU: C. J. Harris, a Cherokee chief, 1891.
In 1956, Miss Hill decided to become a full-time artist. She has remained dedi-
cated to her career, rightly earning national recognition.
EDUCATION: Harris Elementary School, Alice Robertson Junior High
School, and graduated Central High School, Muskogee, Okla., 1948; A.A.,
Muskogee, 1950; B.A. (Ed.), Northeastern, 1952. Additional art study
under Dick West (*q.v.*) at Bacone College, and under George E. Calvert,
John Kennedy, Jack Vallee, Ruth M. White (*q.v.*), Laurie Wallace, Roger
Lee White, John Arthur, Bob Bartholic, Paul Maxwell, and Frederic
Taubes, 1956–64; under Dong Kingman (workshop tour of Europe, 1964);
Famous Artists Commercial Art, Inc.
CAREER: Art instructor, Roosevelt Junior High School, Tulsa, Okla., 1952–
56; adult art instructor, Muskogee Art Guild, 1959; artist, 1956–.

HONORS: Listed in *Oklahoma Artists* and *Leadership Index* (a "Who's Who in Oklahoma"); member, Φ Θ K (honorary scholastic society); art and publicity director, Muskogee Art Guild; publicity director, Annual Muskogee Art Show.

COMMISSIONS: *Commercial Art*: FCTM brochure, 1957; trademark, Cos-Medic Specialities Co., 1959; *Corning Glass Works in the Sooner State* (1960), cover and 30 illustrations. *Portraits*: 34 completed; 11 famous Cherokees, commissioned by Hardin Nelson; FCTM, eight of the Five Tribes Chiefs.

WORK PUBLISHED: Hamm and Inglish (1960), cover; Gregory and Strickland (1967). *The Sunday Oklahoman, Orbit Magazine* (July 21, 1963); *Southwest Review* (Summer 1966), cover.

EXHIBITIONS: 1956–65 (87 non-juried, 39 juried): AIE, BC, FAIEAIP, FCTM, IACB, ITIC, MNM, MNM/T, OAC, PAC, SN, USDI; Bazza Gallery and Oklahoma Museum of Conservative Art, Oklahoma City; Motorola Regional Art Exhibit, Tulsa; Northeastern State Teachers College Library; Annual Six-State Exhibition, Springfield, Mo.; American Indian and Eskimo Cultural Foundation, Agra Gallery, Washington, D.C.; Bartholic Gallery, Benedictine Heights College, Oklahoma Cattlemen's Association, Tulsa, Okla.; Muskogee Annual Art Shows, Art Guild Studio, Muskogee, Okla.; Conners State College; Carl Addington Gallery, Yukon, Okla. *One-man shows*: 1952–65: HM, PAC; Northeastern State College; Western Hills Lodge, Sequoyah State Park, Okla.; Henson Gallery, Yukon, Okla.; Leone Kahl Gallery, Dallas, Tex.; American Embassies abroad, 1965–67.

AWARDS: 1959–65: 34 from major juried shows, 78 from Tulsa and Muskogee State Fairs, also one Sweepstakes and one Grand Award.

COLLECTIONS: *Public*: BC, FCTM, IACB, MAI, MNM, PAC; Western Hills Lodge, Sequoyah State Park; *Private*: Addington, E. Adkins, R. Adkins, A. Baker, Basore, Bock, Bynum, J. Carter, M. Carter, R. Clark, Connelly, Conry, Crickmer, J. Fletcher, M. Fletcher, Florence, Garrett, Girdler, Harvey, Heughland, W. C. Hill, W. M. Hill, Hively, Hohn, Huldermann, E. Jacobson, J. James, N. Jones, O. Jones, Judkins, Kershaw, Leathers, Lynde, Marshall, T. Mason, McCann, McKee, McKeever, McNaught, J. Milburn, Myers, Nelson, B. Oldham, Perdue, D. Perry, Pierce, Rowsey, Satterwhite, Schreiber, J. Snodgrass, Spillers, G. Stevens, W. Stone, Stout, Summers, Swindler, Upton, VanCleve, J. Walker, C. Walkingstick, R. Wheeler, Witkamp.

ADDRESS: Route 3, Box 151, Harris Road, Muskogee, Okla.

Hinds, Patrick Swazo   *Tesuque*
Grey Squirrel

BORN: March 25, 1929, Tesuque Pueblo, N.M. In 1939, at the age of ten, the artist was adopted by Dr. Norman A. E. Hinds, an honorary member of Tesuque, who, for 45 years, was Professor of Geology at the University of California.

MARRIED: Rita Ann Gunther, 1958. Children: Mark Allen, 1959; Marita, 1961.

Not long after he was adopted by Professor Hinds, the artist moved to California where, except for the years he was away at school, he has resided ever since. He usually spends summer vacations at Tesuque Pueblo. He is active in the Society of Western Artists, the Oakland Art Association, the Berkeley Arts and Crafts Cooperative, and American Indian Artists.

EDUCATION: Tesuque; Santa Fe, 1938–39; St. Catherine's, 1940; St. Mary's College High School, Berkeley, Calif., 1941–46; Hill, 1948; Mexico C. C., 1952; Chicago, 1953–55; B.A., California C., 1951.

SERVICE: U.S. Marine Corps, two years.

CAREER: Silk screen processor, Hawkins and Hawkins, Berkeley, Calif., 1961–.

HONORS: Chairman, Arts and Crafts Cooperative, Berkeley, Calif.; Associate Chairman, Painting Committee, American Indian Artists, San Francisco.

EXHIBITIONS: Twenty-two, 1947–63: CAI, CPLH, ITIC, MNM; Cork Wall Gallery, Berkeley, Calif.; Oakland Art Museum, Rental Gallery, Oakland, Calif. *One-man shows*: HM; Gallery Nine, Grey Shop, Oakland, Calif.

AWARDS: SN Grand Award, 1966.

COLLECTIONS: *Private*: Boynoff, D. Brown, Dewey, Elkus, Giannini, D. Griffin, Hammond, Hardy, D. Harris, Hearne, Herwick, Irby, Klick, Krueger, J. Lewis, Little, McGilliway, McIune, Mills, Miner, Morford, Nortner, Ordon, Pina, Regan, Waller, Zeff, Zelonis.

ADDRESS: 1912 McBee Avenue, Berkeley, Calif.

His Battle (*see* Jaw)

His Crazy Horse *Sioux*

COLLECTIONS: *Public*: MPM (pictographic style).

His Fight *Hunkpapa Sioux*

BORN: Date unknown; lived near Fort Buford, Mont., 1868.

WORK PUBLISHED: Smith (1943).

COLLECTIONS: *Public*: MAI (line drawing executed in ink).

Histito, Alonzo *Zuni*

COLLECTIONS: *Public*: MNM.

Hiuwa Tuni ?

COLLECTIONS: *Public*: W/JSC (*ca.* 1940).

Hobah *Comanche*

COLLECTIONS: *Public*: FSM (painting on deerskin in native colors, before 1922).

Ho Chee Nee (*see* Burton, Jimalee)

Hoffman, Delores ?

EXHIBITIONS: AIM, 1964.

Hogoon (*see* Silverhorn)

Ho Haw *Kiowa*

The artist was among the 72 Plains Indians taken as prisoners from Fort Sill, Okla., to Fort Marion, St. Augustine, Fla., in 1875.

WORK PUBLISHED: *Bulletin of the Missouri Historical Society* (October 1950), *St. Louis Post Dispatch* (August 13, 1950).

COLLECTIONS: *Public*: MHS, OAA/SI

Hokeah, Jack *Kiowa*

BORN: 1902, western Oklahoma. GF: White Horse (*q.v.*), the warrior. Orphaned while still a young boy, he was reared by his grandmother. Although Hokeah was one of the Five Kiowas (*q.v.*), he has not recently contributed to the art world.

EDUCATION: St. Patrick's through the ninth grade; Santa Fe; Oklahoma, special non-credit classes.

CAREER: On New York stage for a short period; later employed by BIA.

COMMISSIONS: *Murals*: Santa Fe Indian School.

WORK PUBLISHED: Jacobson (1929; 1964), Jacobson and D'Ucel (1950). *American Magazine of Art* (August 1933), *American Scene*, GM (Vol. VI, No. 3).

EXHIBITIONS: AIE/T; EITA; "The Five Kiowas on the 50th Anniversary of Statehood," PAC.

AWARDS: IACB Certificate of Appreciation, 1966.

COLLECTIONS: *Public*: ACM, DAM, GM, JAM, MAI, MKMcNAI, MNA/KHC, MNM, SPL. *Private*: Denman, Deupree, Dockstader, O. Jacobson, W. S. Price.

ADDRESS: Rural Route, Anadarko, Okla.

Holgate, Eugene, Jr.   *Navaho*
EXHIBITIONS: 1962–63: PAC, SN, USDS.
COLLECTIONS: *Public*: BIA, IACB.
ADDRESS: 4014 North Second Street, Phoenix, Ariz.

Holgate, J.   ?
COLLECTIONS: *Public*: MAI.

Hollowbreast, Donald   *Northern Cheyenne*
Maxhebaho, Big Black
BORN: May 17, 1917, Birney, Mont.
  The artist was interested in painting even as a child. He began to paint with oils in 1950. Since then, he has experimented with other media. [*See* "Donald Hollowbreast: Fighting Cheyenne Editor," *Montana* (Autumn 1964).]

EDUCATION: Birney Day School and La Bré Mission, Ashland, Mont.; Busby Public School and Tongue River Boarding School, Busby, Mont.; Chemawa (Oreg.) Public School, Ashland (Mont.) Public School.

CAREER: Assisted with Indian adult education program, Birney, Mont., 1959; Editor, *Birney Arrow*, 1959–.

WORK PUBLISHED: *Montana* (Autumn 1964).

EXHIBITIONS: 1952–63: 13, including AAID, BNIAS, DAM, ITIC, MHS/H, PAC; Rosebud County Fair, Forsyth, Mont.; Northern Cheyenne Indian Fair, Lame Deer, Mont.; Midland Empire Fair, Billings, Mont.

AWARDS: Many prizes in local fairs.

COLLECTIONS: *Private*: Arbouchon.

ADDRESS: Box 145, Birney, Mont.

Holmes, Art (*see* Lomayaktewa, V.)

Holmes, Gordon   *Hopi*
COLLECTIONS: *Public*: MAI.

Holmes, Roderick   *Hopi*
EDUCATION: Santa Fe.
EXHIBITIONS: JGS, 1955.
COLLECTIONS: *Public*: MNM (dated 1952).
ADDRESS: Tuba City, Ariz.

Holton, Anne Tennyson *Cherokee*
BORN: February 1, 1921, McNairy County, Tenn. Daughter of H. Frank
Tennyson and Mattie Lucille Jernigan. M/GP: Joseph Ingle and Delia.
P/GGP: Hiram Olney Tennison and Sally Ann Vaughters.
MARRIED: Bob Holton, 1955. One son: Mark Douglas, 1958.
EDUCATION: Central High School, Bolivar, Tenn.; Memphis, Tenn., School
of Commerce.
CAREER: Employed by Walgreen Drug Co., five years; sales representative,
Helena Rubinstein, Inc., eight years.
HONORS: Listed in 1964 *Leadership Index* (a "Who's Who in Oklahoma");
La Grande (Oreg.) Arts Festival, 1964, first award in poetry; American
Poets Fellowship Society, New York, N.Y., 1964, third award.
WORK PUBLISHED: Holton (1964).
AWARDS: 1943–65: Several from Okmulgee County Annual Art Exhibit,
Okmulgee, Okla.
EXHIBITIONS: 1963–65: CCHM, FANAIAE, PAC; Okmulgee Art Exhibit,
and Library Art Exhibit, Okmulgee; Fort Gibson, Okla., Arts and Crafts
Exhibit; Tahlequah, Okla., Arts and Crafts Exhibit; AAUW Arts Exhibit
and Book Fair, Bartlesville, Okla.
COLLECTIONS: *Private*: T. Alexander, K. Chandler, H. Davidson, M. Grant,
C. Jones, Lowry, Martin, McElroy, McGilhra, B. Peterson, L. Ross, Shelton,
Simpson, Tennyson.
ADDRESS: 1413 East Eighth, Okmulgee, Okla.

Holy Buffalo (*see* Levings, Martin)

Holy Standing Buffalo *Sioux*
COLLECTIONS: *Public*: MPM (pictographic style on paper).

Home Of The Elk (*see* Martínez, Crescencio)

Homer, Bernard *Zuni*
EXHIBITIONS: MNM, 1965.
ADDRESS: Box 117, Zuni, N.M.

Honahni, Al *Hopi*
COLLECTIONS: *Public*: MNA/KHC (dated *ca.* 1952).

Honahniein, Ramson R. *Hopi*
Suhonva
(Also known as Honahnie.)
BORN: *ca.* 1928, Moenkopi, Ariz.
COLLECTIONS: *Public*: MNM.

Honewytewa, Louis Calvin, Jr. *Hopi*
Queyesva, Sitting Eagle
BORN: June 30, 1930, Keams Canyon, Ariz.
EDUCATION: Hopi.
COLLECTIONS: *Public*: PAC.
ADDRESS: Shungopovi, Second Mesa, Ariz.

Honganozhe (*see* Ballard, Louis Wayne)

Hood, Rance   *Comanche*
Au Tup Ta, Yellow Hair
BORN: February 9, 1941, Lawton, Okla. Son of Tom Hood and June Tene-
guar (Comanche). Son-in-law of Roland Whitehorse (*q.v.*).
MARRIED: Phyllis Whitehorse (Kiowa), February 4, 1963. Two children:
Deanna, 1964; Andrea, 1965.
CAREER: Sequoyah Mills, Anadarko, Okla., 1963–.
EXHIBITIONS: AIE, FAIEAIP, PAC, SN.
AWARDS: AIE; Fourth Annual Texas-Oklahoma Sidewalk Art Exhibit,
Lawton, Okla., 1965.
COLLECTIONS: *Public*: MAI, SPIM.
ADDRESS: General Delivery, Cache, Okla.

Hopkins, Merina Luján (*see* Pop Chalee)

Horn, Miles S.   *Arikara*
White Crow
BORN: Date unknown. GGGF: Chief One Star. Nephew of Red Star, a scout
enlisted in the Seventh Cavalry under Gen. Custer.
    The artist was encouraged to paint by Charles Russell and has been a popular
    artist in the Upper Great Plains area for many years.
SERVICE: WWI; WWII.
CAREER: Solo cornetist with all-Indian band; professional baseball player;
cowboy; range rider; motion picture actor.
EXHIBITIONS: BNIAS painting entitled "Day Before Custer Battle."
COLLECTIONS: *Public*: BIA/B.
ADDRESS: Box 580, Billings, Mont.

Horse, Perry   *Kiowa*
EXHIBITIONS: 1963–64: AAIEAE, USDS.

Horse Chief (*see* Beard, Lorenzo)

Horse Tail   *Crow*
COLLECTIONS: *Public*: DAM.

Hosetosavit, Arden   *Mescalero Apache*
BORN: May 21, 1945, Mescalero, N.M.
EDUCATION: Santa Fe, *ca.* 1962; Institute, 1965–66.
EXHIBITIONS: 1962–64: MNM, PAC, SAIEAIP, SN, USDI, USDS.
AWARDS: *Interior Design Magazine* Award, 1964.
COLLECTIONS: *Public*: BIA, IACB.
ADDRESS: Box 74, Mescalero, N.M.

Hoskie, Larry   *Navaho*
COMMISSIONS: *Murals*: ASF/Coliseum, 1965 (with four other Navahos).

Hoskiel (*see* Abeyta, Narciso Platero)

Hotyee (*see* Byrnes, James Michael)

House Standing Upright (*see* Denetsosie, Hoke)

Houser, Allan C.   *Chiricahua Apache*
Haozous, Pulling Roots
BORN: June 30, 1915, Apache, Okla. Son of Sam Haozous (Apache). GU:
Gerónimo, famous warrior who was imprisoned at Fort Sill, Okla.

MARRIED: Anna Marie Callegos (Navaho). Four children: Roy, Lonnie, Robert, Stephen.

Houser's parents were taken to Fort Sill and held prisoners with Gerónimo's band. Later, after his father started to farm, the boy helped at home and attended school intermittently. From a beginning of many hardships, he has attained an outstanding career and reputation in the art field. He first began painting about 1924 and is today equally well known as a sculptor. O. B. Jacobson regarded Houser as one of the most important artists of his day.

EDUCATION: Boone County (Okla.) School, through 8th grade; Fort Sill; Chilocco; Haskell; Santa Fe. Mural instruction under Olaf Nordmark at Fort Sill.

CAREER: Artist in residence and art instructor, Inter-Mountain Indian School; painting and sculpture instructor, Institute of American Indian Arts, 1962–.

HONORS: John Simon Guggenheim Scholarship for Sculpture and Painting, 1948; Palmes d'Académiques, 1954; represented in *Indians of Today*; Certificate of Appreciation, IACB, 1967.

COMMISSIONS: *Murals*: SPIM, USDI; Fort Sill Indian School; Riverside Indian School; Jicarilla Indian School; Inter-Mountain Indian School. *Sculpture*: Marble war memorial, "Comrades in Mourning," Haskell Institute, 1948; portrait of Gerónimo, capital building, State of Arizona. *Medal*: The Society of Medallists, 59th medal issued, May, 1959. *Dioramas*: SPIM.

WORK PUBLISHED: Jacobson and D'Ucel (1950), Carter (1954), Pierson and Davidson (1960), Arnold (1960) dust jacket, Dockstader (1961), Jacobson (1964). *Arizona Highways* (February 1950; November 1962), *Compton's Pictured Encyclopedia* (Vol. 7, 1957), *Oklahoma Today* (Summer 1958), *Sunday Bonanza, San Francisco Chronicle* (August 22, 1965), *Indians from Oklahoma*, BIA (1966).

EXHIBITIONS: AAIE, AIEC, AIW, CAI, DAM, EITA, ITIC, JGS, MNM, NGA, PAC, PAC/T, SFWF, SN; National Exhibition of American Art, New York, N.Y., 1937 (only Indian represented); New York World's Fair, 1939; Blair House, Washington, D.C., 1964. *One-man shows*: CAI, DAM, MNM, OU, PAC.

AWARDS: DAM, ITIC, PAC, SN; trophy for outstanding work in Indian art, Santa Fe Indian School, senior year; three Grand Awards.

COLLECTIONS: *Public*: AF, BIA, FSM, IACB, JAM, MNA/KHC, MNM. OU/MA, OU/SM, PAC. *Private*: H. Adams, Denman, Elkus, Finley, N, Hunt, O. Jacobson, D. Kramer, Mullan, Neumann, Pritzlaff, Schonwald, Thoeny, Walch, Wyman.

ADDRESS: 1020 Camino Carlos Rey, Santa Fe, N.M.

Howe, Oscar *Yanktonai Sioux*
Mazuha Hokshina, Trader Boy

BORN: May 13, 1915, Joe Creek, Crow Creek Reservation, S. Dak. Son of George T. Howe (Yanktonai) and Ella Not Afraid of Bear (Yanktonai). P/GGF: Bone Necklace, head chief of Yanktonais. M/GGF: White Bear (Yanktonai), awarded medal from federal government for outstanding service to the nation in 1862. M/GF: Not Afraid of Bear, Yanktonai chief.

MARRIED: Heidi Hampel, July 29, 1947. One daughter: Ingre Dawn, 1948.
While a child in government boarding school, the artist developed a serious skin
disease and trachoma. He was sent home and given little chance to escape blind-
ness and disfiguration, but he vowed to get well and "be the best." He returned
to school and completed his education.

EDUCATION: Pierre Indian School, Pierre, S. Dak., through ninth grade;
graduated Santa Fe, 1938; B.A., Dakota Wesleyan University, Mitchell.
S. Dak., 1952; M.F.A., University of Oklahoma, 1953.

SERVICE: WWII, U.S. Army, three and one-half years; European Theater,

CAREER: Instructor in art, Pierre Indian School, 1939; artist in residence
and Assistant Professor of Creative Arts, University of South Dakota,
1957–. The artist conducts the annual American Indian Art Summer Workshops, University of South Dakota.

HONORS: High School Salutatorian; Harvey Dunn Medal of Art; Certificate
of Appreciation, IACB; Artist Laureate of South Dakota; Waite Phillips
Outstanding Indian Artist Trophy, PAC, 1966; listed in *Indians of Today*,
Who's Who in South Dakota, *Who's Who in American Art*. See Pennington,
1961.

COMMISSIONS: *Murals*: Carnegie Library and Corn Palace, Mitchell, S. Dak.;
City Auditorium, Mobridge, S. Dak.; Park Building, Nebraska City, Nebr.;
Proviso High School, Hinsdale, Ill.

BOOKS ILLUSTRATED: Raabe (1942), Clark (1943a), Jacobson (1952) Hassrick
(1964). *Legend of the Mighty Sioux*, South Dakota Writers' Project, (1941).

WORK PUBLISHED: Douglas and D'Harnoncourt (1941); La Farge (1956;
1960); Pierson and Davidson (1960), Pennington (1961). *Oklahoma Today*
(Summer 1958); *Museum News* (June 1962); *Smoke Signals*, IACB (Autumn
1965).

EXHIBITIONS: 1949–65: 75 museums and art associations in North America,
including AIEC, BNIAS, CAI, DAM, MMA, MNM, NGA, OU/ET, PAC,
PAC/T, SAIEAIP, SIECC, SM, SU, USDI, USDS. 1947–66: Indian art
competitions, 22 showings; 1965–67: U.S. Embassies in Europe. *One-man
shows*: 26, including AIW, DAM, HM, JAM, MNM, PAC, USDI.

AWARDS: 1947–65: 28, including five PAC Grand Awards.

COLLECTIONS: *Public*: BIA, DAM, IACB, JAM, MAI, MAM, OU/MA, OU/SM,
PAC, SIECC, SM. *Private*: Bush, Denman, Dietrich, Dockstader, Edwards,
Eisenhower, A. Forbes, Grender, Hassrick, E. Jacobson, O. Jacobson,
McGovern, Merits, Michels, Pickart, W. S. Price, Rue, Schonwald, Schrei-
ber, Yulke.

ADDRESS: 128 Walker Street, Vermillion, S. Dak.

Howling Wolf   *Southern Cheyenne*

BORN: Date unknown. Son of *Minimic (Ma nim ik)*, who was in Black
Kettle's camp at Big Timbers and was chief of his own band, which surrendered to reservation life in 1869.

The artist was among the 72 Plains Indians taken as prisoners from Fort Sill,
Okla., to Fort Marion, St. Augustine, Fla., in 1875. By 1880 he had returned to
the area of the Darlington Cheyenne Agency, Darlington, Okla., where apparently
he did no further painting.

WORK PUBLISHED: Petersen (1968).

COLLECTIONS: *Public*: CMNH, HI, JAM/BL, MAI, YU/BRBML. *Private*: Curtin.

Huan Toa (*see* Momaday, Al)

Hugh, Victor C. *Hopi*

COLLECTIONS: *Public*: AF.

Humetewa, Eric *Hopi*

BORN: Date unknown; from Tuba City, Ariz. area. Uncle of James Russell Humetewa, Jr. (*q.v.*).

COLLECTIONS: *Private*: Dockstader.

Humetewa, James Russell, Jr. *Hopi*

Humetewa, Shelling Corn; *Soo Woea* (or *Saw Whu, Salo Whu*), Morning Star.

BORN: May 28, 1926, east of Grand Canyon, near Tuba City, Ariz. His brother resides at Santo Domingo Pueblo.

Records at the Museum of New Mexico disclose that the artist has exhibited extensively in New Mexico and Arizona. In 1950, he was reportedly the most profilic of the younger Hopi artists.

EDUCATION: Hopi, *ca.* 1940; graduated Santa Fe, 1945.

CAREER: Onetime employee of MNM.

WORK PUBLISHED: Jacobson and D'Ucel (1950).

EXHIBITIONS: FWG, ITIC, MNA, MNM, NMSF, PAC, PAC/T, SFWF.

One-man shows: 1947, MNM.

COLLECTIONS: *Public*: GM, MAI, MNM, PAC. *Private*: Denman, Elkus, A. Forbes.

ADDRESS: Santa Ana Pueblo, Bernalillo, N.M.

Hummingbird, Jerome *Kiowa*

BORN: 1930, Lawton, Okla.

EDUCATION: Riverside.

EXHIBITIONS: PAC.

COLLECTIONS: *Private*: Truex.

ADDRESS: Cache, Okla.

Hunt, Clyde "Sunnyskies" *Acoma*

COLLECTIONS: *Private*: W. S. Price.

Hunt, Wayne Henry (*see* Hunt, Wolf Robe)

Hunt, Wolf Robe *Acoma*

Kewa, Growing Plant

(Also known as Hunt, Wayne Henry.)

BORN: October 14, 1905, on the Acoma Reservation, N.M. Son of Edward Hunt (Acoma), Chief of the Delight Makers, and Morning Star (Acoma), well-known potter and weaver. M/GGF: Martin Vallo, seven-time governor of Acoma Pueblo.

MARRIED: Glenal Davis, 1932. One daughter: Lo Waynenema, 1933.

As a boy on the reservation, Wolf Robe herded sheep for his father and later became a member of the respected Hunters Society. He is an accomplished silversmith, and, yearly since 1936, has exhibited at the Inter-Tribal Indian Ceremonials. Since the 1930's, he has been active in the promotion of authentic

Pueblo dance groups. He is a Charter Member of the Tulsa Pow Wow Club, a member of the Masonic Lodge, Scottish Rite, and Akdar and President of the Masonic Lodge Indian Patrol of Tulsa, Okla.

EDUCATION: Albuquerque; graduated Albuquerque Public High School, Albuquerque, N.M.; studied privately under Carl Redin in Albuquerque and under Frank Von Der Laucken in Tulsa.

CAREER: Lecturer, author, painter, and silversmith. Toured Europe as a member of a dance group with 101 Ranch Circus; organized and led Pueblo dance group presenting educational programs throughout the U.S., 1936; director of Indian dances, Boy Scout Circus Pageant, St. Louis, Mo., 1937; Indian arts and crafts instructor, PAC, 1953; motel owner and operator, Tulsa, Okla., 1957–59; lecturer, University of Kansas, Extension Service; assisted BAE as interpreter; Indian trader, owner and operator of Indian arts and crafts shop, Tulsa, Okla., 1938–.

HONORS: Offered scholarship from University of Chicago, Department of Anthropology; selected by the U.S. Department of Agriculture to represent American Indians at a food exhibition, Hamburg, Germany, 1964; represented in *Indians of Today*.

BOOKS ILLUSTRATED: Rushmore and Hunt (1963).

EXHIBITIONS: AIE, FANAIAE, ITIC, MNM, PAC, SAIEAIP, SN, USDS; United States Food Exhibition, Hamburg, Germany. *One-man shows*: 1964–66, HM, PAC.

AWARDS: 1964: FANAIAE, MNM.

COLLECTIONS: *Public*: BIA, IACB, PAC. *Private*: Mayor (1965) of Segeberg, Germany.

ADDRESS: Box 15606, Tulsa, Okla.

Hunter, Elwood   *Navaho*
EXHIBITIONS: FWG, HM.

Hunting Horse (*see* Darby, Raymond Lee)

Hunting Horse (*see* Tsatoke, Lee Monette)

Hunting Horse (*see* Tsatoke, Monroe)

Hunting Wolf   *Apache*
Hunting Wolf was among the 72 Plains Indian prisoners taken from Fort Sill, Okla., to Fort Marion, St. Augustine, Fla., in 1875; while there, he executed paintings and drawings on writing paper.
COLLECTIONS: *Public*: OHSM.

Hushka Yelhayah (*see* Lee, Charlie)

Huskett, John   *Navaho*
EDUCATION: Chilocco (commercial art course after WWII).
SERVICE: WWII, U.S. Navy, four years.
EXHIBITIONS: PAC; Midwest Rural Conference, Oklahoma State University, 1959.

Hyde, Douglas   *Nez Percé*
BORN: 1946, Hermiston, Idaho.
EDUCATION: Institute, 1965–66.
EXHIBITIONS: SAIEAIP.

Hyeoma, Lucille   *Hopi*
EDUCATION: Institute, 1965–66.
EXHIBITIONS: YAIA.

Ihunter (*see* Orr, Howell Sonny)

Immana, Annie Weokluk   *Eskimo*
Annnanooruk
BORN: 1903, Big Diomede, Siberia.
  The artist's travels along the coast of Siberia in a skin boat have provided her
  with the subject matter for her paintings.
EXHIBITIONS: Nome Skin Sewers, Alaska; Poliet's Store, Nome, Alaska.
ADDRESS: Nome, Alaska.

In The Middle Of Many Tracks (*see* Anko)

Ingram, Jerry Cleman   *Choctaw*
BORN: December 13, 1941, Battiest, Okla. Son of Charley Ingram and Jincy
Cobb (Choctaw).
MARRIED: Veronica Marie Orr, *q.v.* (Colville), February 14, 1964. One child:
Teresa M., 1964.
EDUCATION: Battiest Elementary School; graduated Chilocco, 1963; post-
graduate work at Institute, six months; graduated Oklahoma S. U./S. T.,
1966.
COMMISSIONS: *Murals*: Oklahoma State University, Oklahoma Room.
EXHIBITIONS: CCHM; Okmulgee Pow Wow, Okmulgee Art Show, Oklahoma
State University Art Show.
AWARDS: Okmulgee Art Show, 1965.
COLLECTIONS: *Private*: L. Brock, Frith, Robinett.
ADDRESS: Oklahoma State University, School of Technology, Okmulgee.

Ingram, Veronica Marie   *Colville*
Suctwa Quinkum, Musically Inclined
BORN: January 12, 1945, Omak, Wash. Daughter of Samuel A. Orr (We-
natche) and Caroline Nelson (Colville). Sister of Caroline Louise Orr (*q.v.*).
MARRIED: Jerry Cleman Ingram, *q.v.* (Choctaw), February 14, 1964. One
child: Teresa M., 1964.
EDUCATION: Omak (Wash.) Public School; graduated Institute, 1963; six
months' postgraduate work.
CAREER: Secretary (student trainee) and tourist guide at the Institute of
American Indian Arts.
EXHIBITIONS: CCHM; IAIA Gallery; Okmulgee Art Show, Okmulgee Pow
Wow, Okmulgee Library, Okla.
ADDRESS: c/o Oklahoma State University, School of Technology, Okmulgee,
Okla.

Inn, M. Riding (*see* Riding Inn, M.)

Iromagaja (*see* Rain In The Face)

Iron Tail (Chief)   *Oglala Sioux*
Sinte Maze, Iron Tail
(Also known as Plenty Scalps.)

BORN: 1851; once lived in Pine Ridge, S. Dak. Took part in Battle of Little Big Horn while his name was Plenty Scalps. Died, May 29, 1916 near Ft. Wayne, Indiana.

MARRIED: Indian woman; lived on reservation.

HONORS: Succeeded Sitting Bull as chief.

COLLECTIONS: *Public*: MAI (autograph sketch, see Black Heart).

Itchez Ha Biye (*see* Scott, Johnson Lee)

Itkaminyauke   *Sioux*

COLLECTIONS: *Public*: MPM (pictographic style on paper).

Jackson, Nathan   *Tlingit*

BORN: 1938, Juneau, Alaska.

EXHIBITIONS: SAIEAIP, SN.

AWARDS: SN, 1964.

ADDRESS: Haines, Alaska.

Jake, Albin Roy   *Pawnee*

Ahsey Sututut, War Horse

BORN: June 22, 1922, Skedee, Pawnee County, Okla. Died, July 1960. Brother of John Jake, Pawnee, Okla.

> In 1957, the artist wrote Philbrook Art Center: "My modernistic oil paintings are innovations of age old designs and patterns. The broken color designs bordering some of my paintings are to me representative of the geometric designs, patterns and hide paintings of the Indians of the Great Plains area, a glimpse into and out of something that is by-gone."

EDUCATION: Bacone College, under Dick West (*q.v.*); graduated Haskell, where he studied under Franklin Gritts (*q.v.*); graduated Northeastern; attended Oklahoma.

SERVICE: WWII, U.S. Marine Corps, 34 months; Pacific Theater.

CAREER: Artist-illustrator, Tinker Air Force Base, Oklahoma City, Okla.; resigned in 1957 to devote full-time to freelance art work and mural commissions.

COMMISSIONS: *Murals*: Tinker Air Force Base, conference room (with Bunny Randall, *q.v.*, and LeRoy McAllister).

WORK PUBLISHED: La Farge (1956) (1960), Pierson and Davidson (1960). *The World Book Encyclopedia* (1960).

EXHIBITIONS: 1949–60: DAM, JGS, MNM, PAC, PAC/T. *One-man shows*: PAC, 1957.

AWARDS: 1949–56: MNM, PAC (including one Grand Award).

COLLECTIONS: *Public*: OHSM, PAC. *Private*: Deupree, Schonwald.

James, Sammy   *Navaho*

COLLECTIONS: *Public*: MAI.

Jaramillo, Edward Gilbert   *Isleta*

EDUCATION: Santa Fe, *ca.* 1959.

EXHIBITIONS: MNM, 1959.

Jaramillo, Joseph Louis   ?

EDUCATION: St. Catherine's.

COLLECTIONS: *Public*: MNM (colored pencil on cardboard).

Jaw *Hunkpapa-Sans Arcs Sioux*
Cehu'pa (and *Oki'cize Tawa*, His Battle)
BORN: 1850. His mother was a Hunkpapa, and his father was a Sans Arcs.
The artist was named Cehu'pa by his White brother-in-law; his childhood name
was Mázaho Waste (Loud Sounding Metal), and at the age of 17 he was given
the name of Oki'cize Tawa.
WORK PUBLISHED: BAE, *Bull. 61, 173* (pictographic style).

Jay, Tom *Hopi*
EDUCATION: Santa Fe, *ca.* 1938.
EXHIBITIONS: AIW.
COLLECTIONS: *Private*: Dietrich.

Jefferson, Bennie *Sauk-Fox*
BORN: 1913.
EDUCATION: Chilocco.
EXHIBITIONS: AIEC.

Jenkins, Nathan *Hopi*
EXHIBITIONS: HM (*ca.* 1951, while a student).

Jim, Frank *Navaho*
BORN: September 17, 19?8, Keams Canyon, Ariz. The artist is known to
have exhibited in Flagstaff, Ariz.

Jim, Wilson *Navaho*
BORN: In 1952, near Jeddito Trading Post, Arizona.
EDUCATION: Santa Fe; Albuquerque, seventh grade, *ca.* 1964.
EXHIBITIONS: NMSF.
AWARDS: 1964: NMSF.

Jobie Bear (*see* Byrnes, James Michael)

Joe, Ray *Navaho-Zia*
BORN: November 23, 1945, Fort Wingate, N.M. Son of Tom Joe (Navaho-
Zia) and Mary Houston (Navaho). P/GF: Black Joe (Man With Big Whiskers).
M/GF: Doan Houston. M/GM: Bah James Houston.
Listed as an outstanding art student by Duane O. Berg, Gallup art instructor,
he received his first award in the Gallup Lions' Club Rodeo Poster Contest while
in the fourth grade. He hopes to become an art teacher at the elementary level.
EDUCATION: Houck Mission School, Sanders Public School, Tohatchi
Boarding School, N.M., 1949–58; graduated Gallup, 1964.
EXHIBITIONS: ITIC, NACG, NMSF; Gallup Indian Community Center.
AWARDS: Six from Gallup Indian Community Center; NACG Student
Exhibit.
COLLECTIONS: *Public*: Paramount Resturant, Gallup, N.M.; Manuelito Hall,
Gallup High School. *Private*: Berg, Stanley, M. Woodard.
ADDRESS: General Delivery, Lupton, Ariz.

John, Angelo Marvin *Navaho*
BORN: February 5, 1946, Flagstaff, Ariz. Son of Charlie John (Navaho).
EDUCATION: Ganado Mission, Ganado, Ariz.; Mission School, Cottonwood,
Ariz.; Fort Sill; Institute (senior, 1964–65).

HONORS: Fifth Annual Navaho Youth Conference, Shiprock, N.M., 1965; Student-body President, Institute of American Indian Arts, 1965.
COMMISSIONS: *Murals*: Cedar Point Great Hall, Mackinac Island, Mich.
EXHIBITIONS: PAC, YAIA.
COLLECTIONS: *Public*: BIA, IAIA. *Private*: Bush, Egertson.
ADDRESS: 5–B, Clark Homes, Flagstaff, Ariz.

John, Johnny   *Shawnee*
COLLECTIONS: *Public*: MAI.

Johns, David   *Navaho*
COLLECTIONS: *Public*: MAI. PRIVATE: E. Carter.

Johns, Joe L.   *Seminole*
EDUCATION: Institute, *ca.* 1965.
EXHIBITIONS: YAIA.

Johnson, Alfred   *Cherokee*
Eya
EDUCATION: Bacone College.
EXHIBITIONS: PAC, PAC/T.
AWARDS: PAC.
COLLECTIONS: *Public*: PAC.

Jojola, E.   *Isleta*
COLLECTIONS: *Public*: MAI.

Jones, Laura Asah   *Kiowa-Comanche*
EXHIBITIONS: PAC, 1959.
ADDRESS: 2338 North West 35th, Oklahoma City, Okla.

Jones, Ruthe Blalock   *Delaware-Shawnee*
Chulundit, Little Bird
BORN: June 8, 1939, Claremore, Okla. Daughter of Joe Blalock (Shawnee-Cherokee) and Lucy Parks (Delaware).
MARRIED: Carroll E. Jones Saumty (Kiowa), 1957. (Although his Indian name was Saumty, the artist's father-in-law was given the name of Jones, and the family has used the name ever since.) Three children: Deborah, 1957; Carroll, Jr., 1959; Nancy Ann, 1965.
EDUCATION: Junior high schools in Miami and Dewey, Okla.; Bacone College High School; graduated correspondence school. Private art instruction under Ruth Steincamp.
EXHIBITIONS: AAID, AAUW, AIE, FAIEAIP, FNAIC, ITIC, PAC, SN; Ponca Indian Fair, Ponca City, Okla.; Okmulgee County Annual Art Exhibit; Okmulgee Public Library; Fort Gibson Traders Fair; Tulsa Arts Festival. *One-man shows*: 1964–65: Two at Shirley Paint Co., Okmulgee.
AWARDS: 1953–65: Eight, including AAUW, AIE; Okmulgee County Annual Art Exhibit; Ponca Indian Fair.
COLLECTIONS: *Public*: Murrow Indian Children's Home, Muskogee, Okla. *Private*: T. Alexander, Ann Anderson, Blue Eagle, Dale, Deel, Dolan, W. Foster, Franklin, Holton, S. Jones, Kelly, Kiley, M. Martínez, Milner, Pickett, H. Robinson, Shelton, Strickland, E. Walters.
ADDRESS: 1200 East 13th, Okmulgee, Okla.

Joshongeva *Hopi*
COLLECTIONS: *Public*: CAM.

Jumping Bear (*see* Grass, John)

Kabotie, Fred *Hopi*
Nakayoma, Day After Day

BORN: February 20, 1900, Shungopovi, Second Mesa, Ariz.

MARRIED: Alice Talayaonema (Hopi), 1931. Two children: Hatti Lou, 1939; Michael (*q.v.*), 1943.

> In 1906, Kabotie's family, seeking to escape the efforts of the Government to force them to abandon their customs, joined other people of old Oraibi and established Hotevilla. Eventually they were forced to return to Oraibi and Shungopovi, where, in 1913, the children were placed in schools for the first time. Later, as a disciplinary measure, Kabotie was sent to Santa Fe Indian School. There he was encouraged by Mr. and Mrs. DeHuff to develop his artistic talents. Since 1920, his work and his name have usually appeared wherever Indian art is mentioned. His work as an educator has prevented him from painting extensively since 1959.

EDUCATION: Shungopovi and Santa Fe, 1915–20; graduated Santa Fe Public School, 1924; attended summer sessions, Alfred.

CAREER: Teacher, painter, author, lecturer, craftsman, and good-will ambassador; art instructor, Oraibi High School, 1937–59; in charge of Indian artists exhibiting at SFWF; manager, Hopi Silvercraft Coöperative Guild, 1941–46; field specialist, IACB, 1959–.

HONORS: Guggenheim Foundation Fellowship, 1945–46; Indian Achievement Medal, awarded by Indian Council Fire of Chicago, 1949; Palmes d'Académiques, awarded by government of France, 1954; Certificate of Appreciation, IACB, 1958. Represented U.S. in India as goodwill envoy, 1960; listed in *Who's Who in American Art* and in *Indians of Today*.

COMMISSIONS: *Murals*: Grand Canyon's Desert View Tower; made reproductions of the Awatovi prehistoric murals in original size on panels in fresco for The Peabody Museum, Harvard University, Cambridge, Mass. (late 1930's). *Paintings*: Recorded Indian dances for the School of American Research and the Archaeological Society of New Mexico, 1920–26; commissioned to paint Hopi life and customs for MAI, 1928–29.

BOOKS ILLUSTRATED: DeHuff (1927; 1929; 1932); Kennard (1941); Kabotie (1949).

WORK PUBLISHED: La Farge (1956, 1960), Dockstader (1962), *International Studio* (March 1922), *Travel* (1931), *Introduction to American Indian Art* (1931), *The American Magazine of Art* (August 1932), *Contemporary Arts of the South and Southwest* (November-December 1932), *Cincinnati Art Museum, Bulletin* (January 1938), *Arizona Highways* (July 1951), *Compton's Pictured Encyclopedia* (1957), *News Notes* (December 1961), *Paintings by American Indians*, CPLH (1962).

EXHIBITIONS: ACC, AIW, DAM, DMFA, EITA, ITIC, MAI, MMA, MNA, MNM, NGA, OU/ET, PAC, PAC/T, TM, WRNGA; Society of Fine Arts, Palm Beach, Fla. *One-man shows*: MNA, 1947; the artist's reproductions of the Awátovi murals toured the U.S.

AWARDS: ASF, ITIC, MNM, PAC. Grand Awards: ITIC, PAC.

COLLECTIONS: *Public*: AF, BIA, CAM, CGA, CGFA, DCC, GM, HM, MAI, MKMcNAI, MMA, MNA, MNA/KHC, OU/MA, PAC, TM. *Private*: Denman, Dietrich, Dockstader, Elkus, Waters.

ADDRESS: Box 44, Oraibi, Ariz., *and* Box 37, Second Mesa, Ariz.

Kabotie, Michael   *Hopi*

BORN: 1946. Son of Fred Kabotie, *q.v.* (Hopi) and Alice Talayaonema (Hopi).

MARRIED: Name unknown; two children.

> "Of his son, Fred Kabotie says: 'Michael learned to paint by watching me work in my studio from the time he was a little boy. He had no formal art training other than my work and guidance. In the beginning of his development, Michael was mainly interested in subjects of a humorous nature but of late he has concerned himself with more serious subjects.'" *Arizona Highways* (August 1966).

EDUCATION: Hopi; scholarship to Arizona, "Southwest Indian Art Project," summer, 1960; Arizona, *ca.* 1964–66.

WORK PUBLISHED: *Arizona Highways* (August 1966).

EXHIBITIONS: HM, ITIC, PAC, SN.

AWARDS: ITIC.

COLLECTIONS: *Public*: HM, MNA. *Private*: Elkus.

ADDRESS: c/o Box 44, Oraibi, Ariz.

Kacha Honawah (*see* White Bear)

Kachina Town (*see* Sánchez, Ramos)

Kagige, Francis   *Ottawa*

BORN: 1931, Manitoulin Island, British Columbia, Canada.

> The artist's first work, executed on cardboard from old shoeboxes and on the backs of looseleaf notebooks, depicted Indian symbols in stylized designs. The artist attended school through the fourth grade and has never had formal art training. He first began to paint in 1962.

CAREER: Road construction worker.

EXHIBITIONS: NYWF (Canadian Indian Exhibit); International Institute of Metropolitan Toronto, Ontario, Canada; Solveig West Arts and Crafts Shop, Manitoulin Island.

ADDRESS: Manitoulin Island, B.C., Canada.

Kahgegagahbowh (Chief)   *Ojibway*

WORK PUBLISHED: Hamilton (1950).

Kahirpeya (*see* Runs Over)

Kahn, Chester   *Navaho*

Tso Yazzie, Big Little

BORN: February 24, 1936, Pine Springs, Ariz.

MARRIED: Annie Tsosie, 1955. Six children: Neshah, 1956; Mariana, 1957; Charlotte, 1958; Norma, 1959; Gloria, 1961; Tony, 1962.

> Mr. Kahn recalls doing drawings on cardboards and on canyon walls with great joy while herding sheep when he was about seven.

EDUCATION: Pine Springs Day School, 1943–47; Shiprock, 1947–48; Stewart, 1948–53; scholarship to Arizona, "Southwest Indian Art Project," summers, 1960–61; classes in summer school and night school toward a degree.

CAREER: Painter, fabric designer, and silversmith; Coordinator and teacher-aid, Stewart Indian School; professional sign and billboard painter, 1958–64; designer, Federal Signs and Signals, Corp., 1964–.

COMMISSIONS: *Murals*: Gallup (N.M.) Indian Community Center.

WORK PUBLISHED: Willoya and Brown (1962).

EXHIBITIONS: 1955–64: 17, including AIAE/WSU, ASF, ITIC, MNA, MNM, NTF, PAC; Nevada Artists' Association, Idlewild Park, Reno, Nev.; Coconino County Fair, Flagstaff, Ariz. *One-man shows*: State Library, Carson City, Nev.; Washoe County Library and Tower Theater, Reno, Nev.; Gallup (N.M.) Public Library.

AWARDS: 1956–64: 11 from AIAE/WSU, ASF, ITIC, NTF, PAC; Coconino County Fair, Flagstaff, Ariz.; Nevada Artists Association Exhibit, Reno, Nev.; honorable mention, Fisher Body Craftsmen's Guild, 1957, for a model car design.

COLLECTIONS: *Public*: AU/ASM; Randee Motel, Sedona, Ariz.; Window Rock (Ariz.) Lodge, *Private*: Burdock, Spell, Sward, P. Terry, Thoeny, H. Walters, Wright.

ADDRESS: 301 Woodland Drive, Flagstaff, Ariz.

Kai Sa (*see* Sandy, Percy Tsisete)

Kakarook, Guy *Eskimo*

COLLECTIONS: *Public*: SI (crayon sketches of river steamboats on the Yukon, executed about 1903).

Kallestewa, Wiston *Zuni*

EXHIBITIONS: MNM, 1965.

AWARDS: MNM.

ADDRESS: Box 131, Zuni, N.M.

Kanribeloka (*see* The Crow)

Kapelva, Don *Hopi*

COLLECTIONS: *Private*: Thoeny.

Kasero, Joseph J. *Laguna*

EDUCATION: Bacone College, *ca.* 1960; Santa Fe, *ca.* 1961.

SERVICE: U.S. Army.

EXHIBITIONS: MNM, 1961.

Kaskalla, David *Zuni*

EDUCATION: Zuni, *ca.* 1961.

EXHIBITIONS: MNM, 1961.

Katahke (*see* Palmer, Woodrow Wilson)

Katexac, Bernard T. *Eskimo*

BORN: 1922.

The artist is from an isolated island in the Bering Sea. He branched out from ivory carving to painting in oils and watercolors and has been successful in applying the three-dimensional quality of ivory sculpture to wood.

EDUCATION: University of Alaska, College, *ca.* 1964.

HONORS: First Eskimo to attend University of Alaska on a BIA scholarship for talented native Alaskan artists.

ADDRESS: c/o University of Alaska, Art Department, College, Alaska.

Ka Tside *San Juan*

EXHIBITIONS: AIEC, 1937.

Katsiekodie, Charlie (*see* Washakie, Charles)

Kaw'lahnohndaumah (*see* Odle pah)

Kayarvena, Walter *Hopi*
BORN: Shipaulovi, Second Mesa, Ariz.
COLLECTIONS: *Public*: LMA/BC.

Kaye, Wilmer *Hopi*
COLLECTIONS: *Public*: MAI.

Keahbone, George Campbell *Kiowa*
Asaute
BORN: January 29, 1916, Anadarko, Okla. Son of Mark Keahbone (Kiowa) and Frances Fletcher. M/U: Spencer Asah (*q.v.*).
MARRIED: Tonita Luján, *q.v.* (Taos), 1936. Two children: Robert, 1940; Gordon Keahbone (*q.v.*), 1943.
  While at Bacone, Princess Ataloa, the arts and crafts instructor, encouraged him to develop his artistic talent and to attend Santa Fe Indian School where he could study under Dorothy Dunn. He has lived in the Southwest since going there to attend school.
EDUCATION: St. Patrick's, 1921–27; Chilocco, 1927–28; graduated Bacone College High School, 1934; graduated Santa Fe, 1936; attended Taos, 1947–48.
SERVICE: WWII, U.S. Navy, two and one-half years; South Pacific and Asian Theaters.
WORK PUBLISHED: Jacobson and D'Ucel (1950), LaFarge (1956). *Magazine Tulsa* (May 1948), *Paintings by American Indians*, CPLH (1962).
EXHIBITIONS: AIW, CPLH, ITIC, MNM, NGA, OU/ET, PAC, PAC/T, SFWF; Harwood Foundation, and Blue Door Gallery, Taos, N.M.; Vassar College, Poughkeepsie, N.Y.
AWARDS: AIE, ITIC, MNM, PAC.
COLLECTIONS: *Public*: AMNH, GM, JAM, MAI, MNA/KHC, MNM, MRFM, OU, PAC. *Private*: Denman, Dietrich, Grawe, D. Kramer, La Farge.
ADDRESS: 102 Temblon Drive, Santa Fe, N.M.

Keahbone, Gordon *Kiowa-Taos*
BORN: 1943. Son of George Campbell Keahbone, *q.v.* (Kiowa) and Tonita Luján, *q.v.* (Taos).
EDUCATION: Scholarship to Arizona, "Southwest Indian Art Project," summer, 1960.
ADDRESS: c/o 102 Temblon Drive, Santa Fe, N.M.

Kee (*see* Gorman, Alfred Kee)

Keejana, Oreston *Hopi*
COLLECTIONS: *Public*: OU/SM.

Keep From The Water (*see* Wa Wa Chaw)

Keeti Bahi (*see* Draper, Teddy, Sr.)

Keevama, David *Hopi*
COLLECTIONS: *Private*: Elkus.

Kehdoyah (*see* Battese, Stanley)

Keith, C. Hobart *Sioux*
Blue Horse
EXHIBITIONS: PAC, 1957.
ADDRESS: Pine Ridge, S. Dak.

Keith, Sidney John *Sioux*
Little Chief
BORN: October 15, 1919, near Moreau River, S. Dak.
EDUCATION: Phoenix, Ariz., two years; correspondence art school.
SERVICE: WWII, U.S. Air Force, four years; Asian and Pacific Theaters.
EXHIBITIONS: In Arizona and Wyoming; has not exhibited for many years.
ADDRESS: Box 73, Eagle Butte, S. Dak.

Kelhoyoma, C. T. *Hopi*
COLLECTIONS: *Public*: MAI, MNM.

Keloowise (*see* Kylesdawa, Dennis)

Kemoha (*see* Patterson, Pat)

Keno, Frankie *Paiute-Shoshoni*
BORN: September 13, 1943, Fallon, Nev.
EDUCATION: Stewart, 1950–58, 1960; Woodrow Wilson Junior High School,
Tulsa, Okla., 1959; Las Vegas (Nev.) Public School, 1961; Institute, 1962.
EXHIBITIONS: 1963: PAC, SN, YAIA.
COLLECTIONS: *Private*: McGrath.
ADDRESS: 280 Front Street, Fallon, Nev.

Kerakahi-to (*see* Red Horn Elk)

Kewa (*see* Hunt, Wolf Robe)

Kewanwytewa, Riguel *Zia-Hopi*
EDUCATION: Albuquerque, *ca.* 1962.
EXHIBITIONS: MNM, 1962.

Kewanyouma, Leroy *Hopi*
So Kuva, Morning Star
BORN: October 14, 1922, Shungopovi, Ariz.
EDUCATION: Shungopovi.
SERVICE: WWII, U.S. Navy.
EXHIBITIONS: PAC.
COLLECTIONS: *Public*: MAI, MNA/KHC, MNM. *Private*: D. Maxwell.
ADDRESS: Box 704, Shungopovi, Second Mesa, Ariz.

Kgoo Ya (*see* Gutiérrez, José Leandro)

Khup Khu (*see* Luján, Tonita)

Kicking Bear *Oglala Sioux*
BORN: Date unknown; camped at the Big Bend of the Yellowstone River,
1872. [See Vestal (1932; 1934).]
In 1898, the aging veteran of the Battle of Little Big Horn was asked by Frederic
Remington to paint his version of the fight. Kicking Bear complied, and the
pictographic account is now at the Southwest Museum.
COLLECTIONS: *Public*: MAI, SM.

Kie, Robert A. *Laguna*
BORN: 1948, Winslow, Ariz.
EDUCATION: St. Catherine's, *ca.* 1965.
EXHIBITIONS: 1965: MNM, PAC, SAIEAIP.
COLLECTIONS: *Private*: R. Moore.
ADDRESS: Laguna, N.M.

Kikekah Wahtiankah (*see* Wagoshe, Russell William)

Kills Two *Oglala Sioux*

BORN: 1869. Died 1927 (it is reported that his wife placed a hide painting of a Sioux Winter Count in his coffin).
MARRIED: Eagle Deer.
CAREER: Indian policeman.
WORK PUBLISHED: Alexander (1938) (including the cover).
COLLECTIONS: *Public*: SIECC (a winter count).

Kimball, Yeffe *Osage*
Mikaka Upawixe, Wandering Star
BORN: March 30, 1914, Mountain Park, Okla. Daughter of Other Good-Man (Osage) and Martha Smith.
MARRIED: Harry Slatin, *ca.* 1952.

> In 1946, a New York critic, Henry McBride, said of Miss Kimball: "Georgia O'Keeffe had better watch out. Her rival now appears on the desert horizon" (*The Sun*, New York, 1946). In 1965, Edgar J. Driscoll, Jr., remarked: "She has been involved with the outer reaches of space, fiery comets, and spheres, but in her more recent paintings, using acrylic resin medium and pure pigments, she works in oval shapes with concave and convex surfaces" (*The Boston Globe*, Mass.).

EDUCATION: Richmond (Mo.) Public Elementary School; East; Oklahoma; Art. Private instruction in France and Italy, 1936–39; studied with Fernand Léger intermittently, 1936–41.
CAREER: Painter, illustrator, textile designer, consultant on native arts. Consultant to: Chrysler Art Museum, Provincetown, Mass.; Portland Museum of Art, Portland, Oreg. Selected Indian art section of "America 1953" for the State Department; advisor to Americana Foundation and Young America Films for 13 films, 1951–57; did research and illustrations for *Book of Knowledge* and *World Book of Knowledge*, 1957–58.
HONORS: Represented in *Who's Who in American Art*; life member and former vice-president, now on Board of Control, Art Students League.
BOOKS ILLUSTRATED: Keech (1940), Brindze (1951), Gallenkamp (1954), Leekley (1965), Kimball and Anderson (1965).
WORK PUBLISHED: *Book of Knowledge* (1957), American Indian Section.
Author: Articles on American Indian art, *Art Digest*, 1945–49.
EXHIBITIONS: 1942–65: 101, including AGAA, BMFA, CAM, CIFA, FAIE-AIP, MHDYMM, MJG, MNM, SAIEAIP, SBM, TMA, UG, W, WA, WRNGA. *One-man shows* (first show, RG, 1946; fifty-fifth show, TKG, 1966): CAG, DAI, DAM, DMG, FAG/S, GG, HAU, IDM, JAM, JKA, MHS/W, MNM, PAC, PAM, PAM/C, RAC/M, SBM, TKG, TMA, UNM, UVM, YK/T. *Retrospective*: PAC, 1966.
AWARDS: PAC.
COLLECTIONS: *Public*: BAM, BIA, BMFA, CAM, CAM/M, DAI, EB, IACB, MM, NMAS, PAC, PAM, TWA, WA, WLU. *Private*: Agoos, J. Anderson, Chrysler, Dana, M. Davidson, Fleishmann, Germeshausen, Grossman, B. Kronenberg, W. Rogers, Saltonstall, Slobodkin, Tishman, Weinberg, Wood.
ADDRESS: 11 Bank Street, New York, N.Y.

Kinyeonny Beyeh (*see* Gorman, Carl Nelson)

Kirk, Ernest *Navaho*
COMMISSIONS: *Murals*: ASF Coliseum, 1965 (with four other Navahos).

Kishketon, George *Kickapoo*
Nama Piaska, Splashing Water
BORN: February 1, 1919, McLoud, Okla. Son of George Kishketon (Kickapoo) and Mary Murdock (Kickapoo). GF: Kickapoo chief.
MARRIED: Nemah Tomah, 1952.
EDUCATION: McLoud (Okla.) High School, Bacone College, 1939–41.
CAREER: Farmer, rancher, and artist.
COMMISSIONS: *Murals*: Bacone College.
EXHIBITIONS: PAC; Skirvin Hotel, Oklahoma City, Okla., 1941.
COLLECTIONS: *Public*: GM, PAC.
ADDRESS: Route 3, Walters, Okla.

Kiyaa Nii (*see* Denetsosie, Hoke)

Kiya Ahnii (*see* Denetsosie, Hoke)

Klah Tso (*see* Big Lefthanded)

Knight, L. *Ponca*
COLLECTIONS: *Public*: PAC.

Koba (*see* Wild Horse)

Kocha Honawu *Hopi*
COLLECTIONS: *Public*: DAM.

Kodaseet, Alfred Calisay *Kiowa*
EDUCATION: Bacone College, *ca.* 1938.
EXHIBITIONS: AIW.

Koketha (*see* Murdock, Cecil)

Koo Peen (*see* Atencio, Pat)

Kopeley *Hopi*
COLLECTIONS: *Public*: MNM.

Kucha Honawuh (*see* White Bear)

Kuka, King *Blackfoot*
BORN: 1946, Browning, Mont.
EDUCATION: Institute, 1965–66.
WORK PUBLISHED: YAIA catalog.
EXHIBITIONS: YAIA.

Kummok Quivviokta (*see* Wooden Leg)

Kuofde (*see* Sánchez, Ramos)

Kuperu (*see* Suina, Theodore)

Ku Se Peen (*see* Vigil, Tim)

Kutca Honauu (*see* White Bear)

Kyash Petrach (*see* Byrnes, James Michael)

Kylesdawa, Dennis *Zuni*
Keloowise
COLLECTIONS: *Public*: MNM (student work dated ninth grade, 1930).

Ladd, Edmund J.   *Zuni*
  Fleetfoot; *Helele*; *Lapilakwa*; *Lapilaokya*.
  (Also known as Ladd, Edmond.)
  CAREER: Archaeologist, U.S. National Park Service.
  EDUCATION: Zuni; M.A., New Mexico U.
  EXHIBITIONS: MNM, 1959–60.
  COLLECTIONS: *Public*: BIA, MAI.
  ADDRESS: Box 215, Honaunau, Kona, Hawaii.

Lady In The Sun (*see* Morgan, Judith Phillis)

Lalio, Ernie   *Zuni*
  COLLECTIONS: *Public*: MNM (dated 1951).

Lamar, Elgin W.   *Wichita*
  BORN: June 22, 1918, Anadarko, Okla.
  EDUCATION: Tulsa.
  SERVICE: WWII, U.S. Army, 40 months; South Pacific Theater.
  EXHIBITIONS: PAC.
  ADDRESS: 1116 South Birmingham Avenue, Tulsa, Okla.

Lame Dog   *Teton Sioux*
  Shunga Hushti
  COLLECTIONS: *Public*: OAA/SI.

Lame Man (*see* Cohoe, William)

Lapilakwa (*see* Ladd, Edmund J.)

Lapilaokya (*see* Ladd, Edmund J.)

Larvie, Calvin   *Sioux*
  Umpan Hanska, Tall Elk
  BORN: July 6, 1920, Wood, S. Dak. P/GGF: Joe Larvie, homesteader at
  Hot Springs, S. Dak. with his Sioux wife. M/GF: White Yellow Fox (Brulé
  Sioux), a medicine man who later became a scout for the U.S. Army.
    Woodrow Wilson Crumbo (*q.v.*) has said that Larvie was one of the finest artists
    he had ever had in class. Calvin left school during WWII to take part in the
    invasion of France. He later received the Bronze Star. For the past 18 years, he
    has spent most of his time in government hospitals, during which time he has
    done little painting. In 1963, he submitted his first completed paintings in 21
    years to a show in Bismarck, N. Dak.
  EDUCATION: Rosebud (S. Dak.) High School; graduated Bacone College
  High School, 1940; Wichita, 1965.
  SERVICE: WWII, U.S. Army, six and one-half years; European Theater.
  COMMISSIONS: *Murals*: SFWF.
  WORK PUBLISHED: Jacobson and D'Ucel (1950). *National Geographic Maga-*
  zine (March 1955).
  EXHIBITIONS: 1939–65: BNIAS, FAIEAIP, FNAIC, NGA, OU/ET, PAC,
  PAC/T. *One-man shows*: PAC; Rosebud (S. Dak.) Arts and Crafts Museum.
  AWARDS: Statement of Recognition from the jury, BNIAS; FNAIC.
  COLLECTIONS: *Public*: DAM, GM, IACB, OU/MA, PAC, SIECC. *Private*:
  J. Snodgrass, Solberg, Tarnasky, D. Young.

Laughing Boy (*see* Blue Eagle, Acee)

Laughing Bull (*see* Flores, William Vann)

Lawasewa, V. C.   *Zuni*
The artist was one of the founders of the contemporary Zuni school of art (*ca.* 1922) and apparently has done little painting since that time. He is known for his formal drawings of altars executed in the late 1920's.
COLLECTIONS: *Public*: MNA/KHC, MNM. *Private*: Denman.

Lays Near Hair (*see* Rowell, Charles Emery)

Leader (*see* Burton, Jimalee)

Lean Wolf   *Hidatsa*
BORN: Date unknown. At one time the artist was living in the area of Fort Buford and Fort Berthold, Dakota Territory.
WORK PUBLISHED: BAE, *4th* and *10th AR*.
COLLECTIONS: *Public*: OAA/SI.

Leandro, José (*see* Gutiérrez, José Leandro)

Le Coeur, Leon   *Huron*
BORN: 1924, Hazel Park, Mich. Son of Arthur George Le Coeur and Goldie (Little Cloud) Brandimore. M/GGF: Chief Fleeting Cloud of the Alpena and Saginaw territory. P/GM: Le Coeur, daughter of Silent Cloud, Huron chief. His French ancestors—the Beauchamps, La Fonds, and Brandimores (as well as the Le Coeurs)—were among the first settlers of Fort Detroit.
MARRIED: Niki Doktor, October 17, 1963.
An accident orphaning the artist at the age of seven also caused his loss of speech. Until he reached manhood, he attended numerous orphanages. As a young child, no medium adaptable to artistic creations escaped his imaginative mind. When he was taught to speak again through musical therapy, poetry and music were added to his skills. Although Le Coeur creates through many media, painting seems to be the one art which attracts him most.
SERVICE: WWII, U.S. Navy, two years.
CAREER: Painter, sculptor, playwright, poet and composer; accounting engineer, General Telephone and Electronics Corp.
HONORS: Named Artist of the Year by the American Education Assoc.; Special Award from Liberty Amendment of Greater New York; original board member; Midwest Outdoor Art Exhibition. *Outstanding reviews*: "...not since Picasso has a more definitive style and school of art been seen..." (*Chicago Tribune*); "...LeCoeur showed a unique talent and definite style that personalized his talents to the fullest. It is wonderful to find an artist who THINKS and not just paints" (*Chicago Daily News*).
EXHIBITIONS: Annual Rush Street Art Fair, Chicago, Ill.; Lynn Kottler Galerie, Village Art Show, N.Y. *One-man shows*: Paula Insel Galerie, N.Y.
ADDRESS: 128 East 24th St., New York, N.Y.

Lee, Charlie   *Navaho*
Hushka Yelhayah, Warrior Who Came Out
BORN: April 14, 1926, near the Four Corners area in Ariz.
MARRIED: Coralie Ann Christenson. Three children: Rebecca, Eric, Evan.
As a child on the reservation, herding sheep and taking care of his grandfather's horses occupied the artist's extra hours. The horses became the subjects for his

outstanding paintings. After graduation from high school, he enrolled at Santa Fe for special instruction in art, voice, and piano. While a soloist for a large Santa Fe choir, he developed an interest in the ministry, and is now active as a Christian minister on the Navaho reservation.

EDUCATION: Indian schools; graduated Santa Fe, 1946; graduated Central Bible Institute, Springfield, Mo.

CAREER: Previously a painter and silversmith, he is now a Christian minister on the Navaho reservation.

BOOKS ILLUSTRATED: *Pathway to the Sky.*

EXHIBITIONS: 1947–63: MNM, MNM/T, PAC, PAC/T.

AWARDS: 1947–52: Five in N.M. and Okla.

COLLECTIONS: *Public*: AF, GM, MAI, MNM, MRFM, PAC, SI, UPA. *Private*: Dockstader, Elkus, A. Forbes, E. Hill, Lockett, Thoeny, Truex.

ADDRESS: Box 162, Shiprock, N.M.

Lee, Edward (*see* Natay, Ed)

Lee, Frank   ?

EXHIBITIONS: SN.

AWARDS: SN, 1964.

Lee, J. S.   *Navaho*

EXHIBITIONS: 1961: PAC, MNM.

COLLECTIONS: *Private*: Long.

ADDRESS: Window Rock, Ariz., and 4225 Seeley, Downers Grove, Ill.

Lee, Jerry   *Navaho*

BORN: 1944, Pine Springs, Ariz.

EXHIBITIONS: AIAE/WSU, FAIEAIP, SN.

AWARDS: SN, 1964.

COLLECTIONS: *Private*: Downey, R. Moore, Mount, Thoeny, R. Walker.

Lee, Nancy Isabel   *Navaho-Santo Domingo*

BORN: Date unknown. Daughter of Edward H. Lee and Juanita C. Lee. Her mother retired after 32 years at Santa Fe Indian School and has recently adapted Indian designs to contemporary dress fashions. She is the sister of Edward H. Lee, Jr.

EDUCATION: Public schools in Santa Fe, N.M.; Arizona S. C./F.; currently an undergraduate at New Mexico U.

HONORS: Past-president of Future Teachers of America Club; member of Kiva Club, University of New Mexico; Indian Youth Council secretary, 1961; Santo Domingo Educational Club Scholarship to University of New Mexico, 1963; United Pueblo Agency, scholarship for two years' study. See "Navajo Girl Majors in Art," *The Navajo Times* (June 11, 1964).

EXHIBITIONS: UNM.

AWARDS: UNM, student show, 1964.

COLLECTIONS: *Public*: IABC.

ADDRESS: 423 Cornell, SE, Albuquerque, N.M.

Lee, Nelson   *Navaho*

EDUCATION: Fort Sill, 1962.

EXHIBITIONS: PAC, 1955.

Lee, Paul *Navaho*
COLLECTIONS: *Public*: PAC.

Leekela, Howard *Zuni*
(Also known as Lekeela.)
COLLECTIONS: *Public*: MAI, MKMcNAI, MNA/KHC. *Private*: Denman.

Left Hand *Cheyenne* (?)
Na Mos, Left Hand
BORN: Date unknown; a Left Hand signed the Fort Wise Treaty in 1861; also, a Left Hand was listed as an Arapaho chief at Darlington, Okla., *ca.* 1870.
> The artist was among the 72 Plains Indians taken as prisoners from Fort Sill, Okla., to Fort Marion, St. Augustine, Fla., in 1875.

COLLECTIONS: *Public*: HI.

Lefthanded, Big (*see* Big Lefthanded)

Leholm, Mary Frances Pichette *Colville-Iroquois*
BORN: May 17, 1933, Inchelium, Wash., on the Colville Reservation. Daughter of Joseph Lawrence Pichette (Cree-Colville) and Marquriete Christine MacDonald (Colville-Iroquois). P/GGGF: Louis Dupuois Pichette, a Frenchman, born in 1797, led a Hudsons Bay Co. exploring party in 1817 to Astoria. M/GU: Pierre Pichette, French artist and poet.
MARRIED: Bernard A. Leholm, 1951.
EDUCATION: Public schools in Chemawa, Oreg.; Inchelium High School, Inchelium, Wash.; Columbia Basin College, Pasco, Wash.; B.F.A., Washington State University, Pullman, Wash., 1966. Private instruction in art under Warren Wilder and Edgar Desautel.
CAREER: Housewife; plans to teach art. Employed two years at Colville Indian Agency; freelance commercial artist.
EXHIBITIONS: BNIAS, FAIEAIP, ITIC, MNM, PAC, SAM; Wenatchee (Wash.) Apple Blossom Festival, Benton-Franklin County Fair, Kennewick, Wash.; Central Washington Art Festival, Yakima, Washington Art Association, Spokane. *One-man shows*: Wenatchee; Walla Walla: Pullman (Chamber of Commerce); Pasco; Kennewick; Colville Indian Agency (Coulee Dam). Also in Lewiston, Idaho.
AWARDS: Several at local fairs.
COLLECTIONS: *Public*: BIA, IACB. *Private*: Hatfield.
ADDRESS: Box 316, Pullman, Wash.

Lekeela (*see* Leekela, Howard)

Leleka (*see* Outie, George)

Leno, Marce *Tesuque*
EDUCATION: Tesuque, *ca.* 1959; Institute, 1963.
EXHIBITIONS: MNM, 1959.

Lente, José Bartolo *Isleta*
> A note regarding this artist's work in the collection of MNM states the painter was known to "hang around things he didn't belong to. We used to know he sold paintings. He would come back with money." This work was executed *ca.* 1930. The artist is deceased.

BOOKS ILLUSTRATED: Goldfrank (1962; 1967).
COLLECTIONS: *Public*: MAI, MNM. A quantity of his unsigned work is known to exist, the use of which is restricted.

Leslie, Ernest   *Navaho*
COMMISSIONS: *Murals*: AFS, Coliseum, 1965 (with four other Navahos).

Levings, Martin   *Hidatsa*
Black Cloud; Holy Buffalo.
BORN: October 14, 1892. Son of Hard Horn (Hidatsa), a chief and medicine man.

> Upon his return from military service, Levings was given his second tribal name at a special ceremony to honor his war record. He started painting about 1923, "to while away the long snowbound days of winter."

SERVICE: WWI.
CAREER: Rancher.
EXHIBITIONS: BNIAS.
ADDRESS: c/o George Fox, Sr., Box 145, Mandaree, N. Dak.

Lewis, Albert Artie   *Navaho*
BORN: January 21, 1926.
EXHIBITIONS: Flagstaff, Ariz., 1947.
AWARDS: Flagstaff, 1947.
ADDRESS: c/o Pinedale Store, Gallup, N.M.

Lewis, Jimmy   *Navaho*
BORN: January 1, 1946, Fort Defiance, Ariz.

> Listed as a promising student by Duane O. Berg, his Gallup art instructor, Jimmy has been painting since 1961. He plans to attend a trade school.

EDUCATION: Gallup Public Schools, nine through twelfth grades, Gallup, N.M.; graduated Gallup High School, 1965.
EXHIBITIONS: NACG (student show).
COLLECTIONS: *Private*: Berg.
ADDRESS: Churchrock Store, Churchrock, N.M.

Lewis, Roger   *Navaho*
BORN: February 1, 1948, Pinedale, N.M. GF: Jeff King, Navaho scout.
EDUCATION: Gallup Public Schools, Gallup, N.M.
EXHIBITIONS: Gallup Public Schools, Gallup, N.M.
COLLECTIONS: *Private*: Berg, Shippy.
ADDRESS: Churchrock, N.M.

Leyestewa, Cyrus   *Hopi*
COLLECTIONS: *Public*: MNM.

Lightning (*see* Nahsohnhoya, Thomas Dolwiftema)

Lightfooted Runner (*see* West, Dick)

Limping (*see* Alberty, Dewey)

Little, Bernadette   *Mescalero Apache*
BORN: 1948, Mescalero, N.M.
EDUCATION: St. Catherine's, 1965.
EXHIBITIONS: PAC, 1965; SAIEAIP.
COLLECTIONS: *Public*: MAI. *Private*: Silberman.
ADDRESS: Mescalero, N.M.

Littlebear, Charles   *Plains*
   MARRIED: Esther Side Bear.
   COLLECTIONS: *Public*: GM.

Little Bear (*see* Sett'an)

Little Bear (*see* Decker, Vernon Edward)

Little Bear (*see* Woodring, Carl)

Little Big Man   *Sioux*
   WORK PUBLISHED: BAE, *10th AR*.
   COLLECTIONS: *Public*: OAA/SI (pictorial census drawings prepared under
   the direction of Red Cloud).

Little Bird (*see* Bird, Larry)

Little Chief (*see* Keith, Sidney John)

Little Chief (*see* Standingbear, George Eugene)

Little Chief, Buddy   *Kiowa*
   COLLECTIONS: *Public*: Carnegie High School, Carnegie, Okla.
   ADDRESS: 1603 Euclid, Lawton, Okla.

Little Chief, Daniel   *Northern Cheyenne*
   Wuxpais
   BORN: Date unknown. Died 1906. Son of Little Chief (Northern Cheyenne),
   a head chief who was sent south with his people to the Cheyenne Agency,
   Darlington, Okla., *ca.* 1878–79; the government eventually permitted him
   to return north to the Pine Ridge Agency area, S. Dak., 1880–81, where he
   became head chief in 1891.
   MARRIED: Wool Woman, who had previously been the wife of Walking
   White Man.
     Daniel executed the pictures now at the Smithsonian Institution during the
     time his father's band was at Pine Ridge.
   CAREER: Warrior and artist; "at Custer Battle...killed and wounded many
   soldiers."
   COLLECTIONS: *Public*: OAA/SI (30 drawings with notes of explanation from
   artist, translated by Albert S. Gatschet, 1891).

Little Chief, William   *Southern Cheyenne*
   MARRIED: Niece of William Cohoe, *q.v.* (wife's sister's daughter).
     The artist was among the 72 Plains Indians taken as prisoners from Fort Sill,
     Okla., to Fort Marion, St. Augustine, Fla., in 1875.
   COLLECTIONS: *Public*: YU/BRBML.

Little Cook   *Yankton Sioux*
   COLLECTIONS: *Public*: MAI (watercolor and pencil, 1883).

Little Daughter (*see* Smart, Clara Mary)

Little Dog (*see* Parsons, Neil)

Little Eagle   *Brulé Sioux*
   Wambalee Ches Challah, Little Eagle
   CAREER: Soldier, *ca.* 1879.
   WORK PUBLISHED: Newell (1912).

Little Finger Nail   *Northern Cheyenne*
BORN: Date unknown. Killed in January, 1879, while traveling north with
Dull Knife and Little Wolf.
WORK PUBLISHED: Sandoz (1953).
COLLECTIONS: *Public*: AMNH.

Little Grey (*see* Tsinajinnie, Andrew Van)

Little Mustache's Daughter (*see* Cassady, Ann Virginia)

Little No Shirt (*see* Beatien Yazz)

Little Robe (*see* Yellow Nose)

Little Sheep   *Navaho*
"The first name that can be suggested in the annals of Southwest Indian painting
is Little Sheep. He is credited with the painting of several horsemen low on the
wall in Canyon del Muerto in the early decades of the nineteenth century..."
Tanner (1957).

Little Robe (*see* Yellow Nose)

Little Sky, Dawn   *Sioux*
BORN: 1932, Fort Yates, N. Dak., on the Standing Rock Reservation.
Daughter of John Gates (Hunkpapa-Yankton) and Ethel Brugier (Santee).
P/GGF: Chief Two Bear (Sioux). M/GGF: Chief War Eagle (Sioux).
MARRIED: Eddie Little Sky (Oglala). Four children: Dawn Renee, 1951;
Bruce Linden, 1953; Todd David, 1955; Stephen War Eagle, 1957.
Mrs. Little Sky is a painter and actress. With her actor husband and four children
she has organized a Sioux dance group, which gives exhibition dances for nume-
rous organizations.
EDUCATION: Graduated Haskell, 1949; attended Kansas, one year.
CAREER: Artist, Walt Disney Productions, Burbank, Calif.; Indian enter-
tainer, Disneyland, Inc.; various movie companies as an Indian actress.
EXHIBITIONS: 1955–63: ITIC, PAC.
ADDRESS: Box 393, Palmdale, Calif.

The Little Swan (*see* The Swan)

Lizer, Vera   *Navaho*
BORN: 1942.
EDUCATION: Scholarship to Arizona, "Southwest Indian Art Project," 1960.

Loba Heit (*see* Taulbee, Dan)

Locke, James   *Sioux*
COLLECTIONS: *Public*: MNM (written on the back of the painting is "10th
grade-1946").

Loco, Moses   *Apache*
BORN: 1913, Apache, Okla.
In 1936, the Oklahoma WPA Art Project noted that "Loco has unusual talent,
but does not keep to primitive or original work. He would do more work but his
eyes are weak...."
EXHIBITIONS: Local county fairs.
AWARDS: County fairs.

Lohmahaftewa, Linda   *Hopi*
  BORN: 1948, Second Mesa, Ariz.
  EDUCATION: Institute, 1965–66.
  EXHIBITIONS: 1965: MNM, SAIEAIP, YAIA.
  AWARDS: MNM, 1965.

Loloma, Charles   *Hopi*
  BORN: January 7, 1921, Hotevilla, Ariz. Son of Rex and Rachel Loloma.
  MARRIED: Otellie (Sequafenema), *q.v.*, 1942.
    Initially known as a painter, the artist has received greater recognition since
    ca. 1959 as a potter, silversmith, and designer.
  EDUCATION: Hotevilla; Oraibi High School; graduated Phoenix, 1940;
  mural instruction under Olaf Nordmark, Fort Sill; ceramics instruction,
  Alfred University.
  SERVICE: WWII, U.S. Army, four and one-half years; U.S. and Aleutian
  Islands tours.
  CAREER: Operator of Arts and Crafts Shop, Shungopovi, Ariz., *ca.* 1955;
  operator of Arts and Crafts Shop, Scottsdale, Ariz., 1956–60; instructor,
  special classes, University of Arizona and Arizona State University, Tempe;
  head of Plastic Arts Dept., Institute of American Indian Arts, 1962–65.
  HONORS: John A. Whitney Fellowship, 1955, for research on native raw
  materials used in pottery.
  COMMISSIONS: *Murals*: At 16, assisted with the execution of murals SFWF
  (with Joe Evan Duran and Ignacio Moquino, *qq.v.*); Radio Station KOY,
  Phoenix, Ariz.; Oraibi High School; Kiami Lodge, Scottsdale, Ariz.;
  Phoenix Indian School.
  BOOKS ILLUSTRATED: Kennard (1948).
  EXHIBITIONS: ASF, MMA, NMSF; national exhibitions sponsored by
  American Craftsmen Council.
  AWARDS: State and national competitions.
  COLLECTIONS: *Public*: DAM, IACB. *Private*: Denman.
  ADDRESS: Box 113, Hotevilla, Ariz.

Loloma, Otellie   *Hopi*
  Sequafenema
  BORN: Second Mesa, Ariz., *ca.* 1922.
  MARRIED: Charles Loloma (Hopi), *q.v.*, 1942.
    Best known for her work in ceramic sculpture, the artist has recently also turned
    to painting with great success.
  EDUCATION: Oraibi High School; special classes in ceramics, Alfred.
  CAREER: Co-operator of Arts and Crafts Shop, Shungopovi, Ariz., *ca.* 1955;
  co-operator of Arts and Crafts Shop, Scottsdale, Ariz., 1956–60; head of
  Ceramics Department, Institute of American Indian Arts, 1962–.
  COLLECTIONS: *Public*: IACB, MAI, PAC.
  ADDRESS: Institute of American Indian Arts.

Loma, Helena (*see* Lomayesva, Helena)

Lomadamocvia (*see* Polelonema, Otis)

Lomadesva   *Hopi*
COLLECTIONS: *Public*: AF (a symbolic painting signed Lomadesva; correctly
the name should be spelled Lomayesva).

Lomakema, Marshall   *Hopi*
Lomakema, Rainbow Around The Sun
BORN: 1935, Shungopovi, Ariz. Son of Charles and Jane Lomakema (Hopi).
MARRIED: Gertina McLean (Hopi), February 1957.
EDUCATION: Shungopovi; graduated Oraibi High School.
CAREER: Employed at Sombrero Theater, Phoenix, Ariz.
COMMISSIONS: *Painting Series*: 62 paintings for Hopi Project (Byron Harvey
III, Collection), 1964–65.
COLLECTIONS: *Public*: MAI. *Private*: Harvey.
ADDRESS: 745 East Highland, Phoenix, Ariz. *and* Box 732, Shungopovi, Ariz.

Lomay, Louis (*see* Lomayesva, Louis)

Lomayaktewa, Narron   *Hopi*
BORN: 1946, Shungopovi, Ariz. GF: Mishongnovi, village chief of Shungo-
povi.
MARRIED: Trinidad (Santo Domingo).
EDUCATION: Hopi; graduated Albuquerque, 1964.
EXHIBITIONS: Hopi Craftsmen Exhibition, Phoenix, Ariz., 1959.
COLLECTIONS: *Public*: LMA/BC, MAI, MNM (while in sixth grade).
ADDRESS: Shungopovi, Ariz.

Lomayaktewa, V.   *Hopi*
(Also known as Holmes, Art).
BORN: Shungopovi, Ariz.
COLLECTIONS: *Public*: MAI.

Lomayesva, Helena   *Hopi*
(Also known as Loma, Helena.)
BORN: Shungopovi, Second Mesa, Ariz.
EDUCATION: Santa Fe, *ca.* 1937.
EXHIBITIONS: AIEC, 1937.
COLLECTIONS: *Public*: MAI.

Lomayesva, Louis   *Hopi*
(Also known as Lomay, Louis; Coma Pesva; Pesva, Coma.)
BORN: 1920's. Lived in Old Oraibi, Ariz.
   The artist is known for his fine paintings of Kachinas. He has also been both
   silversmith and house painter. He has often signed his paintings "Louis Lomay,"
   as well as an elaborate rendering that appears to be "Coma Pesva."
EXHIBITIONS: MNM, PAC, PAC/T.
COLLECTIONS: *Public*: BM/B, CU/LMA, MAI, MKMcNAI, MNA/KHC, MNM,
OU/MA, PAC, SM. *Private*: Denman, Pritzlaff.
ADDRESS: 709 Kathryn Street, Santa Fe, N.M.

Lomayesva, William   *Hopi-Mission*
BORN: Ariz.
EDUCATION: Institute.
EXHIBITIONS: FAIEAIP.

Lomayn Do   *Taos*
  COLLECTIONS: *Public*: AF.

Lone Bear   *Oglala Sioux*
  BORN: Date unknown. He may have lived in the area of Fort Phil Kearny
  in the mid-1800's and was possibly a Miniconjou. *See* Vestal (1932; 1934).
  COLLECTIONS: *Public*: MAI (ledger drawings).

Lone Bull (*see* Schildt, Gary Joseph)

Lone Dog   *Yanktonai Sioux*
  Shunka Ishnala, Lone Dog; *Chinosa*, A Lone Wanderer.
  BORN: Date unknown. There were several men named Lone Dog during the
  1800's. Chief White Bull listed a Lone Dog as one who fell during the Custer
  battle at Little Big Horn; however, the artist was in the area of Fort Peck,
  Mont., in 1876. He was the son of Red War Bonnet (Tawapasha) (Sisseton),
  originally from Minnesota. Lone Dog and his father, with a group of immi-
  grant Miniconjou, moved into the camp of the Brulé in the White River
  area in southern South Dakota, *ca.* 1810.
  MARRIED: Name unknown. Two children: Swift Bear, second chief in rank
  in the Brulé tribe after 1865; and a daughter who married James Bordeaux,
  a Sioux trader.
  HONORS: Chief of the Red Lodge group, 1840–55.
  WORK PUBLISHED: Jacobson and D'Ucel (1950). BAE, *4th* and *10th AR*.
  The artist's granddaughter, Mrs. Susan B. Bettelyoun, filed an informative
  manuscript on the Red Lodge (Tishayaote) group at the Nebraska Historical
  Society.
  COLLECTIONS: *Public*: MAI (winter count). It is not thought that Lone Dog
  was old enough in 1800 to paint the winter count. Either he received the
  earlier records from a predecessor, or, when older, he gathered the tribal
  traditions from the elders and worked back (*see* Cloud Shield).

Lone Horse   *Oglala Sioux* (?)
  Sunka Wonka Wanjila
  BORN: Date unknown. From Pine Ridge Agency, S. Dak. (*see* Black Heart).
  COLLECTIONS: *Public*: MAI.

A Lone Wanderer (*see* Lone Dog)

Lone Wolf   *Kiowa*
  BORN: Date unknown. Died 1879.
    In 1868, Lone Wolf and Satanta (*q.v.*) painted a robe which told of their battles
    with the Utes and Navahos (*see* Keim 1870, p. 223).
  CAREER: Chief, warrior, artist; signed Little Arkansas Treaty, 1865; took
  part in Battle of Adobe Walls, 1874; surrendered February 26, 1875, and
  was one of 72 Plains Indians taken as prisoners from Fort Sill, Okla., to
  Fort Marion, St. Augustine, Fla., in 1875.

Lone Wolf (*see* Schultz, Hart Merriam)

Lonesome Polecat (*see* Patterson, Pat)

Long, Charles Vee *Navaho*
EDUCATION: Institute, 1962–63; Arizona.
HONORS: Full scholarship to Arizona (art major).
COMMISSIONS: *Mural*: ASF (with four other Navahos).
ADDRESS: Art Dept., University of Arizona, Tucson, Ariz.

Long Cat (Chief) *Oglala Sioux*
BORN: Date unknown. At various times he was on White River, on Chatren Creek, at Spotted Tail Agency (Camp Sheridan), and at Pine Ridge Agency, S. Dak.
HONORS: Dance chief, soldier chief, drum chief; presided at council meetings.
COLLECTIONS: *Public*: MAI.

Looking Elk (*see* Martínez, Albert)

Looks In The Clouds (*see* Standing, William)

Loon (*see* Palmer, Woodrow Wilson)

Loretto, José Richard *Jémez*
EDUCATION: Santa Fe, *ca.* 1960.
EXHIBITIONS: PAC, 1961.

Loretto, Leonard *Jémez*
BORN: 1948.
EDUCATION: Jémez, *ca.* 1960.
EXHIBITIONS: AAIE, MNM.

Louis, James M. ?
COLLECTIONS: *Public*: CGA.

Louis, Julian J. *Pueblo*
COLLECTIONS: *Public*: MNM.

Lovato, Ambrosio *Santo Domingo*
BORN: 1934.
COLLECTIONS: *Public*: MNM.

Lover Of Home (*see* Orr, Howell Sonny)

Low Black Bird (*see* Amiotte, Arthur Douglas)

Loweka, Bill *Zuni*
COLLECTIONS: *Public*: MNM.

Lucero, Alondo *Jémez*
EDUCATION: Santa Fe, *ca.* 1955.
EXHIBITIONS: ITIC, MNM.
AWARDS: MNM, 1958.
COLLECTIONS: *Public*: MNM. *Private*: Thoeny.

Lucero, Guadalupe *Jémez*
EDUCATION: Santa Fe, *ca.* 1958.
EXHIBITIONS: MNM, 1958.

Lucero, Lupita *Jémez*
BORN: 1949.
EDUCATION: Jémez, *ca.* 1960–63; Institute, 1965–66.
EXHIBITIONS: 1957–64: ITIC, MNM, PAC, SN.
AWARDS: 1960–64. Six, from ITIC, MNM, SN.

Lucero, Mary Rose   *Jémez*
  EDUCATION: Jémez, *ca.* 1963.
  EXHIBITIONS: 1963–64: MNM, SN; Washington, D.C.

Lucero, Nora Alice   *Jémez*
  COLLECTIONS: *Public*: MAI.

Lucero, Victor   *Jémez*
  EDUCATION: Jémez, *ca.* 1962.
  EXHIBITIONS: MNM, 1962.

Luci   *Jémez*
  COLLECTIONS: *Public*: MAI. *Private*: Denman.

Luján, Albert   *Taos*
  (Also known as Luján, Alfred).
  CAREER: Crafts instructor and assistant boys' advisor, Santa Fe Indian
  School; employed at radio station KKIT, Taos, N.M., 1962–.
  EXHIBITIONS: USDS.
  COLLECTIONS: *Public*: MAI.
  ADDRESS: Taos, N.M.

Luján, Alfred (*see* Luján, Albert)

Luján, Alfred   *Taos*
  BORN: July 10, 1922.
  MARRIED: Nettie (Taos). Four children.
    The artist has painted infrequently since a tragic accident in 1950 killed his
    small son.
  EDUCATION: Santa Fe; Taos.
  CAREER: United Pueblo Agency, Albuquerque, N.M.
  COMMISSIONS: *Tourist brochure*: *Things to See and Do*, Kiwanis International
  of Taos, N.M.
  EXHIBITIONS: Taos Art Association; Phoenix, Ariz.; Santa Fe, N.M.
  COLLECTIONS: *Public*: BIA. *Private*: Wyman.

Luján, Gilbert   *Taos*
  EDUCATION: Albuquerque, *ca.* 1960.
  EXHIBITIONS: MNM, 1960–61.
  AWARDS: MNM.
  ADDRESS: c/o Box 1095, Taos, N.M.

Luján, James   *Taos*
  BORN: 1941. Brother of Jerry Luján (*q.v.*).
  EDUCATION: Bacone College; Santa Fe; Arizona, "Southwest Indian Art
  Project," summer, 1960; graduated Arizona S. U./T.
  EXHIBITIONS: 1959–62: MNM, PAC.
  COLLECTIONS: *Public*: IACB. *Private*: Frazier.
  ADDRESS: c/o Box 1095, Taos, N.M., *and* Box 781, Mesa, Ariz.

Luján, Jerry   *Taos*
  BORN: 1945. Brother of James Luján (*q.v.*).
  EDUCATION: Central High Catholic School, Taos, N.M.
  COLLECTIONS: *Public*: MNM (dated 1949).
  ADDRESS: c/o Box 1095, Taos, N.M.

Luján, Lorenzo A.   *Taos*
  Bilokila, Floating Plumes
  BORN: 1922, Taos, N.M. Died, 1962. His daughter is Emille Mirabel.
  EDUCATION: Santa Fe; Taos.
  EXHIBITIONS: Harwood Foundation, Taos, N.M.
  ADDRESS: Ramah, N.M.

Luján, Manuel   *Taos*
  COLLECTIONS: *Public*: WRNGA.

Luján, Margaret   *Taos*
  BORN: *ca.* 1928.
  COLLECTIONS: *Public*: MAI.

Luján, Merina (*see* Pop Chalee)

Luján, Mike   *Taos*
  EXHIBITIONS: FWG, 1943.

Luján, Tonita   *Taos*
  Khup Khu
  MARRIED: George Campbell Keahbone, *q.v.* (Kiowa), 1936. Two sons: Robert,
  1940; Gordon Keahbone (*q.v.,*) 1943.
    The artist has painted very little, if at all, since the late 1930's.
  EDUCATION: Santa Fe, under Dorothy Dunn.
  COMMISSIONS: *Murals*: Assisted with a frieze at Santa Fe Indian School.
  BOOKS ILLUSTRATED: Clark (1940b).
  EXHIBITIONS: AIEC, 1937; AIW, NGA.
  COLLECTIONS:*Private*: Dietrich.
  ADDRESS: 102 Temblon Drive, Santa Fe, N.M.

Luján, Vicente   *Taos*
  COLLECTIONS: *Public*: MAI.

Luján, Wahleah   *Taos*
  EDUCATION: Saint Catherine's, *ca.* 1965.
  EXHIBITIONS: PAC, 1965.
  HONORS: Elected Miss Indian America, 1966.
  ADDRESS: Taos, N.M.

Lumhee Holattee (*see* Blue Eagle, Acee)

Lyons, Oren R.   *Iroquois*
  BORN: 1930, Gowanda, N.Y.
  EXHIBITIONS: FAIEAIP, ITIC, PAC.
  AWARDS: ITIC, 1964.
  ADDRESS: Roselle, N.J.

MacMillan, James H.   *Zia*
  EXHIBITIONS: AIEC, 1937.

Maggino, Waka Ignacio   *Zia*
  COLLECTIONS: *Public*: OU/MA.
  This is probably the same person as Ignacio Moquino, *q.v.*

Mahse Nompah (*see* Red Corn, Raymond Wesley)

Mahthela (*see* Spybuck, Ernest)

Mahtohn Ahzshe (*see* Standingbear, George Eugene)

Mah To Toh Pa (*see* Four Bears)

Making Medicine *Cheyenne*
BORN: *ca.* 1843.
> The artist was among the 72 Plains Indians taken as prisoners from Fort Sill, Okla., to Fort Marion, St. Augustine, Fla., in 1875.

WORK PUBLISHED: Grinnell (1915), De Camp (1960), LaFarge (1960), Dines and Price (1961).
COLLECTIONS: *Public*: MHS/B, OAA/SI, SAHSL, YU/BRBML.

Malegotkuk, Florence (*see* Chauncey, Florence Nupok)

Mammedaty *Kiowa*
> With Lone Wolf and Tohausen (*qq.v.*) (Kiowas) and other warriors, the artist fought in a skirmish known as Lost Valley Fight, in Texas, July 16, 1874. Immediately following this encounter, Lone Wolf "made a gift of his name to Mammedaty" (the preferred family spelling). He succeeded his uncle, Chief Lone Wolf, as chief in 1879. A calendar executed by Mammedaty is in the possession of his descendant, Justin Poolow (*see* Momaday, Al).

Man Alone (*see* Cochran, George McKee)

Man Who Carries The Sword *Oglala Sioux*
COLLECTIONS: *Public*: MAI.

Man With Light Complexion (*see* Mitchell, George Charlie)

Mana *Apache*
Hayokah
COLLECTIONS: *Private*: Thoeny.

Manning, Ferdinand *Ute*
COLLECTIONS: *Private*: Thoeny.

Manuelito, Monte *Navaho*
EXHIBITIONS: MNM, 1963.
AWARDS: MNM, 1963.

Mapera Mohe (*see* Cohoe, William)

Ma Pe Wi (*see* Herrera, Velino Shije)

Marmon, Miriam A. *Laguna*
MARRIED: Wallace Tyner.
EDUCATION: New Mexico U., *ca.* 1936.
COLLECTIONS: *Public*: MNM.

Martin, James, Jr. *Osage*
Night Walker
BORN: September 16, 1927, Pawhuska, Okla. Son of Martin Take Away Gun (Osage) and (?) Logan (Osage). Brother of Mike Martin (*q.v.*). M/GF: John Logan (Osage).
> The artist became interested in art during his elementary school days. An eye injury during military service caused permanent damage to his sight. He returned from the service to Chilocco Indian School where he changed his major from art to business.

EDUCATION: Graduated Chilocco; attended Haskell; Northeastern A.M.
SERVICE: WWII, three years; Pacific Theater.
EXHIBITIONS: PAC; Pawhuska, Okla.

Martin, Mike   *Caddo*
Silvermoon
BORN: Anadarko, Okla. His mother died when he was about six, and he
was reared by his grandmother, Choah.

> Silvermoon began his art career early. As a young boy, he frequently had to leave
> his drawing to hoe corn or herd his grandmother's horses and cattle. In 1936,
> he was responsible for starting a fad for hand-painted hosiery in New York, at
> which time *Collier's Magazine* ran his photograph in full costume on its cover.

EDUCATION: Carlisle.
SERVICE: WWI.
CAREER: Worked with William deForest Brush, New York artist.
EXHIBITIONS: GM, OHSM.
COLLECTIONS: *Public*: GM, OHSM.
ADDRESS: 110½ North West First, Anadarko, Okla.

Martin, Raymond   *Navaho*
COMMISSIONS: *Murals*: ASF Coliseum, 1965 (with four other Navahos).

Martin, Ringlin   *Apache*
EXHIBITIONS: FWG, 1943.

Martine, Bob   *Navaho*
(Also known as Martínez, Bob.)
EDUCATION: Santa Fe, *ca.* 1959.
EXHIBITIONS: 1959–64: MNM, SN.
AWARDS: 1960–64: Two, from MNM, SN.

Martínez, Albert   *Taos*
Looking Elk
BORN: Date unknown. Died *ca.* 1941. His wife died *ca.* 1950. His son is José
R. Martínez (*q.v.*).

> The artist was known to have executed a number of paintings, each of which
> illustrated a creation myth and carried an explanation written by him. He was a
> close friend of the famed Taos artist, Oscar Berninghaus. He often worked in oils.

EDUCATION: Santa Fe (no art training).
HONORS: Served as Governor of Taos Pueblo.
COLLECTIONS: *Public*: MAI, MNM.

Martínez, Anecito (?)   ?
COLLECTIONS: *Public*: MRFM.

Martínez, Bob (*see* Martine, Bob)

Martínez, Crescencio   *San Ildefonso*
Te E, Home Of The Elk
BORN: Date unknown. Died June 20, 1918. Uncle of Awa Tsireh (*q.v.*).
MARRIED: Anna. Their son is José Miguel Martínez (*q.v.*).

> Crescencio first began to draw before 1910, when Dr. Edgar L. Hewett found
> him using the ends of cardboard boxes and gave him paper and watercolors. The
> artist was known to have painted pottery before this time. He is considered to be
> one of a small group at the pueblo who began the modern watercolor movement,
> for he painted extensively after he received Dr. Hewett's gift. His career lasted
> only two years, but during this period he almost completed a series of paintings
> for the Museum of New Mexico and The School of American Research depicting
> all the costumed dances of San Ildefonso's summer and winter ceremonies.

CAREER: Janitor, San Ildefonso Day School, before 1910 (where he first obtained crayons); worked on the Pajarito Plateau excavations, *ca.* 1915. During WWI, he and his wife moved to Santa Fe, N.M., were employed by the Rocky Mountain Camp Co. (owners of the "old" La Fonda Hotel), and kept busy grooming and feeding horses, painting in their spare time.
COMMISSIONS: *Painting Series*: MNM and The School of American Research, Santa Fe, N.M., 1917.
WORK PUBLISHED: *Travel* (1931).
EXHIBITIONS: AMNH (1920 show arranged by Mary Austin); EITA; Society of Independent Artists, New York, N.Y., *ca.* 1918–19.
COLLECTIONS: *Public*: MNM, MRFM. *Private*: A. Henderson; Hewett.

Martínez, Daisy *San Ildefonso*
EDUCATION: St. Catherine's, *ca.* 1964–65.
EXHIBITIONS: PAC.
AWARDS: PAC, student award, 1965.
COLLECTIONS: *Private*: R. Moore.
ADDRESS: San Ildefonso Pueblo, N.M.

Martínez, Dave ?
BORN: N.M.
EDUCATION: Institute.
EXHIBITIONS: FAIEAIP.

Martínez, Jerry *Taos*
BORN: Date unknown. Son of Avelina Luján Martínez.
EDUCATION: Albuquerque, *ca.* 1960.
EXHIBITIONS: MNM, 1960–61.
COLLECTIONS: *Public*: MNM.
ADDRESS: Taos Pueblo, N.M.

Martínez, Joe (*see* Martínez, Jose R.)

Martínez, John D. *San Ildefonso*
(Also known as Martínez, Juan.)
BORN: November 12, *ca.* 1917–20, Santa Fe, N.M.; deceased. Son of Julián Martínez, *q.v.* (San Ildefonso) and María Montoya (San Ildefonso). Brother of Popovi Da, *q.v.*
MARRIED: Clara. Two children: Jeanette, Dennis.
EDUCATION: Bacone College, *ca.* 1945; Santa Fe, *ca.* 1937; Santa Fe High School, *ca.* 1940; Georgia Military Academy, *ca.* 1942; Stanford, *ca.* 1946–48.
SERVICE: WWII, U.S. Army, 1942–44.
CAREER: Road engineer, engineering draftsman.
EXHIBITIONS: AIEC, UNM. *One-man shows*: Atlanta (Ga.) Museum of Fine Arts, Duke University, Durham, N.C.; Stanford University.
COLLECTIONS: *Public*: GM, SU. *Private*: A. Forbes, Kamen-Kaye, Schonwald, Thoeny, Wyman.

Martínez, José Miguel *San Ildefonso*
Wa Chin Cadi
BORN: Date unknown. Son of Crescencio Martínez, *q.v.* (San Ildefonso). Cousin of Julián Martínez, *q.v.* (San Ildefonso).

CAREER: Painter; in 1950 he was painting infrequently.
WORK PUBLISHED: Alexander (1932). *American Magazine of Art* (August 1933).
COLLECTIONS: *Public*: DAM.
ADDRESS: San Ildefonso Pueblo, N.M.

Martínez, José R.   *Taos*
(Also known as Martínez, Joe.)
Paaokela
BORN: Date unknown. Son of Albert Martínez (*q.v.*).
COLLECTIONS: *Public*: MNM. *Private*: A. Forbes.
ADDRESS: Taos, N.M.

Martínez, Juan (*see* Martínez, John D.)

Martínez, Juan José   *Picuris*
COLLECTIONS: *Public*: SM.

Martínez, Julián   *San Ildefonso*
Pocano
BORN: 1897. Died 1943.
MARRIED: María Montoya (San Ildefonso), internationally known potter, 1904. His sons are John D. Martínez and Popovi Da (*qq.v.*).
> Julián decorated his wife's famous pottery. Although he had been painting since before 1920 and had ventured into several periods of "realistic" paintings, his more outstanding works were designs of the type found on María's pottery.

COMMISSIONS: *Murals*: Santa Fe Indian School, among others.
WORK PUBLISHED: Alexander (1932), Jacobson and D'Ucel (1950), Glubok (1964). *American Magazine of Art* (September 1928) (August 1933); *Theatre Arts Monthly* (August 1933).
EXHIBITIONS: ACC, AIEC, EITA, FWG, OU/ET; Corona Mundi International Art Center, New York, 1927; Fair Park Gallery, Dallas, Tex., 1928.
COLLECTIONS: *Public*: AF, AU/ASM, CAM, CGFA, CMA, DAM, DCC, GM, JAM, MAI, MKMcNAI, MNA/KHC, MNM, OU/MA, RM, PU/M, RM. *Private*: Aldridge, Dietrich, Dockstader, A. Forbes, Hogue, Neumann, Patton, Schonwald, Walch.

Martínez, Manuel   *Taos*
Good Rain
BORN: Date unknown. Son of Albert Martínez, *q.v.* (Taos).
CAREER: U.S. Navy.
COLLECTIONS: *Public*: MNM.

Martínez, Miguel   *San Ildefonso*
COLLECTIONS: *Public*: WRNGA.

Martínez, Philip   *San Ildefonso*
COLLECTIONS: *Public*: MAI.

Martínez, R. M. (*see* Martínez, Ralph)

Martínez, Ralph   *Taos*
(Also known as Martínez, R. M.)
BORN: Date unknown. Deceased.
COLLECTIONS: *Public*: MNM.

Martínez, Raymond *San Ildefonso*
BORN: *ca.* 1942.
EDUCATION: Haskell, *ca.* 1963.
COLLECTIONS: *Public*: MNM.

Martínez, Ricardo (*see* Martínez, Richard)

Martínez, Richard *San Ildefonso*
Opa Mu Nu
(Also known as Martínez, Ricardo.)
BORN: 1904.
As one of the original students at Santa Fe Indian School, the artist assisted in the execution of a mural series in the student dining room in 1936. He painted as early as 1920, and, in 1950, he was still painting mythological and ceremonial subjects. He seldom paints now.
COMMISSIONS: *Murals*: Santa Fe Indian School.
WORK PUBLISHED: Alexander (1932). *American Magazine of Art* (September 1928).
EXHIBITIONS: EITA.
COLLECTIONS: *Public*: CAM, CGA, CU/LMA, DAM (82 watercolors), GM, MAI, MNM, MRFM, SM. *Private*: A. Forbes, Howella.
ADDRESS: San Ildefonso Pueblo, N.M.

Martínez, Santana R. *San Ildefonso*
COLLECTIONS: *Public*: MKMcNAI (records say: "wife of the eldest son of María and Julián Martínez (*q.v.*), and one-time decorator of María's pottery").

Martínez, Tony (*see* Da, Popovi)

Mathews, Fadie Mae *Cherokee*
BORN: March 10, 1909, Tenn. Daughter of Tom Blackwell and Alyie. M/ GGGF: Chief Taw (Cherokee). M/GGF: Last name Garrett, killed in Georgia before the Cherokee removal.
MARRIED: Homer H. Mathews, 1939. Three children by previous marriage: Norman Ray Eton, 1928; Mary Helen, 1929; Nelda Elaine, 1931.
EDUCATION: Attended school in Nashville, Tenn.; Ellis and Circle Park Schools, Fort Worth, Tex., 1919–25.
COMMISSIONS: South Wayside Baptist Church, Fort Worth, Tex.
EXHIBITIONS: South Seminary Mall, Crump's Music Store, and Mason's Hobby Shop, of Fort Worth, Tex.; Englewood (Calif.) Art Center, New Orleans Treasure House, Arlington, Tex.
COLLECTIONS: *Public*: Security Life Insurance Co., and Faith Chapel, in Fort Worth, Tex.; New Orleans Treasure House, Arlington, Tex. *Private*: Betts, Michener.
ADDRESS: 2321 McGuire Avenue, Fort Worth, Tex.

Mathews, William P. (*see* Red Corn)

Mato Hunka *Sioux*
COLLECTIONS: *Public*: MPM (pictographic style on paper).

Mato Myaluta (*see* Red Living Bear)

Mato Sapo (*see* Black Bear)

Mato Tope (*see* Four Bears)

Mato Wantakpe (*see* Grass, John)

Mauldin, Carol Jane McCarty   *Choctaw*
> BORN: January 19, 1936, Tulsa, Okla. Daughter of Vernon Clay McCarty
> (Choctaw) and Madelyn Helen Beck. Her sister is Valjean Hessing (*q.v.*)
> MARRIED: Corwin Bobby Mauldin, 1955. Four children: Mark Corwin, 1957;
> Liza Carol, 1960; Jerald Clay, 1961; Steven Carl, 1962.
>> Upon graduation from high school, the artist married and devoted herself to a
>> family and career for about eight years. In 1963, she again began to paint and
>> enter her work in competitions.
> EDUCATION: Elementary schools in Okla. and Calif. Graduated from Tulsa
> Central High School, 1954.
> CAREER: Commercial artist, Floyd Gates Studio, Tulsa, 1953–.
> COMMISSIONS: *Portraits*: Argie Lewis, L. D. Allen, in Tulsa, Okla.
> EXHIBITIONS: 1964–65: FAIEAIP, PAC, SN; Mulvane Art Center, Indepen-
> dence, Kan.; Art Unlimited Exhibitions; Oertle's Outdoor Art Show; Coun-
> cil of American Indians Exhibition, Tulsa, 1965. *One-man shows*: Jones'
> Frame Shop, Tulsa, Okla.
> AWARDS: Five in local exhibits, three in poster contests, and five in school-
> connected exhibitions.
> COLLECTIONS: *Public*: BIA. *Private*: L. D. Allen, Bell, Haworth, Hayes,
> I. Johnson, A. Lewis, Jer. Mauldin, Poser, Stiefel, Woolley.
> ADDRESS: 1549 North Marion, Tulsa, Okla.

Maulson, Gerald   *Chippewa*
> *Bedonni Quid*, Slow Cloud
> BORN: December 7, 1941, Haywood, Wisc.
> EDUCATION: Lac Du Flambeau (Wis.) Public School, 1946–55; graduated
> Lakeland Union High School, Winocqua, Wisc., 1955; Santa Fe, 1960–61.
> CAREER: Roofer, Maulson and Sons. Presently coil winder, Advance Trans-
> former Co., Chicago, Ill.
> EXHIBITIONS: 1962–64: BNIAS, MNM, PAC, USDS.
> AWARDS: MNM, 1962–63.
> COLLECTIONS: *Public*: BIA, IACB. *Private*: Putnam, Thoeny.
> ADDRESS: 3755 North Sheffield, Chicago, Ill.

Maxhebaho (*see* Hollowbreast, Donald)

Mayokok, Robert   *Eskimo*
> EXHIBITIONS: AAIEAE.
> WORK PUBLISHED: AAIEAE catalog.

Mazuha Hokshina (*see* Howe, Oscar)

McBride, Del   *Quinault*
> EXHIBITIONS: PAC, 1961.
> ADDRESS: Box 145, Nisqually, Wash.

McCombs, Solomon   *Creek*
> BORN: May 17, 1913, west of Eufaula, Okla. Son of James McCombs (Creek)
> and Ella McIntosh (Creek). The artist's father was the pastor of Tuskegee

Indian Baptist Church in Oklahoma for more than 30 years. His GGF and GGM traveled the "Trail of Tears" from Georgia to Oklahoma. P/GU: William McCombs (Creek), one of the founders of Bacone College; McCombs Memorial Art Gallery there is named for him. Solomon's mother was a descendant of William McIntosh, Creek chief.

MARRIED: Margarita Sauer, 1961.

> An injury in his youth confined the artist to his bed for considerable time, and it was then that he became interested in art. Mr. McCombs has exhibited in Philbrook Art Center's "Indian Annual" every year since its inception in 1946. He has represented the Indian through exhibits and lectures abroad, as well as in the U.S.

EDUCATION: Attended rural Oklahoma schools; graduated Bacone College High School, 1937; completed one year Bacone College, where he received instruction under "Princess Ataloa" and Acee Blue Eagle (*q.v.*). Attended art classes at Tulsa Downtown College, 1944, studying under Frank von der Lauchen.

CAREER: Douglas Aircraft Co., Tulsa, 1943; U.S. Corps of Engineers, Tulsa, 1944; Clovis (N.M.) Air Force Base, 1947; Bureau of Reclamation, Nebraska, 1948; General Services Administration, Washington, D.C., 1950–56; U.S. Department of State, 1956–. Served as illustrator, architectural draftsman, cartographer, and mockup designer, engaging in audio-visual services in all these positions.

HONORS: Exhibited paintings and explained American Indian contributions to the development of the U.S. and its culture on a tour sponsored by the U.S. Department of State to the Far East and Africa, 1954; member, Society of Federal Artists and Designers, Washington, D.C., and finance auditor and treasurer, 1956–57; a founder and President, American Indian and Eskimo Cultural Foundation, Washington, D.C.; listed in *Indians of Today*. Has presented many illustrated lectures; recipient of Waite Phillips' Special Indian Artist's Trophy Award, PAC, 1965.

COMMISSIONS: *Murals*: U.S. Post Office, Marietta, Okla. Commissioned to execute a painting used in President Kennedy's Inaugural Parade, 1961; commissioned to design the floats representing North American Indians for President Johnson's Inaugural Parade, 1964.

WORK PUBLISHED: Jacobson and D'Ucel (1950), Jacobson (1964). *Sunday Oklahoman, Orbit Magazine* (May 26, 1963); *Smoke Signals*, IACB (Autumn 1965).

EXHIBITIONS: 1940–65: AAIE, AAUW, AIEC, AIE/T, AIW, BC, BNIAS, CGA, DAM, FANAIAE, GM, ITIC, JAM, JGS, MMA, MNM, OU/ET, PAC, PAC/T, SAIEAIP, SI, SN, USDS. *One-man shows*: HM, JAM, PAC, SPIM.

AWARDS: 1948–65: 25, including AAID, ITIC, MNM, PAC, SN.

COLLECTIONS: *Public*: BIA, CCHM, DAM, GM, IACB, JAM, MNM, OU/MA, PAC. *Private*: Arnold, Bouldin, Callaway, Cone, C. Deffer, P. Deffer, Denman, Hedges, Huls, R. Kennedy, Kruss, McKinney, Mertz, Migliaccio, Myle, L. Peterson, Renner, Schonwald, Spielman, Stinson, Stinson, Jr., Wadley, Wallop, Watkins, Wofford.

ADDRESS: 4501 Arlington Boulevard, Apt. 317, Arlington, Va.

McIntosh, Alex C. (*see* Blue Eagle, Acee)

Medicine Crow (Chief)   *Crow*
BORN: Date unknown. Father of Joe Medicine Crow, anthropologist, Crow Reservation.

> The artist was known to have visited Washington, D.C. Upon his return to the reservation, he painted from memory the many animals he had seen in museums there. *See* Jacobson and D'Ucel (1950).

Medicine Mountain (*see* Gonzales, Louis)

Medina, James D.   *Zia*
COLLECTIONS: *Public*: MAI.

Medina, José de la Cruz   *Zia*
(Also known as Medina, José la Cruz.)
EDUCATION: Santa Fe.
EXHIBITIONS: MNM, PAC, SN.
COLLECTIONS: *Public*: MNM. *Private*: Henneke.
ADDRESS: 3313 James Street, Santa Fe, N.M.

Medina, Juan B.   *Zia*
BORN: Date unknown.
EDUCATION: Santa Fe.
EXHIBITIONS: AIW; NGA, 1953; OU/ET.
COLLECTIONS: *Public*: MAI, SM. *Private*: Dietrich, D. Kramer.

Medina, Rafael   *Zia*
Teeyacheena
BORN: September 10, 1929, Zia Pueblo, N.M. Parents active in the culture of the pueblo. P/GM: Trinidad Medina (Zia), the famous potter, toured the U.S. demonstrating Zia pottery-making in 1930–46, under the sponsorship of Wick Miller, a trader in the Southwest.
MARRIED: Sofia Pino, 1954. Eight children.

> As a young man, "barely old enough to hold the weight of a single shotgun," he often hunted. At the same time he studied the appearance of the animals and birds, which he believes has helped him greatly in his art work. While still a young student, he was encouraged and aided by Mary Mitchell.

EDUCATION: Zia, through the fifth grade; Albuquerque; studied under Velino Shije Herrera, José Rey Toledo, and Gerónima Montoya (*qq.v.*); graduated Santa Fe.
COMMISSIONS: His first sale was a commission for 50 Christmas dinner place-cards from Mary Mitchell, while he was still a student at Albuquerque Indian School.
EXHIBITIONS: 1949–66: AIAE/WSU, DAM, ITIC, JGS, MNM, PAC, SN. *One-man shows*: AU.
AWARDS: 1955–66: Six from AIAE/WSU, ITIC, PAC, SN; 1966, PAC Grand Award.
COLLECTIONS: *Public*: AU/ASM, MAI, MNM, PAC. *Private*: E. Adkins, Adlerblum, Holway, Thoeny.
ADDRESS: Zia Pueblo, San Ysidro, N.M.

Meet Me In The Night   *Omaha-Sioux*
  COLLECTIONS: *Public*: MAI (watercolor, 1882).

Melchior, Ray   *Cochití*
  (Also known as Melchior, Reyes.)
  BORN: 1924, Cochití Pueblo.
  EDUCATION: Santa Fe.
  EXHIBITIONS: AIW, MNM; Old Town, Albuquerque, N.M.
  ADDRESS: Cochití Pueblo, Peña Blanca, N.M.

Melchior, Reyes (*see* Melchior, Ray)

Melford, Earl   ?
  EXHIBITIONS: ITIC.
  AWARDS: ITIC, 1964.

Mepaa Kte (*see* Wife Eagle Deer)

Mesquakie (*see* Pushetonequa, Charles)

Mikaka Upawixe (*see* Kimball, Yeffe)

Mike, Judy   *Winnebago*
  BORN: Washington.
  EDUCATION: Institute.
  EXHIBITIONS: FAIEAIP.
  ADDRESS: c/o Institute of American Indian Arts, Santa Fe, N.M.

Miller, Frances   ?
  EXHIBITIONS: ITIC.
  COLLECTIONS: *Private*: Elkus.

Miller, George   *Omaha*
  BORN: Date unknown; he was a member of the *Ictasanda* (Thunder) clan.
  CAREER: Informant and artist for BAE ethnologist James Owen Dorsey.
  WORK PUBLISHED: BAE, *11th AR*.
  COLLECTIONS: *Public*: OAA/SI (original drawings which appear in the above publication).

Minoch, Milo   *Eskimo*
  COLLECTIONS: *Public*: SMNAI.

Mirabel, Eva   *Taos*
  Eah Ha Wa, Green Corn
  BORN: 1920.
  MARRIED: Manuel Gómez.
  Eva, who lives at Taos Pueblo with her children, paints infrequently. Her husband is making the Navy his career.
  EDUCATION: Graduated Santa Fe; attended Taos.
  SERVICE: WWII, WAC.
  CAREER: Artist in residence, Southern Illinois University, Carbondale, Ill.; counselor, girls' camp in Kentucky; active in Girl Scout work at one time.
  COMMISSIONS: *Murals*: Santa Fe Indian School; Veteran Hospital, Library, Albuquerque, N.M.; several in private homes.
  WORK PUBLISHED: Jacobson and D'Ucel (1950). *El Palacio* (August 1950), *G. I. Gertie*, an Army publication.

EXHIBITIONS: AIEC, AIW, GM, MNM, NGA, PAC.
AWARDS: MNM, PAC.
COLLECTIONS: *Public*: GM, MAI, MNM, PAC, UPA. *Private*: Dietrich, A.
Forbes, M. Kramer, Lohman, Schonwald.
ADDRESS: Box 827, Taos, N.M.

Mirabel, Leon   ?
EXHIBITIONS: ITIC.
AWARDS: ITIC, 1964.

Mirabel, Vicente   *Taos*
Chiu Tah, Dancing Boy
BORN: 1918. Deceased *ca*. 1946, WWII, Battle of the Bulge.
MARRIED: Navaho woman. Three sons.
   The artist's career as a painter was so promising when he entered military
   service that he was regarded as the most up-and-coming artist from Taos Pueblo.
EDUCATION: Graduated Santa Fe.
SERVICE: WWII, U.S. Army; European Theater.
CAREER: Assistant painting instructor when he entered the army, Santa Fe
Indian School.
HONORS: While teaching at Santa Fe, won SFWF poster contest, with the
theme "Taos Turtle Dance."
WORK PUBLISHED: Jacobson and D'Ucel (1950). *Arizona Highways* (August
1952).
EXHIBITIONS: AIW, NGA; 1953.
COLLECTIONS: *Public*: CAMSL, MAI, OU. *Private*: H. Adams, Denman,
Dietrich, D. Kramer.

Mis Ta Moo To Va (*see* Blackowl, Archie)

Misty (*see* Ortiz, Joseph)

Mitchell, George Charlie   *Navaho*
Dineh Ligaai, Man With Light Complexion
BORN: March 2, 1926, Lukachukai, Ariz. Son of Charlie Bitsi (Navaho). GF:
Charlie Mitchell, tribal policeman who aided in locating Navaho outlaws
after Fort Sumner; also an interpreter and tribal leader.
MARRIED: Bobby Jo Erwin, 1956. One daughter: Sherry Lane, 1958.
EDUCATION: BIA schools in Ariz.; graduated Chilocco, 1949. After high
school, the artist attended a two-year school for printers, and after eight
years of college courses (taken summers, Saturdays, nights, and by exten-
sion), he graduated from Northeastern, B.A., Ed., 1963.
SERVICE: WWII, U.S. Navy, two years; Pacific Theater.
CAREER: Chilocco Indian School: interpreter for non-English-speaking
students; counselor; elementary teacher, arts and crafts, 1954–58; general
shop, 1957–58. Sequoyah Indian School: arts and crafts instructor, 1963.
Dennehotso Boarding School, Kayenta, Ariz.: instructor, 1963. Tuba City
Public Health Indian Hospital, Tuba City, Ariz.: education specialist, 1964–.
HONORS: National Honor Society; chairman of many school committees
responsible for pageants and class projects.

COMMISSIONS: Illustrated textbooks for BIA; wrote captions and compiled pictures for educational brochure at Chilocco Indian School.
WORK PUBLISHED: Greeting cards, copyrighted by Navaho tribe.
EXHIBITIONS: FAIEAIP, PAC; Indian fairs.
ADDRESS: General Delivery, Tuba City, Ariz.

Mitchell, James *Navaho?*
COLLECTIONS: *Private*: Elkus.

Mitchell, Peter *Navaho*
EDUCATION: Riverside; Good Shepherd's Mission School, Fort Defiance, Ariz.; scholarship to Arizona, "Southwest Indian Art Project," summers, 1961–62.

Mitchell, Stanley C. *Navaho*
Che Chilly Tsosie, Slim Curley Hair
(Has also signed as Chi Chilly Tseiso.)
BORN: 1920, Sail Lee, Ariz. Brother of George Charlie Mitchell (*q.v.*).
The artist began painting at Santa Fe Indian School and has received training as a silversmith. He has exhibited his silverwork regularly at the Inter-Tribal Indian Ceremonials but is no longer an active painter.
EDUCATION: Santa Fe.
SERVICE: WWII.
CAREER: Owner and operator of a silversmith shop in Las Vegas, Nev.
COMMISSIONS: *Murals*: Fort Wingate Vocational High School, Fort Wingate, Ariz.; West Yellowstone business establishment, West Yellowstone, Wyo.
WORK PUBLISHED: Jacobson and D'Ucel (1950).
EXHIBITIONS: AIW, ASF, PAC.
COLLECTIONS: *Public*: AF, MNA/KHC, OU, PAC. *Private*: Dietrich, Lockett.
ADDRESS: 3220A East Patrick Lane, Las Vegas, Nev.

Mofsie, Louis Billingsly *Winnebago-Hopi*
Weepama Quedaecouka, Green Rainbow; *Mofsie*, Sharp Shooting.
BORN: May 3, 1936, Brooklyn, N.Y. Son of Morris Mofsie (Hopi), painter from Second Mesa, Ariz., deceased, and Alvina Lowery (Winnebago), from Winnebago, Nebr. GA: Red Wing St. Cyr, silent screen star.
EDUCATION: Public School 94, and Joan of Arc Junior High School, New York, N.Y.; graduated School of Industrial Arts High School, New York, N.Y.; B.S., State University of New York, Teachers College, Buffalo, N.Y., 1958; Pratt Institute, New York (currently doing graduate work toward M.S. in art education). Special classes, Museum of Modern Art, and Ethical Culture School, New York.
CAREER: Art instructor, East Meadow (N.Y.) Public School, 1957–.
HONORS: Past-president, Indian League of the Americas, New York; chairman, Folk Arts Festival Council, New York.
EXHIBITIONS: ITIC, MMA (school exhibition), MNM, PAC.
AWARDS: MNM.
COLLECTIONS: *Private*: BenAmi, Kimball, Tarrant, Weyr.
ADDRESS: 323 Schermerhorn, Brooklyn, N.Y.

Momaday, Al   *Kiowa*

Huan Toa, War Lance

(Also known as Momaday, Alfred Morris.)

BORN: July 2, 1913, Mountain View, Okla. Son of Mammedaty (Standing High) and A-ho (both Kiowa). P/GGF: Mammedaty, *q.v.* (Kiowa); M/GF: French Canadian. GGM: Non-Indian captured by the Kiowas. GF: First Indian judge when the Kiowa Agency was established, 1888. GF: George Poolaw, Kiowa medicine man.

MARRIED: Natachee Scott, 1933. One son: N. Scott, 1934.

> At Jémez Pueblo, Mr. Momaday initiated a program of arts and crafts which brought international recognition to the school. He organized parent groups to discuss problems and programs within the Pueblo, and was a progressive leader in many educational and Indian art activities.

EDUCATION: Bacone College; New Mexico U.; University of California, Los Angeles.

CAREER: U.S. Corps of Engineers, War Dept., 1942–44; director of arts and crafts, AAID, 1955–57; director of arts and crafts, AIE, 1956–57; assistant director of arts and crafts, NMSF, 1948–; instructor of Indian arts and crafts, PAC, summer, 1958; principal and art teacher, BIA, Jémez Day School, 1947–67.

HONORS: Past chairman, New Mexico Indian Art Commission; Tribe of Teal Wing, Dallas Exchange Club, Outstanding Indian Artist Award, 1956; Ho-ennywe Society, Western (N.Y.) Art Association, Outstanding Indian Artist Award, 1962; listed in *Who's Who in New Mexico* and *Indians of Today*; presented plaques by New Mexico Arts and Crafts Fair for outstanding Indian exhibits, and by African Educators for outstanding art work and public relations; IACB Certificate of Appreciation, 1967.

COMMISSIONS: *Altar Plaques*: St. Luke's Lutheran Church, Albuquerque, N.M., eight plaques with Indian designs representing symbols of the Christian church, 1958.

WORK PUBLISHED: La Farge (1956; 1960), Pierson and Davidson (1960), Haskell (1960), Willoya and Brown (1962). *Tulsa Magazine* (May 1948), *The Lutheran* (May 28, 1958), *Indian Life* (1960), *Region VI American Camping Association Convention Program* (Norman, Okla., 1965), cover.

EXHIBITIONS: AAID, AAIE, AIE, ASF, BG, DAM, DMFA, FAIEAIP, GM, HFA, HM, ITIC, LAIC, MNA, MNM, NMSF, PAC, PAC/T, PSC, SAIEAIP, SN, UNM, UO, USDS. *One-man shows*: BG, DMFA, MNA, OTP, PAC, UO.

AWARDS: AAID (including two Grand Awards), AIE (including two Grand Awards), DAM, DMFA, HFA (best in show), ITIC, MNM, NMSF (including two Grand Awards), PAC, SN.

COLLECTIONS: *Public*: BIA, CWC, GM, IACB, KM, MAI, MNM, MRFM, NMSF, PAC, TWS, WM. *Public*: Ballenger, Bamrook, Boles, Brenner, Briggs, Burshears, Cochran, Conners, Dicus, Deupree, Dustin, Eastman, Eggert, Elkus, Feinwiler, Grammer, Greenblatt, G. Harris, Hertz, F. Johnson, E. Jones, Link, Marriott, Owens, Riley, Wm. Schofield, Schonwald, Seligman, Shepard, Simonton, M. Smith, Smithson, Smoker, J. Snodgrass, Spencer,

Springer, Steffens, J. Stevens, Stokes, Teague, Wayman, Wengard, E.
White, Whiteman, Wisner, Worth, Ydens, Yellowhorse.
ADDRESS: Box 67, Jémez Pueblo, N.M.

Monignok, Gabriel   *Eskimo*
BORN: Mekoryuk, Alaska. Died September 29, 1965 while fishing.
EDUCATION: Santa Fe.
EXHIBITIONS: MNM, PAC.
AWARDS: MNM, PAC.
COLLECTIONS: *Public:* MAI. *Private:* Marriott.

Montana, David   *Papago*
BORN: 1947, Sells, Ariz.
EDUCATION: Institute, 1965–66.
WORK PUBLISHED: YAIA catalog.
EXHIBITIONS: FAIEAIP, SAIEAIP, YAIA.

Montoya, Alfredo   *San Ildefonso*
Wen Tsireh, Pine Tree Bird
BORN: Date unknown. Died May 21, 1913. Brother of Isabelita Montoya.
MARRIED: Tonita Roybal (San Ildefonso), 1910.

> During excavations on Pajarito Plateau, *ca.* 1915, Alfredo was unable to work
> as a digger because of a tubercular condition. Therefore, he became a recorder,
> drawing replicas of the pueblo ceremonial life unearthed there. Bertha Dutton
> said that he was "perhaps the young man from San Ildefonso who initiated
> modern pueblo painting" (*El Palacio*, June 1942).

EDUCATION: San Ildefonso. (In 1911, his instructor, Elizabeth Richards,
sent his paintings to Barbara Freire-Marreco in England for display.)
CAREER: Employed for a time by School of American Research; primarily
an artist.
COLLECTIONS: *Public*: MAI, MNM (gift of the Fred Harveys, *ca.* 1909).

Montoya, Charles   *San Ildefonso*
Oqowamono
COLLECTIONS: *Public*: WRNGA.

Montoya, Gerónima Cruz   *San Juan*
Po Tsunu, Shell
BORN: September 22, 1915, San Juan Pueblo, N.M. Daughter of Pablo Cruz
(San Juan) and Crucita Trujillo (San Juan), the award-winning potter who
exhibited in the Nationwide Pottery Exposition, Syracuse, N.Y., 1941.
MARRIED: Juan A. Montoya, 1939. Three sons: Robert, 1947; Paul, 1950;
Eugene, 1954.

> This highly respected teacher has devoted the major portion of her career in-
> structing others. Only recently did she find the necessary time for her own
> painting. "She does not force their work into any preconceived pattern...she
> allows the student to project his own ideas, simply guides him into a more
> rounded development of his initial creative impulse" [Dorothy Morang, *El Pala-*
> *cio* (May 1940), p. 118].

EDUCATION: Graduated Santa Fe, 1935; New Mexico U.; Claremont; B.S.,
St. Joseph's, 1958. Studied under Dorothy Dunn, Alfredo Martínez, *q.v.*,
and Kenneth Chapman.

CAREER: Teacher, lecturer, and artist; assistant to Dorothy Dunn, Santa Fe Indian School, 1935–37; chairman, art department, Santa Fe Indian School, 1937–61. Currently active in adult education.

HONORS: Credited by many Indian artists as being the teacher who gave them most encouragement; Henry Dendahl Award for Outstanding Student, Santa Fe Indian School; received honorarium when her student, Ben Quintana (*q.v.*), won the National Youth Forum's art contest; listed in *Who's Who in the West* and *Who's Who in American Art*.

WORK PUBLISHED: Jacobson and D'Ucel (1950).

EXHIBITIONS: 1935–65: AIW, BNIAS, ITIC, JGS, MHDYMM, MNM, MNM/T, PAC, SN, USDS. *One-man shows*: MNM, PAC; Yonemoto Art Gallery, Albuquerque, N.M.; Nuremberg, Germany.

AWARDS: 1959–64: Six from ITIC, MHDYMM, MNM, NMSF, PAC, SN.

COLLECTIONS: *Public*: BIA, IACB, MAI, MHDYMM, MNM, MRFM. *Private*: H. Adams, Bluemenshein, Denman, Dietrich, Dixon, Dockstader, T. García, Geis, H. Jones, D. Kramer, Thoeny, Woffard.

ADDRESS: 1008 Calle De Sueños, Santa Fe, N.M.

Montoya, Guadalupe   *San Juan*
COLLECTIONS: *Public*: DAM.

Montoya, Isabelita   *San Ildefonso*
MARRIED: Benjamin Atencio, *ca.* 1925. Five children: one is Gilbert Atencio (*q.v.*).
> During her schooldays in Santa Fe, Isabelita executed charming pencil and crayon sketches.

EDUCATION: Santa Fe.
ADDRESS: San Ildefonso Pueblo, N.M.

Montoya, Joe (*see* Montoya, José L.)

Montoya, José L.   *Isleta*
(Also known as Montoya, Joe.)
BORN: December 12, 1903, Isleta Pueblo, N.M.
MARRIED: Leona F. Montoya.
> The artist was known as a still-life painter. In 1950, he was working in Albuquerque, and no longer painting.

EDUCATION: New Mexico U., B.F.A., 1951.
EXHIBITIONS: MNM, UNM.
ADDRESS: c/o Johnnie Luján's Trading Post, Isleta Pueblo, N.M.

Montoya, Juan B.   *San Juan*
COLLECTIONS: *Public*: MAI.

Montoya, Monty (*see* Montoya, Sidney, Jr.)

Montoya, Ned   *San Juan*
EDUCATION: Santa Fe, *ca.* 1958.
EXHIBITIONS: MNM, 1958.
AWARDS: MNM, 1958.
COLLECTIONS: *Public*: MNM.

Montoya, Nellie   *San Juan*
COLLECTIONS: *Public*: MAI.

Montoya, Sidney, Jr.   *San Juan-Navaho*
Thun Povi, Sun Flower
(Also known as Montoya, Monty.)
BORN: September 4, 1928.
EDUCATION: Graduated Albuquerque; B.A., Journalism, New Mexico; graduate work toward M.A., Drury College, Springfield, Mo.
CAREER: Last known profession, photo-engraver. No longer painting.
EXHIBITIONS: MNA, MNM, NMSF, PAC.
COLLECTIONS: *Public*: MNM.

Montoya, Thomas   *San Juan*
(Also known as Montoya, Tommy.)
EDUCATION: Albuquerque, *ca.* 1960; Institute, *ca.* 1963.
WORK PUBLISHED: YAIA catalog.
EXHIBITIONS: 1960–63: MNM, YAIA.
AWARDS: MNM.
COLLECTIONS: *Public*: BIA. *Private*: McGrath.

Moore, Georgianna   *Chippewa*
EXHIBITIONS: PAC, USDS.

Mootzka, Waldo   *Hopi*
BORN: 1903, near Oraibi, Ariz. Died *ca.* 1935–40.
Mootzka had no formal art training. He often observed Fred Kabotie (*q.v.*) painting at Oraibi Day School, and it may have been there that he learned the technique of watercolor painting. Later, in Santa Fe, he was sponsored by Frank Patania, who taught him silversmithing. At the time of his death, Mootzka was devoting almost all his artistic talents to silverwork.
EDUCATION: Shungopovi; Albuquerque; Santa Fe.
CAREER: Illustrator, painter, and silversmith.
WORK PUBLISHED: Nelson (1937). *Theatre Arts Monthly* (August 1933).
EXHIBITIONS: AIEC, NGA, PAC, PAC/T.
COLLECTIONS: *Public*: AF, BM/B, GM, MAI, MKMcNAI, MNA/KHC, OU, PAC, SM. *Private*: Aldridge, Denman, Dockstader, Elkus, A. Forbes, Lockett, Patania, Pritzlaff, Schonwald, Thoeny.

Mopope, Stephen   *Kiowa*
Qued Koi, Painted Robe
BORN: August 27, 1898, near Red Stone Baptist Mission, on the Kiowa Reservation, Okla. His grandfather was a Spanish captive, kidnaped by the Kiowas from a wagon train crossing the prairie and reared by Chief Many Bears. The artist is a descendant of Appiatan, a noted Kiowa warrior; his granduncles are Silverhorn (Haungooah) and Hakok.
MARRIED: Janet Berry. Two daughters: Vanette and Laquinta.
Mopope's childhood education by his grandmother was in the Kiowa tradition. He is one of the original Five Kiowas (*q.v.*) and has been primarily a painter and dancer most of his life. His granduncles, Silverhorn and Hakok, found him drawing designs in sand and taught him how to paint on tanned skins in the old Kiowa way. His expert and colorful dancing at Indian gatherings, even today, continues to draw the attention of spectators.
EDUCATION: Finished seventh grade at mission school in Anadarko, Okla. Received special non-credit instruction at Oklahoma.

CAREER: Artist; retired farmer.

HONORS: Represented in *Indians of Today*; speaker, National Folk Festival Conference, Chicago, Ill., May, 1957; Certificate of Appreciation, IACB, 1966.

COMMISSIONS: *Murals*: FSM, OHSM, OU, USDI; U.S. Navy Hospital, Carville, La.; Federal Building, Anadarko, Okla.; Northeastern Oklahoma A & M College; Muskogee Junior College, and Federal Building, Muskogee, Okla.; St. Patrick's Mission School and First National Bank of Anadarko, Anadarko, Okla.; Fort Sill Indian School; Northeastern State College, Tahlequah, Okla.

WORK PUBLISHED: Jacobson (1929) (1964), Jacobson and D'Ucel (1950), La Farge (1956). *American Indian Exposition Program*, cover, 1946, 1948.

EXHIBITIONS: AIEC, AIW (frescoes), EITA, OU/ET, PAC, PAC/T, SI; Kermac Mural Design Exhibition, 1965. *One-man shows*: AIE, 1965.

COLLECTIONS: *Public*: ACM, DCC, GM, IACB, MAI, MKMcNAI, MNA/KHC, MNM, OAC, OHSM, OSAF/GC, OU/L, OU/MA, OU/SM, PAC, SPIM, SPL. *Private*: Callaway, Denman, Deupree, Dockstader, Field, Hogue, O. Jacobson, D. Maxwell, R. Moore, Thoeny, Wyman.

ADDRESS: Route 2, Fort Cobb, Okla.

Moqui *Hopi*
Wickahtewah
COLLECTIONS: *Public*: MNM.

Moquino, Delfino *Zia*
Yaka
COLLECTIONS: *Private*: Harvey.

Moquino, Ignacio *Zia*
Waki Yeni Dewa, Stratus Cloud
BORN: May 7, 1917, Zia Pueblo, N.M.
MARRIED: Marie Trujillo (San Juan). Three children.

The artist left school after his father's death to care for his family. While working part-time as a shoemaker, he began his art career by designing and painting pictures of various tribal costumes. He later turned his interests to silversmithing.

EDUCATION: Graduated Santa Fe; two years graduate work in art under Dorothy Dunn and Gerónima Montoya (*q.v.*).

SERVICE: WWII, U.S. Army.

CAREER: Was employed at one time by University of California; taught school for one year.

COMMISSIONS: *Murals*: SFWF (with Charles Loloma and Joe Duran, *qq.v.*).

WORK PUBLISHED: Jacobson and D'Ucel (1950).

EXHIBITIONS: AIW, ITIC, JGS, MNM, OU/ET, PAC, SFWF.

AWARDS: ITIC.

COLLECTIONS: *Public*: DAM, MAI, MNA/KHC, MNM, MRFM, OU, USDI. *Private*: Denman, Dietrich.

ADDRESS: San Juan Pueblo, N.M.

Moquino, Juanito *Zia*
COLLECTIONS: *Public*: MNM.
ADDRESS: Zia Pueblo, N.M.

Moquino, Toribio   *Zia*
COLLECTIONS: *Public*: MNM.

Morez, Mary   *Navaho*
BORN: 1938.
EDUCATION: Scholarship to Arizona, "Southwest Indian Art Project," 1960.

Morgan, Judith Phillis   *Tsimshian*
Simclosh, Lady In The Sun
BORN: April 27, 1930, at Kitwanga, British Columbia, Canada. Both her
parents were hereditary chiefs. Her father was Chief of the Wolf clan whose
family originated in Kitsegukla and moved to Kitwanga to be closer to
their property rights. Her mother was a member of the Grouse clan whose
family originated in Kitwanga on the Skeena River. Her brother, Raymond,
carved the totem crests which still stand at Kitwanga. M/GF: Chief of the
Eagle clan and consultant to the tribe on matters of high decision.
MARRIED: Willis O. Fitzpatrick, 1952. Five children.
  Mrs. Fitzpatrick has been painting since about 1953. She concentrates on depict-
  ing the northwest coast and her family tribe in non-traditional Indian style.
EDUCATION: Kitwanga Day School, Kitwanga, B.C., Canada; Albernie
Indian Residential School, B.C., Canada, four years; Cottey Junior College,
Nevada, Mo.; received Elementary Teacher Certificate for B.C. Studied art
two years under G.N. Sinclair.
CAREER: Housewife; artist.
EXHIBITIONS: Victoria (Canada) Provincial Museum, Pacific National Ex-
hibition, Vancouver; Vancouver Art Gallery, B.C.; National Art Gallery,
Toronto; Little Gallery, Kansas City, Mo.; Portland Art Museum, Portland,
Oreg.; University of British Columbia; represented in a cross-country tour
from Vancouver to Toronto.
AWARDS: Won two poster contests in Victoria, B.C.
COLLECTIONS: *Public*: Provincial Government, Victoria, B.C.
ADDRESS: c/o 1209 West Maple, Enid, Okla.

Morgan, Robert   *Mescalero Apache*
EXHIBITIONS: MNM (student division), 1963.

Morning Star (*see* Humetewa, James Russell, Jr.)

Morning Star (*see* Kewanyouma, Leroy)

Morning Star (*see* Toledo, José Rey)

Morris, Ruth Ella   *Navaho*
BORN: 1944.
EDUCATION: Scholarship to Arizona, "Southwest Indian Art Project," 1960.
ADDRESS: Window Rock, Ariz.

Morrison, George   *Chippewa*
BORN: September 30, 1919, Grand Marais, Minn. Son of James Morrison
(Chippewa) and Barbara Mesaba (Chippewa).
MARRIED: Hazel Belvo, December, 1960. One son: Briand Mesaba, 1961.
  Mr. Morrison has distinguished himself and his tribe by establishing what is
  probably the most outstanding record of any Indian painter in the fine arts field.

EDUCATION: Graduated Grand Marais (Minn.) High School, 1938. Minneapolis (Minn.) School of Art, 1943; Art, 1943–46; University of Aix-Marseille, Aix-en-Provence, France, 1952–53.

CAREER: Teacher, special classes in painting, drawing, and related subjects; Rockport (Mass.) Art School, 1947; Cape Ann (Mass.) Art School, 1948; private art classes, N.Y., 1948–50; Camp Robinson Crusoe, 1949; Wiltwyck School for Boys, 1947; Minneapolis School of Art, 1959; Dayton (Ohio) Art Institute, 1960–61; State College of Iowa, 1961; Cornell University, 1962; Pennsylvania State University, 1963; Assistant Professor of Art, Rhode Island School of Design, 1964–.

HONORS: John Hay Whitney Fellowship, 1953–54; Fulbright Scholarship to France, 1952–53; scholarship grants from Consolidated Chippewa Agency, 1941–42; Bernay's Scholarship, 1943; Vanderlip Traveling Scholarship, 1943; Women's Club Scholarship to Minneapolis Art Institute, 1942; Lucy Gilbert Award, 1941.

EXHIBITIONS: 1946–63: 132 group and invitational exhibitions throughout the world. They include, in New York, the Pyramid Gallery, Grand Central Moderns, Riverside Museum, Whitney Museum Annual, Federation of Modern Painters and Sculptors Annual, Audubon Artists Annual Exhibitions, Brooklyn Museum Print Annual, Davida Gallery Drawing Invitational, Phoenix Gallery Invitational, James Gallery Invitational, the National Arts Club Invitational, Nonagon Gallery Invitational, Art U.S.A. at Madison Square Garden, and Pepsi-Cola Paintings of the Year. In Ohio, Toledo Museum of Art, Columbus Museum of Art, and the International Selected Artists Exhibition at the Dayton Art Museum. In Pennsylvania, the Annual Exhibition of the Pennsylvania Academy of Fine Arts, and at Lehigh University. Other U.S. exhibits include: the Detroit Institute of Arts Annual Exhibition, Detroit, Mich.; Biennial Painting Exhibition, Columbia Museum of Art, Columbia, S.C.; Biennial Exhibition, Colorado Springs Fine Arts Center, Colorado Springs, Colo.; Joslyn Art Museum, Omaha, Nebr.; Washington University, St. Louis, Mo.; M. H. De Young Memorial Museum, San Francisco, Calif.; Houston Museum of Fine Arts, Houston, Tex.; Dallas Museum of Fine Arts, Dallas, Tex.; Twin City Annual Exhibitions, Walker Art Center, Minneapolis, Minn.; Biennial Exhibition, Corcoran Gallery of Art, Washihgton, D.C. *One-man shows*: 1949–62: Twenty, including Cornell University and Grand Central Moderns in New York; State College of Iowa, Cedar Falls, Iowa; Dayton Art Institute, Dayton, Ohio; University of Georgia, Athens, Ga.; Southern Illinois University, Carbondale, Ill. *Two and three-man shows*: 1945–58: Philadelphia, Art Alliance, Philadelphia, Pa.; Stephens College, Columbia, Mo; Karlis Gallery, Provincetown, Mass.; Birmingham Museum of Art, Birmingham, Ala.; Ashby Gallery, New York, N.Y.

AWARDS: 1965, First Award, Rhode Island Arts Festival, Providence, R.I.

COLLECTIONS: *Public*: AH, AHM, AK, BMJ, CAM/M, CCH, CCHS, DAI, DFNB, GCG, GO, IACB, IBM, JAM, LJMA, LS, MIA, MPWI, MSIC, NMAS, NYU, PMA, PSU, SCI, SC/MA, UM, VMA, W, WAC, WM/CU.

Private: Abe, Bedlaender, Benacerraf, Bing, Brownstone, Colt, Cotner, Elsohn, Gershenson, Gess, Gomberg, Graubarth, Greene, Guillaume, M. Johnson, Koenig, S. Kramer, Bor. Kronenberg, Lannon, Leng, Lockwood, Neilson, Nevelson, Olson, C. Pereyma, E. Pereyma, Primrose, Roach, B. Rogers, Rouillon, A. Scott, Stueland, J. Weber, Whiteford, G. Williams.
ADDRESS: 12 Cole Farm Court, Providence, R.I.

Moses, James Kivetoruk *Eskimo*
Kivetoruk, Bark Dye
(Also known as Moses, Kivetoruk.)
BORN: February, 10 1903, near Cape Espenberg, Alaska. Son of Kivoluk, who, with his partner Charlie Browers, established whaling stations along the arctic coast using Eskimo crews and skin boats.
MARRIED: Bessie Ahgupuk, 1933. Children: James, Jr., 1934; Charles, 1936.
EDUCATION: At Shishmaref, Alaska, through the third grade.
CAREER: Deerherder, trapper, and hunter until he was crippled in a plane crash "back of Shishmaref," at Ear Mountain, 1953. Executed sketches of Eskimo life on ivory carvings and, in 1954, began painting professionally.
EXHIBITIONS: BNIAS, FNAIC, MNM, PAC, SAIEAIP, USDS.
AWARDS: 1959–64: BNIAS, FNAIC, MNM, PAC.
COLLECTIONS: *Public*: IACB. *Private*: Elkus, Leno, Solberg, L. Stewart.
ADDRESS: Box 814, Nome, Alaska.

Moses, Kivetoruk (*see* Moses, James Kivetoruk)

Mountain Cougar (*see* Shipshee, Louis)

Mountain Of The Sacred Wind (*see* Atencio, Gilbert Benjamin)

Mountain Rock (*see* Atencio, Pat)

Moving Whirlwind (*see* Whirlwind)

Murdock, Cecil *Kickapoo*
Koketha, Turning Bear (*or* Running Bear)
BORN: October 13, 1913, McLoud, Okla. Died December 14, 1954. The artist lived with his grandmother until he was 16, and "she developed and nourished my learning and the love of being an Indian."
MARRIED: Ida Mae Fredericks (Hopi).
In 1946, Murdock wrote Philbrook Art Center that his accomplishments in art were "greatly due to Oscar B. Jacobson's guidance and encouragement." His military service resulted in 20 per cent disability, and he consequently painted less frequently after the war.
EDUCATION: Chilocco; Friends University, Wichita, Kans.; Oklahoma.
SERVICE: WWII, Fifth Air Force, four years; New Guinea, the Netherlands, and India.
CAREER: Demonstrated mural techniques at the Palmer House, Chicago, Ill., 1940–41.
COMMISSIONS: *Murals*: Painted murals two years, WPA Project, Lawton and Anadarko, Okla.; University of Oklahoma; Ohio State University, Columbus, Ohio.
WORK PUBLISHED: Jacobson and D'Ucel (1950).

EXHIBITIONS: AIW, HM, PAC, PAC/T; Chicago, Ill.; Washington, D.C.; Oklahoma City, Okla.; Lawton, Okla.; New York World's Fair, 1939–40.
AWARDS: PAC, 1946.
COLLECTIONS: *Public*: GM, MNA/KHC, OU/MA, PAC. *Private*: Denman, J. Young.

Murray, Alice Hearrell   *Chickasaw-Choctaw*
COLLECTIONS: *Public*: OHSM.

Murray, Daniel M.   *Iowa-Oto*
Nhuschingyay, No Heart
BORN: May 28, 1934, Perkins, Okla. Son of Frank Murray (Iowa) and Martha McGlasin (Iowa-Oto). M/GF: Ben McGlasin, last Oto chief. GGGF: One of several Iowa chiefs. Descendant of Chief White Cloud.

> The artist has just recently begun to exhibit his three-dimensional oil paintings. It is his ambition to "expose the honors and the downfalls committed upon his people, to paint Indians of Oklahoma as well as the state's heritage and present daily life."

EDUCATION: High school; Oklahoma S.U./S.T., one year.
SERVICE: Korean War, U.S. Marine Corps, three years.
CAREER: Previously employed by Pennsylvania Rubber Co., Cleveland, Ohio; currently a freelance landscape artist.
WORK PUBLISHED: *Sunday Oklahoman, Orbit Magazine* (February 2, 1964).
EXHIBITIONS: PAC, 1965.
COLLECTIONS: *Public*: GWS. *Private*: Asip, J. Ross.
ADDRESS: Perkins, Okla.

Musically Inclined (*see* Ingram, Veronica Marie)

Mus Truwi (*see* Toledo, José Rey)

Nagawbo (*see* Des Jarlait, Patrick Robert)

Naha, Archie A.   *Hopi*
Mr. Naha is the uncle of Raymond Naha (*q.v.*).
EXHIBITIONS: HM.
COLLECTIONS: *Private*: Bialac.

Naha, Raymond   *Hopi*
BORN: 1933, Hopi Reservation, Ariz.
EDUCATION: As a high school student, he studied under Fred Kabotie (*q.v.*).
WORK PUBLISHED: *Arizona Highways* (August 1966).
EXHIBITIONS: AIAE/WSU, FAIEAIP, ITIC, MNM, PAC, SAIEAIP, SN, USDS.
AWARDS: AIAE/WSU, ITIC, MNM, PAC, SN.
COLLECTIONS: *Public*: AF, BIA, IACB, MAI, MNA/KHC. *Private*: Dockstader, Hanks, McGee, Sangster, J. Snodgrass, Thoeny.
ADDRESS: Box 374, Zuni, N.M.

Nahsohnhoya, Thomas Dolwiftema   *Hopi*
Dolwiftema, Lightning
(Also known as Nahsonhoya, Thomas Dolwiftema; Nasonhoya, Thomas Dolwiftema.)
BORN: October 15, 1929, Sichomovi, First Mesa, Ariz.

EDUCATION: Hopi.
EXHIBITIONS: PAC, 1948.
ADDRESS: Polacca, Ariz.

Nahsonhoya, Thomas Dolwiftema (*see* Nahsohnhoya, Thomas Dolwiftema)

Naiche (Chief) *Chiricahua Apache*
BORN: Date unknown. Son of Cochise, hereditary Apache chief.
Naiche was Chief of the Apaches at Fort Sill, Okla., in 1899, and was well-known at that time as an artist. He lived to an old age at Mescalero. *See* Sonnichsen (1958).
CAREER: In the spring of 1885, as prisoners of the Government, Naiche and Geronimo escaped near White Mountain Reservation in Arizona and began a campaign of resistance against White settlement. In September, 1886, he surrendered, and was taken to Fort Pickens, Fla. In May, 1888, he was transfered to Vermont, Va., where he worked for the Government until October, 1894. *See* Barrett (1906).
WORK PUBLISHED: La Farge (1956). *American Heritage* (October 1956).
COLLECTIONS: *Public*: FSM, MAI, OHSM, SI/MNH.

Nailor, Gerald *Navaho*
Toh Yah, Walking By The River
BORN: 1917. Pinedale, N.M. Died, August, 1952.
MARRIED: A woman from Picurís. Their son may be Jerry Nailor (*q.v.*).
In 1937, Nailor shared a studio in Santa Fe with Allan Houser (*q.v.*). His paintings were exhibited in the home of Mrs. Hall Adams from 1943 to 1952. At the time of his death, he was living with his family at Picurís Pueblo, N.M.
EDUCATION: Elementary grades at mission boarding schools; attended Gallup (N.M.) Public School, on scholarship; graduated Albuquerque; attended Santa Fe (supplementary courses); Oklahoma. Special instruction under Dorothy Dunn, Kenneth Chapman, and the Swedish muralist, Olaf Nordmark.
SERVICE: WWII.
COMMISSIONS: *Murals*: USDI; Mesa Verde Post Office, Mesa Verde, Colo.; Navaho Tribal Council House, Window Rock, Ariz.
WORK PUBLISHED: Jacobson and D'Ucel (1950). *Compton's Pictured Encyclopedia* (1957); *Arizona Highways* (February 1950); *Indian Life* (1960); *American Scene* (Vol. VI, No. 3), cover. Paintings have been silk-screened by Tewa Enterprises.
EXHIBITIONS: AIEC, AIW, DAM, ITIC, MAI, MMA, MNM, NGA, OU/ET, PAC, PAC/T.
COLLECTIONS: *Public*: BIA, GM, MAI, MNM, MRFM, OU, PAC, SM. *Private*: H. Adams, Bates, Crawford, Denman, Dietrich, Elkus, Finley, A. Forbes, Hurr, D. Kramer, Lockett, Pritzlaff, Rosenwald, Rust, Thoeny, Woffard.

Nailor, Jerry *Picurís*
BORN: Date unknown. May be the son of Gerald Nailor (*q.v.*).
EDUCATION: Santa Fe, 1958.
EXHIBITIONS: MNM.

Nakayoma (*see* Kabotie, Fred)

9

Nakowhoadoniulzi (*see* Bushyhead, Allan)

Nama Piaska (*see* Kishketon, George)

Namingha, Grifford   *Hopi*
  BORN: Date unknown. The artist is from Hotevilla, Ariz.
  COLLECTIONS: *Public*: MAI (painting executed at about age 15).

Na Mos (*see* Left Hand)

Nape Sica Hoksila (*see* Claymore, Thomas William)

Naranjo, Adolph   *Santa Clara* (?)
  Ogowee, Road Runner
  BORN: 1916, Santa Clara Pueblo, N.M.
  EDUCATION: Santa Fe.
  WORK PUBLISHED: Jacobson and D'Ucel (1950).
  EXHIBITIONS: AIW.

Naranjo, Balardo   *Santo Domingo*
  COLLECTIONS: *Public*: SM.

Naranjo, Ben   *Santa Clara*
  COLLECTIONS: *Public*: WRNGA.

Naranjo, José Dolores   *Santa Clara*
  Ce Komo Pyn
  EXHIBITIONS: NGA.
  COLLECTIONS: *Private*: Dietrich.
  ADDRESS: Santa Clara Pueblo, Española, N.M.

Naranjo, Louis   *Santa Clara*
  EDUCATION: Santa Fe, 1937.
  EXHIBITIONS: AIEC.

Naranjo, Victor   *Santa Clara*
  COLLECTIONS: *Public*: MNM.

Nash, Daniel   *San Carlos Apache*
  EDUCATION: Mescalero High School, N.M.
  COLLECTIONS: *Public*: MAI, MNM. *Private*: Dockstader, Elkus.
  ADDRESS: Box 143, San Carlos, Ariz.

Nash, Joel   *Hopi*
  EXHIBITIONS: FWG (student) 1951; HM.

Nash, Wesley   *Apache*
  BORN: September 22, 1926, San Carlos, Ariz.
  MARRIED: Anne Goombi (Kiowa), 1953. Four children: Janet, 1954; Sharon,
  1958; Cynthia, 1960; George Wesley, 1963.
    Nash recalls an interest in art as early as the third grade. In 1942, Wilma Fergu-
    son, now Mrs. James Watson, encouraged the artist to enter Santa Fe Indian
    School, where he remembers especially the help received from Vicente Mirabel,
    Gerónima Cruz Montoya (*qq.v.*), and a Miss Kerwin.
  EDUCATION: San Carlos; graduated Santa Fe, 1948; Bacone College, 1952–
  53; Utah S., 1959–60.
  SERVICE: WWII, U.S. Navy, 1944–46. U.S. Army Paratroopers, 1948–52.
  EXHIBITIONS: MNM, NGA, PAC, SN; tribal fairs.

AWARDS: Tribal fairs.
COLLECTIONS: *Public*: MRFM. *Private*: Wyman.
ADDRESS: 16 Freeman, Ardmore, Okla.

Nashboo, William *Zuni*
EDUCATION: Albuquerque, 1963.
EXHIBITIONS: MNM.

Nasonhoya, Thomas Dolwiftema (*see* Nahsohnhoya, Thomas Dolwiftema)

Natachu, Fred *Zuni*
EXHIBITIONS: MNM, 1965.
AWARDS: MNM, 1965.
ADDRESS: Box 533, Zuni, N.M.

Natatches, James J. *Navaho-Mohawk*
EDUCATION: Santa Fe, 1960–61; Rock Point Mission School, Chinle, Ariz.;
scholarship to Arizona, "Southwest Indian Art Project," summers, 1961–62.
EXHIBITIONS: MNM; PAC, 1961.
ADDRESS: Rock Point Mission, Chinle, Ariz.

Natay, Ed *Navaho*
Nat Tay Yelth Le Galth, Walking Leader
(Also known as Lee, Edward.)
BORN: December 15, 1915. Died, January 15, 1967. His father was a medicine man and Indian scout, and his mother was known for her fine weaving.
MARRIED: Pop Chalee (*q.v.*).
CAREER: Instructor, Santa Fe High School, Santa Fe, N.M.; iron worker;
journeyman combination welder; recording artist of native songs; radio
announcer; promoter for MGM movie studios and Santa Fe Railroad Co.
EXHIBITIONS: ASF, CAA, CU, ITIC.
AWARDS: First award and bronze medal of honor, CAA, 1956.

Nat Tay Yelth Le Galth (*see* Natay, Ed)

Naumoff *Eskimo*
The drawing illustrated in the BAE, *10th AR* was made in 1882. The "designs
were traced upon a strip of wood, which was then stuck upon the roof of the
house belonging to the draftsman." (BAE, *10th AR*, p. 350).
WORK PUBLISHED: BAE, *10th AR*.

Nazia (*see* Blackmore, Bill)

Nehakije (*see* Vicenti, Steven)

Nequatewa, Eddie *Hopi*
EXHIBITIONS: AIW, OU/ET.
COLLECTIONS: *Public*: OU/MA, SM.
ADDRESS: Box 106, Hotevilla, Ariz.

Netostimi (*see* Schildt, Gary Joseph)

Nevamokewesa (*see* Saufkie, Morgan)

Newini *Zuni*
(Also known as Newmi.)
It has been recorded that the artist was painting in 1927.
COLLECTIONS: *Public*: MNM.

Newmi (*see* Newini)

Newton, Ranzy Alison   *Kiowa*
Chief Charging Skunk
BORN: April 21, 1894, Weatherford, Tex. During childhood, lived in Altus and Olustee, Okla.
SERVICE: WWII, Sixth Field Artillery, U.S. Army, eight years.
EXHIBITIONS: PAC; Spring Hill (Ala.) College; Desert Gallery, Palm Desert, Calif.
ADDRESS: 2324 North F Street, Stockton, Calif.

Nez, D. M.   *Navaho*
COLLECTIONS: *Public*: MAI.

Nez, Ford   *Navaho*
COLLECTIONS: *Public*: MNM.

Nhuschingyay (*see* Murray, Daniel M.)

Nichols, Katie   *Miwok*
BORN: December 5, 1905, Merced, Calif.
EDUCATION: Karl Thorpe Art School; Polytechnic High School, Riverside, Calif.; Adult Evening College, Sacramento, Calif.
EXHIBITIONS: CSF; Northern California Art Fair, Sacramento, Calif.

Nichols, Milton   *Hopi*
EXHIBITIONS: HM (student) 1951.

Nick   *Cheyenne*
The artist was among the 72 Plains Indians taken as prisoners from Fort Sill, Okla., to Fort Marion, St. Augustine, Fla., in 1875.
COLLECTIONS: *Public*: YU/BRBML.

Nieto, Balardo   *Santo Domingo*
SERVICE: The artist was killed in WWII.
COLLECTIONS: *Public*: MNM.

Nieto, Harry   *Zuni*
COLLECTIONS: *Public*: CU/LMA.

Night Walker (*see* Martin, James, Jr.)

Nilchee, Betty Jean   *Navaho*
EDUCATION: Institute, 1962–63.
EXHIBITIONS: MNM, 1963.
AWARDS: MNM, 1963.

Nitoh Mahkwii (*see* Schultz, Hart Merriam)

Nix, Bill (*see*) Red Corn)

No Braid (Chief)   *Sioux*
COLLECTIONS: *Public*: MPM (pictographic style on paper).

No Heart (*see* Murray, Daniel M.)

No Heart (*see* Tinzoni)

No Heart   *Sioux*
Cante Wani Ca
BORN: Date unknown. A medicine man from Standing Rock Reservation.
COLLECTIONS: *Public*: SHSND (pictographic style drawings on cotton of the Dakota Sun Dance).

No Two Horns *Hunkpapa Sioux*
BORN: Date unknown. From Standing Rock Reservation.
HONORS: Important chief and warrior who kept a winter count.
COLLECTIONS: *Public*: SHSND (43 paintings depicting Indian battles).

Nofchissey, Alberta *Navaho*
BORN: Ariz.
EDUCATION: Institute, *ca*. 1954.
EXHIBITIONS: FAIEAIP, YAIA.
COLLECTIONS: *Private*: McGrath.

Nohnicas (*see* Cohoe, William)

Northcutt, Harrell *Chickasaw*
EDUCATION: Bacone College, *ca*. 1951.
EXHIBITIONS: DAM; PAC, 1951–52.

Norton, Jerry R. *Eskimo*
BORN: July 20, 1942.
EDUCATION: Santa Fe.
EXHIBITIONS: MNM, PAC, USDS.
AWARDS: MNM, two.
COLLECTIONS: *Public*: BIA, IACB, MNM. *Private*: Elkus.
ADDRESS: Kivalina, Alaska.

Nosie, Montie *Apache*
COLLECTIONS: *Public*: MAI.

Notah, Ned *Navaho*
EDUCATION: Santa Fe, *ca*. 1936–38.
EXHIBITIONS: AIW; NGA, 1953.
COLLECTIONS: *Private*: D. Kramer.

Nova, A. M. *Hopi*
BORN: Date unknown. From Shungopovi, Ariz.
COLLECTIONS: *Public*: MAI.

Noyes, Phyllis *Colville*
BORN: 1947, Omak, Wash.
EDUCATION: Institute, 1965–66.
EXHIBITIONS: SAIEAIP, YAIA.

Numkena, Lewis, Jr. *Hopi*
(Also known as Junior, Lewis Numkena; Junior, Lewis N.)
BORN: July 24, 1927, Moenkopi, Ariz. Son of Lewis Numkena (Hopi), a
village leader at Moenkopi.
EDUCATION: Santa Fe.
WORK PUBLISHED: *Arizona Highways* (February 1950).
EXHIBITIONS: MNA, MNM, PAC.
AWARDS: MNA; PAC, 1948.
ADDRESS: Tuba City, Ariz.

Nupok, Florence (*see* Chauncey, Florence Nupok)

Nutchuck *Eskimo*
WORK PUBLISHED: The artist wrote and illustrated *Back to the Smoky Sea*
and *Son of the Smoky Sea* (no dates available).

Nuvayouma, Arlo   *Hopi*

Nuvayouma, Snow Carry

BORN: September 6, 1923, Shungopovi, Ariz.

MARRIED: Elizabeth Tawamuniya (Hopi). Two children.

EDUCATION: Second Mesa.

CAREER: Employed at Arizona Country Club, Phoenix, Ariz.

COMMISSIONS: *Painting Series*: 30 paintings illustrating Hopi village life
(Byron Harvey III Collection), 1964–65.

COLLECTIONS: *Public*: MAI. *Private*: Harvey.

ADDRESS: 4015 North Sixth Street, Phoenix, Ariz., *and* Shungopovi, Ariz.

Oau Nah Jusah (*see* Gritts, Franklin)

Octuck, J.   *Eskimo*

COLLECTIONS: *Public*: MAI (with the note: "Point Hope, Alaska, 1905").

Odle Pah   *Kiowa*

Kawlahnohndaumah, Footprints Of A Buffalo

MARRIED: Chief Satanta's second son.

> The artist executed a calendar history of the Kiowas, drawn with colored cray-
> ons in a ledger book. She began *ca.* 1885, and continued until her death in 1934.

COLLECTIONS: *Public*: FSM.

Of The Dawn (*see* Smoky, Lois)

Ogowee (*see* Naranjo, Adolph)

Ohet Toint   *Kiowa* (?)

> The artist was among the 72 Plains Indians taken as prisoners from Fort Sill,
> Okla., to Fort Marion, St. Augustine, Fla., in 1875.

COLLECTIONS: *Public*: YU/BRBML (listed as Charles Chet-toint). *Private*:
R. Robinson.

O'John, Calvin   *Ute*

EDUCATION: Institute, 1965–66.

EXHIBITIONS: YAIA.

Okicize Tawa (*see* Jaw)

Okie, John   *Eskimo*

The following comment appears in a letter to Philbrook Art Center from
Wilbur Wright Walluk (*q.v.*), written August 22, 1946:

> "....he draws art pictures once in a great while. As matter of fact, he always
> have other works to do. He especially does ivory carving. He likes ivory business
> during the war, but now the ivory conditions are change after the war is over.
> The price of ivory is low down since the war is over. He probably give up his
> ivory business and start painting. Jack Okie is a very good Eskimo artist. His
> works use to be better than Ahgupuk (*q.v.*) and my works. My dear mama is
> Jack's cousin. Mama use to tell me that Jack sure like to draw pictures when he
> was a kid. He sure can draw pictures with a pen and ink and watercolor. He pro-
> bably knows how to work with oils too."

Okuwasta (*see* Baca, Henry)

Old Buffalo   *Sioux*

Tatankehanni

BORN: 1845. In 1913, the artist, with Swift Dog (*q.v.*), went to McLaughlin,
S. Dak., to confer with Frances Densmore.

WORK PUBLISHED: BAE, *Bull. 61* (pictographic style).

Old Bull, Moses *Sioux*

COLLECTIONS: *Public*: Iowa State Department of History and Archives, Des Moines, Iowa (a calendar, dated 1812–79, marked "Bullhead, S. Dak."; also a pictographic listing cataloged as "the dead and wounded since coming to Standing Rock Reservation," 1831–33).

Old Dog *Sioux*

COLLECTIONS: *Public*: SHSND (a muslin drawing labeled as "a party of Hidatsa Indians with Sioux in 1856").

Olney, Nathan Hale, III *Yakima*

BORN: January 30, 1937, Wapato, Wash. Son of Nathan Hale Olney, Jr. (Yakima), and Alice Pratt (Hupa). P/GGGF: Capt. Nathan H. Olney, Indian agent at Dallas, Oreg., in 1855, who married a Washo girl.

EDUCATION: Graduated from Wapato (Wash.) High School, 1955; attended Washington S.C., 1956–59; University of Würzburg, Germany, during military service.

SERVICE: U.S. Army, 1960–62. Battle group artist.

CAREER: BIA, four years.

EXHIBITIONS: 1955–64: AAID, FNAIC, ITIC; Central Washington and Western Washington Fairs; La Grande (Oreg.) Arts and Crafts Festival; Southern Command Art Show, Schweinfurt, Germany; Anacortes (Wash.) Arts and Crafts Show; Larson Gallery, Yakima (Wash.) Junior College; Ohio Art Congress Exhibition. *One-man shows*: Yakima (Wash.) Library; Kamiath-Trinity High School, Hoopa, Calif.; Seattle (Wash.) Indian Center; Federal Building, Portland, Oreg.

ADDRESS: 512 West Sixth St., Wapato, Wash.

Oon Na Susah (*see* Gritts, Franklin)

Ootskuyva (*see* Qotskuyva, R.)

Opa Mu Nu (*see* Martínez, Richard)

Oquwa (*see* Roybal, José D.)

Oqwa Owin (*see* Sánchez, Ramos)

Oqwa Pi *San Ildefonso*

Oqwa Pi, Red Cloud
(Also known as Sánchez, Abel.)

BORN: *ca.* 1899–1902.

"I, Oqwa Pi, have been painting since the early 1920's. As I found that painting was the best among my talents, I decided to do my best to win me fame as an Indian artist.... as an artist, I have raised a big healthy family for my painting brought in good income..." (letter from artist to Philbrook Art Center).

EDUCATION: Santa Fe.

CAREER: Painter and farmer.

HONORS: Served as lieutenant governor, and later as governor, of his pueblo.

COMMISSIONS: *Murals*: Santa Fe Indian School.

WORK PUBLISHED: Alexander (1932), Jacobson and D'Ucel (1950). *American Magazine of Art* (August 1933), *Encyclopedia Britannica* (1954).

EXHIBITIONS: AIEC, AIW, CGA, EITA, GCG, ITIC, MMA, MNM, NGA, NJSM, PAC, SU; Muskegon (Wis.) Gallery of Fine Arts, Yale University;

Milwaukee (Wis.) Art Institute; Philadelphia (Pa.) Art Alliance Exhibition of Contemporary Pueblo Indian Art.

AWARDS: ITIC, MNM.

COLLECTIONS: *Public*: AF, AMNH, BM/B, CAM, CGFA, CIS, DAM, JAM, MAI, MKMcNAI, MNA/KHC, MNM, RM, W/JSC. *Private*: Dietrich, Dockstader, Elkus, A. Forbes.

ADDRESS: Route 1, Box 315, Santa Fe, N.M.

Oriole (*see* Herrera, Velino Shije)

Orr, Caroline Louise   *Colville-Wenatchee*

BORN: August 21, 1943, Republic, Wash. Daughter of Samuel A. Orr (Wenatchee) and Caroline Nelson (Colville). Descendant of Moses, famous Wenatchee chief. M/GGGF: Long Alec, Colville chief, U.S. Marshall and pony express rider.

> Miss Orr has been actively engaged in painting her people, in non-traditional Indian style, since 1956. She has completed two collections of Indian portraits and has taken courses in anthropology to further her knowledge of Indian cultures.

EDUCATION: Public schools in Omak, Wash.; B.A., Washington, 1965.

CAREER: Staff member, University of Washington, Art Gallery, 1963–64; assistant reader for design class, University of Washington; staff artist, Fort Okanogan Museum; raises Hereford cattle and Quarter Horses.

HONORS: Four-year scholarship from Colville tribe to attend college; delegate to Career Planning for Minority Groups, U.S. Labor Department, Washington, D.C., 1962.

COMMISSIONS: *Murals*: University of Washington.

BOOKS ILLUSTRATED: Brown (1961).

WORK PUBLISHED: "Goldmark Trial," *Omak Chronicle*, illustrator, 1964; *Spokesman Review* (Western Edition), 1961, portrait of Long Alec; "Sacred Root Feast," *Wenatchee World* (1952), illustrator; *An Okanogan Drying Venison* (1961), illustrator, Okanogan Vocational publication booklet.

EXHIBITIONS: AAID, FAIEAIP, ITIC, MNM, PAC. *One-man shows*: 1957–64: 16, including the Library, County Fair, and Caribou Inn, Okanogan, Wash.; the North Central Washington Museum, and Rocky Reach Dam, Wenatchee, Wash.; The Carey Museum, Cashmere, Wash.; Gonzaga University and Peltier Gallery, Spokane, Wash.; Fort Okanogan Museum, Brewster, Wash.; the Art Club, Republic, Wash.; the Indian Center, Seattle, Wash.; St. Mary's Mission, and Okanogan Valley League of Arts and Crafts, Omak, Wash.; Grand Coulee Dam, Spokane, Wash.

AWARDS: University of Washington, "Arts Award"; Human Education Poster Contest, Stanford, Calif.

COLLECTIONS: *Public*: BIA, BIA/P, CBC, CM/C, FOM, GCD, OL, OPS, WHCO. *Private*: Benson, Barb. Brown, Barc. Brown, C. Brown, E. Brown, M. Casey, T. Casey, Keith, J. Kennedy, Mendhall, Nash, R. Rogers, Rosallini, Tisserant, Turner, VanDivort.

ADDRESS: Box 500, Omak, Wash.

Orr, Howell Sonny   *Chickasaw-Cherokee*
Ihunter, Lover of Home
BORN: May 20, 1929, Washington, Okla. Son of a Cherokee father and
Chickasaw mother. M/GGF: Hatak Shauee, last chief of the Chickasaw
Nation.
> The artist is particularly interested in the work of Mexican muralists and in
> the technique of batik painting, in which he was trained at Instituto San Miguel
> de Allende.

EDUCATION: Public schools in Madill, Okla.; Chilocco; Bacone College;
B.A., Northeastern; graduate study, Tulsa; M.A. (thesis: *American Indian
Art in the United States*), Instituto San Miguel de Allende.
SERVICE: Korean War, U.S. Ski Patrol, three years; Korea and Europe.
CAREER: Art instructor, Derby (Kans.) Junior High, three years; Kukun-
sion Junior High School, Las Vegas, Nev., *ca.* 1962–65; Valley High School,
Las Vegas, Nev., 1965–.
HONORS: Indian tribal dance coordinator, National American Folk Festival,
Oklahoma City, Okla., 1957.
COMMISSIONS: Program cover, Pickens Inter-Tribal Pow Wow, Madill,
Okla., July, 1956.
EXHIBITIONS: AIE, FANAIAE, ITIC, MNM, PAC, SAIEAIP, SN, USDS;
Instituto Nacional de las Bellas Artes, Mexico City, Mexico; Instituto San
Miguel de Allende, Guanajuato, Mexico; Cuarto Exposición Anual de San
Miguel de Allende. *One-man shows*: Las Vegas (Nev.) Art League, 1965.
AWARDS: AIE, ITIC, MNM.
COLLECTIONS: *Public*: BIA. *Private*: Farmer, Story.
ADDRESS: c/o Annie B. Orr, Madill, Okla.

Ortiz, Joseph   *San Juan*
So Whay, Misty
BORN: March 21, 1939, Santa Fe, N.M. Son of Esther Martínez.
> Mr. Ortiz believes that Dick West (*q.v.*) at Bacone College, Mr. and Mrs. James
> E. Watson (formerly of Santa Fe Indian School), and Mrs. J. A. Armstrong
> encouraged him most in his art career. He wishes to continue in the field of
> education and teach art education and biology.

EDUCATION: Attended San Juan, 1946–51; Santa Fe, 1952–58; Bacone
College, 1960; B.S. (Ed.), Arizona S.C./F., 1963; M.S., Arizona S.C./F.,
1964; scholarship to Arizona, "Southwest Indian Art Project."
HONORS: Scholarship to Bacone, from Mrs. J. A. Armstrong, Berkeley, Calif.
EXHIBITIONS: 1956–64: ASC, BC, ITIC, MNM, NMSF, PAC.
AWARDS: 1956–64: Six, from ASC, ITIC, MNM, NMSF.
ADDRESS: c/o Box 715, San Juan Pueblo, N.M.

Ortiz, Louis   *Cochiti*
BORN: Date unknown. Died *ca.* 1943.
COLLECTIONS: *Public*: MNM.

Osapana (*see* Whiteman, James Ridgley)

Osborne, Gerald   *Pawnee*
BORN: Date unknown. Died *ca.* 1964.
EXHIBITIONS: PAC.

AWARDS: PAC, 1950–52.
COLLECTIONS: *Public*: PAC.

Osceola, Mary Gay   *Seminole*
BORN: March 16, 1939.
EDUCATION: Santa Fe, 1960–61; Institute, 1961–65.
EXHIBITIONS: MNM, PAC.
AWARDS: MNM, 1963.
COLLECTIONS: *Public*: BIA. *Private*: Woffard.
ADDRESS: 6320 Northwest 36th, Hollywood, Fla.

Otelaleya   *Cochití*
EXHIBITIONS: AIEC.

Outah, Lawrence   *Hopi*
The artist is reportedly from Oraibi, Arizona. While in the tenth grade at Santa
Fe Indian School in 1948, he was cited for "outstanding ability in art."
EDUCATION: Santa Fe; Haskell.
EXHIBITIONS: MNM, PAC.
COLLECTIONS: *Public*: GM, MAI, MNM.

Outie, George   *Hopi*
Leleka, Snake
BORN: November 16, 1926, Winslow, Ariz.
EDUCATION: Bacone College, 1949.
SERVICE: WWII, U.S. Air Corps; European Theater.
EXHIBITIONS: PAC, PAC/T.
AWARDS: PAC.
COLLECTIONS: *Public*: MAI, PAC.
ADDRESS: Hopi Agency, Keams Canyon, Ariz., *and* Box 113, Tuba City,
Ariz.

Owen, Narcissa Chisholm   *Cherokee*
COLLECTIONS: *Public*: OHSM (oil portraits).

Owl Eagle (*see* Eagle Feather, Elijah)
Owu Tewa (*see* Chávez, Manuel "Bob")
Oye Gi (*see* Herrera, Senofre)
Oysla (*see* García, Ernest P.)
Ozistalis (*see* Speck, Henry)
Paaokela (*see* Martínez, José R.)

Pablito, Thomas   *Zuni*
(Also known as Pablito, Tomás.)
COLLECTIONS: *Public*: MAI.

Pablito, Tomás (*see* Pablito, Thomas)

Packer   *Arapaho* or *Cheyenne*
Sto Ko Wo
The artist was among the 72 Plains Indians taken as prisoners from Fort Sill,
Okla., to Fort Marion, St. Augustine, Fla., in 1875.
COLLECTIONS: *Public*: HI.

Paddock, Hugh   *Navaho*
COLLECTIONS: *Public*: MAI.

Padilla, Michael   *Santa Clara*
EDUCATION: Albuquerque, 1961–62.
EXHIBITIONS: MNM, 1961–62.
AWARDS: MNM, two.
COLLECTIONS: *Private*: Elkus.

Pahsetopah, Loren Louis   *Osage-Cherokee*
Shapa Nazhi, Stands Brown (Buffalo)
BORN: September 10, 1934, Pawhuska, Okla., on the Osage Reservation.
Son of Chris Pahsetopah (Osage) and Lorraine (Cherokee). P/GF: Great
Hunter Pahsetopah. Brother of Paul Pahsetopah (*q.v.*).
MARRIED: Virgie Reed (Chickasaw), 1952. Seven children: Lorna Ann, 1954;
Paul Anthony, 1955; Teresa, 1956; Christopher, 1957; Mary Katherine,
1958; Monette, 1960; Elaine, 1962.
  The artist's interest in drawing and painting began when he was about seven
  years old. Participation in pow-wows has aided him in depicting tribal costuming.
EDUCATION: Pawhuska Public Schools; Chilocco.
CAREER: Painting contractor and interior decorator.
WORK PUBLISHED: *Oklahoma Today* (Winter 1965).
EXHIBITIONS: 1952–65: ITIC, MNM, PAC, SN, USDS. *Three-man shows*:
PAC.
AWARDS: First award, Oklahoma School Students Competition, 1949; PAC,
1962–65.
COLLECTIONS: *Public*: IACB; St. Louis (Mo.) Children's Hospital. *Private*:
Brawner, Cheshewalla, Clearman, Connell, Lake, MacKay, K. McCormick,
Pahsetopah, H. Potter, Reed, R. Smith, H. West.
ADDRESS: 2146 East Newton Street, Tulsa, Okla.

Pahsetopah, Paul   *Osage-Cherokee*
Pahsetopah, Four Hills
BORN: September 10, 1932, Pawhuska, Okla., on the Osage Reservation.
Son of Chris Pahsetopah (Osage) and Lorraine (Cherokee). P/GF: Great
Hunter Pahsetopah, active in aiding his people to make peace with the
Whites and in preserving customs of the tribe. Brother of Loren Louis Pah-
setopah (*q.v.*).
MARRIED: Jean Bevenue (Yuchi-Creek), 1955. Three sons: Mike, 1958;
Russell, 1961; Jon, 1962.
  At the age of 14, the artist showed an interest in painting and drawing. He had
  already made his first dance costume. It was not until Acee Blue Eagle (*q.v.*)
  encouraged him to paint in the 1950's, that he worked seriously in art.
EDUCATION: Pawhuska (Okla.) High School, Chilocco; parochial schools in Okla.
SERVICE: WWII and Korean War.
CAREER: Painting contractor and interior decorator.
EXHIBITIONS: 1952–65: MNM, PAC, SN. *Three-man shows*: PAC..
AWARDS: PAC, 1963; several in high school shows.
COLLECTIONS: *Private*: Biggers, Boshell, I. Brown, Jean Brown, Chamberlin,
Collins, Koch, A. Kramer, K. McCormick, Orr, I. Peterson, Ryan, Schaefer,
Shaeber, Wolaver.
ADDRESS: 1400 East 34th St., Tulsa, Okla.

Painted Arrow (*see* Atencio, Tony)

Painted Robe (*see* Mopope, Stephen)

Pajoma, Peni   *Tesuque*
   Paintings by the artist are said to be dated as early as 1920.
   COLLECTIONS: *Public*: MNM.

Paladin, Dave   *Navaho* (?)
   COLLECTIONS: *Private*: Thoeny.

Palmenteer, Theodore   *Colville-Nez Percé*
   EDUCATION: Institute, 1962–63.
   WORK PUBLISHED: YAIA catalog, including cover.
   EXHIBITIONS: MNM, 1963; YAIA.
   ADDRESS: Nespelem, Wash.

Palmer, Dixon   *Kiowa*
   EXHIBITIONS: PAC, 1959.
   ADDRESS: Box 356, Anadarko, Okla.

Palmer, Ignatius   *Mescalero Apache*
   EXHIBITIONS: 1957–62: MNM, PAC, SN.
   AWARDS: SN, 1962.
   COLLECTIONS: *Public*: LMA/BC, MAI, MNM, UPA. *Private*: Denman.

Palmer, Woodrow Wilson   *Miami-Peoria*
Katahke, Loon
BORN: December 1, 1916, Miami, Okla. Son of Harvey T. Palmer (Spotted
Loon), Miami chief, 1910–63, and Ada Moore, second chief of the Peoria
tribe, 1930–51. P/GGF: Peshewa (or Richardville), a nephew of Little
Turtle, who defeated Gen. Washington, and Gen. St. Clair. P/GF: Chief
T. F. Richardville, who named the town of Miami, Okla., and secured land
from the Government for the purpose of founding Bacone College. M/GF:
Senator James K. Moore, charter member of Oklahoma's Legislature, 1907.
MARRIED: Theresa Goggles, 1940; divorced, 1947. Married Virginia Shoemaker, 1949. Two children: Harley Thomas, 1942; Eva Levina, 1944.
   Mr. Wilson is the inventor of "dualism," a modern painting style using Indian
   motifs. Its fundamental stages are a careful underpainting with wax and an
   overlay of the initial composition with a major theme. "The final step is the
   engraving or scoring of the overlay, causing a release of the 'inner light' and an
   orchestration of color over the entire work. For the most part the palette con-
   sists of the primary colors and black."
EDUCATION: Seneca, 1931; Haskell, 1932–33. Graduated Sherman, 1934.
Studied mural painting under Harold Ashodian, landscape painting under
Elton Furlong, and anatomy under Karnig Nalbandian, in Providence, R.I.
SERVICE: WWII, Korean War, U.S. Navy.
CAREER: Newspaper columnist and proofreader.
COMMISSIONS: *Murals*: Club El Rio, Baby Grande Lounge, Celebrity Club,
Jimmy's Place, home of Louis Monterio, all in Providence, R.I.
EXHIBITIONS: 1948–64: BNIAS, ITIC, MNM, PAC, SN; Contemporary
Artists of Rhode Island; Providence (R.I.) Art Club; Boston (Mass.) Arts
Festival.

COLLECTIONS: *Public*: GM. *Private*: T. Baker, Brennan, Buck, Colby, Dalgren, Hyam, Mellor, F. Miller, Rouse, Shoemaker, Yarborough.
ADDRESS: 1231 Janes Lane, Colorado Springs, Colo.

Panana, Gerald *Jémez*
EDUCATION: Jémez.
EXHIBITIONS: MNM, 1958–59.
AWARDS: MNM, two.

Panana, Sophie *Jémez*
BORN: 1945.
EDUCATION: Jémez.
EXHIBITIONS: PAC (student exhibit).
COLLECTIONS: *Public*: MNM.

Panana, Veronica *Jémez*
BORN: 1945.
EXHIBITIONS: MNM, PAC.

Pan Yo Pin (*see* Vigil, Thomas)

Pa O Kelo *Pueblo*
COLLECTIONS: *Public*: AF.

Paradis, Rena *Navaho*
BORN: 1945.
The artist has received no formal art education other than a one-year high school art class. She particularly enjoys painting children in non-traditional Indian style because "they don't hide their feelings." (See *The Navajo Times*, January 2, 1964, p. 9.).
EDUCATION: Graduated Roosevelt High School, Seattle, Wash., 1961.
CAREER: Co-owner of Las Canastas Shop; painter and ceramist.
ADDRESS: c/o Las Canastas Shop, Tucson, Ariz.

Parks *Delaware* (?)
COLLECTIONS: *Public*: PU/M (pencil and crayon drawings of the Bear Feast, 1930).

Parsons, Neil *Blackfoot*
Little Dog
BORN: March 2, 1938, Browning, Mont. Son of Henry T. Parsons and Florence DeGuire (Blackfoot). M/GGGF: Charles "Rondine" Mercier, a keelboat builder from France who came up the Missouri River to Old Fort Benton and married a Blackfoot woman.
MARRIED: Patricia Dell McCamish, February 16, 1963. Two children: Anthony Neil, 1963; Andrea Dell, 1964.
EDUCATION: Browning Elementary and High School, Browning, Mont.; graduated high school, 1956; B.S. (Art), Montana State College, Bozeman, 1961; M.A.A., Montana State University, Missoula, 1964.
SERVICE: U.S. Air Force, Air National Guard.
CAREER: Graphic artist, Boeing Aircraft Co., Seattle, Wash.; painting instructor, Institute of American Indian Arts, 1964–.
HONORS: Joseph Howard Kinsey Memorial Scholarship, 1963.

COMMISSIONS: *Murals*: MPI (thesis project).
WORK PUBLISHED: MNM; USDI exhibition catalogs; Seattle Art Museum, Seattle, Wash.
EXHIBITIONS: ASPS, DAM/I, IPSE, MNM, SAIEAIP, SAM, SIAC, SN, UW/G; represented in three sales galleries.
AWARDS: Inter-Mountain Printmakers Exhibition, Salt Lake City, Utah, Purchase Award, 1963.
COLLECTIONS: *Public*: BIA, IACB, SLAC. *Private*: New.
ADDRESS: 513 Salazar, Santa Fe, N.M.

Patkotak, Paul *Eskimo*
Patkotak, A Fan
BORN: November 24, 1892, Snowhouse, Utukok River, Alaska.
MARRIED: Wife deceased. Five children.

> Mr. Patkotak is a self-taught artist. In 1958, he said, "I do not draw any more. My eyes are getting dull." At one time in his career his work sold well at Point Barrow, Alaska.

CAREER: Once served as marshal of his village.
HONORS: Served on village council.
EXHIBITIONS: PAC; Alaska Native Service Office, Juneau, Alaska; Wainwright Day School, Wainwright, Alaska.
ADDRESS: Wainwright, Alaska.

Patterson, George W. Patrick (*see* Patterson, Pat)

Patterson, Pat *Apache-Seneca*
Kemoha, Lonesome Polecat
(Also known as Patterson, George W. Patrick.)
BORN: December 29, 1914, Centralia, Ill.
MARRIED: Patricia Cain, 1949. Three children: Bill, 1950; Patrick, 1951; Sally, 1953.

> Patterson's father was a "frustrated artist" who rebelled at long hours of practice and ran away to join a circus as a balloonjumper and wirewalker. Pat was born on the old Sells-Floto Circus circuit enroute to an Illinois engagement. Pat's father decided his son would be the artist he had not been and proceeded to expose him to every teacher available.

EDUCATION: B.F.A., Oklahoma, 1940.
CAREER: Director, Woolaroc Museum, Bartlesville, Okla., 1938–.
COMMISSIONS: *Murals*: St. John's Church, Bartlesville, Okla.
Portraits: More than 500.
WORK PUBLISHED: Ke Motta (1952).
ADDRESS: 912 Osage, Bartlesville, Okla.

Paukei, George *Kiowa*
Paukei, Gifts (or Donations)
BORN: 1918, Anadarko, Okla.
EDUCATION: Mountain View Public School, Mountain View, Okla.
CAREER: Electrician.
EXHIBITIONS: AIE, PAC.
AWARDS: AIE.
COLLECTIONS: *Public*: ACM.

Paytiamo, James P. *Acoma*
Flaming Arrow
"The author-illustrator has recorded many of the Pueblo folk tales for Columbia
University, later published in the *American Folk Lore Journal*. He is a well-
known entertainer who has traveled with his own Pueblo company under the
Swarthmore Chautauqua." *Indians of Today* (1947).
EDUCATION: Haskell.
CAREER: Instructor, School of Indian Wisdom (founded by Ernest Thompson
Seton); author and illustrator.
HONORS: Represented in *Indians of Today*.
WORK PUBLISHED: Paytiamo (1932).

Paz, Carol *Mescalero Apache*
BORN: 1948, Mescalero, N.M.
EDUCATION: St. Catherine's, *ca.* 1965.
EXHIBITIONS: PAC; SAIEAIP, 1965.
ADDRESS: Bent, N.M.

Pecos, José D. *Cochití*
EXHIBITIONS: AIEC, 1937.

Peina, Dan *Zuni*
EXHIBITIONS: FWG.

Peña, Christino *San Ildefonso*
Soqueen
BORN: November 24, *ca.* 1942, San Ildefonso Pueblo, N.M. Son of José
Encarnación Peña (*q.v.*).
EDUCATION: Pojoaque (N.M.) School, *ca.* 1957; Arizona, "Southwest Indian
Art Project," summers, 1960–61 (textile major).
COLLECTIONS: *Private*: R. Moore.
ADDRESS: Route 1, Box 318 A, Santa Fe, N.M.

Peña, José Encarnación *San Ildefonso*
Soukwawe, Frost On The Mountain
(Also known as Soqueen; Soqween.)
BORN: March 25, 1902, San Ildefonso Pueblo, N.M.
Mr. Peña is known to have signed his paintings in the following manner: *Soqueen*
and *Soqween*. He was painting in the early 1920's and still paints occasionally.
EDUCATION: Santa Fe.
WORK PUBLISHED: Alexander (1932).
EXHIBITIONS: AIM, DAM, JGS, MNM, PAC.
AWARDS: AIM, 1964; MNM, "Best example of original use of traditional
material," 1957.
COLLECTIONS: *Public*: CGFA, DAM (41 works), MAI, MNM.
ADDRESS: Route 1, Box 318 A, Santa Fe, N.M.

Peña, Tonita *San Ildefonso*
Quah Ah, White Coral Beads
BORN: June 13, 1895, San Ildefonso Pueblo, N.M. Died September, 1949.
Daughter of Ascención Vigil and Natividad Peña. Reared by her aunt,
Martina Vigil. Niece of Florention Montoya.

MARRIED: Juan Rosario Chávez, 1909; died *ca.* 1911. Married Phelipe Herrera, and later, Epitacio Aquerro, farmer, who served as governor of Cochití. Six children: Cecilia, Margaret, Sam, Victoria, Richard, and Joe Hilario Herrera (*q.v.*).

> Tonita began painting when she was seven years old. Surrounded by artistic relatives, such as Martina Vigil the potter, it is not surprising that by the age of 21, she was selling and exhibiting widely. She was the only woman painter in her generation and was one of the original group who participated in the contemporary watercolor movement. Oscar B. Jacobson referred to her as the "grand old lady of Pueblo art." Tonita often said that she preferred to paint children and animals. In 1934, Oren Arnold stated in the *Los Angeles Times*, "The canvases of Miss Peña and her associates [Awa Tsireh, Fred Kabotie, and Oqwa Pi *qq.v.*] depict figures which are not unlike the figures of Greek vase painters."

EDUCATION: San Ildefonso; St. Catherine's.

CAREER: Painter and housewife; art instructor, Santa Fe Indian School and Albuquerque Indian School.

HONORS: One of the artists who made copies of the Pajarito murals preparatory to the restoration work.

COMMISSIONS: *Murals*: James W. Young's Rancho La Cañada, *ca.* 1933; Society of Independent Artists, 1933; Chicago World's Fair; Santa Fe Indian School.

WORK PUBLISHED: Jacobson and D'Ucel (1950), La Farge (1960). *Introduction to American Indian Art* (1931), *The American Magazine of Art* (August 1932), *Theatre Arts Monthly* (August 1933), *School Arts Magazine* (September 1933), *St. Louis Post-Dispatch* (October 1, 1933), *Los Angeles Times, Sunday Magazine* (February 11, 1934), *Cincinnati Art Museum Bulletin* (January 1938).

EXHIBITIONS: AIEC, AIM, AIW, EITA, HM, ITIC, MNM, NGA, NMSF, OU/ET, PAC.

COLLECTIONS: *Public*: AMNH, CAM, CAMSL, CGA, CGFA, CIS, CU/LMA, DAM, DCC, GM, MAI, MKMcNAI, MNA/KHC, MRFM, OU/MA, PAC, PU/M, SM; La Fonda Hotel, Santa Fe, N.M. *Private*: Adlerblum, Dietrich, Dockstader, Elkus, A. Forbes, Hogue, H. Hoover, Lockett, D. Maxwell, Rockefeller, Thoeny, Woffard, Wyman.

Penrod, Michael   *Apache*
EDUCATION: Attended Arizona S. C./T.; scholarship to Arizona, "Southwest Indian Art Project," summer, 1962; scholarship to Rochester, 1962–64.
ADDRESS: Fort Apache, Ariz.

Pentewa, Dick R.   *Hopi*
Sitsgoma, Pumpkin Flower
(Also known as Pentewa, Richard S.)
BORN: April 12, 1927, New Oraibi, Ariz. Son of a Kachina carver.
EDUCATION: Hopi.
EXHIBITIONS: ASF, ITIC, MNA, PAC.
AWARDS: ASF, MNA.
COLLECTIONS: *Public*: GM. *Private*: Dockstader, D. Maxwell.
ADDRESS: (Richard S.), Box 145, Oraibi, Ariz.

Pentewa, Richard S. (*see* Pentewa, Dick R.)

Pen Yo Pin (*see* Vigil, Thomas)

People From The Green Valley (*see* Sakyesva, Harry)

Pepion, Dan   *Blackfoot*
EDUCATION: Institute, 1965–66.
EXHIBITIONS: YAIA.

Pepion, Victor   *Blackfoot*
Double Shields
BORN: March 10, 1907, Birch Creek, Mont., on the Blackfoot Reservation.
Died March 4, 1956, at Cut Bank, Mont. Son of John Pepion, pioneer resi-
dent of Birch Creek. Nephew of Lone Wolf, descendant of the last hereditary
chief of the Blackfoot.
MARRIED: Lucy Goes In Center.
  Pepion painted a style which bordered on the primitive. His untimely death by
  accident cut short a colorful career.
EDUCATION: Elementary schools at Birch Creek and Browning, Mont.;
Army Art School, Shrivenham, England, 1945; Oklahoma, 1945; New
Mexico U., 1946–47; art school in Los Angeles, Calif., one semester; private
instruction under Winold Reiss, two years. B.A. and M.A. degrees; M.A.
thesis: mural at Highland University, Las Vegas, Nev.
SERVICE: WWII, U.S. Air Corps, four years; European Theater (participated
in the invasion of France).
CAREER: Art instructor, Chilocco Indian School, 1951; art instructor,
Phoenix Indian School.
COMMISSIONS: *Murals*: MPI; Oglala Boarding School; Pine Ridge Indian
Agency, Pine Ridge, S. Dak.; Fort Sill Indian School. *Diorama*: MPI.
WORK PUBLISHED: Jacobson and D'Ucel (1950).
EXHIBITIONS: MPI, PAC, PAC/T.
AWARDS: PAC.
COLLECTIONS: *Public*: MPI, OU/MA, PAC.

Perry, Angela Lee   *Choctaw-Osage*
EXHIBITIONS: PAC, SN.
AWARDS: SN (student division), 1962.
COLLECTIONS: *Private*: Waterhouse.
ADDRESS: 613 Canyon Road, Apt. 4, Santa Fe, N.M.

Péshlakai, Fred   *Navaho*
COLLECTIONS: *Private*: Dockstader.

Pesva, Coma (*see* Lomayesva, Louis)

Pete, Andy   *Navaho*
COLLECTIONS: *Public*: MAI.

Pete   *Shoshoni*
  The chief's personal exploits are recorded in BAE, *4th AR*. He is known to have
  visited Washington, D.C., in 1880.
WORK PUBLISHED: BAE, *4th AR*.

Pete Three Legs   *Sioux*
  COLLECTIONS: *Public*: MAI (colored pencil drawing, "Sioux Grass Dance,
  1889, Fort Bennett, S. Dak.").

Peters, Johnston   *Pima*
  COLLECTIONS: *Public*: SM.

Pezi (*see* Grass, John)

Phillips, Dwight E.   *Choctaw*
  CAREER: Commercial art instructor, Oklahoma State University, School of
  Technology, 1951.
  EXHIBITIONS: 1949–51: DAM, PAC.
  COLLECTIONS: *Public*: PAC.

Phillips, Oliver   *Sioux*
  COLLECTIONS: *Public*: PAC.

Pilli, Donna   *Navaho*
  COLLECTIONS: *Public*: CU/LMA.

Pin, Pagna   *Tesuque*
  COLLECTIONS: *Public*: AU/ASM.

Pinayo Pin (*see* Vigil, Thomas)

Pincion, Peter   *Zuni*
  COLLECTIONS: *Public*: MAI.

Pine Tree Bird (*see* Montoya, Alfredo)

Piño, Barbara   *San Ildefonso*
  BORN: 1947, Santa Fe, N.M.
  EDUCATION: St. Catherine's, *ca.* 1965.
  EXHIBITIONS: MNM; PAC; SAIEAIP, 1965.
  ADDRESS: San Ildefonso Pueblo, N.M.

Piño, Juan Isidro   *Tesuque*
  (Also known as Piño, Juan Ysidro.)
    The artist died *ca.* 1953. In 1950, he was employed at Los Alamos, N.M., by
    which time he was no longer working in art. He was an accomplished, self-
    taught artist in the medium of woodblock prints.
  EXHIBITIONS: DAM.
  COLLECTIONS: *Public*: CU/LMA, DAM, MNM.

Piño, Kathy   ?
  EDUCATION: St. Catherine's, *ca.* 1965.
  EXHIBITIONS: PAC, 1965.
  ADDRESS: San Ildefonso Pueblo, N.M.

Piño, Lorenzo   *Tesuque*
  EDUCATION: Albuquerque, 1960–61.
  EXHIBITIONS: MNM.
  AWARDS: MNM, 1960.

Pinto, Dennis Paul   *Navaho*
  EDUCATION: Santa Fe, 1959; Albuquerque, 1950–63.
  EXHIBITIONS: 1959–63: ITIC (student division); MNM.
  AWARDS: MNM, 1959.
  COLLECTIONS: *Public*: MAI.

Pinto, Emily *Zuni*
COLLECTIONS: *Public*: MAI.

Platero, Lorenzo *Navaho*
EDUCATION: Albuquerque, 1959.
EXHIBITIONS: MNM, 1959.

Platero, Raymond *Navaho*
EDUCATION: Santa Fe, 1960.
EXHIBITIONS: MNM, 1960.
AWARDS: MNM, 1960.

Platero, Tom *Navaho*
EDUCATION: Albuquerque, 1958–59.
EXHIBITIONS: MNM, 1958–59.

Plenty Chief, Walter, Sr. *Arikara*
EXHIBITIONS: BNIAS.
COLLECTIONS: *Private*: M. Peterson.
ADDRESS: New Town, N. Dak.

Plenty Coups (Chief) *Nez Percé*
The artist was captured by the Crow Indians when a baby. He grew to manhood with the Crows and became wealthy. For him, painting was a practical tool— he owned a grocery store but, because he could not compute effectively, he kept books by drawing the names of buyers and purchases made. *See* Jacobson and D'Ucel (1950).

Plenty Scalps (*see* Iron Tail)

Pocano (*see* Martínez, Julián)

Polan Yi Katon *Kiowa-Apache*
Polan Yi Katon, Rabbit Shoulder
The artist is known to have executed and maintained a calendar which was said to have been buried with him.

Polelonema, Otis *Hopi*
Lomadamocvia, Springtime; *Polelonema*, Making Ball.
BORN: February 2, 1902, Shungopovi, Ariz. Son of Tawamenewa (Hopi) and Quiuysio (Hopi).
MARRIED: Jessie Salaftoche, 1925. Six children: Walter, 1932; Lawrence, 1934; Benjamin, 1937; Julia, 1939; Erma, 1941; Tyler (*q.v.*), 1944.
The artist believes his experience at Santa Fe Indian School and his contact with Mrs. Willis DeHuff have encouraged him most in the art field. He has painted since 1917 and was active for a time in the WPA Art Project.
EDUCATION: Santa Fe, 1914–20; Santa Fe High School, Santa Fe, N.M.
WORK PUBLISHED: Jacobson and D'Ucel (1950). *The American Magazine of Art* (August 1932), *Magazine Tulsa* (May 1948).
EXHIBITIONS: ACC, ASF, DAM, DMFA, EITA, ITIC, JGS, MNM, OU/ET, PAC, PAC/T, SAIEAIP, SFWF, SI, SN.
AWARDS: AIM, DAM, ITIC, MNA, MNM, PAC, SN.
COLLECTIONS: *Public*: AF, CGFA, DAM, GM, IACB, MAI, MKMcNAI, MNA/KHC, MNM, OU/MA, PAC, SM, SMNAI. *Private*: H. Adams, Denman, Dockstader, Elkus, C. Fenton, O. Jacobson, Lockett, Thoeny, Waters.
ADDRESS: Box 758, Second Mesa, Ariz.

Polelonema, Tyler   *Hopi*
Duvayestewa, Praying For All
BORN: January 24, 1940, Second Mesa, Ariz. Son of Otis Polelonema (*q.v.*)
(Hopi) and Jessie Salaftoche (Hopi).
MARRIED: April 19, 1965. One child: Jeffery, 1965.
EDUCATION: Second Mesa; Oraibi High School; graduated from Stewart.
CAREER: Kitchen helper, Fred Harvey Co., May, 1965.
EXHIBITIONS: SAIEAIP, 1965; Reno, Nev., 1962.
AWARDS: Three, Reno, Nev.; received Awards Day pin, Stewart Indian
School.
COLLECTIONS: *Public*: Hopi Arts and Crafts Guild Shop, Second Mesa, Ariz.
ADDRESS: Box 758, Second Mesa, Ariz.

Poleyestewa, E. D.   *Hopi*
COLLECTIONS: *Public*: AF.

Pollock, William   *Pawnee*
Tayloowayahwho
BORN: 1870. Died March 1899, Pawnee, Okla.
  Pollock was given his non-Indian name at the Agency school. At Haskell Insti-
  tute, he was an outstanding student, played in the band, and painted pictures
  on the wagons used by the Indians. At the age of 22, he received a Government
  land allotment, and, about six years later, just before his death by pneumonia,
  he signed a contract to join Buffalo Bill's Wild West Show.
EDUCATION: Pawnee (Okla.) Agency School, Haskell.
SERVICE: Spanish-American War, First Volunteer Cavalry. *See* Roosevelt
(1899).
CAREER: For a short time he was employed at the Pawnee Agency Office,
Pawnee, Okla.
HONORS: Pawnee Post, Veterans of Foreign Wars, was named for him.
EXHIBITIONS: SI.

Poodry, C. Earl   *Sauk-Fox* and *Seneca*
Quenipea, Fish In Water
BORN: 1915, Akron, N.Y. GF: Last chief of the Senecas.
  Mr. Poodry lived in eastern Oklahoma during his childhood. He is known for
  his paintings and his woodcarvings and cartoons.
EDUCATION: Elementary schools in Cushing and Muskogee, Okla.; Haskell;
Bacone College.
WORK PUBLISHED: Jacobson and D'Ucel (1950).
COLLECTIONS: *Public*: OU, PAC.

Poolheco, Sidney   *Hopi*
EDUCATION: Hopi.
EXHIBITIONS: PAC, 1959.

Pop Chalee   *Taos*
Pop Chalee, Blue Flower
(Also known as Luján, Merina, and Hopkins, Merina Luján.)
BORN: 1908, Castle Gate, Utah. Daughter of Joseph Luján (Taos) and an
East Indian woman.

MARRIED: Otis Hopkins. Edward Lee (*see* Natay, Ed). Two children: Jack, Betty Jean.

The artist long ago developed a unique style of painting which combines Oriental and Amerindian motifs. She has traveled extensively, exhibiting and selling her work. In November, 1936, *School Arts Magazine* published one of her many articles.

EDUCATION: Graduated Santa Fe; two years training to be an art instructor.

CAREER: Active in radio work in the 1950's.

COMMISSIONS: *Murals*: Nine in Albuquerque Airport Terminal Building, Albuquerque, N.M.

WORK PUBLISHED: Jacobson and D'Ucel (1950), Tanner (1957). *Arizona Highways* (February 1950).

EXHIBITIONS: 1937–58: AIEC, AIW, FWG, HM, ITIC, MNM, NGA, SAIEAIP, SM; Elliott O'Hara School, Biddeford, Me.; Russell Sage Foundation, Gallery of Living Artists, New York, N.Y.

AWARDS: ITIC Grand Award, 1938.

COLLECTIONS: *Public*: GM, MNA/KHC, MNM, SU. *Private*: Bennett, Denman, Dietrich, Lockett, Mullan, Thoeny, Woffard, Wyman.

ADDRESS: 424 Fifth Street, Manhattan Beach, Calif.

Pop Wea *Taos*

(Also known as Tanner, Lo Ree.)

EXHIBITIONS: ITIC, 1963.

COLLECTIONS: *Private*: Thoeny.

ADDRESS: Box 36, Newberry, Calif.

Po Qui (*see* Tafoya, Teofilo)

Poquin Tahn (*see* Trujillo, Ascensión)

Porter, Bob *Pima*

BORN: 1938.

EDUCATION: Scholarship to Arizona, "Southwest Indian Art Project," 1960.

ADDRESS: Phoenix, Ariz.

Poseyesva, Raymond *Hopi*

The artist is well-known for his paintings of Kachinas. Originally from Shungopovi, Ariz., he lived in Winslow, Ariz. at one time.

COLLECTIONS: *Public*: AF, MAI, MNM, SM. *Private*: Denman, Dockstader.

Po Tsunu (*see* Montoya, Gerónima Cruz)

Po Ye Gi ?

COLLECTIONS: *Public*: MNM.

Prairie Flower (*see* Darling, Marcell J.)

Preston, Bert *Hopi*

Tenakhongva, Standing Rainbow

BORN: December 6, 1930, Hotevilla, Ariz. Son of Lloyd Tenakhongva (Hopi), from Old Oraibi, Ariz.

MARRIED: A Navaho woman.

EDUCATION: Bacone College.

CAREER: Schoolteacher.

EXHIBITIONS: PAC, PAC/T, SN; Muskogee, Okla.
AWARDS: 1948–53: Six from PAC; Muskogee State Fair.
COLLECTIONS: *Public*: KM, PAC. *Private*: C. Wilson.

Preston, Daniel　　　　　　　　　　　　　　　　　　　*Papago*
COLLECTIONS: *Public*: SM.

Pretty Hawk (Chief)　　　　　　　　　　　　*Yanktonai Sioux*
　　Pretty Hawk's work at the Peabody Museum, executed about 1864, had been
　　used at one time as an inner hanging in a lodge.
WORK PUBLISHED: Alexander (1938).
COLLECTIONS: *Public*: HU/PM.

Pringle, Wilma Jane Reed　　　　　　　　　　*Choctaw-Chickasaw*
BORN: 1928, Wilberton, Okla. Daughter of George W. Reed (Choctaw-
Chickasaw) and Ida Blalack (Choctaw).
MARRIED: John David Pringle, 1964.
EDUCATION: Eufaula (Okla.) Boarding School, 1945; Haskell; St. Joseph's
Academy, Dallas, Tex., 1948; Los Angeles (Calif.) City College; Sculpture
under Jon Raymond, Topanga, Calif., 1966.
CAREER: Kelly Girl Service, and Aames Temporary Agency, Los Angeles,
Calif.
EXHIBITIONS: 1962–65: FAIEAIP, FANAIAE, ITIC, MCA, MNM, PAC,
SAIEAIP, WAA. *One-man shows*: Dallas Osteopathic Hospital, *ca.* 1962.
AWARDS: 1963–65: PAC; SN (poetry).
ADDRESS: 20316 Pacific Coast Highway, Malibu, Calif.

Pucunubbi (*see* Collins, Martha Adele)

Puerto, Leonard　　　　　　　　　　　　　　　　　　*Apache*
EXHIBITIONS: MNM (student division), 1961.
ADDRESS: Dulce, N.M.

Pulling Roots (*see* Houser, Allan)

Pumpkin Flower (*see* Pentewa, Dick R.)

Push, Charlie (*see* Pushetonequa, Charles)

Pushetonequa, Charles　　　　　　　　　　　　　　*Sauk-Fox*
Pushetonequa; *Wawabano Sata*, Dawn Walker; *Mesquakie*, Red Earth
People.
(Also known as Push, Charlie.)
BORN: 1915, Tama, Iowa.
MARRIED: Name unknown. Four children.
　　The artist lives on the Tama Indian Settlement. His paintings depict the life
　　and environment of the Sauk-Fox tribe and have been reproduced and widely
　　distributed by the Tama Indian Crafts organization.
EDUCATION: Pipestone, Minn.; Haskell; Santa Fe.
SERVICE: WWII, U.S. Air Force, three and one-half years; Pacific Theater.
EXHIBITIONS: 1946–59: PAC; Hawaiian Islands (during WWII); special
PAC show at the Association on American Indian Affairs, Inc., New York,
N.Y., 1963.
COLLECTIONS: *Public*: DAM, HSMC, PAC. *Private*: Rowland.

Pu Yo Pin (*see* Vigil, Thomas)

Qotskuyva, R.   *Hopi*
    COLLECTIONS: *Public*: AF; CU/LMA (signed Quatskuyva); MAI (signed
    Robert); SEMNAI (signed Ootskuyva). *Private*: Denman (signed Ralph);
    Dockstader (signed Qotskuyva).

Quah Ah (*see* Peña, Tonita)

Quamahongnewa, Redford   *Hopi*
    COLLECTIONS: *Public*: MAI.

Quameomah (*see* Harvier, Michael)

Quandelacy, Wilmer   *Zuni*
    EXHIBITIONS: MNM, 1965.
    ADDRESS: Zuni, N.M.

Quannie, Emerson T.   *Hopi*
    COLLECTIONS: *Public*: MKMcNAI. *Private*: Denman.

Quannie, Lorenzo H.   *Hopi*
    BORN: Date unknown; possibly from Oraibi, Ariz.
    COLLECTIONS: *Public*: MAI, MNA/KHC (signed Quannie), MNM (signed
    Quannie, 1934, Oraibi), SM (signed Quannig).

Quannig (*see* Quannie, Lorenzo H.)

Quatskuyva, R. (*see* Qotskuyva, R.)

Quenipea (*see* Poodry, C. Earl)

Qued (*see* Archuleta, Betty Keener)

Qued Koi (*see* Mopope, Stephen)

Quetone (*see* Quoetone, Jimmy)

Quetoque, Jefferson   *Zuni*
    EXHIBITIONS: A "Quetoque" exhibited at NGA, 1953.
    COLLECTIONS: *Public*: MNM.

Quetoque, Leo   *Zuni*
    EXHIBITIONS: A "Quetoque" exhibited at NGA, 1953.
    COLLECTIONS: *Public*: MNM.

Queyesva (*see* Honewytewa, Louis Calvin, Jr.)

Quick Thunder   *Sioux*
    COLLECTIONS: *Public*: MPM (pictographic style on paper).

Quin Cha Ke Cha   *Ute*
    COLLECTIONS: *Public*: MNM.

Quintana, Ben   *Cochiti*
    Ha A Tee
    BORN: *Ca.* 1923, Cochití Pueblo, N.M. Died November 9, 1944, in combat,
    WWII.
    EDUCATION: Santa Fe; Cochití. Received art instruction under Tonita Peña
    and Gerónima Montoya (*qq.v.*).
    SERVICE: WWII; Pacific Theater.
    HONORS: Won National Youth Forum art contest while a student at Santa
    Fe Indian School; awarded Silver Star posthumously for heroism under fire.

WORK PUBLISHED: Jacobson and D'Ucel (1950). *Arizona Highways* (August 1952). *American Scene*, GM (Vol. VI, No. 3).
COMMISSIONS: *Murals*: Cochití Day School; Santa Fe Indian School.
EXHIBITIONS: AIW, FWG, NGA, OU/ET, PAC, PAC/T.
AWARDS: At 15, won first prize over 80 contestants with a poster for the Coronado Quadricentennial Celebration; at 17, in competition with 50,000 entries, won $1000 prize in a poster contest sponsored by *American Magazine*.
COLLECTIONS: *Public*: GM, MAI, MNA/KHC, OU/MA, PAC, UPA. *Private*: Denman, Dietrich, Elkus, Hogue, O. Jacobson, D. Kramer.

Quintana, Joe A.   *Cochití*
EXHIBITIONS: AIW.
COLLECTIONS: *Public*: MNA/KHC. *Private*: Wyman.

Quintana, Johnnie   *Cochití*
EDUCATION: Santa Fe, *ca.* 1958.
EXHIBITIONS: MNM, 1958.

Quintana, Marcelino   *Cochití*
COLLECTIONS: *Public*: MNM.

Quintana, Trinidad   *Cochití*
BORN: *ca.* 1916.
COLLECTIONS: *Public*: MNM.

Qui Tone (*see* Quoetone, Jimmy)

Quiver, Dan   *Sioux*
COLLECTIONS: *Public*: MAI.

Quiver, Robert A.   *Sioux*
Wagacho, Cottonwood Tree
BORN: February 18, 1936, Hisle, S. Dak.
EDUCATION: Oglala Community High School, Pine Ridge, S. Dak.
SERVICE: WWII, U.S. Navy, 18 months.
EXHIBITIONS: In S. Dakota.
ADDRESS: Wanblee, S. Dak., and Pine Ridge, S. Dak.

Quiyavema (*see* Sunrise, Riley)

Quoetone, Jimmy   *Kiowa*
(Also known as Qui Tone; Quetone.)
BORN: Date unknown. Died *ca.* 1955, Okla. GF: Anzahte (Kicking Bird), Kiowa participant in the Cut Throat Massacre. Brother of Tah Bone Mah (Iseeo), a member of the U.S. Cavalry and Kiowa scout at Fort Sill, Okla.; also interpreter for James Mooney in the 1890's. Grandfather of Jimmy Quoetone (Kiowa) of Anadarko, Okla.

> Quoetone took the *Haw vahte* calendar from the latter's grave before it was covered and kept it up-to-date with the aid of Charles Emery Rowell (*q.v.*), a relative.

Quoyavema (*see* Sunrise, Riley)

Qussay Yah   *Comanche*
COLLECTIONS: *Public*: FSM (colored crayon on paper, *ca.* 1930).

Rabbit Shoulder (*see* Polan Yi Katon)

Racine, Albert Batiste   *Blackfoot*
Apowmuckcon, Running Weasel
BORN: April 19, 1907, Browning, Mont.
MARRIED: Inez Neet, *ca.* 1957. Three children: Albert T., 1931; Adrian W.,
1933; Frank W., 1947.
   The artist began painting in 1926, but in 1936 he turned to sculpture. During
   WWII he did no art work. In 1956 he began sculpting again and has not devoted
   much time since to painting. He has carved gavels for Presidents John F. Ken-
   nedy and Lyndon B. Johnson, and for Senator Robert Kennedy and Governor
   Edmund G. Brown.
EDUCATION: Graduated Browning (Mont.) Public High School, 1928;
Haskell, 1921–22. Studied under Winold Reiss, Edward Everett Hale, Jr.,
Adrian Voision, Carl Hutig, Sr., and John L. Clark.
SERVICE: WWII, U.S. Army, 1942–45.
CAREER: Commercial sign painter and woodcarver.
EXHIBITIONS: BNIAS; PAM (Northwest Invitational Exhibition); Fair-
mont Hotel, San Francisco, Calif.; Glacier National Park Hotel, Mont.;
Great Falls and Helena, Mont.
COLLECTIONS: *Public*: MPI; Methodist Mission, Browning, Mont. *Private*:
Art Anderson, Chambers, Duncan, Guthrie, Lang, McCord, Thurton.
ADDRESS: Box 502, Browning, Mont.

Rafael, Donald   *Navaho*
EDUCATION: Albuquerque, 1962–63.
EXHIBITIONS: MNM, 1963.

Rain God (*see* Roybal, José D.)

Rain God Town (*see* Sánchez, Ramos)

Rain In The Face   *Hunkpapa Sioux*
Iromagaja
BORN: *Ca.* 1825, "near the forks of the Cheyenne River." Died September 14,
1904, at Standing Rock Agency, N. Dak.
   Rain In The Face was in the Custer Battle of 1876. Work by the artist in the
   MAI is dated Standing Rock, Dakota Territory, 1885.
COLLECTIONS: *Public*: GM, MAI.

Rainbow Around The Sun (*see* Lomakema, Marshall)

Randall, Bunnie   *Creek*
Wiyo
BORN: 1923. Deceased.
EDUCATION: Oklahoma S. U./S. T. (commercial art major).
CAREER: Instructor, Graphic Office, Tinker Air Force Base, Oklahoma City.
COMMISSIONS: *Murals*: Tinker Air Force Base, with Albin Roy Jake (*q.v.*) and
LeRoy McAllister.
EXHIBITIONS: 1958–61: MNM, PAC.
AWARDS: PAC, 1958.

Rani, Bist   *Zuni*
COLLECTIONS: *Public*: PU/M.

Rave, Austin *Sioux*
BORN: 1946, Lantry, S. Dak.
EDUCATION: Institute, 1965–66.
WORK PUBLISHED: *Smoke Signals*, IACB (Autumn 1965).
EXHIBITIONS: SAIEAIP, YAIA.

Raw Hide Rattle (*see* Washakie)

Red Bird (*see* Hill, Joan)

Red Bird (Chief) *Cheyenne*
COLLECTIONS: *Public*: SPIM (a skin painting reputed to depict the war exploits of Chief Red Bird, which apparently was primarily painted by him, although several other hands may have been involved in the work; it is dated somewhere between 1865 and 1880).

Red Bird, Robert *Southern Plains*
BORN: Date unknown; reportedly "in his twenties" in 1965; reared in Gotebo, Okla.
MARRIED: Name not known. Two children.
CAREER: Mechanic.
COLLECTIONS: *Public*: Carnegie High School, Okla. *Private*: R. Moore.
ADDRESS: Dallas, Tex.

Red Buffalo (*see* Romero, Frankie)

Red Bull, Elmer *Sioux*
EXHIBITIONS: BNIAS.
ADDRESS: Box 577, Eagle Butte, S. Dak.

Red Cloud (*see* Oqwa Pi)

Red Cloud (*see* Silva, Marcus)

Red Cloud (Chief) *Cheyenne*
BORN: Winter of 1821–22, between the Dakota Black Hills and the Missouri River.
　Paintings on an MAI buffalo robe, dated 1871, represent a fight with the Shoshoni.
COLLECTIONS: *Public*: MAI.

Red Corn *Osage*
Hadaɔŭtse
(Also known as Bill Nix *and* Mathews, William P.)
BORN: Date unknown. In childhood, Red Corn was adopted by William P. Mathews.
WORK PUBLISHED: BAE, *4th AR*.

Red Corn, Raymond Wesley *Osage*
Mahse Nompah, Straight Reed
BORN: August 22, 1911, Pawhuska, Okla. Son of Raymond Red Corn (Osage) and Bertha Hudson (Cherokee). Nephew: Jim Lacy Redcorn (*q.v.*). P/GF: Wahinglainkah (Red Corn).
MARRIED: Waltema C. Myers, 1932. Two children: Wakon, 1934; R. W., 1955.
　The artist specializes in portraits and has done many through the years as gifts.

EDUCATION: Pawhuska (Okla.) High School, eleventh grade; Chillicothe (Mo.) Business College, 1934.

CAREER: General contractor; Baptist Minister, 1950–.

HONORS: First Osage to be ordained to the Ministry.

EXHIBITIONS: PAC, 1948; county fairs; Osage Museum, Pawhuska, Okla.

COLLECTIONS: *Public*: Osage Indian Agency, Pawhuska.

ADDRESS: Box 206, Pawhuska, Okla.

Red Crane   *Blackfoot*

WORK PUBLISHED: Grinnell (1896).

COLLECTIONS: *Public*: MAI (illustrations of the artist's coups; on the lining of a hide lodge, collected by George B. Grinnell, 1889).

Red Dog   *Sioux*

COLLECTIONS: *Public*: OAA/SI (record of the artist's exploits drawn in a sketch book).

Red Earth People (*see* Pushetonequa, Charles)

Red Elk, Herman   *Yanktonai Sioux*

Hehaka Wambdi, Eagle Elk

BORN: March 27, 1918, Fort Peck Reservation, Poplar, Mont. Son of Herman Red Elk, Sr. (Yanktonai), and Maggie Iron Cloud (Yanktonai). P/GF: Joseph Red Elk (Hehaka Duta), participant in the Battle of the Little Big Horn.

MARRIED: Alberta F. Kennedy (Sioux); divorced. Four children: Loretta, E. 1948; Valerie F., 1950; Eugene L., 1953; Herman A., 1954. Married Loretta Mae Cox (Assiniboin-Sioux); divorced. Two children: Marlon J., 1957; Kim L., 1958.

EDUCATION: Attended Poplar (Mont.) Public School, Chemawa (Oreg.) Indian School.

CAREER: General construction worker, Fort Peck Dam, Glasgow Air Base, Mont., Garrison Dam.

WORK PUBLISHED: *Smoke Signals*, IACB (Summer 1965).

EXHIBITIONS: PAC, SAIEAIP, SN; Black Hills Exposition, Rapid City, S. Dak., 1965.

AWARDS: 1965: Eight from Black Hills Exposition.

COLLECTIONS: *Public*: IACB.

ADDRESS: Box 571, Rapid City, S. Dak.

Red Feather (*see* Colbert, Frank Overton)

Red Fish (Chief)   *Oglala Sioux*

Hogan Luta, Red Fish

BORN: Date unknown; Fort Laramie. Prominent *ca.* 1840, but lost prestige following a defeat at the hands of the Crows in 1841. Lived at Cannon Ball, North Dakota, and was an old man in 1880, at Standing Rock Agency. Met with Father De Smet at Fort Pierre in 1841.

COLLECTIONS: *Public*: MAI (winter count), SHSND.

Red Hail   *Sioux*

COLLECTIONS: *Public*: MPM (pictographic style on paper).

Red Hawk   *Sioux*
Cetan Luta
WORK PUBLISHED: *Sioux Indian Drawings*, Milwaukee Public Museum
(1961).
COLLECTIONS: *Public*: MPM (pictographic style on paper).

Red Horn Bull Buffalo   *Oglala Sioux*
Tantaha Heluta
BORN: Date unknown; from Pine Ridge Agency, S. Dak. (*see* Black Heart).
Wounded in the Battle of Little Big Horn, 1876.
COLLECTIONS: *Public*: MAI (bull buffalo with red horn).

Red Horn Elk   *Oglala Sioux*
Kerakahi-to
BORN: Date unknown; from Pine Ridge Agency, S. Dak. (*see* Black Heart).
COLLECTIONS: *Public*: MAI (green elk with red antlers).

Red Horse (Chief)   *Miniconjou Sioux*
BORN: Date unknown; he was on the Yellowstone, below the mouth of the
Little Big Horn River, Wyo., 1865, on the Tongue River, Mont., 1876, and
went to Cheyenne River Agency, S. Dak. He surrendered his camp in 1877.
See Hyde (1961).
HONORS: Member, Miniconjou Tribal Council; chosen to act as a buffalo
scout from Cheyenne River Agency, *ca.* 1882.
WORK PUBLISHED: BAE, *10th AR*.
COLLECTIONS: *Public*: GM; OAA/SI (series of sign language accounts and
drawings of the Battle of Little Big Horn).

Red Living Bear   *Sioux*
Mato Myaluta
COLLECTIONS: *Public*: MPM (pictographic style on paper).

Red Moon (*see* Sandy, Percy Tsisete)

Red Robin   (?)
BORN: *ca.* 1918. Deceased.
The artist is known to have resided in Taos and Santa Fe, N.M., Denver, Colo.,
and New York City, his last known residence and where he was engaged as a
textile designer. Although claiming relationship with many tribes, his actual
tribal origin is unknown.
EXHIBITIONS: PAC, 1951.
AWARDS: PAC, 1951.
COLLECTIONS: *Public*: CHS/FG, DAM, GM, MNM, *Private*: Thoeny.

Red Star, Kevin   *Crow*
BORN: 1943, Montana.
EDUCATION: Institute, *ca.* 1965.
EXHIBITIONS: FAIEAIP, MNM, YAIA.
AWARDS: MNM, special award, 1965.
COLLECTIONS: *Public*: IACB. *Private*: Eders, McGrath.

Redcorn, Jim Lacy *Osage*
Walanke, No Sense
(Also known as Redcorn, James.)
BORN: May 9, 1938, Pawhuska, Okla. Nephew of Raymond Red Corn (*q.v.*).
MARRIED: Joby Henry, 1961. One child: Frank, 1962.
EDUCATION: Pawhuska Public Schools; Oklahoma, 1958–61; Arizona, "Southwest Indian Art Project," summers, 1961–62; Northeastern, 1963; graduated Oklahoma, 1965.
CAREER: Arizona schoolteacher, 1965–1968; University of Oklahoma, 1968–.
HONORS: Scholarships to attend the University of Oklahoma, the University of Arizona, and Northeastern State College; International Award for Design, from the Association of Interior Decorators and Designers, 1962.
COMMISSIONS: *Dust Jacket*: Willoya and Brown (1962).
EXHIBITIONS: 1961–65: ITIC, PAC, SN; State University of Iowa, Iowa City, Iowa; University of Oklahoma; University of Arizona; Pacific Art Conference, 1961, Seattle, Wash.; Association of Interior Decorators and Designers, 1962, Chicago, Ill. *One-man shows*: The Fort, Denver, Colo. *Three-man shows*: PAC.
AWARDS: ITIC, PAC.
COLLECTIONS: *Public*: AU/ASM, HM, OU/L. *Private*: Kallon.
ADDRESS: 215 S. Webster, Norman, Okla., 73069.

Riddles, Leonard *Comanche*
Black Moon
BORN: June 28, 1910, Walters, Okla. Son of a White man and a Comanche woman. M/GGF: Pahkuuh (Dried Robe), Comanche medicine man. His foster mother was Mrs. W. A. Williams.
MARRIED: Eva Mae Poitillo (Comanche) 1947. Three children: Carrie Joy, 1948; Sharon Lynn, 1949; Darney Gayle, 1955.
> Mr. Riddles states his major desire is to depict the Comanche people authentically and extensively. "My own set requirement is that my paintings meet the approval of my elder relatives and friends."

EDUCATION: Elementary schools in Indiahoma and Cache, Okla.; South Rose Valley High School, Okla.; graduated Fort Sill, 1941; mural instruction under Olaf Nordmark, Fort Sill.
SERVICE: WWII, U.S. Army, 34 months; Alaskan and European Theaters.
CAREER: Rancher, carpenter, and artist; active in farm programs and Indian affairs.
HONORS: High School Valedictorian; Comanche Council historian; Comanche representative to Kiowa-Comanche-Apache Business Committee.
COMMISSIONS: *Murals*: Fort Sill Indian School; Anadarko Indian School.
WORK PUBLISHED: Jacobson and D'Ucel (1950). *Museum News* (June 1962), *The Sunday Oklahoman, Orbit Magazine* (March 31, 1963).
EXHIBITIONS: AAIE, AIE, AIW, FAIEAIP, FANAIAE, ITIC, PAC, SN, SPIM, USDS; Lyman Allyn Museum, New London, Conn.; Lawton Chamber of Commerce, Okla.
AWARDS: AIE (Grand Award, 1964); BNIAS; ITIC; PAC; SN.

COLLECTIONS: *Public*: BIA, IACB, OU, PAC, SPIM. *Private*: Cone, Ekberg, Fitchoway, Frovis, Harmon, F. Harris, Libhart, R. Moore, Morrow, Reynolds, B. Terry, Walch, H. Walkingstick, Washburn, Wermy, Wilkins.
ADDRESS: Rural Route 1, Walters, Okla.

Riding Inn, M. *Pawnee*
(Also known as Inn, M. Riding, and Supernaw, Marlene Mary.)
BORN: March 5, 1933, Council Valley, Okla.
MARRIED: Charles A. Supernaw, 1952.
> The artist began painting *ca.* 1949 and credits Dick West (*q.v.*) as having most encouraged her.

EDUCATION: Bacone College; graduated Chilocco, 1949.
CAREER: Editor, *Talking Leaves* (Indian magazine published in Skiatook, Okla.); housewife and artist.
EXHIBITIONS: AIE, BNIAS, ITIC, MNM, MNM/T, PAC, PAC/T, SI.
AWARDS: AIE (Grand Award, 1963); MNM; PAC.
COLLECTIONS: *Public*: PAC. *Private*: C. Harris, Jefferson.
ADDRESS: 117 West Fourth Street, Skiatook, Okla.

Ridourt, Lucile *San Ildefonso*
COLLECTIONS: *Public*: MNM.

Riley, Victor *Laguna*
EDUCATION: Santa Fe, *ca.* 1958.
EXHIBITIONS: MNM, 1958.
AWARDS: MNM.

Ringo, Good ?
COLLECTIONS: *Public*: MRFM.

Ripley, David J. *Arikara-Blackfoot*
BORN: September 12, 1947, Emmet, N. Dak.
EDUCATION: Emmet (N. Dak.) High School, *ca.* 1963.
EXHIBITIONS: BNIAS; North Dakota State Fair, Minot, N. Dak.
COLLECTIONS: *Private*: Bullard, Hodges, Nykolayow.
ADDRESS: c/o Jackson Ripley, Emmet, N. Dak.

Road Runner (*see* Naranjo, Adolph)

Roan *Navaho*
EXHIBITIONS: MNM, 1957.
ADDRESS: c/o Pine Springs Trading Post, Houck, Ariz.

Roanhorse, Ralph (?) *Navaho*
> The Priests at St. Michaels Indian Mission taught the artist to read, write, and speak English. It was at Albuquerque Indian School that he had his first opportunity to draw and paint. *See* Roanhorse, (1931).

EDUCATION: Albuquerque; Otis *ca.* 1928–31.
SERVICE: WWI.
CAREER: In his youth, he was a mail-carrier (on horseback) on the reservation; after WWI, he returned to the reservation and wrangled horses, punched cattle, built hogans, painted, and sold pictures to tourists. While attending Otis Art Institute, he was a carpenter's helper and painted signs and trucks.
EXHIBITIONS: FWG.

Roaring Thunder (*see* Warrior, Antowine)

Roberts, F. (*see* Roberts, Frank)

Roberts, Frank   *Mohawk*
Young Deer
BORN: Date unknown. Originally from Caughnawaga, Québec, Canada,
he lived at one time in Brooklyn, N.Y.
COLLECTIONS: *Public*: MAI. *Private*: Stiles.

Robinson, John   *Haida*
Bear
BORN: Possibly in British Columbia, Canada.
COLLECTIONS: *Public*: MAI (pencil drawings of Haida designs, "Skidegate,
1892").

Robinson, Rose   *Hopi*
EXHIBITIONS: USDS, 1963.

Robson   *Haida*
COLLECTIONS: *Public*: MAI.
Rocky Mountain (*see* Vigil, Tim)

Rogers, Will Paul   *Cherokee*
BORN: December 28, 1927, Fort Gibson, Okla. Son of Charlotte Rogers
(Cherokee).
 Acee Blue Eagle (*q.v.*) once said, "Rogers is a young genius who has the right to
 call himself an artist." He paints infrequently.
EDUCATION: Bacone College.
EXHIBITIONS: 1946–50: PAC; Northeastern State College; Oklahoma State
University at Stillwater; Oklahoma State Fair, Muskogee, Okla.
AWARDS: PAC, 1947.
COLLECTIONS: *Public*: FCTM, GM, PAC. *Private*: M. Moore, B. Smith.
ADDRESS: Fort Gibson, Okla.

Roman Nose (Chief)   *Miniconjou Sioux*
Woohkinih
(Also known as Crow Nose.)
BORN: Date unknown. Half brother of Chief Red Cloud (Sioux).
CAREER: Warrior-artist (among hostiles on the Powder River and around
Whitestone Agency, S. Dak., *ca.* 1869–73).
HONORS: Chief of his own band.
COLLECTIONS: *Public*: OAA/SI (sketch book of drawings taken from the
artist at the time of his capture in 1866).

Roman Nose, Henry Caruthers   *Southern Cheyenne*
Who Whinny
BORN: June 30, 1865. Died, Okla., June 13, 1917. Son of Shot In Nose
(Cheyenne), also known as Naked Turkey, and Day Woman (Cheyenne).
His stepmother was Eating Bull (Cheyenne) and his half-brother was Little
Bird. GF: Limber Nose (Cheyenne). GM: Big Crow Woman (Cheyenne).

MARRIED: Red Paint Woman (Cheyenne), 1881. Their two children died in infancy. His second wife was Standing (Cheyenne). Two children: Amanda (White Bead), 1887; John (Head Bear), 1891. Standing's two children by previous marriage were Little Woman and Bob-tail.

> After being released from prison and attending schools in the East, the artist returned to Darlington Agency in 1881. He had adopted the "white man's ways," had a good knowledge of English, and was a trained tinsmith. He had taken his name, Henry Caruthers, from a good friend and patron, as did many Indians away at school. Adverse circumstances prevented his working steadily as a tinsmith, and eventually he reverted almost completely to "Indian ways." He was made a chief, *ca.* 1898. He executed his paintings and sketches while a prisoner at Fort Marion, St. Augustine, Fla., in 1875, and apparently did not paint after leaving prison.

EDUCATION: At Fort Marion, equivalent of third grade; Hampton, after his release; Carlisle, *ca.* 1879; returned Carlisle, 1883 (for "refresher" course in tinsmithing), four and one-half months.

CAREER: Employed at Darlington Agency sawmill, 1881; served twice as a scout for the command stationed at Fort Reno, Okla., 1882, 1886; policeman at Darlington Agency, 1884, 1887–88, and 1894; in 1890, for a short period, the artist was making tinware for the tribe, at $20 per month.

HONORS: Roman Nose State Park and Roman Nose Canyon, Okla., are named for him; he, William Cohoe (*q.v.*), and ten other Cheyennes went to Washington in 1899 as a delegation to see the President, to express their dissatisfaction with government treatment. (*See* Petersen, 1968).

COLLECTIONS: *Public*: MAI, YU/BRBML.

Romero, Cipriana   *Cochití*

EDUCATION: Santa Fe.

COLLECTIONS: *Private*: A. Forbes; El Rey Motor Court, Santa Fe, N.M.; Stone's Trading Post, Angostura, N.M.

ADDRESS: Cochití Pueblo, Bernalillo, N.M.

Romero, Frankie   *Taos*

Red Buffalo

> The artist received postgraduate instruction at the Institute of American Indian Arts, where he majored in painting. He also studied exhibition arts and assisted with the installation of displays in the school art gallery.

EDUCATION: Institute, postgraduate, 1963.

EXHIBITIONS: MNM, 1963; YAIA.

COLLECTIONS: *Public*: BIA. *Private*: McGrath.

Romero, Richard   *Pueblo (Tewa)*

BORN: 1949, Española, N.M.

EDUCATION: St. Catherine's, 1965.

EXHIBITIONS: MNM, PAC, SAIEAIP.

ADDRESS: Alcalde, N.M.

Romero, Santiago   *Cochití*

EXHIBITIONS: AIEC, 1937.

Rope, Vine   *Cheyenne*

COLLECTIONS: *Public*: MAI.

Rowell, Charles Emery *Kiowa*
Adol Beak Ka, Lays Near Hair
BORN: April 3, 1909, north of Old Meers, Okla. Son of James Frederick Rowell and Mabonia (or Maude) Narbonee (Kiowa). His mother was a member of the Sun Boy family. His father was a prominent physician, rancher, farmer, and political leader, who came to Okla. in 1897 and built the "little red store" on Medicine Creek. P/U: George Preso Rowell, who at 21 was the youngest attorney ever admitted to the Connecticut bar and U.S. Supreme Court. M/GU: Atotain (White Cowbird) participated in the Wagon Train Massacre, 1871. M/GU: Pai Tolyi (Sun Boy), Kiowa chief. M/GU: Jimmy Quoetone (*q.v.*). The Rowell genealogy has been traced to John Rowell, 1683.
> Since about 1944, the artist has been painting prolifically, executing in 1964 alone 59 watercolors and 27 oils. He assisted Jimmy Quoetone (*q.v.*) in recording Haw Vahte's calendar. He has continued the entries alone since Quoetone's death, and has recently completed a copy of the Anko Calendar.

SERVICE: WWII, U.S. Army, 18 months.
CAREER: Stonemason, carpenter, laborer; currently full-time artist.
EXHIBITIONS: PAC; regional fairs and sidewalk shows.
COLLECTIONS: *Public*: ACM, GM.
ADDRESS: Star Route L-7, Lawton, Okla.

Roybal, Alfonso (*see* Awa Tsireh)

Roybal, José D. *San Ildefonso*
Oquwa, Rain God
(Also known as Roybal, J. D.; Roybal, Dissy; Roybal, Disiderio.)
BORN: November 7, 1922, San Ildefonso Pueblo, N.M. Son of Juan Cruz Roybal (*q.v.*) and Tonita. P/U: Alfonso Roybal (*q.v.*).
MARRIED: Julia Dasheno, 1951. Two children: Gary Steven, 1952; Leon Thaddeus, 1960
> The artist's day school teacher, Helen Culley, was first to encourage him to paint in 1930. He began to paint more seriously *ca.* 1955.

EDUCATION: San Ildefonso, 1927–34; graduated St. Catherine's, 1942; Santa Fe Business College, 1959–60.
SERVICE: U.S. Army, four years; 100% disability discharge.
HONORS: Council member, San Ildefonso Pueblo.
EXHIBITIONS: AIM, MNM, SN, PAC.
AWARDS: AIM, 1942.
COLLECTIONS: *Public*: MAI, MNM. *Private*: Lantre, T. Martínez, Rena, Thoeny.
ADDRESS: Route 1, Box 306, Santa Fe, N.M.

Roybal, Juan Cruz *San Ildefonso*
MARRIED: Tonita. One son: José D. Roybal (*q.v.*).
COLLECTIONS: *Public*: MNM.

Roybal, Louis ?
WORK PUBLISHED: Alexander (1932).

Roybal, Seferino *San Ildefonso*
COLLECTIONS: *Public*: MNM.

Runner, O. B.   *Sioux*
COLLECTIONS: *Public*: MAI.

Running Antelope   *Hunkpapa Sioux*
The chief was at Grand River, Dakota Territory, in 1873. His exploits as a
warrior are recorded as early as 1853.
WORK PUBLISHED: Hamilton (1950). BAE, *4th* and *10th AR*.

Running Deer   *Sioux*
COLLECTIONS: *Public*: MPM (pictographic style on paper).

Running Weasel (*see* Racine, Albert Batiste)

Running Wolf (*see* Davis, Jessie Edwin, II)

Runs Over   *Oglala* (?) *Sioux*
Kahirpeya
BORN: Date unknown; from Pine Ridge Agency, S. Dak. (*see* Black Heart).
COLLECTIONS: *Public*: MAI.

Sah Quo Dle Quoie (*see* Turkey, Moses)

Sah Wa (*see* Vigil, Rufina)

St. Pierre, Rodger   *Chippewa* (?)
COLLECTIONS: *Public*: SHSND (pictographic style painting on canvas of a
buffalo hunt). Museum files indicate that St. Pierre was possibly a member
of the Turtle Mountain Band of the Chippewa of N. Dak.

Sakyesva, Harry   *Hopi*
Sakyesva, People From The Green Valley
BORN: 1921, Hotevilla, Ariz.
The artist is known not only as a painter, but also as a maker of Kachina dolls
and as a silversmith. He has had no formal art training.
EDUCATION: Hopi.
EXHIBITIONS: MNM, PAC; Guadalupe Gallery, Albuquerque, N.M.
COLLECTIONS: *Public*: MNA/KHC, PAC. *Private*: Elkus.
ADDRESS: 1550 East Indian School Road, Phoenix, Ariz.

Sakyewa, Henry   *Hopi*
It is possible that Henry Sakyewa and Harry Sakyesva (*q.v.*) are the same man,
for both last names are apparently variations of the phonetic spelling of *Saky-
estewa* (meaning, literally, the People From The Green Valley).
COLLECTIONS: *Public*: MNM.

Salas, Diego   *Zia*
BORN: 1948.
EDUCATION: Santa Fe.
EXHIBITIONS: FWG, MNA, MNM.
COLLECTIONS: *Public*: MNA/KHC, MNM, *Private*: Denman.
ADDRESS: Zia Pueblo, N.M.

Salo Whu (*see* Humetewa, James Russell, Jr.)

Salt, Freddie   *Navaho*
BORN: December 14, 1940.
EDUCATION: Santa Fe, 1960–61.
EXHIBITIONS: 1961–62: MNM, PAC.
COLLECTIONS: *Private*: Humphrey, Weinicke.
ADDRESS: Tsegi Trading Post, Tonalea, Ariz.

Sampson, William, Jr. *Creek*
BORN: September 27, 1933, Okmulgee, Okla. Son of William Sampson (Creek) and Mabel Lewis (Creek). P/GGF: George McKinley Hill, Creek chief.
MARRIED: Yannah Marshall; divorced, 1958. Married Dolores Dailey; divorced, 1962. Three children: Timothy James, 1956; Shirley Ann, 1961; William, III, 1962.
EDUCATION: Preston (Okla) High School; Haskell; Oklahoma S. T., 1949–50; Los Angeles Art Center School, Calif. 1950–51.
SERVICE: U.S. Navy, two years.
CAREER: Painter, sculptor, and rodeo performer.
COMMISSIONS: *Murals*: CCHM; Wagon Wheel Restaurant, Kansas City, Mo.; International Oil Exposition, Tulsa, Okla.
EXHIBITIONS: DMFA, PAC, USDI. Okla.: Fort Gibson Traders Show; Okmulgee Art Guild; Muskogee State Fair; McAlester Union Stock Yards. Downtown Art Gallery, Fort Worth, Tex. *One-man shows*: Downtown Art Gallery, Muskogee Country Club, Okla. *Two-man shows*: PAC.
AWARDS: Okmulgee Art Guild Annual, 1963, "most popular painting"; Tulsa State Fair.
COLLECTIONS: *Public*: CCHM, PAC; Ramsey Winch, Tulsa, Okla. *Private*: Askew, Bailey, Beaver, H. Carter, M. Chandler, Coleman, Crain, Crisler, Dailey, Downing, Factor, Fincher, Hillman, Holmes, Howe, Lasley, Leibensperger, R. Miller, Mishler, Peller, Shipley, Talley, H. Thorne, I. White, Wilf, I. Williams.
ADDRESS: Route 1, Box 293, Okmulgee, Okla.

Samuel *Sioux*
COLLECTIONS: *Public*: MAI (ledger sheet).

Samuel, Tony *Tesuque*
EDUCATION: Santa Fe, *ca.* 1958.
EXHIBITIONS: MNM, 1958.

Sánchez, Abel (*see* Oqwa Pi)

Sánchez, Arsenio *Pueblo*
COLLECTIONS: *Public*: RM.

Sánchez, Guadalupito *San Ildefonso*
EXHIBITIONS: FWG, 1943.

Sánchez, Laura *Pueblo (Tewa)*
BORN: 1951, Santa Fe, N.M.
EDUCATION: St. Catherine's, 1965.
EXHIBITIONS: PAC, 1965; SAIEAIP.
ADDRESS: San Ildefonso Pueblo, N.M.

Sánchez, Ramos *San Ildefonso*
Oqwa Owin, Kachina Town (or Rain God Town); *Kuofde*, Branded Corn.
BORN: March 17, 1926, San Ildefonso Pueblo, N.M. Son of Oqwa Pi (*q.v.*).
MARRIED: Marie Gertrude Montoya, 1949. Three children: Ann Elizabeth, 1941; Ronnie Patrick, 1957; Randy Paul, 1959.

The artist achieved his desire to see the world outside the pueblo culture when an opportunity to complete school in Pasadena was provided by Mr. and Mrs. Harry James.

EDUCATION: Santa Fe; graduated Pasadena Junior College, Pasadena, Calif., 1944.

SERVICE: WWII, U.S. Navy, two and one-half years; Pacific Theater.

CAREER: Carpenter's apprentice and painter, Los Alamos, N.M., 1946–47; bulldozer operator for past nine years, Zia Co., Los Alamos, N.M.

HONORS: Assisted in establishing the present pueblo government, 1957; served on Pueblo Council; appointed lieutenant governor of the pueblo, 1962; served as sheriff at the pueblo; Vice-chairman, Pojoaque (N.M.) Valley School Board, 1964.

EXHIBITIONS: ITIC, OU/ET; Philadelphia (Pa.) Art Alliance Exhibition of Contemporary Pueblo Indian Art, 1961.

COLLECTIONS: *Public*: MAI (41, postcard size), OU/MA, PU/M, SM. *Private*: C. Grant, H. James, Loo, McKing, Packer, Walton.

ADDRESS: Route 1, Box 315, Santa Fe. N.M.

Sand Burr (*see* Brave, Franklin P.)

Sand Generation (*see* Talahytewa, Gibson)

Sanderville, Richard   *Blackfoot*
(Also known as Chief Bull.)

BORN: *ca.* 1864. Died February, 1951. Reared in Browning, Mont., by a Quaker family. Son of Isodore Sandoval, Jr. (Blackfoot). P/GF: Isodore Sandoval, Sr., who traveled from Spain to join the American Fur Co. at Old Fort Union. He married a Blackfoot woman and became an interpreter for Prince Maximilian, 1833.

MARRIED: Kootena (Nancy Sheppard); deceased. Anna Alberton (Blackfoot), 1917. Four children: Noble, Robert, Agnes, and another daughter.

EDUCATION: Carlisle, 1890–93.

CAREER: Employed as a farmer "at the old agency;" official government interpreter, 1895–1932; assistant director of summer woodcraft school, Culver (Ind.) Military Academy, 1943.

HONORS: Wrote "entire genealogy of the families of the Blackfoot tribe;" assisted Gen. Hugh L. Scott for one year in recording Indian sign language.

COLLECTIONS: *Public*: OAA/SI.

Sandoval, Benny   *San Felipe*
EDUCATION: Albuquerque, *ca.* 1960.
EXHIBITIONS: MNM, 1960.
AWARDS: MNM, 1960.

Sandoval, Ronald   *Navaho*
BORN: June 4, 1947, Crownpoint, N.M.
EDUCATION: Gallup (N.M.) Public Schools.
EXHIBITIONS: NACG.
AWARDS: NACG, honorable mention.
ADDRESS: Jones Ranch School, Gallup, N.M.

Sandoval, Tony   *Navaho*
  EDUCATION: Institute, *ca.* 1965.
  EXHIBITIONS: YAIA.

Sandy, Percy Tsisete   *Zuni*
  Kai Sa, Red Moon
  (Also known as Tsisete, Percy Sandy.)
  BORN: 1918, Zuni Pueblo, N.M.
  MARRIED: Peggy Mirabal (Taos), 1940. One daughter and three sons.
    It was at Zuni Day School that the artist was told to paint, and he found he
    enjoyed it. However, he was 18 when his formal art instruction began at Albu-
    querque. "As an Indian artist, I hope to be instrumental in artistically and
    authentically depicting the customs of my people. This, I hope, will be my small
    contribution to a great race," said the artist in 1940. In 1959 he was severely
    injured in an accident and has periodically been unable to paint since then. When
    he can, he paints and exhibits extensively in the Southwest.
  EDUCATION: Zuni Pueblo Day School; Black Rock, N.M.; graduated Albu-
  querque, 1940; Santa Fe; Sherman Institute.
  COMMISSIONS: *Murals*: La Fonda Hotel, Taos, N.M.; Black Rock School
  and Black Rock Hospital, N.M.
  BOOKS ILLUSTRATED: Clark (1945).
  EXHIBITIONS: ITIC, JGS, MNM, NMSF, PAC, PAC/T, SN, USDS; Blue
  Door Gallery, Taos, N.M.; Paul Elder Gallery, San Francisco, Calif. *One-
  man shows*: Ebell Galleries, Los Angeles, Calif.
  COLLECTIONS: *Public*: AF, BIA, GM, IACB, KM, MAI, MNA/KHC, MNM,
  MRFM, OU/MA, PAC, SMNAI, UPA; Taos Inn. *Private*: Dockstader,
  Haddock, Lockett, D. Maxwell, Rena, Sewell, Thoeny.
  ADDRESS: Taos, N.M.

Sa Pa (*see* Abeyta, Emiliano)

Sapiel Selmo (Chief)   *Passamaquoddy*
  BORN: Date unknown; in 1887, lived at Pleasant Point, Maine. Son of Selmo
  Soctomah (corruption of St. Thomas), who commanded 600 Passamaquoddy
  Indians in the Revolutionary War. When a young man, Sapiel and his
  father had a temporary camp at Machias Lake, Maine.
  WORK PUBLISHED: BAE, *10th AR*.

Saryerwinnie, Houston   *Comanche*
  BORN: September 17, 1929, Apache, Okla.
  MARRIED: Betty Louise Molz, *ca.* 1953. Four children: Dennis Ray, 1954;
  James Lynn, 1956; Kathy Sue, 1958; Judy Ann, 1960.
    The artist began painting about 1953, encouraged by Mrs. Susie Peters and Ten-
    nyson Eckiwaudah (*q.v.*). Since leaving the reservation, about 1958, he has been
    active in Indian lore as a dance instructor and councilman for the Boy Scouts
    in Russell, Kansas.
  EDUCATION: Cyril (Okla.) Elementary School; Fort Sill; graduated Riverside
  Indian School; Kansas State University, extension course in art, 1960.
  SERVICE: Korean War, U.S. Navy, three years; China, Japan, Korea, Guam,
  Hawaii, Okinawa.
  CAREER: House painter and interior decorator, 1957–.

EXHIBITIONS: AIE, MNM, PAC; Downs, Kan.

AWARDS: AIE; Downs, Kan.

COLLECTIONS: *Public*: Museum of Cottonwood Falls, Kan. *Private*: Denman.

ADDRESS: 1454 North Lincoln, Russell, Kan.

Satanta   *Kiowa*

Satanta, White Bear

(Also known as Set T'ainte.)

BORN: Date unknown. Committed suicide in prison at Huntsville, Tex., October 11, 1878. Father of Tsalaute.

> In 1868, Satanta and Lone Wolf (*q.v.*) painted a robe which told of their battles with the Utes and Navahos.

CAREER: Chief, warrior, artist; raided the Utes on the upper Canadian River, 1858–59; led Wagon Train Massacre in Texas, 1871, and arrested for his raids there; took part in Battle of Adobe Walls, Texas, 1874.

HONORS: War chief; signed Little Arkansas Treaty, 1865; became known as "Orator of the Plains" after his speech at the signing of the Medicine Lodge Treaty, 1867.

Satsewa, Paul   *Laguna*

> While a student at the Albuquerque Indian School, the artist was chosen to execute a sketch based on Coronado's first night in the Zuni village. This sketch was used for publicity purposes by the Coronado Quadricentennial Commission of New Mexico.

EDUCATION: Albuquerque, 1938.

Saufkie, Morgan   *Hopi*

Nevamokewesa, Snow Carry

BORN: August 20, 1936, Shungopovi, Ariz.

EDUCATION: Hopi, *ca.* 1951–52.

EXHIBITIONS: PAC, 1956.

AWARDS: PAC, 1956.

COLLECTIONS: *Public*: LMA/BC.

ADDRESS: c/o Paul Saufkie, Shungopovi, Ariz.

Saul, C. Terry   *Choctaw-Chickasaw*

Tabaksi, Ember of Fire (or Coal)

(Also known as Saul, Chief T.; Saul, Chief Terry.)

BORN: April 2, 1921, Sardis (Bunchtown), Okla. Reared at Tuskahoma, Okla. Son of John B. Saul and Nona Anderson (Choctaw-Chickasaw). The artist's given name, not title, is Chief.

MARRIED: Anna Laura Petersen, 1940. Two children: William Terry, 1943; John Bendixen, 1949.

> About 1961, he began to perfect an oil-on-gesso technique using dentist tools to etch away the oil over-painting to form the picture. In 1964, he received his highest fee for an Indian *Madonna and Child* in this technique. In May 1963, Mr. Saul said, "Each painting should be a departure from the one before. You've got to keep improving and growing. An artist cannot afford to become stagnant."

EDUCATION: Jones Male Academy, Hartshorne, Okla.; graduated Bacone High School and College, 1940, with instruction under Acee Blue Eagle and Woodrow Wilson Crumbo (*qq.v.*); B.F.A., Oklahoma, 1948; M.F.A., Oklahoma, 1949; Art, 1951–52, with instruction under Piening and Baer.

SERVICE: WWII, U.S. Army, five years; European and African Theaters.
CAREER: Owner and operator, Village Arts Studio, Bartlesville, Okla., 1950;
technical illustrator and staff artist, Curtis-Wright Co., Garfield, N.J.,
1952–55; commercial artist, Phillips Petroleum Co., Bartlesville, 1955–.
HONORS: Life member, Art Students League.
COMMISSIONS: *Murals*: Union National Bank, Bartlesville, Okla. *Dust
Jacket*: Maloney (1955).
WORK PUBLISHED: Jacobson and D'Ucel (1950). *Art Digest* (August 1947),
Tulsa Magazine (May 1948), *The American Indian* (Spring 1952), Associa-
tion on American Indian Affairs, Inc.; Orbit Magazine, *The Sunday Okla-
homan* (March 10, 1963); *13th Annual Tulsa Pow Wow* (August 1964), cover;
Philnews (September 1964); *Indians of Oklahoma*, BIA (1966); *America
Illustrated*, USDS (No. 33).
EXHIBITIONS: BNIAS, DAM, FANAIAE, FNAIC, MNM, OU, PAC, PAC/T,
SI, SN, USDI; Addison Museum, Andover, Mass.; Art Association, Village
Arts Studio, and Fine Arts Studio and Gallery, Bartlesville, Okla.; Art
Students League; Syracuse Museum of Fine Arts; "The Eight Artists,"
YWCA, Bartlesville; Agra Gallery, Washington, D.C.; The Kermac Mural
Design Competition Exhibition, PAC, 1965. *One-man shows*: HM, PAC; No
Man's Land Museum, Goodwell, Okla.
AWARDS: AAID, DAM, FNAIC, GM, ITIC, PAC, SN.
COLLECTIONS: *Public*: BIA, DAM, GM, IACB, OU, OU/SM, PAC. *Private*:
Ambrister, Deighton, Holch, Mullan, Murphey, Syrier, Tucker.
ADDRESS: 1536 Maple Avenue, Bartlesville, Okla.

Saupity, Larry *Comanche*
BORN: 1924, Okla.
The artist had been drawing and painting since childhood. Injuries received at
St. Lô, France, forced him to withdraw from the School of Art at the University
of Oklahoma, where he had enrolled after WWII.

Saves Life, George ?
COLLECTIONS: *Public*: SIECC (hide painting, covering 1880–1920).

Saw Whu (*see* Humetewa, James Russell, Jr.)

Schildt, Gary Joseph *Blackfoot*
Netostimi, Lone Bull
BORN: June 5, 1938, Helena, Mont.
MARRIED: Arlene Joanne Lightfield, 1963. One child by a previous marriage:
Robin Lynn, 1959.
Mr. Schildt, painting since 1961, is a full-time, freelance artist who prefers por-
trait work.
EDUCATION: Browning (Mont.) High School; Missoula (Mont.) High School;
Haskell, 1958; A.A., Healds Business College, San Francisco, Calif., 1962;
San Francisco Academy of Fine Arts, 1962.
SERVICE: Montana National Guard.
CAREER: Artist.
HONORS: Scholarship, Academy of Fine Arts, San Francisco, Calif.

EXHIBITIONS: BNIAS, PAM; East Glacier (Mont.) Hotel; C. M. Russell Gallery, Great Falls, Mont.; East Glacier 1963 Western Art Show; Ace Powell Gallery, Hungry Horse, Mont.; Trailside Gallery, Jackson, Wyo.; Blackfoot Tribal Office, Browning, Mont.; First Savings and Loan, Kalispell, Mont.

COLLECTIONS: *Private*: Kalispell, D. Vance.

ADDRESS: Hot Springs, Mont., *and* c/o Box 43, Browning, Mont.

Scholder, Fritz   *Mission*

BORN: October 6, 1937, Breckenridge, Minn. Son of Fritz Scholder (Mission) and Ella Mae Haney.

MARRIED: Peggy. One son: Fritz, 1959.

> In 1959 the artist said, "...it is my intention not only to set up graphically a new visual experience for the viewer, but also to make a statement in regard to the society and land in which we, the descendants of the American Indian, live. I am well aware that my paintings are not literal, for to me some ideas require unique statements. I try to capture not only the physical, but the inner and even the spiritual." The artist, encouraged by Oscar Howe (*q.v.*) and Wayne Thiebaud, has been painting since 1950.

EDUCATION: Elementary school in Wahpeton, N. Dak.; high school in Pierre, S. Dak., and Shawano, Wisc.; graduated Ashland High School, 1956; Sacramento (Calif.) State College, A.A., 1958; B.A., 1960; M.F.A., Arizona, 1964; Wisconsin State University, 1956–57; Arizona, "Southwest Indian Art Project," summers, 1961–62.

CAREER: Assistant instructor, University of Arizona, 1962–64; instructor of design and advanced painting, Institute of American Indian Arts, 1964–.

HONORS: John Hay Whitney Opportunity Fellowship, 1962–63; represented in *Who's Who in American Art*, *Who's Who in The West*, *International Directory of Art*, and *Prize Winning Paintings*.

EXHIBITIONS: AU/ASM, BI, CPLH, DAM, DG, DMFA, FAIEAIP, FWAC, HMFA, KU, MNM, NDU, PAC, RAC, SAIEAIP, SDU, USDI, WRNGA, WU/S; Palacio de la Virreina, Barcelona, Spain. *One-man shows*: AU (Art Gallery); Barrios Gallery, Sacramento, Calif.; Hali's 261 Gallery, Tucson, Ariz.; E. B. Croker Art Gallery, Sacramento, Calif.

AWARDS: HMFA, MNM; 10th Southwest Painter's Annual, $500 Festival Award; Tucson Art Center, first award in oils; California Festival Exhibition, Sacramento, 1961; Ford Foundation Purchase Award, 1962; DMFA, 13th Annual Southwestern Drawing and Print Show, Purchase Award, 1963; West Virginia Centennial, 1st National Painting Award, 1963; 15th Mid-America Annual Exhibition, Nelson Gallery of Art, Kansas City, Mo., Hallmark Purchase Award, 1965.

COLLECTIONS: *Public*: BIA, DMFA, HMFA, WU/S; Hallmark Card Collection, Kansas City, Mo. *Private*: G. Clark, Hundley, Pitts, Suzuki.

ADDRESS: 841 El Caminito, Santa Fe, N.M.

Schultz, Hart Merriam   *Blackfoot*
Nitoh Mahkwii, Lone Wolf

BORN: February 18, 1882, on the Blackfoot Reservation, Mont. Son of the author James Willard Schultz, who married a Blackfoot woman. Died *ca.* 1965.

MARRIED: Naomi Tracy, 1917.

Until he left the reservation in 1904, the artist, a range rider, often amused his fellow cowboys with his sketches. Although he had painted since 1893, Mr. Schultz recalled especially the encouragement of the noted art criticand editor of the *Los Angeles Times*, Harry Carr, and that of Thomas Moran. He often sketched "for his father's books" and continued to sign his paintings and sculpture with a line drawing of a wolf's face. His work has been compared with that of Remington and Russell.

EDUCATION: Reservation schools; Fort Shaw Indian School, Fort Shaw, Mont.; Portland Public Schools, Portland, Oreg.; Los Angeles Art Students League, Los Angeles, Calif., 1910; Chicago, 1914–15.

CAREER: Commercial artist; full-time artist working in oil, watercolor, and bronze; maintained a studio in Tucson, Ariz.

COLLECTIONS: *Public*: AF, GM, NU, SFRR. *Private*: Coolidge, Heckscher, Herb. Hoover, Monroe, O'Brien, O. Wister.

Scott, Duard ?

EXHIBITIONS: PAC, 1960.

Scott, Johnson Lee *Creek-Seminole*
Itchez Ha Biye, Beaver

BORN: October 21, 1938, Sasakwa, Okla. Son of Peter Scott and Lena Wolf, a leader of the Ribbon Dance.

MARRIED: Billey Louis Tiger, 1959. Seven children: Gwendy, 1961; Saundra, 1963; Gordon Lee, 1964; (the following four are stepchildren), Sharon, 1957; Terry, 1958; Larry, 1959; Sevina, 1960.

EDUCATION: Oklahoma schools at Spaulding, Oklahoma City, Shawnee, and Holdenville, 1944–59; Oklahoma S. U./S. T.

CAREER: Painter and writer of short stories, poems, and song lyrics.

EXHIBITIONS: Roosevelt Junior High School, Seminole, Okla.; Wetumka (Okla.) Indian Museum.

COLLECTIONS: *Public*: OSU/TL; Wetumka (Okla.) Trading Post.

ADDRESS: 521 East Hickory St., Holdenville, Okla.

Seabourn, Bert D. *Cherokee*

BORN: July 9, 1931, Iraan, Tex. Son of James A. Seabourn (Cherokee) and F. Leeper Thompson.

MARRIED: Bonnie Jo Tompkins, July 30, 1950. Two children: Connie Jo, 1951; Angela Renae, 1954.

EDUCATION: McCamey (Tex.) Public School, 1937–42; Van Buren (Ark.) Public School, 1944: graduated Purcell (Okla.) High School, 1950; Oklahoma C. U., certificate of art, 1960; Famous Artists Correspondence Art School, currently enrolled.

SERVICE: Korean War, U.S. Navy, four years.

CAREER: Draftsman, and later established art department, publicity and advertising section, and continued as artist and director, Oklahoma Gas and Electric, Co., 1955–.

EXHIBITIONS: 1960–65: ITIC, PAC. Oklahoma City, Oklahoma Art Exhibition; Exhibition of Oklahoma Artists; All Oklahoma Exhibition; 6th

National Exhibition of Contemporary American Art; 7th Annual Eight State Exhibition of Painting and Sculpture. Kansas National Printmakers Exhibition, Wichita, Kans. 1st Annual Muskogee (Okla.) Art Show. *One-man shows*: First Presbyterian Gallery, Mangun, Okla.; Henson Gallery, Yukon, Okla.; McClain County National Bank, Purcell, Okla.; Exchange National Bank, Moore, Okla.; St. Paul's Episcopal Gallery, All Souls Gallery, and Mummers Theater, Oklahoma City, Okla.; Chandler (Okla.) Galleries. The Allis-Chalmers Company Show (tour), "The Art of Extra High Voltage."
AWARDS: 1960–65: Three from ITIC; Penn Square Art Show and Festival of the Arts, Oklahoma City, Okla., 1960.
COLLECTIONS: *Public*: OAC.
ADDRESS: 3123 Southwest 63rd, Oklahoma City, Okla.

Searching (*see* Weckeah)

Secatero, McCoy *Navaho*
EDUCATION: Albuquerque, 1958.
EXHIBITIONS: MNM, 1958.

Seekyesva *Hopi*
BORN: Date unknown; the artist was living and painting in 1930.
COLLECTIONS: *Public*: MAI.

See Ru (*see* Herrera, Joe Hilario)

Sekaho (*see* Shelton, Peter H., Jr.)

Servilican, Richard *Washo*
BORN: October 9, 1932, Carson City, Nev.
MARRIED: Florence Sarracino, *ca.* 1955. Three children: David R., *ca.* 1958; Bernice H., *ca.* 1960; Esther M., *ca.* 1962.
EDUCATION: Graduated Ganado (Ariz.) Mission High School, 1950; B.A., St. Joseph's, 1960.
SERVICE: U.S. Navy, 1950–55.
CAREER: Teacher in guidance work.
EXHIBITIONS: CSF, MNM, NMSF; St. Joseph's College.
AWARDS: MNM, 1965; ribbons at state fairs.
ADDRESS: Box 65, Paguate, N.M., *and* 351 Carol Drive, Reno, Nev.

Seton, Thomas *Eskimo*
Kahsahyuli
EXHIBITIONS: MNM, 1965.
AWARDS: MNM, 1965.
ADDRESS: Hooper Bay, Alaska.

Set T'ainte (*see* Satanta)

Sett'an *Kiowa*
Sett'an, Little Bear
BORN: Summer 1833.
MARRIED: In 1851. One daughter: Virginia, 1863.
Sett'an's calendar was inspired by, but not copied from, the Tohausen (*q.v.*) Calendar.

WORK PUBLISHED: Mayhall (1962). BAE, *17th AR* (a calendar which records the tribal history for the years 1833–93).

Shapanazhi (*see* Pahsetopah, Loren Louis)

Sharp Shooting (*see* Mofsie, Louis Billingsly)

Shave Head   *Cheyenne* or *Arapaho*
Chenenaete, Shave Head
> An Arapaho named Shave Head signed the Fort Wise Treaty in 1861. The artist was among the 72 Plains Indians taken as prisoners from Fort Sill, Okla., to Fort Marion, St. Augustine, Fla., in 1875.

COLLECTIONS: *Public*: YU/BRBML.

Shebola, Dixon   *Zuni*
EDUCATION: Santa Fe, a senior high student in 1955; Albuquerque, 1956.
COMMISSIONS: *Murals*: Barelos Community Center, with Charles Vicenti and James Michael Byrnes (*qq.v.*).
EXHIBITIONS: ITIC, NMSF.
AWARDS: ITIC, 1964.
COLLECTIONS: *Public*: MNM, PAC, SMNAI. *Private*: Elkus, Thoeny.
ADDRESS: Zuni Pueblo, N.M.

Shebola, Philbert   *Zuni*
EXHIBITIONS: AIAE/WSU.

Shebola, Sullivan   *Zuni*
EXHIBITIONS: PAC, SN.
AWARDS: SN, 1964.
COLLECTIONS: *Public*: MAI.

Shell (*see* Montoya, Gerónima Cruz)

Shelling Corn (*see* Humetewa, James Russell, Jr.)

Shelton, H.   *Hopi*
(Also known as Shelton, Henry.)
COLLECTIONS: *Public*: MAI. *Private*: Doyle (a Kachina doll by Henry).
ADDRESS: (Henry), Box 1389, Flagstaff, Ariz.

Shelton, Peter H., Jr.   *Hopi*
Sekaho, Yellow Arrow
BORN: Oraibi, Ariz. Son of Peter Shelton (Hopi) and Lillie Seumptewa (Hopi). Brother of H. Shelton (*q.v.*), well-known Kachina doll carver.
EDUCATION: Oraibi Day School, Oraibi, Ariz.; Santa Fe, four years; instruction under Fred Kabotie (*q.v.*).
CAREER: Freelance artist; designer, Hopi Enterprises, Oraibi, Ariz.
WORK PUBLISHED: *Modern American Indian Painting*, MPI (June–September 1963), cover; *Petroleum Today* (Winter 1965); *Region VI American Camping Association Convention Program* (February 17–20, 1965), Norman, Okla.
EXHIBITIONS: GM, ITIC, MNA, MNM, NMSF, PAC, PAC/T.
AWARDS: ITIC, NMSF.
COLLECTIONS: *Public*: GM, LMA/BC, MAI, MNM, PAC. *Private*: Denman, D. Maxwell.
ADDRESS: New Oraibi, Third Mesa, Ariz.

Shendo, Joe Ray   *Jémez*
BORN: 1948.
EDUCATION: Jémez, *ca.* 1962.
EXHIBITIONS: MNM, 1962; PAC, student show, 1957.
AWARDS: MNM, two, 1962.

Sheyka, P.   *Zuni* (?)
EXHIBITIONS: SN.
AWARDS: SN, 1964.

Shije, Marcus   *Zia*
COLLECTIONS: *Public*: MNM. *Private*: Dietrich.

Shinagi (*see* Yellow Blanket)

Shipshee, Louis   *Potawatomi*
Shipshee, Mountain Cougar
BORN: *Ca.* 1900, on the Potawatomi reservation in Oklahoma. Son of Ship-
shee (Kickapoo-Potawatomi?), who was given this name when young,
served in the Spanish-American War, and later became a U.S. Deputy
Marshal. M/GP: Lucian (Sioux-French), scout for U.S. Army, and his
Potawatomi wife. M/GGF: French explorer, Great Lakes area.
MARRIED: Bonnie. Two sons: Vernon; Louis, Jr.
  Mr. Shipshee is now a freelance artist who travels extensively throughout the
  Southwest painting in various media, often on velvet or buckskin. He does land-
  scape paintings and woodcarvings but prefers portrait work.
EDUCATION: Neadreau, Okla. (no longer exists), where he learned to speak
English; Haskell; Chilocco.
SERVICE: WWI.
CAREER: Industrial crafts instructor (conducted painting classes in free
time), Haskell Institute; house painter, interior decorator, freelance artist.
EXHIBITIONS: AAID, AIE, ITIC; Lawton, Okla., 1960; William J. Alexander
Gallery, Oklahoma City, Okla.
AWARDS: AAID, AIE, ITIC.
COLLECTIONS: *Public*: SMNAI; Biltmore Hotel, Oklahoma City, Okla.
Private: Dittemore.
ADDRESS: 1270 Lincoln, Topeka, Kan.

Shirley, Charles Keetsie   *Navaho*
(Also Shirley, Charles Kitsie.)
BORN: March 1909, in Ariz., on the Navaho Reservation in the vicinity of
Aspen Water Springs.
MARRIED: A Navaho woman. Several children.
EDUCATION: Reservation school until seventh grade; attended Haskell,
early 1920's; graduated Albuquerque, 1929; studied art at University of
Denver, Denver, Colo.; trained as a draftsman at Fort Defiance, Ariz.
CAREER: Head draftsman during WWII, Williams Field, Ariz.; continuing
in drafting profession.
COMMISSIONS: *Murals*: Arizona Title and Trust Company, Tucson, Ariz.
WORK PUBLISHED: *The Desert Magazine* (January 1948); *Arizona Highways*
(February 1950).

COLLECTIONS: *Public*: DAM. *Private*: Lockett.
ADDRESS: Shiprock, N.M.

Shirley, Walter *Navaho*
EDUCATION: Bacone College, *ca.* 1951; Northeastern.
EXHIBITIONS: 1951–53: PAC.
AWARDS: PAC, 1952.

Shobah Woonhon (*see* Toledo, José Rey)

Short Bull (Chief) *Oglala Sioux*
BORN: Date unknown, lived for a period on the Pine Ridge Reservation, S. Dak. Died July 6, 1923. Grandfather of Norman Shortbull (*q.v.*).
COLLECTIONS: *Public*: AMNH.

Shortbull, Norman *Oglala Sioux*
BORN: March 11, 1918, Wanblee, S. Dak. GF: Short Bull (*q.v.*).
MARRIED: Elizabeth G. Prue, 1945. Ten children: Thomas, 1946; Norma J., 1948; Linda A., 1950; Marilyn L., 1951; David W., 1953; Norman, Jr., 1955; Marietta, 1957; Timothy A., 1959; Vonny Jo Ann, 1961; Lisa, 1962.
The artist has been painting since 1951 and prefers portrait work. He has been strongly encouraged in his career by Angelo Di Bennedetto and Phil Steele.
EDUCATION: Art school, Denver, Colo.
SERVICE: U.S. Army, three years.
CAREER: House painter; conducts art classes during the winter.
EXHIBITIONS: BNIAS. Igloo, Rapid City, Spearfish, and Kadoka, S. Dak.; Vogue Theater, Denver, Colo.
AWARDS: Shows in: Rapid City and Igloo, S. Dak.; Denver, Colo.
COLLECTIONS: *Public*: St. Francis Museum, and Mother Butler Center, S. Dak. *Private*: Riggert, Sundet, Tiffany.
ADDRESS: Box 742, Igloo, S. Dak., *and* c/o Mrs. Alice Coffee, Harrington, S. Dak.

Shows The Feather *Sioux*
COLLECTIONS: *Public*: MPM (pictographic style on paper).

Shunka Ishnala (*see* Lone Dog)

Shunka Sapa (*see* Black Horse)

Shupela, Douglas *Hopi*
(Also known as Shupla, Douglas.)
BORN: August 22, 1932, First Mesa, Ariz., where he often painted the decorative motifs on his mother's pottery.
EDUCATION: Hopi.
CAREER: Employed by *Arizona Sun*, 1961.
EXHIBITIONS: PAC, 1948.
COLLECTIONS: *Public*: PAC.
ADDRESS: Polacca, Ariz.

Sikchida (*see* Yellow Feather)

Silva, Anthony *Laguna*
BORN: 1947, Albuquerque, N.M.
EDUCATION: St. Catherine's, *ca.* 1965.

EXHIBITIONS: MNM; PAC; SAIEAIP, 1965.
COLLECTIONS: *Private*: R. Moore.
ADDRESS: Old Laguna, N.M.

Silva, Marcus   *Santa Clara*
Red Cloud
BORN: 1921.
EDUCATION: Santa Fe.
EXHIBITIONS: 1948–63; FAIEAIP, MNM, SN.
ADDRESS: Box 14, Española, M.N.

Silver Horns (*see* Silverhorn)

Silverhorn   *Kiowa*
Haungooah (and *Haungoonpau*; *Hogoon*; *Hawgone*)
(Also known as Silver Horns.)
BORN: 1861. Died, *ca.* 1941. Descendant of Tohausen (*q.v.*).
   Silverhorn was one of a delegation of Kiowas taken to the Congress of the United
   States. While in Washington, he sketched what he saw. His work usually
   portrays religious ceremonies and tribal myths.
CAREER: Participated in last Kiowa outbreak, 1874; medicine man and
guard to a "grandmother medicine pouch;" soldier under Gen. Hugh L.
Scott, 1889–94.
WORK PUBLISHED: Alexander (1938), Mayhall (1962).
COLLECTIONS: *Public*: AMNH, CC, MKMcNAI, NL, OAA/SI.

Silverhorn, Arthur   *Kiowa*
COLLECTIONS: *Public*: GM.

Silverhorn, George   *Kiowa*
(Also known as Silverhorn, Dutch.)
EXHIBITIONS: PAC.
COLLECTIONS: *Public*: GM, MRFM. *Private*: Schonwald.
ADDRESS: Anadarko, Okla.

Silvermoon (*see* Martin, Mike)

Simbola, Irene   *Picurís*
BORN: August 25, 1942.
EDUCATION: Institute, 1962–63.
EXHIBITIONS: PAC, 1962.
ADDRESS: Box 26, Peñasco, N.M.

Simclosh (*see* Morgan, Judith Phillis)

Sine, David   *Apache*
BORN: Date unknown; originally from San Carlos, Ariz.
EXHIBITIONS: FWG, HM.

Singer, James   *Navaho-Santa Clara*
BORN: 1937.
EDUCATION: Arizona, "Southwest Indian Art Project," summer, 1960.
ADDRESS: Box 465, Española, N.M.

Sinte   *Sioux*

The Cronau album consists of 112 individual original drawings, by American Indians, commissioned and collected by an illustrator for a German periodical, Rudolf Cronau, at Standing Rock Agency, Pine Ridge Agency, Fort Randall, etc., 1880–83. In 1886, a number of these artists, including Sinte, were taken on a tour of Europe by Cronau, who was especially impressed by Sinte's uncanny ability to draw from memory. Among this artist's 19 drawings was an original map, of which Cronau said: "This map [was] made by Sinte in my presence from memory without the Indian having seen a cartographic representation in our concept. This sheet shows a tremendous testimony for the orthographic development of the man's mind." Other artists represented in the album are The Crow, Fast Deer, Yellow Blanket, and Black Horse (*qq.v.*).

COLLECTIONS: *Public*: AMNH (Cronau album).

Sinte Maze (*see* Iron Tail)

Sisneros, Marie   *Santa Clara*

EDUCATION: Haskell.

EXHIBITIONS: PAC, 1951.

Sitsgoma (*see* Pentewa, Dick R.)

Sitting Bear (*see* Whiteman, A.)

Sitting Buffalo Bull (*see* Sitting Bull)

Sitting Bull (Chief)   *Hunkpapa Sioux*

Tatanka Iyotanka, Sitting Buffalo Bull

BORN: *Ca.* 1834, near old Fort George or on Grand River, S. Dak. Died, December 15, 1890. Son of subchief Jumping Bull (and/or Sitting Bull). His uncles were Chiefs Four Horns and Hunting His Lodge.

MARRIED: Three wives, including She That Was Seen By The Nation and She That Had Four Robes. Nine children, including two sons—Black Bird and Crow Foot (who was killed during the same skirmish which took his father's life)—and a daughter, Standing Holy.

In 1870, a series of autobiographical drawings by Sitting Bull, admittedly stolen, were sold by a group of Yankton Sioux to an army officer at Fort Buford, Mont., for $ 1.50. The pictures were outlined in ink and shaded with colored chalk and colored pencils. In the corner of each was a buffalo bull on his haunches, the artist's "totem" or signature. This book of drawings, later sent to the Army Medical Museum Library, Washington, D.C., is now known as the Kimball Pictographic Record.

EDUCATION: Received art instruction from Rudolf Cronau (*see* Sinte).

CAREER: Chief, medicine man, Indian politician; sold autographs for $1.00 while on a four-month tour with Buffalo Bill's Wild West Show.

HONORS: Became chief, *ca.* 1868.

WORK PUBLISHED: Dunn, Jr. (1886), Kelly (1926), Vestal (1932), Smith (1943), Schmitt and Brown (1948), La Farge (1956; 1960), Ewers (1965). *Harpers Weekly* (1876); Stirling (1938); *American Heritage* (June 1964).

COLLECTIONS: *Public*: MAI, OAA/SI.

Sitting Crow   *Teton Sioux*

COLLECTIONS: MAI (pencil and color sketch, *ca.* 1880); MPM (pictographic style on paper).

Sitting Eagle (*see* Honewytewa, Louis Calvin, Jr.)

Sitting Eagle   *Miniconjou Sioux*
(Also known as Harry Hand.)
BORN: Date unknown; at one time was at Pine Ridge, S. Dak. (*see* Black
Heart) and on Rosebud River (*sic*) in 1867. His brother-in-law, Steamboat,
began a Miniconjou calendar and taught Sitting Eagle to interpret it. When
Steamboat died, Sitting Eagle took possession of this record.
COLLECTIONS: *Public*: MAI (autograph sketch).

Sitting Hawk   *Sioux*
Cetaniyatake (?)
COLLECTIONS: *Public*: MPM (pictographic style on paper).

Slim Curley Hair (*see* Mitchell, Stanley C.)

Slim Navaho (*see* Denetsosie, Hoke)

Slow Cloud (*see* Maulson, Gerald)

Smallcanyon, Evelyn   *Navaho?*
EDUCATION: Richfield High School, Utah, *ca.* 1964.
EXHIBITIONS: NACG.
AWARDS: NACG, 1964.

Smart, Clara Mary   *Eskimo*
Buniyuk, Little Daughter
BORN: January 16, 1841, Hooper Bay, Alaska. Daughter of Knute Smart,
Sr., and Irene Bunyan.
    Miss Smart has been painting since 1962 and has been encouraged by her in-
    structors to continue. She also writes poetry, another potential career.
EDUCATION: Hooper Bay (Alaska) School, 1958; St. Mary's High School,
1959; Mt. Edgecumbe High School, *ca.* 1961–62; Institute, 1962–.
EXHIBITIONS: MNM; Institute of American Indian Arts.
COLLECTIONS: *Public*: IAIA.
ADDRESS: 1286 South Bryant, Denver, Colo.

Smith, Ernest   *Seneca*
Gaon Yah, From The Middle Of The Sky
BORN: 1907, on the Tonawanda Reservation, N.Y. Son of Pete Smith
(Seneca). Brother of Kidd Smith, a gifted carver, and Rose Spring, an out-
standing beadwork artist.
    The Rochester *Democrat and Chronicle* (August 21, 1950) reviewed the artist's
    show at RMAS as follows: "...he has been painting since he was 10.... titles
    of his paintings indicate the wide range of daily life covered by legends and fairy
    tales of the Senecas. ...much of his work was produced under the Federal Indian
    Art Project...."
EDUCATION: Buffalo Public Schools, Buffalo, N.Y.
CAREER: Painter, sculptor; informant and illustrator for published works
by William N. Fenton. Employed for a short period by RMAS, in the
Temporary Emergency Relief Administration Project, 1930's; U.S. Gypsum
Mines, Oakfield, N.Y., 1950; Akron Parks Dept., Akron, N.Y., 1961.
WORK PUBLISHED: LaFarge (1960), Underhill (1965). BAE *Bull. 156*.
EXHIBITIONS: *One-man shows*: RMAS (100 watercolors).
COLLECTIONS: *Public*: RMAS (200 paintings, 24 sculptures); SI. *Private*:
W. Fenton.

Smith, Gibson R. *Apache-Navaho-Yuma*
EDUCATION: Arizona, "Southwest Indian Art Project," summers, 1961–62.
ADDRESS: General Delivery, McNary, Ariz.

Smith, Johnny *Eskimo*
Donvirak
EXHIBITIONS: MNM.
AWARDS: MNM, 1965.
ADDRESS: Bureau of Indian Affairs School, Hooper Bay, Alaska.

Smith, Patronella *Quechan*
EDUCATION: Santa Fe, 1960–61; Institute, 1962–63; Arizona, "Southwest Indian Art Project."
EXHIBITIONS: MNM, 1961.
ADDRESS: Box 401, Winterhaven, Calif.

Smoky, Lois *Kiowa*
Bougetah (and *Bougeta, Boudetah*), Of The Dawn
(Also known as Bougetah Smoky.)
BORN: 1907, near Anadarko, Okla. Daughter of Enoch Smoky. GU: Chief Appiatan (Kiowa).

Lois was one of the Five Kiowas (*q.v.*) who received special art training at the University of Oklahoma. It has long been customary among the Plains Indians that women not draw or paint in a representational style. Because of this feeling Lois fought some resentment on the part of the Kiowa group at the University. Although her family, renowned as warriors, became well-known as craftsmen, Lois's art career was brief. She married and devoted her full time to her husband and family.

EDUCATION: Oklahoma Indian schools; special non-credit instruction, Oklahoma, 1927.
WORK PUBLISHED: Jacobson (1929), Jacobson and D'Ucel (1950), Blue Eagle (1959).
HONORS: IACB Certificate of Appreciation, 1966.
EXHIBITIONS: AIE/T; throughout the U.S. with the Five Kiowa exhibits.
COLLECTIONS: *Public*: GM, MAI, MKMcNAI. *Private*: O. Jacobson, Schonwald.
ADDRESS: c/o Enoch Smoky, Virden, Okla. (?)

Snake (*see* Outie, George)

Snow (*see* Suina, Theodore)

Snow Carry (*see* Nuvayouma, Arlo)

Snow Carry (*see* Saufkie, Morgan)

Soaring Eagle *Cheyenne*
The artist was among the 72 Plains Indians taken as prisoners from Fort Sill, Okla., to Fort Marion, St. Augustine, Fla., in 1875.
COLLECTIONS: *Public*: YU/BRBML.

So Hah Ney (*see* Wilkinson, Douglas)

So Kuva (*see* Kewanyouma, Leroy)

Son Of Milk (*see* Begay, Apie)

Son Of The Star (*see* White Bear, Alton)

Son of The Towering House People (*see* Gorman, Carl Nelson)

Soo Woea (*see* Humetewa, James Russell, Jr.)

Soqueen (*see* Peña, Christino)

Soqween (*see* Peña, José Encarnación)

Soukwawe (*see* Peña, José Encarnación)

So Whay (*see* Ortiz, Joseph)

Speck, Henry (Chief)   *Kwakiutl*
(Also known as The Greatest; Ozistalis.)
BORN: August 12, 1908, Turnour Island, Canada.
MARRIED: Name unknown, 1927. Eleven children.
>   "My art talent was handed down to me from my mother's father. I just grew up
>   with it. When I was a little boy I used to copy everything from mail order
>   catalogue," said Speck in 1963. Chief Speck has turned from native tools to
>   paint and paper. His art forms are seldom used in traditional ceremonies but he
>   has recorded them honestly and prolifically.

EDUCATION: Fourth grade, Alert Bay, Canada.
HONORS: Chief of the Tlawitsis (Powerful People), a Kwakiutl group on
Turnour Island, Brit. Col., Canada.
WORK PUBLISHED: *Kwakiutl Art by Chief Henry Speck*, New Design Gallery,
Vancouver, B.C. (1964).
EXHIBITIONS: *One-man shows*: 1964: New Design Gallery.

Spencer, Jeri   *Yakima*
EDUCATION: Bacone College.
EXHIBITIONS: DAM; PAC, 1952.

Spencer, Marlene R.   ?
EXHIBITIONS: MNM, 1965.
ADDRESS: Cooper Hall 788, Fort Lewis College, Durango, Colo.

Splashing Water (*see* Kishketon, George)

Spotted Elk, Leo   *Sioux*
EXHIBITIONS: PAC, 1951.
COLLECTIONS: *Public*: SMNAI.
ADDRESS: St. Francis, So. Dakota.

Spotted Horse   *Oglala* (?) *Sioux*
Sunkklesha
BORN: Date unknown; from Pine Ridge Agency, S. Dak. (*see* Black Heart).
COLLECTIONS: *Public*: MAI (horse with spots).

Spotted Tail   *Crow*
COLLECTIONS: *Public*: MAI (personal exploits of several warriors, painted
on elkskin). *See* Wildschut, William (1926).

Springtime (*see* Polelonema, Otis)

Spybuck, Ernest   *Shawnee*
Mahthela
BORN: 1883, one mile west of Tecumseh, on the Potawatomi and Shawnee
Reservation, Okla. Son of John Spybuck and Peahchepeahso. Died, 1949,
on his Indian allotment land, 16 miles west of Shawnee, Okla.

Spybuck never studied art, but painted from the age of six. Harriet Patrick Gilstrap, his teacher at Shawnee, mentioned him in her memoirs and said that when he was eight, he did nothing but draw and paint pictures recounting events in his life. In 1937, it was noted that he had never been out of the county of his birth. He is buried in the family burial ground near his home.

EDUCATION: Shawnee Boarding School, Shawnee, Okla.; Sacred Heart Mission in south-central Okla.

COMMISSIONS: *Murals*: CCHM, OHSM. *Ethnographic series*: MAI.

WORK PUBLISHED: Harrington (1921), LaFarge (1956; 1960), Underhill (1965).

EXHIBITIONS: AIEC.

COLLECTIONS: *Public*: CCHM, GM, MAI, OHSM, OSAF/GC. *Private*: Marriott.

Squint Eyes *Cheyenne*

The artist was among the 72 Plains Indians taken as prisoners from Fort Sill, Okla., to Fort Marion, St. Augustine, Fla., in 1875.

COLLECTIONS: *Public*: YU/BRBML.

Standing, William *Assiniboin*

Fire Bear; Looks In The Clouds

BORN: July 27, 1904, near Oswego, Mont. Died, June 27, 1951, Fort Belknap (Mont.) Indian Reservation. Son of Stephen Standing (Standing Rattle) (Assiniboin). M/U: Lance, Sioux medicine lodge painter. Accounts concerning his mother and his wife are conflicting: one states that his mother was Fire Bear (Canadian Sioux), and another says that this was his wife's name. Through his paternal lineage, the artist's direct ancestor is Iron Arrow Point, Chief of the Stone Band during the Revolutionary War, and whose son, In-the-Light (Azan Zan Na) was the first Assiniboin ambassador from Fort Union to visit the capital, 1831–32.

"...in the White man's custom I am William Standing after the first name of my father. My father called me Looks In The Clouds. My own choice of names is Fire Bear: this was my grandmother's name...it makes no difference to me. If people want me to sign a name on pictures in White man's way and buy more pictures that is alright. But I'd rather be Fire Bear...I like to do what is called an independent artist and draw and paint what I see." After completing high school, the artist traveled extensively throughout the U.S. exhibiting his oils, watercolors, and sketches. He returned to the reservation where he married and remained until his death.

EDUCATION: Fort Peck Reservation schools, Mont.; Wolf Point Presbyterian Mission, Mont.; Haskell, 1920–24.

COMMISSIONS: Illustrations in the 1930's for the Federal Art Program in Montana.

BOOKS ILLUSTRATED: Kennedy (1961).

EXHIBITIONS: Washington (D.C.) Art Club, *ca.* 1932; Colonial Exposition, Paris, France, 1930's; WPA Art Center, Great Falls, Mont.; Trailside Galleries, Idaho Falls, Idaho (sold more than 1600 examples of his work in various media); Colorado; Oklahoma. *One-man shows*: MHS/H; Trailside Galleries, Idaho Falls, Idaho.

COLLECTIONS: *Public*: MHS/H; Hotel Sherman, Wolf Point, Mont.; Trading Post, Oswego, Mont. *Private*: J. W. Anderson, Flood, M. Kennedy.

Standing Alone (*see* Dick, Cecil)

Standing Bear (*see* Byrnes, James Michael)

Standing Bear (*see* Standingbear, George Eugene)

Standing Bear *Miniconjou Sioux*
BORN: December, 1868.
> A leader among the Sioux and ancestor of Arthur Douglas Amiotte (*q.v.*), Standing Bear was well known as an illustrator and storyteller.

WORK PUBLISHED: Neihardt (1932), Hamilton (1950).
COLLECTIONS: *Public*: AMNH (?); DAM (tipi, signed Standing Bear); MPM; St. Joseph Museum, St. Joseph, Mo.

Standing Bear, Andrew *Sioux*
BOOKS ILLUSTRATED: Clark (1942a).

Standing Buffalo *Ponca*
Totay Gonai, Standing Buffalo
WORK PUBLISHED: BAE, *Bull. 195* (copy of a drawing, by a young warrior, showing a battle between the Ponca and the Sioux).

Standing Chief, Robert *Cree*
EXHIBITIONS: BNIAS.
COLLECTIONS: *Private*: R. Henderson.
ADDRESS: Belcourt, N. Dak.

Standing Leaf ?
COLLECTIONS: *Public*: W/JSC.

Standing Rainbow (*see* Preston, Bert)

Standing-Soldier, Andrew *Sioux*
> The artist is married and has three children. He is well known among the Rosebud Sioux for reproducing and interpreting Sioux Winter Counts.

CAREER: Commercial sign painter.
COMMISSIONS: *Murals*: Valentine (Nebr.) Post Office and a local cafe.
BOOKS ILLUSTRATED: Clark (1942a; 1947).
WORK PUBLISHED: *Compton's Pictured Encyclopedia*, Vol. 7 (1957).
COLLECTIONS: *Public*: BIA/R, SIECC.
ADDRESS: c/o Bureau of Indian Affairs, Rosebud, S. Dak.

Standingbear, George Eugene *Osage-Sioux*
Zshingka Heka, Little Chief (Osage name); *Mahtohn Ahzshe*, Standing Bear (Sioux name).
BORN: October 31, 1929, Pawhuska, Okla. Son of Eugene George Standingbear (Sioux) and Mary Nora Lookout (Osage). The artist was given his Osage name by Chief Bacon Rind (Osage) when he became an official member of the Bear Clan. M/GM: Julia Ann Mongre. M/GF: Fred Lookout (*Wahtsake Tumpah*, He May Be Going On The Warpath And Others Are Looking Him Over), last hereditary chief of the Osage. M/GGGF: Nathaniel Pryor, a member of the Lewis and Clark Expedition and for whom the city of Pryor, Okla., was named. P/GGM: Sister of American Horse. P/GGF: Standing Bear (*Mahtohn Ahzshe*) (Sioux).
MARRIED: Barbara Wright, August, 1952. Four children: Geoffrey, 1953; Eugene Sean, 1955; Patrick Spencer, 1958; Margaret Mary, 1961.

EDUCATION: Elementary school, Immaculate Conception, Pawhuska, Okla., and Ponca Military Academy, Ponca City, Okla.; Oklahoma Military Academy, high school, Claremore, Okla.; graduated Pawhuska High School, 1947; B.A., Tulsa, 1952; graduate work, Tulsa, 1954–.

CAREER: Technical editor, Engineering Publications Department, Douglas Aircraft Co., Tulsa, 1952–64; fencing and art instructor, Benedictine Heights College, Tulsa, 1955–57; technical illustrator and instructor, University of Tulsa, 1963–; Engineering Publications Technical Analyst, North American Rockwell Corp., Tulsa, 1964–.

HONORS: Art director, Tulsa Philharmonic Cinderella Ball.

COMMISSIONS: *Murals*: Catholic Information Center, Tulsa.

WORK PUBLISHED: Tulsa Charity Horse Show, publicity director, designed brochure, posters, etc., 1964.

EXHIBITIONS: PAC; University of Tulsa. *One-man shows*: Benedictine Heights College, Tulsa.

AWARDS: 1964 Grand Award, Tulsa Fine Arts Festival.

COLLECTIONS: *Public*: Thayer (Mo.) High School, E. A. Meyer Associates, Caracas, Venezuela. *Private*: Lindstrom, Proctor, Rubin, Rucinski, B. C. Von Aspe, B. W. Von Aspe.

ADDRESS: 2403 East 25th Place, Tulsa, Okla.

Stands Brown (*see* Pahsetopah, Loren Louis)

Steatuma, Tony   *Santo Domingo*
COLLECTIONS: *Public*: SM.

Sterne, Mabel   *Zuni*
COLLECTIONS: *Public*: MNM.

Stevens, Jim   *Apache*
BORN: 1937, outside Globe, Ariz., near San Carlos Reservation.

MARRIED: Christine (Pima). Seven children.

> While in the fifth grade, the artist executed a painting, the face of a crowned and bleeding Christ, which is preserved at St. Peter's Mission in Bapchule Brophy Preparatory College, Phoenix, Ariz. To finance his education, the artist must maintain various jobs and has little time to paint. He hopes to devote full time to his art work when he is no longer able to farm his land.

EDUCATION: St. John's Indian Mission School, Komatke, Ariz., until junior year.

CAREER: Farmer.

COMMISSIONS: *Murals*: 20 murals in six Arizona missions.

ADDRESS: Ariz.

Stevens, Leroy   *Navaho*
EXHIBITIONS: USDS, 1963.
COLLECTIONS: *Public*: BIA, IACB, SMNAI.
ADDRESS: Crystal, via Fort Defiance, Ariz.

Stewart, Albert   *Navaho*
EDUCATION: Fort Sill.
EXHIBITIONS: PAC, 1955.
COLLECTIONS: *Private*: W. S. Price.

Stewart, Richard   *Paiute*
  BORN: 1944, Bishop, Calif.
  EDUCATION: Institute, 1964–66.
  EXHIBITIONS: SAIEAIP; MNM, 1965.

Stimone (*see* Herrera, Justino)

Sto Ko Wo (*see* Packer)

Stone Man   ?
  BORN: *ca.* 1864. From Fort Yates area.
  COLLECTIONS: *Public*: SHSND (pictographic painting executed in 1917).

Straight Reed (*see* Red Corn, Raymond Wesley)

Stratus Cloud (*see* Moquino, Ignacio)

Sturr, Jonathan   ?
  EXHIBITIONS: ITIC (juvenile class).
  AWARDS: ITIC, 1964.

Sua Peen (*see* Aguilar, José Vicente)

Suctwa Quinkum (*see* Ingram, Veronica Marie)

Suetopka, Elliot   *Hopi*
  EDUCATION: Eighth grade student in 1951.
  COLLECTIONS: *Public*: MNM.

Suhonva (*see* Honahniein, Ramson R.)

Suina, Herman   *Cochití*
  EDUCATION: Santa Fe.
  EXHIBITIONS: MNM, 1958.

Suina, Theodore   *Cochití*
  Kuperu, Snow
  BORN: February 26, 1918, Cochití Pueblo, N.M.
  MARRIED: Lucy Romero, 1953. Two adopted children: Evangeline Frances,
  1960; James Simon, 1962.
    While recovering from a broken neck, a result of an accident, the artist began
    to paint seriously. His teachers, Mary Mitchell at the Day School and Gerónima
    Montoya (*q.v.*) at the Santa Fe Indian School, encouraged him to continue. He
    has had less time to paint since becoming Governor of Cochití Pueblo.
  EDUCATION: Cochití; St. Catherine's; Hill; graduated Santa Fe, 1942; B.S.,
  St. Joseph's, 1953.
  SERVICE: WWII, U.S. Army, three years; Pacific Theater.
  CAREER: Draftsman, Los Alamos (N.M.) Atomic Laboratory.
  WORK PUBLISHED: Jacobson and D'Ucel (1950).
  EXHIBITIONS: DAM, FAIEAIP, ITIC, JGS, MNM, NMSF, OU/ET, PAC,
  PAC/T, SFWF, SN, UNM, USDS; Civic Center, San Francisco, Calif.;
  Villita Gallery, San Antonio, Tex.; Southern Illinois University, Carbondale.
  AWARDS: DAM, ITIC, MNM, NMSF, PAC, SN; Terry National Art Exhibi-
  tion, Miami, Fla., 1952.
  COLLECTIONS: *Public*: DAM, GM, IACB, MAI, MKMcNAI, MNA/KHC,
  MNM, MRFM, OU/MA, PAC, UPA. *Private*: Denman, Elkus, A. Forbes,
  Dockstader, Marriott, D. Maxwell, Thoeny, Yulke.
  ADDRESS: 1875 B 24th St., Los Alamos, N.M.

Summer Mountain (*see* Vigil, Thomas)

Sundust (*see* Dewey, Wilson)

Sunka Luzahan (*see* Swift Dog)

Sunka Wonka Wanjila (*see* Lone Horse)

Sunkklesha (*see* Spotted Horse)

Sun Flower (*see* Montoya, Sidney, Jr.)

Sun Rise (*see* Sunrise, Riley)

Sunrise (*see* Byrnes, James Michael)

Sunrise, Riley   *Hopi*
   Quoyavema (and *Quiyavema*)
   (Also known as Sun Rise.)
     While in the third grade at Anadarko, the artist submitted a series of Hopi
     symbols in a statewide newspaper contest and received second award. Adopted
     by a Kiowa family, his work seems to reflect the influence of Kiowa painting.
   EDUCATION: St. Patrick's.
   CAREER: Executed paintings for the permanent collection, MAI, 1930's;
   SM, for a short period; worked as an extra in Hollywood movies.
   BOOKS ILLUSTRATED: Nelson (1937).
   COLLECTIONS: *Public*: CIS, DAM, GM, MAI, MKMcNAI, SM. *Private*:
   Dockstader.

Supernaw, Marlene Mary (*see* Riding Inn, M.)

Susunkewa, Manfred   *Hopi*
   Susunkewa, Beautiful
   BORN: October 10, 1940, Second Mesa, Ariz.
   EDUCATION: Graduated Stewart (Ariz.) High School, 1959; Haskell, 1959–
   61; Santa Fe; graduated Institute, 1964; scholarship to Arizona, "South-
   west Indian Art Project," summers, 1960–62; currently on scholarship at
   Arizona, art major.
   SERVICE: ROTC Cadet, University of Arizona.
   CAREER: Was employed and encouraged in an art career by Charles Loloma
   (*q.v.*) and Lloyd New at their respective shops in Scottsdale, Ariz.
   ADDRESS: University of Arizona, Department of Art, Tucson, Ariz.

Su Ta (*see* Atencio, Tony)

The Swan   *Miniconjou Sioux*
   (Also known as The Little Swan; The Swanor.)
   BORN: Date unknown. At Cheyenne Agency, Dakota Territory, in 1872,
   when he recorded his calendar for Mallery.
     The Swan, a chief, kept a calendar record on a dressed skin of an antelope or
     deer, claiming it had been maintained in his family for 70 years. The calendar
     was called "History of the Miniconjou Dakotas," and represented the events of
     1800–71.
   WORK PUBLISHED: BAE, *4th AR*.
   COLLECTIONS: *Public*: OAA/SI.

The Swanor (*see* The Swan)

Swazo, Juan G.   *Tesuque*
BORN: Date unknown. Deceased.
EDUCATION: Santa Fe, *ca.* 1938.
EXHIBITIONS: AIEC, AIW.

Sweet Fruit (*see* Zotigh, Barbara Tallamonts)

Sweet Potato (*see* Anderson, Jimmy)

Sweezy, Carl   *Arapaho*
Wattan, Black
BORN: *Ca.* 1879, on old Cheyenne-Arapaho Reservation near Darlington,
Okla. Died, May 28, 1953, Lawton, Okla. During most of his adult life, he
spent the summer months at Washington Crossing, Okla. Son of Hinan Ba
Seth (Big Man), whose wife died when Carl was very young.
MARRIED: Hattie Powless (Oneida), who was employed as a matron at
Rainy Mountain School, Okla., when they met.

> The artist's older brother, while at the Mennonite school in Halstead, Kan.,
> took the name of Fieldie Sweezy (Sweezy being the name of the railway agent
> there). The other children of the family were given the same surname, and Wattan
> became Carl Sweezy. At 14, the artist returned from school to the reservation
> with a baseball, a hat, catcher's mitt, and a box of newly-acquired watercolor
> paints, which a White woman at the agency had taught him to use. His most
> prolific period came during and after he worked for James Mooney. To the end
> of his life he continued to paint in what he called "the Mooney way." His oils
> and watercolors, often unsigned, are excellent ethnographic examples.

EDUCATION: Mennonite Mission Schools in Darlington, Okla., and Halstead,
Kan.; Carlisle; Chilocco.
CAREER: Member of the Indian police who lived in their own tipis near
the agency's main street; at 14, returned to the reservation to test his
knowledge of farming; farmer and dairyman, Rainy Mountain School, St.
Patrick's Mission, and Concho, Okla.; informant, Oklahoma Historical
Society; recorder and informant at 20 for James Mooney, Smithsonian
Institution anthropologist; professional baseball player, two seasons, Enid,
Okla.; member, all-Indian baseball team on tour of U.S.; BIA, Rainy
Mountain School and other schools, more than 20 years; retired to paint
full-time in 1920.
WORK PUBLISHED: Jacobson and D'Ucel (1950). *Oklahoma State Health
Department, Annual Report* (July 1951), frontispiece.
EXHIBITIONS: AIE, AIW, ITIC, MPI, PAC, PAC/T; "Louis and Clark Ex-
position," Portland, Oreg. (work lent by SI); OU, Dept. Anthropology.
COLLECTIONS: *Public*: CMNH (not confirmed), GM, MAI, OHSM, OU/L,
OU/MA, OU/SM, PAC, SI (unsigned), SM. *Private*: O. Jacobson, R. Moore,
Neumann, Schonwald.

Swift Dog   *Hunkpapa Sioux*
Sunka Luzahan
BORN: 1845. Son of Running Fearlessly (Kagi Sniin Yanka), a Hunkpapa
chief, who received a medal from the U.S. Government while in Washington,
D.C. Swift Dog was a member of the Bad Bow Band (Sitting Bull's people).

MARRIED: Woman's Neck (Wita'hu).
WORK PUBLISHED: BAE, *Bull. 61* and *173* (a pictographic Winter Count representing the years 1797–98 to 1911–12), Praus (1962).

Tabaksi (*see* Saul, C. Terry)

Tafaga, Joseph *Santa Clara*
(Perhaps also known as Tafoya, Joseph.)
COLLECTIONS: *Private*: Mullan.
ADDRESS: Santa Clara Pueblo, N.M.

Tafoya, Camilio *Santa Clara*
COLLECTIONS: *Public*: WRNGA.

Tafoya, Francis *Pueblo*
BORN: 1947, Santa Fe, N.M.
EDUCATION: St. Catherine's, 1965.
EXHIBITIONS: PAC; SAIEAIP, 1965.
ADDRESS: Española, N.M.

Tafoya, Joseph (*see* Tafaga, Joseph)

Tafoya, Mary Agnes *Santa Clara*
COLLECTIONS: *Public*: SM.

Tafoya, Rosita *Santa Clara*
EXHIBITIONS: AIW.
COLLECTIONS: *Public*: MNM, OU/MA.

Tafoya, Teofilo *Santa Clara*
Po Qui
(Also known as Tafoya, Teo.)
BORN: May 15, 1915, Santa Clara Pueblo, N.M. Son of Cleto and Severa Tafoya.
MARRIED: Grace Paisano. His son is Charles Dale.
EDUCATION: Santa Fe, 1933–36; degree in art education, New Mexico U., 1941.
CAREER: Teacher: Phoenix Indian School; Oglala Community High School, Pine Ridge, S. Dak.; Jémez Day School; Albuquerque Indian School.
COMMISSIONS: *Murals*: Santa Fe Indian School; Santa Clara Day School; Julius Rosenwald Building, Chicago, Ill.; Maxwell Public School.
EXHIBITIONS: AIM, ITIC, MMA, MNM, NMSF, UNM.
AWARDS: AIM, ITIC, NMSF.
COLLECTIONS: *Public*: MAI, MKMcNAI.
ADDRESS: c/o Albuquerque Indian School, 362 Tyler Road, Albuquerque, N.M.

Tahalytewa, Stacy *Hopi*
EXHIBITIONS: FWG.

Tahcawin *Sioux*
Tahcawin, Fawn
(Also known as de Cinq-Mars, Tahcawin Rosebud Josephine Marie Louise.)
BORN: January 10, 1929, New York, N.Y. Daughter of Arthur Edmond de Cinq-Mars, actor and theatrical director in New York, and Rosebud Yellow

Robe (Sioux), lecturer on Sioux history and customs. M/GF: Chauncey Yellow Robe, hereditary Sioux chief. M/GGGU: Sitting Bull, *q.v.* (Sioux). MARRIED: Kenneth B. Moy, 1951; died 1956. One child, Karen Winona, 1951. EDUCATION: Graduated Bayside High School, N.Y., 1947; attended Naum Los School of Art, N.Y., 1947–48; Brooklyn Museum Art School, N.Y., 1948–49; Art, 1949–51. Studied photography under Maurice Lehv and ethnic dance under La Meri. CAREER: Painter, dancer, and photographer; assistant recreation director, Long Island (N.Y.) Park Commission, 1945–50; dancer, NBC/TV, 1950; style colorist, Cohn-Hall-Marx, N.Y., 1951; receptionist, Lightoliers, Ernest and Ernest, N.Y., 1956. HONORS: Chosen to represent the "First Americans" in the dedication ceremony of the American Common, New York World's Fair, 1939. EXHIBITIONS: WRNGA, PAC; Carlebach Gallery, N.Y. AWARDS: PAC. COLLECTIONS: *Public*: MAI, PAC. *Private*: Holway. ADDRESS: 50 Prospect Park, SW, Brooklyn, N.Y.

Taho, Mark   *Hopi*
EXHIBITIONS: FWG, 1951.

Taho, Wilbert   *Hopi*
BORN: Date unknown; from Oraibi, Ariz.
EXHIBITIONS: 1949–51: FWG, PAC.

Tahoma, Quincy   *Navaho*
Tahoma, Water Edge
BORN: 1921, near Tuba City, Ariz. Died, November, 1956, Santa Fe, N.M.
  While at Santa Fe Indian School, the artist developed his unique painting style.
  He was active in sports and set a district track record in 1940. After WWII, he
  established himself as a full-time artist and shared his studios in the Southwest
  with artists who are now well-established. Clara Lee Tanner rightly said he was
  "..one of the most dynamic, imaginative, and gifted of Southwest artists."
  During most of his life, he experienced misfortune, and died at the age of 35.
EDUCATION: Albuquerque, 1936–40; postgraduate work at Santa Fe.
SERVICE: WWII, U.S. Armed Forces; overseas.
CAREER: For a short period he worked in Hollywood movie studios; painter.
COMMISSIONS: *Murals*: Santa Fe Indian School. *Posters*: MNM, "Man Becomes an Artist," Laboratory of Anthropology Exhibition.
WORK PUBLISHED: Jacobson and D'Ucel (1950); La Farge (1957), Tanner (1957), Dockstader (1961). *Encyclopedia Britannica Junior*, 1946; *Arizona Highways* (February 1950; July 1956), *Indian Ceremonial Magazine*, ITIC, Gallup, N.M. (1957).
EXHIBITIONS: AIW, FWG, JGS, MNM, PAC, PAC/T, SFWF, UNM; Foundation of Western Art, Los Angeles, Calif., 1941; J. W. Young Galleries, Chicago, Ill.
AWARDS: ITIC, NMSF, PAC; two Grand Awards.
COLLECTIONS: *Public*: AF, CU/LMA, GM, KM, MAI, MNA/KHC, MNM, MRFM, OU, PAC, SM, UPA. *Private*: Dietrich, A. Forbes, Mullan, Thoeny, Vinson, Waters, Wyman.

Tail Feathers (*see* Feathers, Gerald T.)

Takilnok, Richard Davis   *Eskimo*
   BORN: February 25, 1927, Nunivak Island, Mekoryuk, Alaska.
   SERVICE: Alaska National Guard, two years; Mekoryuk, Alaska.
   EXHIBITIONS: MHDYMM, PAC,
   AWARDS: MHDYMM.
   COLLECTIONS: *Public*: MHDYMM.

Takotokasi (*see* Warrior, Antowine)

Takzi   *Apache*
   BORN: *Ca.* 1862. Lived in the area of Anadarko, Okla., 1884.
   COLLECTIONS: *Public*: OAA/SI.

Talahytewa, Gibson   *Hopi*
   Dewayesva, Sand Generation
   BORN: March 10, 1934, Moenkopi Village, Ariz.
   EDUCATION: Santa Fe, *ca.* 1954.
   EXHIBITIONS: AAID, MNM, NGA.
   AWARDS: MNM, 1951.
   COLLECTIONS: *Public*: MNM. *Private*: Dietrich.
   ADDRESS: Box 234, Tuba City, Ariz.

Talaswaima, Terry   *Hopi*
   (Also known as Talaswazma, Terry.)
   BORN: *Ca.* 1940, Second Mesa, Ariz.
   EDUCATION: Arizona, "Southwest Indian Art Project," summer, 1960.
   COLLECTIONS: *Public*: LMA/BC (signed Terence).

Talaswazma, Terry (*see* Talaswaima, Terry)

Taliwood, Richard   *Navaho*
   BORN: 1942.
   EDUCATION: Arizona, "Southwest Indian Art Project," summer, 1960.
   EXHIBITIONS: 1960–64: AIAE/WSU, ITIC, SN.
   AWARDS: 1960–65: ITIC, SN.
   ADDRESS: Box 672, Gallup, N.M.

Tall Elk (*see* Larvie, Calvin)

Tallas, Terrance   *Hopi*
   BORN: Shungopovi, Ariz.
   COLLECTIONS: *Public*: MNM.

Taller, Herman   *Hopi*
   BORN: *Ca.* 1939.
   COLLECTIONS: *Public*: MNM.

Tanner, Lo Ree (*see* Pop Wea)

Tantaha Heluta (*see* Red Horn Bull Buffalo)

Tanuga Shinga (*see* White, Clarence A.)

Tartsah, Jim   *Kiowa* (?)
   COLLECTIONS: *Private*: R. Moore.

Tasumke Witka   *Sioux*
   COLLECTIONS: *Public*: MPM (pictographic style on paper).

Tatanka Cante Sice (*see* Bad Heart Buffalo, Amos)

Tatanka Iyotanka (*see* Sitting Bull)

Tatankehanni (*see* Old Buffalo)

Taulbee, Dan   *Comanche*
  Loba Heit, Wolf Alone
  (Also known as Taulbee, Daniel J.)
  BORN: April 7, 1924, St. Ignatius, Mont.
  MARRIED: LaVerne Eva Hanson, 1946. Three children: Mallory, 1948;
  Mitchell, 1950; Janelle, 1953.
    The artist works in oil, watercolor, and ink. In 1963 he said, "I am a breed. I
    paint what I see and what I hear from the old people of many tribes. I'm usually
    known as a 'Montana Historical Indian Artist'—strictly a realist."
  EDUCATION: Elementary school at Polson and Charlo, Mont., 1930–38;
  graduated Polson High School, 1942.
  SERVICE: U.S. Army, two and one-half years.
  EXHIBITIONS: BNIAS, FAIEAIP, PAC; Great Falls (Mont.) National Bank;
  Williston National Bank, N. Dak.; Deer Lodge Bank and Trust (Mont.).
  One-man shows: 1959–65: nine, including HM; Burr Gallery, New York,
  N.Y.; Butte (Mont.) Junior League; Farnsworth Museum, Rockland, Me.;
  Peabody Museum, Salem, Mass.; Russell Gallery, Great Falls, Mont.;
  Statesville (N.C.) Museum. *Two-man shows*: PAC.
  AWARDS: Burr Gallery, N.Y., 1959.
  COLLECTIONS: *Public*: IACB, MAI. *Private*: Bott, Cochoran, Huntington,
  Stallman.
  ADDRESS: 22 East Center, Butte, Mont.

Tayloowayahwho (*see* Pollock, William)

Taylor, Virginia   *Cherokee*
  BORN: September 15, 1922, Los Angeles, Calif.
  EDUCATION: High school; Los Angeles Art Center School.
  CAREER: Commercial artist, Walt Disney Studios, and Buzza-Cardoza
  Greeting Card Co., in California; medical and scientific illustrator; office of
  publications staff artist, Oregon State University, ten years; department
  of art faculty, Oregon State University, two years.
  WORK PUBLISHED: *The West* (February 1966).
  EXHIBITIONS: *Ca.* 1964–66, in Oregon.
  ADDRESS: Oregon State University, Department of Art, Corvallis, Oreg.,
  and Route 4, Box 411, Albany, Oreg.

Te E (*see* Martinez, Crescencio)

Teeyacheena (*see* Medina, Rafael)

Tega, Charles   *Eskimo*
  BORN: April 10, 1942, Tanacross, Alaska.
  EDUCATION: Wrangell (Alaska) Institute, Mt. Edgecumbe (Alaska) High
  School, Institute, postgraduate student (major in painting and textile
  painting).
  EXHIBITIONS: FAIEAIP, MNM; Mt. Edgecumbe, Alaska; New York, N.Y.
  ADDRESS: Fairbanks, Alaska.

Telese, Gilbert   *Zuni*
  COLLECTIONS: *Public*: MNM.

Tenakhongva (*see* Preston, Bert)

Terasaz, Marian   *Comanche*
  Aukemah
  BORN: 1916. In 1950, the artist had a family and was no longer painting.
  EDUCATION: Bacone College, *ca.* 1938.
  WORK PUBLISHED: Jacobson and D'Ucel (1950).
  EXHIBITIONS: AIW.
  COLLECTIONS: *Public*: MAI.

Terrazas, Helen Hardin (*see* Hardin, Helen)

Tewaquaptewa   *Hopi*
  HONORS: Village chief, Oraibi, Ariz.; played a major role in the 1906 village
  split between the Hostile and Conservative factions.
  WORK PUBLISHED: Dockstader (1954).
  COLLECTIONS: *Private*: Dockstader.

Thayhaiya (*see* Darby, Raymond Lee)

They Have Gone Back (*see* Gritts, Franklin)

They Have Returned (*see* Gritts, Franklin)

Thomas, Clifford   *Tlingit*
  EDUCATION: Santa Fe.
  EXHIBITIONS: MNM, 1962.
  ADDRESS: Box 23, Haines, Alaska.

Thomas, Edson   *Onondaga*
  BORN: New York. Son of George Thomas, Chief of the Onondaga Iroquois.
  COLLECTIONS: *Public*: MAI.

Thomas, Evans S.   *Eskimo*
  EXHIBITIONS: PAC, 1956.

Thomas, Kenneth   *Paiute*
  EDUCATION: Santa Fe, 1960–61.
  EXHIBITIONS: MNM; PAC, 1961.
  AWARDS: MNM ("artist showing outstanding promise"), 1961.
  COLLECTIONS: *Private*: Maddy.

Thompson, Alex   ?
  EDUCATION: Ganado (Ariz.) Public School, *ca.* 1964.
  EXHIBITIONS: NACG.
  AWARDS: NACG, 1964.

Thompson, Robert   *Laguna*
  EXHIBITIONS: AIW.
  COLLECTIONS: *Public*: SM.

Thompson, Thomas   *Laguna*
  EXHIBITIONS: AIEC, AIW.

Thorn (*see* Brave, Franklin P.)

Thornton, Clinton Evan *Cherokee*
BORN: April 7, 1941, Rose, Okla. Son of C. R. Thornton.
MARRIED: Meredith Ann Swimmer (Cherokee), *ca.* 1960.
EDUCATION: Salina High School, Okla.; Northeastern A. & M., 1958–59; graduated Northeastern, 1962.
EXHIBITIONS: PAC; Springfield (Mo.) Art Center; Muskogee Annual Art Show, Northeastern State College.
AWARDS: Muskogee Annual Art Show.
COLLECTIONS: *Public*: BIA, IACB.
ADDRESS: c/o C. R. Thornton, Box 213, Jay, Okla.

Thun Povi (*see* Montoya, Sidney, Jr.)

Tia Na (*see* Toledo, José Rey)

Tichkematse *Cheyenne* (?)
The artist was among the 72 Plains Indians taken as prisoners from Fort Sill, Okla., to Fort Marion, St. Augustine, Fla., in 1875.
COLLECTIONS: *Public*: HI, OAA/SI.

Tiger, Jerome Richard *Creek-Seminole*
BORN: July 8, 1941, Tahlequah, Okla. Died, August 13, 1967. Son of John Tiger (Seminole) and Lucinda Lewis (Creek).
MARRIED: Peggy Lois Richmond, 1960. Two children: Dana Irene, 1961; Lisa Lou, 1965.
The artist first began to paint "Indian style" in 1962, and submitted his initial works to the Philbrook Indian Annual that year. Much credit for Tiger's recognition must be given Miss Nettie Wheeler of Muskogee, Okla., who has worked tirelessly in his behalf throughout the country.
EDUCATION: Public school in Eufaula, Okla.; Alice Robertson Junior High School and Central Senior High School, Muskogee, Okla., 1956–58; Eufaula High School, 1961; Cleveland (Ohio) Engineering Institute, 1963–64.
SERVICE: U.S. Naval Reserve, 1958–60.
CAREER: Full-time artist.
HONORS: Scholarship to Cleveland Engineering Institute.
COMMISSIONS: *Murals*: Calhoun's Department Store, Muskogee, Okla.
BOOKS ILLUSTRATED: Gibbons (n.d.).
WORK PUBLISHED: Anon. (1965). Smyth, Ed (1965).
EXHIBITIONS: AAID, FAIEAIP, ITIC, MNM, PAC, SN; Agra Gallery, Washington, D.C.; Presbyterian Convention, Ridgecrest, N.J.; Marymount College, Tarrytown, N.Y. *One-man shows*: PAC; the Public Library and Calhoun's Department Store, Muskogee, Okla.; Central National Bank, and Don Paul Cafeteria, Enid, Okla.; Fort Smith (Ark.) Art Center.
AWARDS: AAID (Grand Award, 1965); ITIC, MNM, PAC, SN.
COLLECTIONS: *Public*: BIA, MAI, PAC. *Private*: E. Adkins, Bartleson, Bass, Bellman, Bixby, Buddrus, Ju. Campbell, Carlson, Cocke, Curry, Dockstader, Edmondson, Elkins, Foreman, Gephardt, J. Griffin, J. Hall, Jacobs, A. Johnson, P. Johnson, Kirshner, Lacy, Leake, Luton, Magee, D. Mason, B. Oldham, Rice, Silberman, Slack, Smyth, J. Snodgrass, Swinchatt, Tarpley, W. Weber, N. Wheeler, M. White, Wyman.

Timeche, Bruce   *Hopi*

BORN: November 9, 1923, Shungopovi, Ariz.

Through Mrs. C. V. Whitney, the artist received a scholarship making formal art training possible for 30 months. He is a portrait artist, a carver of excellent Kachina dolls, and is equally adept in the execution of ethnographic Hopi paintings. He has been painting since about 1955.

EDUCATION: Graduated Kachina School of Art, Phoenix, Ariz., 1958.

CAREER: Employed at Bright Angel Curio Shop, Grand Canyon, Ariz.

HONORS: Scholarship, Kachina School of Art.

COMMISSIONS: *Murals*: Assisted his instructor with a mural at First National Bank, Phoenix, Ariz., and Desert Hills Motel, Phoenix, Ariz.

EXHIBITIONS: ASF, FAIEAIP, ITIC, MNA, MNM, PAC, SN; Maricopa County Fair, Mesa, Ariz.; Visitors Center, Grand Canyon, Ariz.; Artist-in-Particular, Town and Country, Phoenix, Ariz.; Waldorf-Astoria Scholarship Fund Exhibition, New York, N.Y.

AWARDS: 1955–65: ITIC, MNM, PAC, SN.

COLLECTIONS: *Public*: IACB, LMA/BC, MAI, MNA, SMNAI. *Private*: Denman, Frazier, Johnet, L. Stewart, Thoeny, Whitney.

ADDRESS: 2407 West Papago, Phoenix, Ariz.

Timeche, Harold   *Hopi*

BORN: June 23, 1924. Died, March 7, 1948.

For many years the artist's father was employed at Hopi House in Grand Canyon. A frail boy most of his life, Harold was in several tuberculosis sanitariums before he returned to his home in Shungopovi, Ariz. It was during this time that he did most of his paintings. Shortly after completing a painting for Philbrook's Indian Annual in 1948, the artist contracted flu and died.

EDUCATION: Hopi, 1941–43; Phoenix, 1938–41.

COLLECTIONS: *Public*: GM.

Tinzoni   *Shoshoni*

(Also known as No Heart.)

The artist was painting in the area of the Shoshoni Reservation, Wyo., in 1885.

WORK PUBLISHED: BAE, *Bull. 61*.

COLLECTIONS: *Public*: DAM.

Ti Ookeah Bahze (*see* Fireshaker, Franklin)

Toahty, Zachary   *Kiowa-Oto*

EDUCATION: Institute, 1965–66.

EXHIBITIONS: YAIA.

Todacheenie, Barry   *Navaho*

The artist prefers to execute landscapes and portraits in oils. He believes he has inherited his art ability from his mother, a fine weaver living near Leupp, Ariz.

EDUCATION: Graduated Oklahoma S. U./S. T., 1965.

CAREER: Before school in Okla., the artist worked for an outdoor advertising company in Ariz. engaged in the layout and painting of large billboards.

HONORS: Navaho Tribal Scholarship to attend Oklahoma State University.

Toddy, Jimmy (*see* Beatien Yazz)

Todea, Rocky *Navaho*
COMMISSIONS: *Murals*: The Navaho Tribal Museum, Window Rock, Ariz.
WORK PUBLISHED: BAE, *17th AR*.
COLLECTIONS: *Public*: OAA/SI.

Tohasan (*see* Tohausen)

Tohausen *Kiowa*
Tohausen, Top of the Mountain, Little Mountain, or Little Bluff (Also
known as *Tohasan*; *Dohasan*; *Doha*; *Dohate*; *Aanote*.)
BORN: *Ca.* 1835; was a member of the Kata or Arikara band. Died *ca.*
1866–68, in Okla. Father: Chief Old Tohausen (the spelling preferred by his
descendants).

> The chief was known to have made a Kiowa calendar on heavy manila wrapping
> paper using colored pencils. After his death, his nephew and namesake kept the
> calendar. Drawings by Haungooah (*q.v.*), represent Tohausen in the collection
> of the Marion Koogler McNay Art Institute.

HONORS: The fourth (and last) Kiowa head chief in tribal history, from
1833 until his death; prominent at the Medicine Lodge Treaty signing.

Toh Yah (*see* Nailor, Gerald)

Toledo, Jerome *Kiowa*
EDUCATION: Santa Fe.
EXHIBITIONS: MNM, 1958.

Toledo, José Rey *Jémez*
Shobah Woonhon, Morning Star; *Tia Na*, Northeast Place (used by his
father's people); *Aluh Hochi*, Lightning; *Mus Truwi*, literally, "a little
mountain creature with great power."
BORN: June 28, 1915, Jémez Pueblo, N.M. Son of Ortiz Toledo (Pecos-
Jémez) and Rufugia Moquino (Zuni-Hopi). His father was chief of the
Jémez Arrow Society, a warrior lodge, and the first Jémez Indian to own
a modern general store in Jémez Pueblo. M/GF: José Moquino (Hopi)
married at Zia Pueblo. M/GGF: A Zia scout for Kit Carson during the
Bosque Redondo period when the Navahos were taken to Fort Sumner.
MARRIED: Amelita Toya (Pecos-Jémez), 1938. Eight children: Adelina, 1938;
Allen, 1940; Stephen (deceased); Wilma, 1944; Mary, 1946; Michael, 1948;
Junie, 1950; James Ernest (Oglala), 1961 (foster child, descendant of Chief
Red Elk (Oglala).

> In his youth, the artist's observations of his cousin, Velino Shije Herrera (*q.v.*),
> painting stimulated his interest in art. His career has become well established.
> In 1965, after several years of little painting activity, the artist said, "I have
> not lost hope to again paint seriously."

EDUCATION: Santa Fe; graduated Albuquerque, 1935; B.A., New Mexico U.,
1951; M.A., Art Ed., New Mexico U., 1955; New Mexico, summer, 1955.
CAREER: Painted under WPA, 1940–41; arts and crafts instructor, Santa Fe
Indian School, 1949–56; art instructor, Albuquerque Indian School, 1956–
57; U.S. Public Health Service, Department of Indian Health, 1947; in
1959, transferred from New Mexico to Aberdeen, S. Dak. area as Health
Education Specialist; Education Specialist (Community Health), Laguna
Service Unit, Laguna, N.M., 1964–.

COMMISSIONS: *Murals*: The Bernalillo (N.M.) Mercantile Co., Albuquerque Indian School; Seligman Indian Store, Albuquerque, N.M.

HONORS: One-year grant to University of New Mexico.

WORK PUBLISHED: Jacobson and D'Ucel (1950). *Arizona Highways* (February 1950); "Pine Tree Ceremonial Dance," postal card of the last authentic Pine Tree Ceremonial Dance performed by the Jémez Indians, painted by the artist at the dance and printed by OU/MA.

EXHIBITIONS: AIE, AIEC, DAM, HM, ITIC, MNM, NGA, NMSF, OU/ET, PAC, PAC/T, UNM.

AWARDS: 1947–56: ITIC, MNM, NMSF, PAC.

COLLECTIONS: *Public*: GM, MAI, MNM, OU/MA, OU/SM, PAC, SM. *Private*: K. Adams, Denman, Dietrich, A. Forbes, Schroeder, Woodward.

ADDRESS: Box 186, Laguna, N.M.

Toledo, Mike *Jémez*

EXHIBITIONS: FWG, 1943.

Tom, Herbert. Jr. *Navaho*

BORN: July 15, 1928, Klagetoh, Ariz.

EDUCATION: Fort Wingate (N.M.) Vocational High School, *ca.* 1948; graduated Santa Fe.

EXHIBITIONS: FWG, 1951.

COLLECTIONS: *Public*: MNM.

ADDRESS: Klagetoh Trading Post, Ganado, Ariz.

Tomahawk, A. E. (*see* Edaakie, Anthony P.)

Tomo ?

COLLECTIONS: *Public*: MNM.

Tomossee, T. *Hopi*

COLLECTIONS: *Public*: MAI (46 paintings of Kachinas).

Tonepahhote, Billy *Kiowa*

EXHIBITIONS: PAC, 1958.

ADDRESS: c/o Ruth Cox, Box 89, Anadarko, Okla.

To'oan *Kiowa*

BORN: Date unknown. He lived in the area of Fort Sill, Okla., *ca.* 1886.

CAREER: Warrior and artist.

COLLECTIONS: *Public*: MAI (ledger).

Top Of The Mountain (*see* Tohausen)

T'o Pove (*see* Atencio, Lorencita)

Toppah, Herman *Comanche-Kiowa-Apache*

Al Qua Kou, Yellow Hair

BORN: August 17, 1923, Carnegie, Okla.

MARRIED: Pauline Kaubin (Kiowa) 1952. Three children: Byron, 1953; Jerry, 1957; Janice, 1960.

EDUCATION: Carnegie (Okla.) Elementary School, St. Patrick's; Riverside; Chilocco. Mural instruction under Olaf Nordmark; studied under James Auchiah, Spencer Asah, Leonard Riddles, Archie Blackowl, and Cecil Murdock (*qq.v.*).

WORK PUBLISHED: Jacobson and D'Ucel (1950).
EXHIBITIONS: AIE, BNIAS, FANAIAE, ITIC, PAC; Regional and National Motorola Art Shows.
AWARDS: ITIC, PAC; Regional Motorola Art Show.
COLLECTIONS: *Public*: PAC, SPIM; Carnegie (Okla.) High School. *Private*: Bush, R. Moore, Powell.
ADDRESS: General Delivery, Carnegie, Okla.

Torivio, Lolita *Acoma*
EDUCATION: Santa Fe.
EXHIBITIONS: AIEC, NGA.
COLLECTIONS: *Private*: D. Kramer.

Tosa, Lawrence *Jémez*
BORN: 1947.
EDUCATION: Jémez.
EXHIBITIONS: 1958–60: AAIE, MNM.
AWARDS: MNM, 1959.

Tosa, Mary *Jémez*
EDUCATION: Jémez, *ca.* 1959.
EXHIBITIONS: 1959–60: MNM.

Tosa, Paul *Zia*
EXHIBITIONS: AAIEAE.

Tosa, Tony *Jémez*
BORN: 1947.
EDUCATION: Jémez.
EXHIBITIONS: 1958–60: AAIE, MNM.

Toshewana, Robert Leo *Zuni*
EDUCATION: Santa Fe, *ca.* 1960.
EXHIBITIONS: 1961–62: MNM, PAC.
AWARDS: MNM, 1962.
COLLECTIONS: *Private*: Adlerblum, Humphey, Marriott, D. Maxwell.

Tosque (*see* Williams, David Emmett)

Tough Soldier *Sioux*
Zuyaterila
COLLECTIONS: *Public*: MPM (pictograph on paper).

Toun Keuh *Kiowa* (?)
The artist was among the 72 Plains Indians taken as prisoners from Fort Sill, Okla., to Fort Marion, St. Augustine, Fla., in 1875.
COLLECTIONS: *Public*: YU/BRBML.

Townsend, Roger *San Felipe*
EDUCATION: Albuquerque, *ca.* 1959.
EXHIBITIONS: MNM, 1959.

Townsend, Roy C. *San Felipe*
EDUCATION: Santa Fe, *ca.* 1958.
EXHIBITIONS: MNM, 1958.

Toya, Johnny *Jémez*
COLLECTIONS: *Public*: MAI (a 1956 painting).

Toya, José María   *Jémez*
  COLLECTIONS: *Public*: MAI.

Toya, Mary Isabel   *Jémez*
  COLLECTIONS: *Public*: MNM (acquired when the artist was 11).

Toya, Patricio   *Jémez*
  EXHIBITIONS: ACC, EITA.
  COLLECTIONS: *Public*: CGA, MNM.

Toya, Pete   *Jémez*
  BORN: 1945, Jémez Pueblo, N.M.
  EDUCATION: Jémez.
  EXHIBITIONS: 1960–61: MNM; PAC (Jémez School Exhibit), 1957.
  AWARDS: MNM, 1960.
  COLLECTIONS: *Private*: Jameson.

Toya, Rosie   *Jémez*
  BORN: 1947, Jémez Pueblo, N.M.
  EDUCATION: Jémez.
  EXHIBITIONS: 1958–60: AAIE, MNM.

Tracy, E.   *Pueblo*
  COLLECTIONS: *Public*: RM.

Tracy, Edmund   *Navaho*
  Owipo
  COLLECTIONS: *Public*: DAM (30 paintings); RM.

Tracy, Jo Ellis   *Cherokee*
  EXHIBITIONS: PAC, 1961.
  ADDRESS: 830 South El Molino, Pasadena, Calif.

Trader Boy (*see* Howe, Oscar)

Treas, Byron L.   *Apache* (?)
  COLLECTIONS: *Public*: AF.

Treas, Rudolph   *Mescalero Apache*
  EDUCATION: Santa Fe.
  EXHIBITIONS: 1947–63: AIAE/WSU, MNM, PAC, SI, SN.
  AWARDS: 1957–63: MNM, PAC, SN.
  COLLECTIONS: *Public*: AF, MAI. *Private*: Thoeny.

Trujillo, Andy   *Cochití*
  EDUCATION: Santa Fe.
  COLLECTIONS: *Public*: MAI.
  ADDRESS: Cochití Star Route, Peña Blanca, N.M.

Trujillo, Ascensión   *San Juan*
  Poquin Tahn
  BORN: May 23, 1933, San Juan Pueblo, N.M. Died *ca.* 1959.
  EDUCATION: Graduated Santa Fe, 1953; attended New Mexico U.
  EXHIBITIONS: 1956–59: FWG, MNM, PAC.
  AWARDS: 1957: MNM, PAC.
  COLLECTIONS: *Private*: Wyman.

Trujillo, Jennie   *Taos*
  EDUCATION: Institute.
  EXHIBITIONS: FAIEAIP.
Trujillo, Gregory   *Pueblo*
  EDUCATION: Santa Fe, *ca.* 1958.
  EXHIBITIONS: MNM, 1958.
Trujillo, Manuel   *San Juan*
  Peen Tseh, White Mountain
  BORN: December 21, 1927, San Juan Pueblo, N.M.
  EDUCATION: Graduated Santa Fe, 1947.
  SERVICE: WWII, U.S. Army, Airborne Paratroopers, five and one-half
  years; South Pacific Theater.
  EXHIBITIONS: FWG, ITIC, JGS, MNM, PAC.
  AWARDS: PAC, 1954.
  COLLECTIONS: *Public:* MNM.
  ADDRESS: San Juan Pueblo, N.M.
Tsabetsaye, Roger   *Zuni*
  Tsabetsaye, Eagle's Tail
  BORN: October 29, 1941, Zuni Pueblo, N.M. GF: Henry Gasper, Governor
  of Zuni Pueblo in the 1930's.
  MARRIED: Rosie Epaloose, 1962. Two children: Darrel Davis, 1962; Roderick
  Mark, 1963.

> The artist started painting in 1957 and has made exceptional progress in his
> chosen field of arts and crafts. His contemporary designs in silver are outstanding.
> He hopes to continue his education and become permanently connected with
> art education.

  EDUCATION: Zuni Day School; Albuquerque, 1957–60; Arizona, "Southwest
  Indian Art Project," summer, 1961; Institute, 1962; Rochester S. T., 1963–.
  HONORS: Scholarship to special classes, University of Arizona, 1961; $1500
  scholarship to Rochester School of Technology; Albuquerque Indian School;
  awards night certificate and student service certificate, Arts and Crafts
  Department Certificate of Merit; Institute of American Indian Arts, Out-
  standing Student, 1963.
  COMMISSIONS: *Necklace:* President Lyndon B. Johnson commissioned a
  silver necklace for presentation to Señora Orlich, wife of the President of
  Costa Rica.
  EXHIBITIONS: 1957–65: 25, including ITIC, MNM, NMSF, PAC, SN, USDI,
  YAIA.
  AWARDS: 1957–65: 20 from ITIC, MNM, NMSF, PAC, SN (Award to
  the Student with the Greatest Promise).
  COLLECTIONS: *Public:* AU/ASM, BIA, IACB, MNM, PAC. *Private:* Adler-
  blum, Thoeny.
  ADDRESS: Zuni Pueblo, N.M.
Tsadeltah   *Kiowa*
> The artist was among the 72 Plains Indians taken as prisoners from Fort Sill,
> Okla., to Fort Marion, St. Augustine, Fla., in 1875.

  COLLECTIONS: *Public:* HI.

Tsait Kope Ta *Kiowa*

The artist was among the 72 Plains Indians taken as prisoners from Fort Sill, Okla., to Fort Marion, St. Augustine, Fla., in 1875.

COLLECTIONS: *Public*: MHS/B.

Tsa Sah Wee Eh (*see* Hardin, Helen)

Tsate Kongia (*see* Bosin, Blackbear)

Tsa To Kee (*see* Tsatoke, Lee Monette)

Tsa To Kee (*see* Tsatoke, Monroe)

Tsatoke, Lee Monette *Kiowa*

Tsa To Kee, Hunting Horse

BORN: March 21, 1929, Gotebo, Okla. Son of Martha Koomsa (or Koomsataddle), and Monroe Tsatoke, *q.v.* (both Kiowa). M/GGF: Satanta, Kiowa chief. GGGF: Satank, Kiowa war chief. P/GF: Tsa To Kee (Hunting Horse), Kiowa scout for Custer. M/GF: Bob Koomsataddle (or Koomsa), outstanding drummer of many Kiowa chants and songs.

MARRIED: Donna Jean Mopope (Kiowa), 1948. Five children: Martha, 1953; Anna Mae, 1956; Ladonna, 1958; Lois, 1960; Rita, 1963.

The artist inherited his interest and talent in art from his famous father; however, he did not become actively engaged in art as a career until 1943. He credits his teachers at Riverside—-Acee Blue Eagle (*q.v.*), Ruth Cox, and Mrs. Susie Peters (the government worker who did much to encourage his father)—as having encouraged him most through the years.

EDUCATION: Graduated Riverside, 1948.

CAREER: Guide, Indian City, U.S.A., Anadarko, Okla.; freelance artist.

WORK PUBLISHED: *American Indian Tradition* (Issue 52, 1963), cover.

EXHIBITIONS: AAIE, AIE, BNIAS, ITIC, MNM, PAC, PAC/T. Kirkwood (Mo.) Sidewalk Show, Stix-Bher and Fuller; Public Library, St. Louis, Mo. *One-man shows*: PAC; Conners College, Warner, Okla.

AWARDS: ITIC, PAC; Kirkwood (Mo.) Sidewalk Show.

COLLECTIONS: *Public*: BIA, IACB, MAI, OHSM, PAC, SPIM; Carnegie (Okla.) High School. *Private*: Bush, Cox, Denman, Deupree, Dockstader, Douney, Elkus, Hughes, R. Moore, Schonwald, Thoeny, Walch, M. Wilson.

ADDRESS: 114 West Texas, Anadarko, Okla.

Tsatoke, Monroe *Kiowa*

Tsa To Kee, Hunting Horse

BORN: September 29, 1904, Saddle Mountain, Okla. Died, February 3, 1937. Son of Tsa To Kee, a Kiowa scout for Custer. GM was a White captive.

MARRIED: Martha Koomsa (or Koomsataddle) (Kiowa), *ca.* 1924. Four children: Jewel, 1926; Lee Monette (*q.v.*), 1929; Ross Maker (Buddy), 1934; John Thomas.

Monroe was one of the Five Kiowas (*q.v.*). It was recorded in 1936 that "he could always draw pictures, but never took any art lessons until Mrs. Susie Peters organized a Fine Arts Club of Indian boys and girls who showed talent in drawing and painting, beadwork, and other native work. Mrs. Willie Baze Lane also gave them lessons and encouragement." He worked hard at his art, responding with all his spirit to the sympathy and encouragement of his teachers at Anadarko and later at the University of Oklahoma. He took great delight in his work, painting the things he knew first-hand. While seriously ill with tuberculosis, the

artist joined the Peyote faith, becoming a member of the Native American
Church, and began the series of paintings which expressed his religious experiences (published after his death). Music was also important to him; he loved
to sing and, for many years, was chief singer at Kiowa dances.

EDUCATION: Rainy Mountain Indian School, near Anadarko, Okla.; Bacone
College; special non-credit classes at Oklahoma.

CAREER: Farmer until given the opportunity to attend the University of
Oklahoma. Began painting *ca.* 1915.

HONORS: University of Oklahoma Press adopted his painting as a colophon;
represented in *Indians of Today*.

COMMISSIONS: *Murals*: OHSM, OU/A; St. Patrick's Mission School; Anadarko Federal Building.

WORK PUBLISHED: Jacobson (1929; 1964), Jacobson and D'Ucel (1950),
Tsatoke (1957), LaFarge (1960). *Smoke Signals*, IACB (No. 42, 1964).

EXHIBITIONS: AIE/T, NGA, OU/ET, PAC, PAC/T, SFWF; United Nations
Conference, San Francisco, Calif., 1945.

COLLECTIONS: *Public*: ACM, GM, MAI, MKMcNAI, MNA/KHC, MNM,
MRFM, OHSM, OU/MA, OU/SM, PAC, SPL. *Private*: Callaway, Denman,
Deupree, Dockstader, Elkus, Hogue, O. Jacobson, D. Maxwell.

Tse Ko Yate (*see* Big Bow, Woody)

Tse Tsan (*see* Velarde, Pablita)

Tsen T'ainte (*see* White Horse)

Tse Ye Mu (*see* Vigil, Romando)

Tsina   *Navaho*
COLLECTIONS: *Public*: MAI.

Tsihnahjinnie (*see* Tsinajinnie, Andrew Van)

Tsinajinnie, Andrew Van   *Navaho*
Yazzie Bahe, Little Grey
(Andrew [or Andy] has spelled his last name at least five different ways:
Tsihnahjinnie, Tsinajinie, Tsinajininie, Tsinajinnie, and Tsinnaijinnie.)

BORN: November 19, 1918, Rough Rock, Ariz.

MARRIED: Minnie McGirt, *ca.* 1945. Five children: Hulleah June, 1954;
Welake Jane, 1956; Tsosie Van, 1957; Miquagekee, 1961; Bahe Jim, 1963.
At about the age of five, "Andy" learned there were such things as pencils and
asked his mother to buy one when she went to the trading post for supplies. He
then drew on wrapping paper and the backs of labels from cans. Until that time,
the youngster had used "stone-on-stone" to produce charming drawings. He
has been a serious painter since about 1940, and is well known for his "color
periods"—blue, pink, etc. As an outlet for his other creative interests, he is a
member of the Navaho Salt River Band, Scottsdale, Ariz., and The Navaho
Tribal Band, Window Rock, Ariz.

EDUCATION: Fort Apache (Ariz.) Indian School, graduated Santa Fe, 1936;
attended Oakland.

SERVICE: WWII, U.S. Army Air Force, five years; South Pacific and Asian
Theaters.

CAREER: Illustrator, Navaho Agency, Window Rock, Ariz.; has maintained
his studio in Scottsdale, Ariz., since WWII; full-time artist.

HONORS: Palmes d'Académiques, 1954.
COMMISSIONS: *Murals*: Phoenix Indian School; Navaho Sanitorium, Winslow, Ariz.; Fort Sill Indian School; Navaho Museum, Window Rock, Ariz.; one mural in Japan. *Silk Screens*: Tewa Enterprises, Santa Fe, N.M.
BOOKS ILLUSTRATED: Clark (1940a; 1960); Schevill (1956); Wyman (1966).
WORK PUBLISHED: Jacobson and D'Ucel (1950), La Farge (1956; 1960), Pierson and Davidson (1960), Bahti (1965). *Arizona Highways* (February 1950; December 1958); *The Tie-In* (1st Quarter 1960), cover.
EXHIBITIONS: AIAE/WSU, AIEC, FAIEAIP, HM, ITIC, MNA, MNM, OU/ET, PAC, PAC/T, SN, USDS.
AWARDS: ITIC, MNM, PAC, SN; in the 1930's, award in a national competition conducted by *American Magazine*; has received several grand awards in Indian art competitions.
COLLECTIONS: *Public*: AF, AMNH, BIA, CGA, GM, IACB, LMA/BC, MAI, MKMcNAI, MNCA, MNM, OU/MA, OU/SM, PAC, SMNAI. *Private*: H. Adams, Berg, Denman, Dietrich, Elkus, A. Forbes, Freeman, Goff, Jameson, D. Kramer, Lockett, Maxwell, F. McCormick, Mullan, Neely, Schonwald, Sewell, Thoeny, Wyman.
ADDRESS: Box 542, Scottsdale, Ariz.

Tsisete, Percy Sandy (*see* Sandy, Percy Tsisete)

Tso, John *Navaho*
BORN: Date unknown. Son of Mrs. Ason Gladys Tso, Oraibi, Ariz.
EDUCATION: Graduated Holbrook (Ariz.) High School, 1964; Eastern Arizona Junior College, Thatcher, Ariz., 1964–.
HONORS: Art award from Eastern Arizona Junior College, May, 1965.
EXHIBITIONS: Student Center, Eastern Arizona Junior College.
ADDRESS: c/o Mrs. Ason Gladys Tso, Oraibi, Ariz.

Tsoodle, James *Kiowa*
EXHIBITIONS: AIEC.

Tsosie, George *Navaho*
EXHIBITIONS: ITIC.
AWARDS: ITIC, 1964.

Tsosie, Paul *Navaho*
COLLECTIONS: *Public*: SM.

Tso Yazzie (*see* Kahn, Chester)

Tucson, Loren *Zuni*
EXHIBITIONS: MNM, 1965.
ADDRESS: Zuni, N.M.

Tullma (*see* C.D.T.)

Tune (*see* Two Hatchet, Spencer Lee, Jr.)

Turkey, Moses *Kiowa*
Sah Quo Dle Quoie
EXHIBITIONS: PAC, 1956.
AWARDS: PAC.
COLLECTIONS: *Public*: ACM.

Turning Bear (*see* Murdock, Cecil)

Turning Bear (Chief)   *Brulé Sioux*

BORN: Date unknown. He was on the Yellowstone with Sitting Bull's camp, 1870 (*see* Grass, John). The artist was a prisoner at Fort Omaha, Nebr., awaiting trial for murder in October, 1880; he later stood trial and was released. *See* Hyde (1961; 1956).

COLLECTIONS: *Public:* AMNH. *Private:* Hay (colored drawing executed for Capt. Leonard Hay, Ninth Infantry).

Tuvahoema, Kyrate   *Hopi*

(Also known as Tuvahoema, Kyrat.)

BORN: 1914, Old Oraibi, Ariz. Died January 1, 1942.

The artist's paintings were few; he contracted tuberculosis shortly after leaving school and spent much of his remaining life in sanatoriums in Arizona.

EDUCATION: Oraibi Day School, Oraibi, Ariz.; Albuquerque, 1927; Santa Fe, 1933–35.

WORK PUBLISHED: *Search Magazine* (September 1965).

COLLECTIONS: *Public:* MAI, GM.

Twakuku   *Zuni* (?)

COLLECTIONS: *Public:* AF.

Two-Arrows, Tom   *Onondaga*

Ga Hes Ka, Two Arrows

(Also known as Dorsey, Tom.)

BORN: February 2, 1920, on the Onondaga Reservation, N.Y.; member of the Onondaga Wolf Clan and False Face Society. His son is Tom Dorsey, Jr. (*q.v.*), Tatoganta (Little Turtle). His daughter is Okanta (Little Owl).

In 1946, the artist expressed interest in the need for a revival of traditional Woodland art forms, using such designs in their original state or modifying them for decorative use in interior decoration, clothing, and the like. "The use of authentic design motifs is essential, of course; but it is equally important to use them intelligently, with full awareness of their symbolic significance. I feel, too, that the Indian artist is not being fully creative if he merely copies or compiles these motifs in decorative form. Designs can be analyzed, separated into their symbolically significant parts, and reassembled according to the originality, taste and purpose of the artist. If we are to have a developing art instead of a static, backward-looking one, we must feel free to use the same artistic ingenuity that helped to form that art...." The artist works in tempera because of its "earthy quality" and with an established palette in which "red and black, the religious color combinations of the Eastern Indians, is most used." Two-Arrows' talents range from painting to creating Indian garments, hand-carving, silverwork, musical instruments, jewelry, and beadwork.

EDUCATION: Albany (N.Y.) Institute of History and Art, studied painting techniques eight years, under Herbert Steinke.

SERVICE: WWII, U.S. Army Air Force, two years; China-Burma-India Theater. Taught art at the Armed Forces Institute, Calcutta, India.

CAREER: Illustrator, decorator, designer; display specialist, AMNH; lecturer on Indian folklore for schools, libraries, museums, and civic groups; artist (established display center for Pakistan arts and crafts), Pakistan Consulate, New York, N.Y.; guest teacher of dance at summer schools in Mass.; has performed in films on Indian dancing.

Honors: He and his wife were sent on a good-will mission to Asiatic nations, under the sponsorship of the USDS; introduced a silk-screen method for making a useful machine-gun target.

Commissions: *Textiles*: Designs, Textron, Inc. *Dinnerware*: Designs, Arzberg Porcelain. *Murals*: Post Library, Seymore Johnson Air Field.

Work Published: *Masks and Men,* AMNH (1946), catalog; illustrated many U.S. Army booklets.

Exhibitions: AFA, DAM, JGS, MAI, NGA, PAC, PAC/T; University of Minnesota, Minneapolis, Minn.; Smith Gallery, Springfield, Mass.; "Indian Art in Industry of India," Calcutta. *One-man shows*: AFA, CPLH, MAM.

Awards: DAM, PAC; Carnegie Scholastic Award.

Collections: *Public*: AIHA, AMNH, GM, MAI, MAM, PAC.

Address: 25 Second Street, Albany, N.Y. 12210

Two Eagle, Violet   *Sioux*
Exhibitions: BNIAS.
Address: Parmelee, S. Dak.

Two-Hatchet, Spencer Lee, Jr.   *Kiowa*
Tune (Kiowa nickname)
Born: August, 6 1943, Lawton, Okla. Son of Spencer Two-Hatchet (Kiowa) and Peggy Lois Payahsote (Kiowa.) GGM: Niece of Hunting Horse (Kiowa) and descendant of Mokeen (Mexican captive who played a prominent role in Kiowa history). P/GGF: Edward Two-Hatchet (Pahdongkie) (Kiowa).
Mrs. Susie Peters purchased the artist's first painting, encouraging him, as did Mr. and Mrs. Hardy of the Hardy Gallery, to continue to paint.
Education: Graduated Institute, 1965.
Exhibitions: AIE, FAIEAIP, ITIC, PAC, SN.
Awards: SN.
Collections: *Private*: R. Moore, Peters.
Address: Box 878, Carnegie, Okla.

Twoitsie, Hansen   *Hopi*
Education: Santa Fe.
Exhibitions: NGA, 1953.
Collections: *Private*: Dietrich, D. Kramer.

Two Strikes   *Oglala Sioux*
The artist's "Partisan" drawing is reproduced in the BAE, *4th AR*. This is a drawing illustrating the man's authority, or leadership of a war party, by an elevated pipe or war club.
Work Published: BAE, *4th AR*.

Tyndall, Calvin T.   *Sioux* or *Omaha*
Umpah, Elk
Exhibitions: *One-man shows*: JAM, 1930's.
Collections: *Public*: HMFA. *Private*: Denman.
Address: Macy, Nebr.

Umpah (*see* Tyndall, Calvin T.)

Umpan Hanska (*see* Larvie, Calvin)

Upright Post (*see* Chauncey, Florence Nupok)

Used As A Shield (*see* Grass, John)

Vacit, Gary   *Zuni*
  COLLECTIONS: *Public*: MNM.

Valencia, Anna Lou   ?
  EDUCATION: St. Catherine's, 1965.
  EXHIBITIONS: PAC, 1965.
  ADDRESS: Box 1883, Santa Fe, N.M.

Vallo, Pedro   *Acoma*
  COLLECTIONS: *Public*: MNM.

Velarde, Neito   *Santo Domingo*
  COLLECTIONS: *Public*: UPA.

Velarde, Pablita   *Santa Clara*
  Tse Tsan, Golden Dawn
  BORN: September 19, 1918, Santa Clara Pueblo, N.M. Daughter of Herman
  Velarde (Santa Clara) and Marianita Chavarría (Santa Clara).
  MARRIED: Herbert O. Hardin, 1942; divorced. Two children: Helen Hardin
  (*q.v.*), 1943; Herbert, Jr.

> Tonita Peña (*q.v.*), the "mother" of Pueblo painting, introduced Pablita to the
> world of art. There was a period in childhood when an eye disease caused a loss
> of sight. Upon regaining her eyesight she explained, "temporary darkness made
> me want to see everything.... I have trained myself to remember, to the small-
> est detail, everything I see...." In 1938, Pablita benefited greatly from a four-
> month tour of the U.S., accompanied by Ernest Thompson Seton, the famous
> naturalist and lecturer, and his wife. During the tour, she exhibited her paintings,
> selling several. Upon returning to New Mexico, she built her first studio at the
> pueblo and began her painting career. Dorothy Dunn, in speaking of the artist's
> work, said that her "style evokes the poise and gentle strength of a Pueblo
> woman."
>
> In 1956, Pablita began her unique earth paintings, made from various colored
> rocks that she grinds to powder on a *metate*, mixes with water and glue for a
> plastic effect, and applies to Masonite. In 1964, the artist expressed herself in
> the following way: "I have not gone to the new trend nor do I wish to do so in
> the near future. I cannot contribute thoughts of value without appreciating and
> understanding the past." She feels there is still very much beauty and dignity
> to draw upon from the past, and that even if she were to "catch-up" with the
> present, she would never have enough time to paint the beauty she sees in
> yesterday.

  EDUCATION: Española; St. Patrick's; graduated Santa Fe, 1936.
  CAREER: Assistant art teacher, Santa Clara Day School, 1938; lectured
  about her paintings and the exhibits at Bandelier National Monument
  Museum, N.M.; full-time freelance artist.
  HONORS: Palmes d'Académiques, 1954; represented in *Indians of Today*;
  special recognition from 20th Century Art Club, St. Louis, Mo., 1955; *Old
  Father, the Story Teller*, voted one of the Best Western Books of 1961.
  COMMISSIONS: *Murals*: Bandelier National Monument, N.M.; Western Skies
  Hotel, Albuquerque, N.M.; Santa Clara Day School; First National Bank,
  Los Alamos, N.M. *Building Façade*: Maisel Building, Albuquerque, N.M.
  (with other artists).
  BOOKS ILLUSTRATED: Velarde (1960).

WORK PUBLISHED: Jacobson and D'Ucel (1950), La Farge (1956; 1960). *Women Speaking* (April 1959), *New Mexico* (December 1960); *Arizona Republic* (March 2, 1963), *Indian Life*, ITIC (August 1961), *American Artist* (April 1965).

EXHIBITIONS: AIAE/WSU, AIM, CCP, DAM, GM, ITIC, JGS, MHDYMM, MNM, NMSF, OU, OU/ET, PAC, PAC/T, SN, USDS; University of California, Berkeley; Bandelier National Monument Museum, N.M. *One-man shows*: MNM, PAC; Enchanted Mesa, Albuquerque, N.M.

AWARDS: 1946–65: DAM, ITIC, MNM, NMSF, PAC. One Grand Award.

COLLECTIONS: *Public*: AF, BIA, DAM, GM, IACB, KM, LMA/BC, MAI, MHDYMM, MNM, OU/MA, PAC, SMNAI, UPA; State of New Mexico. *Private*: H. Adams, Adlerblum, Cosgrove, Elkus, A. Forbes, Goff, Lockett, W. S. Price, Schonwald, Thoeny, Verryden, M. Williams.

ADDRESS: 805 Adams, NE, Albuquerque, N.M.

Velino Shije (*see* Herrera, Velino Shije)

Venego, Florenzo   *Apache*
COLLECTIONS: *Public*: MNM.

Vicenti, Carl A.   *Jicarilla Apache*
BORN: January 8, 1930, Dulce, N.M.
MARRIED: Norine Isidora Verhagen, 1953. Five children: Carey, 1954; Carson, 1955; Noraleen, 1957; Carlisle, 1959; Carlson, 1962.
EDUCATION: Dulce (N.M.) Public School, Albuquerque; Haskell; Brigham Young University, Provo, Utah; Utah S.; B.A., Utah.
CAREER: Art Instructor, Inter-Mountain Indian School, *ca*. 1963–.
EXHIBITIONS: ITIC, MNM, PAC, SN.
AWARDS: PAC, SN.
COLLECTIONS: *Public*: BIA; Jicarilla Apache Tribe. *Private*: Blake, Jorgensen, Rousch, Schreiber, L. Smith.
ADDRESS: c/o Inter-Mountain Indian School, Brigham City, Utah.

Vicenti, Charles   *Zuni*
EDUCATION: Albuquerque, *ca*. 1956.
COMMISSIONS: *Murals*: Barelas Community Center (with other artists).
COLLECTIONS: *Public*: MAI.

Vicenti, Steven   *Jicarilla Apache*
Nehakije
(Also known as Vicenti, Stephen.)
BORN: 1917, Dulce, N.M. Died, 1948, at Santa Fe, N.M.
Clara Lee Tanner (1957) refers to the artist as the "first modern painter of the Apache tribe."
EDUCATION: Santa Fe.
EXHIBITIONS: First exhibited in 1934 at Santa Fe, N.M. Later exhibited widely among such institutions as AGAA, AIW, MNM, NGA, SUAG.
COLLECTIONS: *Public*: CGFA. *Private*: Dietrich.

Vigil, Albert   *San Ildefonso*
BORN: Date unknown. Son of Romando Vigil (*q.v.*).
EDUCATION: Santa Fe.

COLLECTIONS: *Public*: GM, MAI, MNA/KHC.
ADDRESS: 1708½ South Vermont Avenue, Los Angeles, Calif.

Vigil, Alfred *Jémez*
EDUCATION: Jémez
EXHIBITIONS: MNM., 1961.

Vigil, Andrea *Jémez*
EDUCATION: Jémez.
EXHIBITIONS: MNM, 1962.
AWARDS: MNM.

Vigil, Calvin *Jicarilla Apache*
BORN: June 19, 1924, Dulce, N.M.
EDUCATION: Dulce (N.M.) Indian School, 1939–43; Santa Fe, 1946–47.
SERVICE: WWII, U.S. Navy; South Pacific Theater.
CAREER: Farmer and rancher.
EXHIBITIONS: DAM, ITIC, MNM, PAC.
COLLECTIONS: *Public*: DAM, PAC. *Private*: Deem, Feemster, D. Maxwell, W. S. Price.
ADDRESS: Box 32, Dulce, N.M.

Vigil, Frank Paul *Jicarilla Apache*
BORN: 1921.
EXHIBITIONS: 1950–63: AAIE, ITIC, PAC, SN, USDS.
AWARDS: PAC, 1950.
COLLECTIONS: *Public*: BIA, SMNAI. *Private*: Dixon.
ADDRESS: Box 29, Dulce, N.M.

Vigil, Jo *Tesuque*
(Also known as Vigil, Jo Gabriel.)
EDUCATION: Santa Fe.
EXHIBITIONS: AIW, OU/ET.
COLLECTIONS: *Public*: AU/ASM, CU/LMA, OU/MA.
ADDRESS: Tesuque Pueblo, N.M.

Vigil, Juanita *Tesuque*
EDUCATION: Tesuque, *ca.* 1959.
EXHIBITIONS: MNM, 1959.

Vigil, Lucy *Tesuque*
EDUCATION: Tesuque, *ca.* 1959.
EXHIBITIONS: MNM, 1959.

Vigil, Marco *Zuni*
COLLECTIONS: *Public*: MAI.

Vigil, Pete *Tesuque*
BORN: July 16, 1919.
MARRIED: Lila. Three children: Kanchee, David, Thomas.
EDUCATION: Santa Fe.
CAREER: Technician, University of California; painter, silversmith, and woodcarver.
EXHIBITIONS: AIEC, AIW, PAC.

COLLECTIONS: *Public*: CU/LMA, GM, OU/SM. *Private*: A. Forbes, Denman, Thoeny.

ADDRESS: Route 1, Box 57A, Santa Fe, N.M.

Vigil, Priscilla *Jémez*
BORN: 1958, N.M.
EDUCATION: Jémez.
EXHIBITIONS: AAIE, 1960.

Vigil, Ralph *Jémez*
COLLECTIONS: *Public*: MNM.

Vigil, Ramon *Tesuque*
EDUCATION: Tesuque, *ca.* 1959.
EXHIBITIONS: MNM, 1959.

Vigil, Romando *San Ildefonso*
Tse Ye Mu, Falling In Winter
BORN: 1902. Father of Albert Vigil (*q.v.*). Brother of Tonita Peña (*q.v.*).
The artist was painting as early as 1920 at the pueblo. In 1950, he was apparently in California. His style is that of the San Ildefonso school of painting. Some of his work could be found for sale in New Mexico galleries in 1952.
EDUCATION: Santa Fe.
CAREER: Artist, for a short time at Walt Disney Studios, Hollywood, Calif.
COMMISSIONS: *Murals*: The Corcoran Gallery of Art, EITA; with Velino Shije Herrera and Oqwa Pi (*qq.v.*), 1933; Santa Fe Indian School; La Fonda Hotel, Santa Fe, N.M.
WORK PUBLISHED: Alexander (1932). *American Magazine of Art* (August 1933).
EXHIBITIONS: ACC, AIEC, EITA, MNM, OU/ET.
COLLECTIONS: *Public*: AF, AMNH, DAM, GM, JAM, MAI, MNA/KHC, MNM, MRFM, OU/MA, PAC, PU/M, RM. *Private*: Denman, Elkus, Hinchman, Thoeny.

Vigil, Rufina *Tesuque*
Sah Wa
Rufina painted and exhibited in Santa Fe and in Chicago. She received training under Dorothy Dunn. In 1950, however, it was reported that she had stopped painting "long ago."
EDUCATION: Santa Fe.
CAREER: Draftsman, Los Alamos, N.M., "at one time."
EXHIBITIONS: NGA, OU/ET.
COLLECTIONS: *Public*: MNM, OU/MA. *Private*: Denman, D. Kramer.

Vigil, Thomas *Tesuque*
Pan Yo Pin, Summer Mountain (and *Pen Yo Pin*; *Pu Yo Pin*; *Pinayo Pin*). (Also known as Vigil, Tomás.)
BORN: *Ca.* 1889, Tesuque Pueblo, N.M. Died, 1960. Father of Tim Vigil (*q.v.*) and Paul Vigil.
The artist was painting at the pueblo as early as 1920. In 1950, he occasionally painted on special orders only.
EDUCATION: St. Catherine's, 1904–07 (did not complete school).
WORK PUBLISHED: Jacobson and D'Ucel (1950).

EXHIBITIONS: ACC, EITA, SI/T.
COLLECTIONS: *Public*: AMNH, CAM, CGFA, DAM, GM, MAI, MNM, MRFM, OU, PU/M, RM. *Private*: Elkus, A. Forbes, W. Henderson.

Vigil, Tim   *Tesuque*
  Ku Se Peen, Rocky Mountain
  BORN: Date unknown. Son of Thomas Vigil (*q.v.*).
  CAREER: Employed at Los Alamos, N.M., "at one time."
  EXHIBITIONS: PAC, SN.
  COLLECTIONS: *Private*: Neely.
  ADDRESS: Route 1, Box 59, Santa Fe, N.M.

Vigil, Tom   *Jémez*
  BORN: 1945.
  EDUCATION: Jémez, *ca.* 1957.
  EXHIBITIONS: AIE, PAC.
  AWARDS: AIE, 1957.
  COLLECTIONS: *Private*: Jameson, J. Snodgrass.
  ADDRESS: Route 1, Box 59, Santa Fe, N.M.

Vigil, Tomás (*see* Vigil, Thomas)

Vigil, Ultimio (*see* Vigil, Utimio)

Vigil, Utimio   *Tesuque*
  (Also known as Vigil, Ultimio.)
  EXHIBITIONS: AIEC (listed as Ultimio).
  COLLECTIONS: *Public*: CU/LMA (signed Utimio, executed at 18). *Private*: Walch.

Waano-Gano, Joe T. N.   *Cherokee*
  Waano-Gano, Bow-Arrow
  BORN: March 3, 1906, Salt Lake City, Utah. Son of James Noonan (and Noonah), and Rena May Lash-Heart (both Cherokee). His godmother was Ah Wahn U (Seneca).
  MARRIED: Christine Ruben (Karok), March 15, 1935.

  > As far back as he can remember, from the time he could hold a pencil or brush, Waano-Gano has drawn or painted. Many of his early creative works were in the medium of clay. His studies were given assistance and guidance by anthropologists Arthur Woodward, Frederick W. Hodge, and M. R. Harrington. As the result of a car accident in 1961, the artist must now force his fingers and wrists to "work."

  EDUCATION: Public schools in Salt Lake City, Utah, and graduated Los Angeles (Calif.) Metropolitan High School, 1922,; Von Schneidau School of Art, 1924–28; extension courses, University of Southern California at Los Angeles. Studied under Hanson Puthoff and Theodore N. Lukits.
  SERVICE: WWII, U.S. Air Force, three years.
  CAREER: Décor designer, Western Air Lines, 1944–46; member of an all-Indian radio cast which presented dramatic adaptations from Indian legends, *ca.* 1939–41; outdoor display artist; commercial and advertising artist, 1924–41; designer of textiles with Indian motifs for manufacturer; lecturer; stage director and actor, *Song of Hiawatha*, Hollywood Bowl, Los Angeles; designer of more than 30 combat and transport plane insignia.

HONORS: Represented in *Who's Who in American Art, Indians of Today*; received "Best Picture to Live With" Award, Biltmore Annual, 1952, Hermosa Beach, Calif.; past president, San Fernando Valley Artist's Guild; past president, Painters and Sculptors, Los Angeles; Chairman, California International Flower Show Art Exhibition, 1958; on Honor Roll of the "Greatest Living American Indians," 1933; portrait in CCP Hall of Fame, Indian section.

COMMISSIONS: *Medal*: Designer of Indian Council Fire Achievement Annual Award, 1933. *Masthead*: *The Amerindian*, designer. *Cover*: *California Authentics, Santa Fe Trail Series* (September 14, 1946), fabric and fashion design brochure, fabric designs also by the artist. *Outdoor Mural*: Community Chest, Los Angeles, Calif. *Indoor Murals*: Sherman Institute, Riverside, Calif.; Los Angeles General Hospital; Los Angeles Public Library, assisted Dean Cornwell in completion of his murals. *Paintings*: "Green Virgin of Mexico," unveiled 1948 and used to raise funds for Mexican education, now in Mexico City after touring Mexico and South America.

WORK PUBLISHED: *California Stylist* (September 1946); "Art of the American Indian," *Western Art Review* (October 1951), author and illustrator.

EXHIBITIONS: 1926–65: AAA/T, CAC, CCP, CSF, DMFA, FAIEAIP, FMC, GTA, ITIC, LAIC, LBAG, LH, MAF, MAG, MNM, PAC, SAIEAIP. One-man shows: 1940–63: 45, including BA, BHH, CBMM, CFS, CG, CI, CIFS, DSG, GPL, HB, LACC, LACM, LBAG, MAG/H, MG, MSAC, MVAG, RRG, SFNB, SGAG, SM, TAC, UC, UWC, WCH, WFS.

AWARDS: FMC, GTA, HBBA, ITIC, KCF, LACF, LAIC, LBAG, MAF, PAC. First Award For Outstanding Textile Design, "Kachina Masks," worldwide competition.

COLLECTIONS: *Public*: Gardena (Calif.) Public Schools. *Private*: Andrews, Burridge, Ja. Campbell, Fraser, Gosfeldt, Welch.

ADDRESS: 8926 Holly Place, Hollywood, Calif.

Wabliska (*see* White Eagle)

Wa Chin Cadi (*see* Martínez, José Miguel)

Wade, Bobby *Choctaw*

BORN: March 22, 1940, Broken Bow, Okla.

Mr. Wade began painting in 1961 and credits Dick West (*q.v.*) as having encouraged and inspired him most. Information on the Choctaws, from his mother, provides authentic subject matter for his paintings.

EDUCATION: Graduated Broken Bow (Okla.) Public High School; attended Bacone College.

EXHIBITIONS: PAC; McCurtain County Fair, Idabel, Okla.

AWARDS: McCurtain County Fair, Idabel, Okla.

COLLECTIONS: *Public*: BIA/M. *Private*: O. Evans, G. Maxwell.

ADDRESS: 111 West Morgan, Apt. 11, Broken Bow, Okla.

Wagacho (*see* Quiver, Robert A.)

Wagoshe, Russell William *Osage*

Kikekah Wahtiankah, Chief Of Humor

BORN: September 6, 1911, on Salt Creek, Osage County, Okla. Son of John Wagoshe (Osage) and Agnes Bigheart (Osage). P/GF: Whip Hitter (Wagoshe),

Osage chief in 1869, who received his name after killing 13 soldiers with a rawhide whip ornamented with sharpened weights.

MARRIED: Naomi Evelyn Guinn (Cherokee), 1952.

> The artist began painting when he was a small boy. "One teacher got tired of punishing me so she had me draw pictures on the black board." He painted only what he knew about the Osages and signed his paintings with a sketch of a horizontal feather. Because of failing eyesight, the artist is retired.

EDUCATION: Graduated Osage Boarding School, Pawhuska, Okla.

EXHIBITIONS: OHSM.

COLLECTIONS: *Public*: OHSM.

ADDRESS: Whiting Apartments, #18, Pawhuska, Okla.

Waha Canka Yapi (*see* Grass, John)

Wah Peen (*see* Atencio, Gilbert Benjamin)

Waiting Up (*see* Arkeketa, Benjamin)

Wa Ka   *Zia*

EXHIBITIONS: FWG (listed as Wa Kai).

COLLECTIONS: *Public*: JAM.

Waki Yeni Dewa (*see* Moquino, Ignacio)

Walanke (*see* Redcorn, Jim Lacy)

Walker, Thomas, Jr.   *Winnebago*

EXHIBITIONS: PAC, 1951.

ADDRESS: Box 111, Winnebago, Nebr.

Walking By The River (*see* Nailor, Gerald)

Walking Leader (*see* Natay, Ed)

Walluk, Wilbur Wright   *Eskimo*

BORN: January 24, 1928, Shishmaref, Alaska. The artist's father was a reindeer herder whose native village was Walluk. Nephew of Kivetoruk Moses, and cousin of Jack Okie (*qq.v.*).

> The artist began painting "secretly" at the age of six. In 1946, he wrote: "I find myself a thin man artist and funny face artist—once I win first prize on funny face drawing. Then when I am 14 year old I learned how to paint with oil paints at school. When I am 10 to 13 year old Mrs. Russell Government school teacher of Native help me little on arts. When I am 14 I finally give up art and start my own Ivory Business more than arts. Ivory Business was more fun to me. I was on Ivory Business 3 year. At the year 1944 I broke my back bone and I quit Ivory carving." The artist was in the hospital one and one-half years and drew pictures which he gave away and sold. In 1951, when he was not in school, he helped "mama to make fur parkas" and clean and repair them as well. He also painted neckties and made ivory and wood carvings, which he etched and painted with brush and ink.

EDUCATION: Shismaref, Alaska; Mt. Edgecumbe Vocational School, Alaska.

CAREER: Reindeer herder, ivory carver, painter, maker and cleaner of parkas.

EXHIBITIONS: DAM, PAC; Northwest Alaska Fair, Nome.

AWARDS: PAC; Northwest Alaska Fair, Nome.

COLLECTIONS: *Public*: GM.

Walter, Roy M.   ?

COLLECTIONS: *Public*: MAI.

Walters, Harry *Navaho*
  BORN: March 10, 1943.
  EDUCATION: Institute, 1962–63.
  EXHIBITIONS: 1963: MNM, PAC, SN.
  AWARDS: MNM, SN (for student showing the greatest achievement).
  ADDRESS: Post Office Box 447, Kirtland, N.M.

Walz, Peter Frank *Chippewa*
  BORN: June 14, 1912, on the White Earth Reservation, Minn.
  MARRIED: Erma Opal Hicks (Cherokee), *ca.* 1951.
  CAREER: Various administrative positions, BIA, 1934–.
  EXHIBITIONS: MNM, USDS.
  AWARDS: MNM, 1963.
  ADDRESS: 1605 Sigma Chi Road, NE, Albuquerque, N.M.

Wambalee Ches Challah (*see* Little Eagle)

Wanble Orko (*see* Fast Eagle)

Wapah Nahyah (*see* West, Dick)

Wapostangi (*see* Good, Baptiste)

War Horse (*see* Jake, Albin Roy)

War Lance (*see* Momaday, Al)

Ward, Victor *Tlingit*
  BORN: September 22, 1943.
  EDUCATION: Santa Fe.
  EXHIBITIONS: 1961–62: MNM, PAC.
  AWARDS: 1961–62: two from MNM.
  COLLECTIONS: *Private*: Mayer-Oakes.
  ADDRESS: East 2 Cedar Park, Juneau, Alaska.

Ware, Woodrow ?
  COLLECTIONS: *Public*: OHSM.

Warm Mountain (*see* Aguilar, José Vicente)

Warner, Fred ?
  COLLECTIONS: *Public*: MAI.

Warpa Tanka Kuciyela (*see* Amiotte, Arthur Douglas)

Warrior, Antowine *Sauk-Fox*
  Takotokasi, Roaring Thunder
  BORN: January 4, 1941.
  EDUCATION: Bacone College; Haskell; Arizona, "Southwest Indian Art Project," summers, 1960–62.
  EXHIBITIONS: 1958–63: AAIE, AIE, ITIC, MNM, PAC; University of Arizona, Museum of Art; Central State College, Edmond, Okla. *One-man shows*: PAC, 1958.
  AWARDS: 1958–63: Ten from AIE, ITIC, PAC.
  COLLECTIONS: *Public*: AU/ASM, BIA, PAC. *Private*: W. S. Price, V. Smith, L. Stewart, R. Walker, Yulke.
  ADDRESS: Rural Route 1, Box 123, Stroud, Okla.

Warrior Who Came Out (*see* Lee, Charlie)

Warrior Who Walked Up To His Enemy (*see* Begay, Harrison)

Wasaba Shinga (*see* Woodring, Carl)

Wasconadie (*see* Darling, Marcell J.)

Washakie (Chief)   *Flathead-Umatilla*
Washakie, Rawhide Rattle
(Also known as White Haired Chief With Scarred Face.)
BORN: "Born into the Flathead tribe in 1798" in Montana and lived with
them until he was about eight. Died, February 20, 1900. Son of Paseego
(Flathead) and a woman thought to have been an Umatilla or Shoshoni.
MARRIED: A Shoshoni woman; later married Ahawhy Persie (a Crow cap-
tive), *ca.* 1872. Twelve children, among whom were Naun Nang Gai (Snow
Bird); Coocoosh (Dick), *ca.* 1859; Wobaah (Charles), 1873; Conna Yah
(Bishop); and Enga Peahrora, the only daughter whose full name is known.
  The chief produced numerous "artistically decorated" elkskins depicting his
  hunts, buffalo chases, battles, and personal history. It cannot be determined
  whether some paintings, signed "Washakie" are by the chief or by his sons (*see*
  Charles Washakie and George Washakie), for the styles are very nearly identical.
  The name *Washakie* (and *Wussikhe*, The Rattler) came to the artist when he
  killed his first buffalo, making from it a rattle which he always used when riding
  to war. His second name, White Haired Chief With Scarred Face, was given
  him when his hair suddenly turned white following the death of his favorite son.
  (His scarred face was the result of a Blackfoot arrow.) There are 30 official and
  unofficial ways of spelling Washakie. Many references refer to the Chief as Shoshoni, but he did not join this tribe until *ca.* 1826–30.
CAREER: Elected a sub-chief of the Shoshoni, 1840; chief of the Shoshoni
at Wind River Valley, Wyo. (with land rights granted him by the Government in 1863 to 44,672,000 acres in parts of Colo., Wyo., Idaho, and Utah),
1844–1900; set up military system of training men of the tribe; assisted the
U.S. in efforts to quell Indian uprisings; signed six major treaties, 1851–96;
received signed commendation from 9000 Whites who testified to his kindly
aid; orator; Indian scout with Fourth Infantry, 1874; enlisted in army for
several "hitches" during his life, the last of which was in 1889, when he was
91; Crazy Horse regarded Washakie as "the greatest general of them all;"
wrangler for Hudson Bay Co.; employed by American Fur Co.
HONORS: Elected chief of the Shoshoni; united several groups of Eastern
Shoshoni; old Camp Brown was officially designated Fort Washakie, and
Washakie National Forest was also named for him; received gifts and com-
mendations from two presidents; monument erected in his honor, 1905.
WORK PUBLISHED: Alexander (1938). Del Monte (no date).
COLLECTIONS: *Public*: MAI, SDMM, SI/MNH, SM; Newark (N.J.) Museum.

Washakie, Charles   *Flathead-Umatilla-Crow*
Wobaah
(Also known as Washakie, Charlie; Katsiekodie, Charlie.)
BORN: 1873, near Crow Heart Butte, Wyo. Son of Washakie (*q.v.*) and
Ahawhy Persie (a Crow captive). P/GF: Paseego (Flathead).

Because he lived with the tribe, Charles was generally assumed to have been Shoshoni. It is quite possible that many paintings attributed to his father were actually his work, for their styles are similar.

WORK PUBLISHED: Alexander (1938).

COLLECTIONS: *Public*: MAI. *Private*: C. Carter, A. White (skin painting signed Charlie Katsiekodie).

Washakie, George *Shoshoni*

It is probable that George is one of the 12 children of Washakie (*q.v.*), for the names of all 12 have not been determined.

COLLECTIONS: *Public*: MAI.

EXHIBITIONS: CCP (exhibited and sold paintings).

Wa Shun Keh (*see* Brave, Franklin P.)

Watchetaker, George Smith *Comanche*

Watchetaker, Hide Away

BORN: March 1, 1916, Elgin, Okla. Son of Walter Hoke Smith Watchetaker and Dana Tahtahdarsy (Small and Pitiful, or Cute).

MARRIED: Eva Tooahnipah, August 24, 1953.

EDUCATION: Mt. Scott (Okla.) Rural School, 1923–27; Fort Sill, 1927–32; Haskell, 1932–35 (graduated 1935).

CAREER: Painter, decorator, sign painter.

HONORS: 1966–67 holder of "World's Championship Indian Dancer."

EXHIBITIONS: AIE, PAC; in Lawton and Clinton, Okla., Wichita Falls, Tex., Albuquerque, N.M.

AWARDS: AIE, 1963; Southwest Sidewalk Show, Lawton, Okla., 1964–65.

COLLECTIONS: *Public*: FSM (charcoal portrait).

ADDRESS: Rural Route 1, Box 76, Elgin, Okla.

Water Edge (*see* Tahoma, Quincy)

Water Elk (*see* Cohoe, William)

Wattan (*see* Sweezy, Carl)

Wawabano Sata (*see* Pushetonequa, Charles)

Wa Wa Chaw (Princess) *Rincón*

Wa Wa Chaw, Keep From The Water

BORN: December 25, 1885, Valley Center, Calif. Adopted by Dr. C. Duggan, who delivered her, and his sister, Mary.

The artist worked many years with Dr. Carlos Montezuma. Her foster parents encouraged her interest in the study of "anatomy and free brush strokes." Albert P. Ryder taught her to "tone down" her colors. She has painted all her life, and, for at least 70 years, she has been involved in the art of America and Europe. "The expression of a hobby has to find its way to our youthful minds so that our Indian youth is not misled to thinking they can make a life of art— it is not bread—it is the art of keeping the mind alive" (1963).

EDUCATION: Sherman; "eastern schools;" instruction under Albert P. Ryder.

EXHIBITIONS: PAC; Greenwich Village Out-Door Exhibitions, New York, N.Y.; Europe.

COLLECTIONS: *Public*: PAC.

ADDRESS: 2060 Third Avenue, Apt. #12, New York, N.Y.

Weahkie, Teddy (*see* Weakee, Teddy)

Weakee, Teddy   *Zuni*
Weakie and *Wiacke*

BORN: 1900, Zuni Pueblo, N.M. Died 1965.
  The artist was known to have painted in oils in the European perspective, but
  was painting infrequently by 1950. He was best known as a carver of fetishes.
EDUCATION: Studied art at home for nearly 25 years.
WORK PUBLISHED: *American Magazine of Art* (August 1933).
EXHIBITIONS: ITIC.
AWARDS: ITIC.
COLLECTIONS: *Public*: MAI, SMNAI (deerskin paintings).

Weakie (*see* Weakee, Teddy)

Webster, David   ?
EDUCATION: Phoenix, 1964.
EXHIBITIONS: FAIEAIP.

Weckeah   *Comanche*
Weckeah, Searching
(Also known as Bradley, Roberta C.)

BORN: 1920, Lawton, Okla. Daughter of Edward H. Clark (Comanche) and
Mary Pache Parker (Comanche). M/GF: Quanah Parker, Comanche chief.
M/GM: Weckeah, wife of Parker. M/GGF: Petak Nocona, Comanche chief.
M/GGM: Cynthia Ann Parker, captured at age of nine by Comanches. P/GF:
E. L. Clark, principal interpreter at the Jerome Agreement, 1892. P/GM:
Waumaconnie (Comanche).
MARRIED: William B. Bradley, Jr. Three children: Robert Stanwood, 1946;
Cynthia Ann, 1949; Roberta Helen, 1960.
  Mrs. Bradley is best known in art circles as Weckeah. She seldom paints in the
  flat Indian style but prefers instead to use oils, pastels, watercolors, and char-
  coal to depict her history-based art work. She is also a sculptor.
EDUCATION: Graduated Cameron High School, Lawton, Okla.
EXHIBITIONS: 1955–65: AIE, MNM, PAC; Duncan Art Show, Ponca Indian
Fair, Ponca City, Okla. *One-man shows*: 1959–65: Fort Sill (Okla.) Post
Service Club; Lawton (Okla.) Chamber of Commerce; Carnegie Library,
Lawton, Okla.
AWARDS: Five; at Duncan, Ponca City, and Anadarko, Okla.
COLLECTIONS: *Public*: FSM, MNM; Southwestern State College, Weather-
ford, Okla.
ADDRESS: 414 Ferris, Lawton, Okla.

Weepama Quedaecouka (*see* Mofsie, Louis Billingsly)

Wen Tsireh (*see* Montoya, Alfred)

West, Dick   *Cheyenne*
Wapah Nahyah, Lightfooted Runner
(Also known as West, W. Richard; West, Walter Richard.)

BORN: September 8, 1912, on the banks of the North Canadian River, near
Darlington, western Okla. Son of Lightfoot West (Cheyenne), track star
and marathon runner, and Rena Flying Coyote, also known as Emily Black
Wolf (Cheyenne). M/GF: Thunder Bull. M/GA: Ghost Woman, who with

Sioux Left Hand and Walter and John Tassel (his maternal uncles) reared the artist. M/GM: Big Belly Woman.

MARRIED: Maribelle McCrea, May 29, 1940. Two children: Richard, Jr., 1943; James Lee, 1946.

> Dick West is an accomplished artist who is never content to stand still by working only in one medium and one style. He is known for his traditional Indian paintings, as well as for his portraits, abstractions, and other European-derived style paintings and sculpture. Upon receiving the Grand Award at Philbrook Art Center in 1955, Mr. West wrote: "I do not profess to have established anything definite in my experimental dabblings, but I do feel that the Indian artist must be allowed freedom to absorb influences outside of his own art forms and to develop them in his own manner. I do realize the dangers involved, but I also see the promise of a new lane of expression that should keep the Indian's art alive and closer to a more contemporary existence. I, too, would want to preserve the art form termed 'native Indian painting,' and I give my students every opportunity to execute it....I believe that Indian artists with formal art background will be going more and more in the direction of the European interpretational influences."

EDUCATION: Graduated Haskell, 1935; one year vocational training, 1936; graduated Bacone College, 1938; B.A., Oklahoma, 1941; M.F.A., Oklahoma, 1950; graduate work, University of Redlands, Calif., summers, 1946, 1952; Northeastern, summer, 1953 (teaching credentials); extension course, graduate education, Oklahoma, 1951–52; Tulsa, summers, 1951, 1957. Mural instruction under Olaf Nordmark, Phoenix, Ariz., 1941–42.

SERVICE: WWII, U.S. Navy, four years; European Theater.

CAREER: Painter, sculptor, lecturer, teacher; director of camp activities, Boys Camp, East Hebron, N.H., summers, 1938, 1941; art instructor, Phoenix Indian School, 1941–42, 1946–47; Chairman of Art Department, Bacone College, 1947–.

HONORS: Student body president, Haskell Institute. Represented in *Who's Who in American Art, Who's Who in the West and Southwest, Who's Who in Oklahoma, Indians of Today*. Featured in TV program produced by National Council of Churches, 1956. Recipient of Certificate of Appreciation, IACB, 1960; honorary degree, Doctor of Humane Letters, Eastern Baptist College, St. Davids, Pa., 1963; Waite Phillips Outstanding Indian Artists Award Trophy, PAC, 1964. Past president, Muskogee Art Guild.

COMMISSIONS: *Murals*: BC, OU (North Campus); U.S. Post Office, Okemah, Okla.; Boys Camp, New Hebron, N.H.; Phoenix, Indian School; H. Dub Stewart home, Muskogee, Okla. *Seals*: Designer of official seal, AIE.

BOOKS ILLUSTRATED: Bass (1950), Penney (1953), Lyback (1963).

WORK PUBLISHED: Llewellyn and Hoebel (1941), dust jacket; Jacobson and D'Ucel (1950), Carter (1955), La Farge (1956; 1960), Pierson and Davidson (1960), Berthrong (1963), Bleeker (1963), Jacobson (1964). *Denver Post, Empire Magazine* (September 1953); *National Geographic Magazine* (March 1955), *Oklahoma Today* (Summer 1958), *Life International* (March 16, 1959), *Baptist Leader* (November 1961), *Today* (March 1963), *The Sunday Oklahoman, Orbit Magazine* (April 14, 1963), *Saturday Review* (June 15, 1963).

EXHIBITIONS: 1946–65: AIE, AIEC, AIW, DAM, ITIC, JAM, JGS, MHDY-MM, MNM, NGA, OAC, PAC, PAC/T, SAIEAIP, USDI, USDS, WRNGA;

Agra Gallery, Washington, D.C.; Mulvane Art Center, Topeka, Kan.; The
Kermac Mural Design Competition Exhibit, Oklahoma City, Tulsa, Okla.
One-man shows: BC, DAM, PAC; Esquire Theater Art Gallery, Celebrity
Art Gallery, Oakbrook Theatre, Chicago, Ill.; Oshkosh Museum, Oshkosh,
Wisc.; Muskogee Art Guild, Muskogee, Okla.; Choppels Art Gallery, Pasa-
dena, Calif.; University of Redlands, Art Club of Palos Verdes Estates,
Calif.; Telfair Academy of Arts and Sciences, Savannah, Ga.
AWARDS: 1946–63: 19, (and two Grand Awards) from DAM, PAC; Oklahoma
state fairs.
COLLECTIONS: *Public*: BC, BIA, DAM, IACB, JAM, KM, MAI, MNA/KHC,
OU/L, OU/MA, PAC, SPIM, SPL; St. Augustine's Center, Chicago, Ill.;
Muskogee Art Guild; Commercial National Bank of Muskogee; Eastern
Baptist College, St. Davids, Pa. *Private*: E. Adkins, Albert, Ansara, Capps,
Cross, Edmondson, Elwell, Gaston, Green, J. Hall, Harbour, Hart, Hen-
schen, Hurley, O. Jacobson, Johnet, Leathers, Lindsey, D. Maxwell,
McAlister, Melville, K. Miller, Moreland, B. Oldham, Oliphant, Palmer,
Powell, H. Price, D. Ramsey, Ruby, Schonwald, Schreiber, Shaw, Shillin,
Spraker, J. Stone, Thompson, R. West, Woodburn, R. Young.
ADDRESS: Bacone College, Bacone, Okla.

Whirlwind (Chief)   *Southern Cheyenne*
Hevovitastamiutsts, Moving Whirlwind
BORN: Date unknown. Died, 1891. Old Whirlwind was a chief of the Southern
Cheyenne living at Darlington, Indian Territory (now Oklahoma), in 1872.
    The artist's work in Montgomery is a set of pencil and crayon sketches collected
    by Lt. Samuel Goode Jones at Fort Reno, I.T., 1890. *See* Grinnell (1915; 1923).
CAREER: Chief, warrior, and artist, who recorded scenes of battle, Indian
life, and travel.
HONORS: Whirlwind Indian Day School and Mission, Blaine County, Okla.,
was named for him.
COLLECTIONS: *Public*: MMFA.

Whirlwind Hawk   *Sioux*
COLLECTIONS: *Public*: MPM (pictograph on paper).

White, Clarence A.   *Omaha*
Tanuga Shinga, Little Bull
EDUCATION: Bacone College.
EXHIBITIONS: PAC, 1954.

White, Riley   *Cherokee*
BORN: 1912, DeQueen, Ark.
EDUCATION: Chouinard Art Institute, Los Angeles, Calif., *ca.* 1945; B.F.A.,
Oklahoma S. U., 1950; M.F.A., Oklahoma S. U., 1954; summer courses
toward M.A., New Mexico U.
SERVICE: WWII, U.S. Army, and U.S. Air Force, five years.
CAREER: Art instructor, Sequoyah Indian School, 1951–.
EXHIBITIONS: PAC; Western Hills Lodge, Sequoyah State Park, Okla. *One-
man shows*: Conners College, Warner, Okla.; Tahlequah, Stillwater, Okla.
ADDRESS: c/o Sequoyah Indian School, Tahlequah, Okla.

White, Ruth M.   *Sauk-Fox*

BORN: Date unknown. Daughter of Walter Emmitt McKitrick and Alta Virginia Holmes (Sauk-Fox).

> The artist has demonstrated her original spoon-painting technique throughout the Southwest and South. She has completed a series of Oklahoma Indian portraits in oil and lent them to various educational institutions in the area. She believes artists are made, not born, and "heartily endorses the study of art as a hobby and for therapeutic value."

EDUCATION: Elementary public schools, Tulsa, Okla.; graduated Gorman (Tex.) High School, 1927; Hardin-Simmons College, Abilene, Tex.; Chicago; Morris Harvey College, Charleston, W. Va.; School of Arts and Sciences, Trenton, N.J.; Philadelphia (Pa.) Fine Arts Academy, Del Mar College, Corpus Christi, Tex.; Connors State College; Oklahoma; Utah S.; Northeastern; Bacone College. Private instruction under Henry Clayton Staples, Elliot O'Hara, and Frederick Taubes.

CAREER: Painter, sculptor, teacher, lecturer, writer; art instructor, Connors State College, Warner, Okla., 1950–65. Conducted 17 art workshops at Ruidoso, N.M.; Northwest State College, Alva, Okla.; Galveston, Tex.; Telluride, Dolores, Colo., 1952–64. Conducted art classes at Muskogee, Warner, Stigler, and Wagoner, in Okla., 1946–63.

HONORS: Oklahoma Education Association: consultant for art program; vice-chairman of art section; member of the council; program chairman for art section; art chairman for eastern district; associate editor for *Art Lines*, the association's art magazine. Invited to participate in National Teachers Art Program, Miami Beach, Fla., 1961. Art chairman, Conference of Junior Colleges, Norman, Okla., 1962. Represented in *Who's Who in American Education, Who's Who in the South and Southwest, Who's Who in American Women*; listed in *International Directory of Arts, Directory of International Biography*. Chosen by M. Grumbacher, Inc., for *Palette from Renaissance to Modern Times*; elected to National Association of Women Artists.

EXHIBITIONS: 1947–65: AEOP/T, GM, MNM, NAWA/T, PAC, RM, SMNAI, SPIM, WM/T. National Academy of Design, New York, N.Y.; Continental Museum, Corpus Christi, Tex.; Connors State College; Galveston (Tex.) Watercolor Exhibits, M. Grumbacher, Inc., Original Palette Permanent Collection Exhibit, Grand Central Art Galleries, N.Y. Texas Watercolor Society Exhibit, San Antonio, Tex.; 70th Exhibition of National Association of Women Artists, National Academy of Art, N.Y.; represented in Ruskin Rental Gallery, PAC; Muskogee Annual Art Show. *One-man shows*: 1947–60: 16, including Amarillo Senior High School, Amarillo, Tex.; Galveston Art League, Rosenburg Library; Connors State College; Muskogee Semi-Centennial Fair; Professional Artists' League, and National Arts Club, in N.Y.; Western Hills Lodge, Sequoyah State Park, Okla.; Adoue Park, Galveston, Tex.; Downtown Galleries, New Orleans, La.; Argent Gallery, N.Y.

AWARDS: OAC, SN; Allied Artists of West Virginia Exhibition; Witte Memorial Museum, San Antonio, Tex.; Muskogee and Tulsa State Fairs,

Sweepstakes awards, 1958–59; Muskogee Annual Art Show, Grand Award; state fairs in Oklahoma, totaling 200 awards.

COLLECTIONS: *Public*: Connors State College, Fort Gibson (Okla.) Museum, *Private*: C. Snodgrass.

ADDRESS: 417 Locust St., Alva, Okla.

White Bear   *Arapaho*

The artist was among the 72 Plains Indians taken as prisoners from Fort Sill, Okla., to Fort Marion, St. Augustine, Fla., in 1875.

COLLECTIONS: *Public*: HI.

White Bear   *Crow* (?)

COLLECTIONS: *Public*: GM (crayon drawings on paper, *ca.* 1921).

White Bear   *Hopi*

Kutca Honauu, White Bear

BORN: 1869.

White Bear was among the first Indian artists of the Southwest. Between 1899 and 1900, the artist, and several other Hopis, were persuaded by Dr. J. Walter Fewkes to make drawings representing the Hopi gods and to explain the symbolism of the dance rituals. The project resulted in the publication, in 1903, of about 180 Kachina drawings on some 50 color plates. The artist was assisted by his uncle, Homovi.

WORK PUBLISHED: BAE, *21st AR*.

COLLECTIONS: *Public*: MAI, SMNAI (by a Hopi named White Bear).

White Bear   *Hopi*

Kucha Honawah, White Bear

(Also known as Fredericks, Oswald.)

BORN: February 5, 1906, Old Oraibi, Ariz. Son of Charles Fredericks Tu-wahoyiwma (Hopi) and Anna Tuvengyamsi, (Hopi).

MARRIED: Naomi.

EDUCATION: Oraibi, and Phoenix (Ariz.), Indian Schools; Phoenix High School; Bacone College; Haskell, 1933–37.

CAREER: Arts and crafts instructor, Boys Club of Phoenix, Ariz., *ca.* 1959; art teacher, YMCA in New Jersey, 15 years; Kachina carver; lecturer, writer; teacher of dancing and interpretive music, Fred Waring Workshop.

COMMISSIONS: *Murals*: YMCA in New Jersey.

WORK PUBLISHED: Waters (1963). *Arizona Highways* (July 1959), *The Arizona Republic, Sunday Magazine* (June 7, 1964).

COLLECTIONS: *Public*: MAI [original 72 paintings and drawings published in Waters (1963)]; SMNAI (by a Hopi named White Bear).

ADDRESS: Box 162, Oraibi, Ariz.

White Bear, Alton   *Arikara*

Son of the Star

BORN: March 27, 1933. Son of Joseph White Bear. GF: Raymond Red Bear, scout for Custer, who participated in the Battle of the Little Big Horn. GGF: Son of Star.

MARRIED: García Lee Hale, 1960. One child: Connie Agnes, 1962.

The artist has been interested in art most of his life. He first began to paint *ca.* 1958. During the winter months he feeds cattle and draws pictures.

EDUCATION: Elwoods, N. Dak.
CAREER: Truck driver and mechanic, 1953–.
EXHIBITIONS: BNIAS.
COLLECTIONS: *Private*: Arrow, Chase, Gierke, O. Keene, Swift Eagle.
ADDRESS: Box 242, Mandaree, N. Dak.

White Bird   *Northern Cheyenne-Nez Percé*
BORN: *Ca.* mid–1800's.
> Capt. Richard L. Livermore's quarters at Fort Keogh in 1890 was a log cabin.
> To make his cabin more presentable, he covered the inside walls with unbleached
> muslin. During his stay at the Fort, his Indian friends came to visit and painted
> pictures on it, many of which were by White Bird. Livermore took the paintings
> with him when he left the Fort "...some are in the possession of his wife in
> Denver." *See* Grinnell (1915).

CAREER: Warrior, possibly in the Battle of the Little Big Horn when he
was 15 years old.
HONORS: Second chief of the Nez Percé.
COLLECTIONS: *Public*: DAM, OAA/SI; U.S. Military Academy Museum,
West Point, N.Y. (not confirmed).

White Buffalo (*see* Hill, Bobby)

White Buffalo, Herbert   *Cheyenne*
BORN: 1917. Lived at Concho, Okla. GF: Kish Hawkins.
EXHIBITIONS: AIAE/WSU, AIEC.
AWARDS: AIAE/WSU.
COLLECTIONS: *Private*: Aaron.

White Bull   *Teton Sioux*
WORK PUBLISHED: BAE, *Bull. 173*.

White Coral Beads (*see* Peña, Tonita)

White-Cow Killer   *Teton Sioux*
> The artist kept a winter count which represented about the same years as the
> counts kept by American Horse and Baptiste Good (*qq.v.*). He was known to
> have been at Pine Ridge Agency *ca.* 1880.

WORK PUBLISHED: BAE, *4th AR*.

White Crow (*see* Horn, Miles S.)

White Eagle   *Oglala* (?) *Sioux*
Wabliska
BORN: Date unknown; from Pine Ridge Agency, S. Dak. (*see* Black Heart).
Chief White Bull reported that a White Eagle was killed in the Battle of the
Little Big Horn, June 25, 1876.
COLLECTIONS: *Public*: MAI (a white eagle).

White Eagle, Charles W.   *Winnebago*
EXHIBITIONS: 1963–64: AAIEAE, USDS.
ADDRESS: 8240 14th Avenue, Apt. 202, Hyattsville, Md.

White Haired Chief With Scarred Face (*see* Washakie)

White Horse   *Kiowa*
Tsen T'ainte, White Horse
BORN: Date unknown (probably early 1800's). Brother of Chief Big Bow
(*q.v.*).

CAREER: Warrior, artist; the Anko calendar records that White Horse killed a Navaho, *ca.* 1867–68. He refused to settle on a reservation, 1873, participated in the Battle of Adobe Walls, 1874, and, with other Plains Indians, was sent to prison at Fort Marion, St. Augustine, Fla., in 1875 (*see* Cohoe, William).

COLLECTIONS: *Public*: JAM; YU/BRBML (previously credited to "White Goose," now thought to be by White Horse).

Whitehead, Ernest   *Mescalero Apache*
EDUCATION: Institute, *ca.* 1964.
EXHIBITIONS: FAIEAIP.

Whitehorse, Roland N.   *Kiowa*
Hanemi Da, Charging Man.
BORN: April 6, 1921, Carnegie, Okla. Son of Charlie Whitehorse (Kiowa) and Laura (Kiowa). P/GGF: Chief Tohausen (*q.v.*). P/GGF: Mamanti (Sky Walker), the famed Kiowa medicine man and war leader. M/GF: Rainy Mountain Charlie, son of Sky Walker (Kiowa), keeper of Grandmother Medicine Bundle. GF: Hanemi Da (Kiowa). P/GU: Chief Whitehorse (*q.v.*).
MARRIED: June L. Carson (Oto-Potawatomi). Four children: Charles, 1953; Susan, 1955; Janet, 1957; Manila, 1963.
EDUCATION: Graduated Washita High School, west of Anadarko, Okla., 1942; attended Bacone College, 1947; Dallas (Tex.) Art Institute, 1957.
SERVICE: WWII, U.S. Army, 40 months; North African and European Theaters.
CAREER: Illustrator, Fort Sill (Okla.) School Training Aids, 1956–59; graphic supervisor, Fort Sill Fourth Army Training Aids, 1959–.
HONORS: Arts and crafts director, AIE, 1960–64; chairman, American Indian Artists Association, 1965.
BOOKS ILLUSTRATED: Marriott (1952), Madrano (1955).
WORK PUBLISHED: *Compton's Pictured Encyclopedia* (1951).
EXHIBITIONS: AIE, PAC, PAC/T, SPIM; Underwood's, Wichita Falls, Tex.; Harris Shopping Center, Dallas, Tex.; Carpenter's Gallery, Dallas, Tex.; Skirvin Tower, Oklahoma City, Okla., joint show with Mopope and Blue Eagle (*qq.v.*).
AWARDS: PAC.
COLLECTIONS: *Public*: FSM, GM, PAC. *Private*: Arkeketa, Bayne, Davis, Knickerbocker, Pappio, E. Roberts.
ADDRESS: Box 265, Elgin, Okla.

White Man (*see* Ahsit)

Whiteman (*see* Ahsit)

Whiteman, A.   *Cheyenne-Arapaho*
Sitting Bear
(Also known as Whiteman, Alfred, Jr.)
BORN: August 28, 1928, Colony, Okla. Son of Alfred Whiteman, Sr. (Arapaho) and Nellie R. Rouse (Cheyenne). P/GGF: Chief Little Raven (Arapaho), who signed the Medicine Lodge Treaty in 1867, and was awarded the Medal of Honor by the U.S. Government.

MARRIED: Henrietta Verle Mann, 1959. Four children: Mark Alan (stepson), 1956; Alden Alfred, 1960; Montoya Ann, 1962; Jackie Ladean, 1963.
Two small White boys, lost on the prairie, were adopted by different Arapaho families. One died shortly thereafter, and the surviving boy, who was given the name White Man (Neotha), grew to manhood and married the chief's daughter, Anna Little Raven. White Man was the artist's paternal grandfather.

EDUCATION: Central and Irving Schools, El Reno, Okla., 1936–44; graduated El Reno High School, 1948; Naval Preparatory Schools in Corpus Christi, Tex., and Memphis, Tenn.; Naval Air Technical Training Center, Memphis, Tenn.; graduated Oklahoma S. U./S. T., 1962.

SERVICE: WWII, U.S. Navy, four years; South Pacific Theater.

CAREER: Jet engine mechanic, Tinker Air Force Base, Oklahoma City, Okla.; artist and designer, Oklahoma State University, Stillwater, Public Information Division, 1962–.

WORK PUBLISHED: *The Sunday Oklahoman, Orbit Magazine* (August 2, 1964), *Oklahoma State Alumnus Magazine* (November 1964).

EXHIBITIONS: BNIAS, FAIEAIP, MNM, PAC; Sporting Gallery, Middleburg, Va.; Yukon (Okla.) Gallery, Oklahoma State University, Stillwater, Okla.; YWCA, Oklahoma City, Okla.; St. Andrews Episcopal Chirch, Stillwater, Okla.; University of Arkansas. *One-man shows*: 1962–65: Oklahoma State University, Sherwin-Williams, First National Bank, and National Conference of American Farm Economics Association (Oklahoma State University), in Stillwater, Okla.; Citizens National Bank, Okmulgee, Okla.

AWARDS: FNAIC, MNM.

COLLECTIONS: *Public*: Oklahoma State University, Student Union, Stillwater, Okla. *Private*: Belford, Berkeley, Bond, H. Campbell, Cowling, R. Dennis, Frusti, Gatliff, Gay, I. Jones, King, Kroll, Leno, Marks, Meyers, Milberger, Morrissette, S. Ramsey, H. Sanders, Simank, Solow, Spurlock, Stryker, Todd, Twins, Webster.

ADDRESS: 805 S. Orchard Lane, Stillwater, Okla.

Whiteman, Alfred, Jr. (*see* Whiteman, A.)

Whiteman, James Ridgley   *Powhatan* (?)
Osapana

BORN: January 15, 1910, Portales, N.M. Son of Levi Whiteman and Katherine Great House.

EDUCATION: New Mexico U., 1930; studied sculpture under Brice Sewell, portrait painting under Neils Hogner, Indian art under Kenneth Chapman, and archaeology under Edgar L. Hewett; Federal Art Project, under Vernon Hunter, 1937–41; private study, Oklahoma City, Okla., one winter; studied under Ann W. Keener, Gallup, N.M., 1940; ceramics training, Anaheim, Calif., 1963–65.

CAREER: Seasonal work as commercial artist since the 1930's, the Western Decorating Co., Los Angeles, Calif.; lecturer, painter, sculptor, and commercial artist; employed at Knott's Berry Farm, Los Angeles, *ca.* 1960–.

HONORS: Honorary member, Creek Nation of Oklahoma; council member, Western *Kee Too Wah*; did handprinting and color plates for Spanish Colonial Art of New Mexico, Federal Art Project, *ca.* 1939.

EXHIBITIONS: FAIEAIP, ITIC, LAIC, MNM, PAC, USDI. *One-man shows*: MNM.
AWARDS: ITIC, LAIC.
ADDRESS: 6757 Val Verde, Buena Park, Calif.

Who Whinny (*see* Roman Nose, Henry Caruthers)

Wiacke (*see* Weakee, Teddy)

Wickahtewah (*see* Moqui)

Wife Eagle Deer *Oglala Sioux*
Mepaa Kte, Wife Eagle Deer
BORN: *ca.* 1869. Died *ca.* 1929.
The artist painted skins depicting Sioux dance scenes and battles between the Crow and Sioux. *See* Jacobson and D'Ucel (1950).

Wild Hog (Chief) *Cheyenne*
COLLECTIONS: *Public*: KSHS (manuscript division: notebook of sketches, dated 1879); OAA/SI (copy of a drawing by Wild Hog).

Wild Horse *Kiowa*
Koba
The artist was one of many Plains Indians arrested at Salt Fork, Red River, Indian Territory, February 18, 1875, and imprisoned at Fort Marion, St. Augustine, Fla. (*see* Cohoe, William). Wild Horse, primarily a warrior rather than an artist, participated in raids into the Brazos country in 1872, and attacked the Wichita Agency, August 22, 1874.
EDUCATION: At Carlisle, he was a student in the tinshop, with Henry Caruthers Roman Nose (*q.v.*).
WORK PUBLISHED: BAE, *17th AR*.
COLLECTIONS: *Public*: HI, MHS/B, OAA/SI, YU/BRBML. *Private*: Walsh.

Wilder, Leonard *Karok-Assiniboin*
COLLECTIONS: *Public*: IACB.

Wilkie, Laurence *Chippewa*
BORN: September 29, 1922, Belcourt, N. Dak. P/GGF: Alexander "Scotch" Wilkie, leader of many buffalo hunts in N. Dak.
MARRIED: Ema Davis, 1951. Six children: Julianne, 1952; Leslie, 1953; Larry, 1955; Tracy, 1957; Russell, 1958; Lee, 1960.
Mr. Wilkie has always been interested in art, but did not start painting until about 1946. He usually does not exhibit his work, preferring to paint for pleasure and for his friends and family.
EDUCATION: Attended Walker's Art Institute, Minneapolis, Minn.
SERVICE: U.S. Navy, four years.
CAREER: Tabulator operator.
EXHIBITIONS: BNIAS (also designed catalog cover).
ADDRESS: Box 301, Belcourt, N. Dak.

Wilkinson, Douglas *Sioux* (?)
So Hah Ney
COLLECTIONS: *Public*: MAI.

Williams, David Emmett   *Kiowa-Tonkawa-Apache*
Tosque, Apache Man
BORN: August 20, 1933, Lawton, Okla. Son of Emmett Williams (Tonkawa-Apache), singer and leather designer. His mother is Kiowa. The artist is descended from the Kiowa war chief Satanka (Sitting Bear).
MARRIED: Norma Jean Eubanks, 1961.
EDUCATION: Bacone College.
CAREER: Painter.
EXHIBITIONS: BNIAS, FANAIAE, PAC, SPIM, SM, USDI; Sporting Gallery, Williamsburg, Va.; Stouffer's Manor Gate House, Pittsburgh, Pa. *One-man shows*: HM. *Two-man shows*: Pasadena, Calif., 1964.
COLLECTIONS: *Public*: MAI, SM; St. Augustine's Center, Chicago, Ill.; Carnegie (Okla.) High School. *Private*: Bialac, Christensen, J. McAlpin.
ADDRESS: Muskogee, Okla.

Williams, Sharon Pilcher   *Potawatomi*
COLLECTIONS: *Public*: St. Augustine's Center, Chicago, Ill.

Wilson, Cynthia Judy   *Quechan*
BORN: September 22, 1942.
EDUCATION: Santa Fe, *ca.* 1962.
EXHIBITIONS: PAC, 1962.
ADDRESS: Box 152, Winterhaven, Calif.

Wilson, J.   ?
EDUCATION: Albuquerque.
EXHIBITIONS: ITIC, 1959.
AWARDS: ITIC.

Wilson, John   *Navaho*
EDUCATION: Santa Fe, 1960.
EXHIBITIONS: MNM, 1960.

Wilson, Lucy   *Navaho*
EDUCATION: Albuquerque, 1959.
EXHIBITIONS: MNM, 1959.
AWARDS: MNM.

Wiyo (*see* Randall, Bunnie)

Wobaah (*see* Washakie, Charles)

Wolf Alone (*see* Taulbee, Dan)

Wolf Face   *Apache*
While a prisoner of war at St. Augustine, Fla., in 1879, he executed paintings on writing paper with watercolor and colored pencil (*see* Cohoe, William).
COLLECTIONS: *Public*: OHSM.

Wolfe, Edmond Richard   *Creek-Seminole*
Este Songah, Gone Man
BORN: September 29, 1928.
EDUCATION: Bacone College; Haskell.
SERVICE: WWII, U.S. Navy, three years; Pacific Theater.
EXHIBITIONS: PAC, 1957.
ADDRESS: Wetumka, Okla.

Wood, Harvy   *Navaho*
BORN: 1944.
EDUCATION: Inter-Mt.
EXHIBITIONS: FAIEAIP.

Wooden Leg   *Northern Cheyenne*
Kummok Quivviokta, Wooden Leg
BORN: 1858, near the Cheyenne River, Black Hills, N. Dak. Deceased. Son
of White Buffalo Shaking Off The Dust (also called Many Bullet Wounds)
(Northern Cheyenne) and Eagle Feather On The Forehead (Northern Chey-
enne).
WORK PUBLISHED: Marquis (1931). *Montana* (Spring 1963).
COLLECTIONS: *Public*: Custer Battlefield National Monument.

Woodring, Carl   *Osage*
Wasaba Shinga, Little Bear
(Also known as Woodring, Carlton Delmas.)
BORN: December 6, 1920, Arkansas City, Kan. Son of Orville Woodring and
Gladys Fagen. Cousin of Harry Woodring, Secretary of War under President
Franklin D. Roosevelt and former Governor of Kansas.
MARRIED: Margaret; divorced, 1964. Four children: Rose, David, Nikkie,
Shawn.
> Reared in Pawhuska, Okla., the artist began painting in 1956, under the tutelage
> of Acee Blue Eagle (*q.v.*). Within a year, he was exhibiting throughout the U.S.
> and Europe and had become a prolific painter. During 1964 and most of 1965,
> he virtually ceased to paint, but late in 1965 he began again.

EDUCATION: Pawhuska, Okla.; colleges in Okla., Tex., Ala., and Oreg.
SERVICE: WWII and Korean War, U.S. Air Corps, 11 years.
CAREER: Architectural engineer, McCune and McCune, Architects, Tulsa,
Okla., *ca.* 1959–64; painter, sculptor.
HONORS: Received more awards in a single year than any artist ever to enter
the PAC Indian Artists' Annual Exhibition; Past-President, Tulsa Pow
Wow Club; arts and crafts director, AIE.
WORK PUBLISHED: *Oklahoma Today* (Summer 1959).
EXHIBITIONS: AAID, AAIE, AIE, ITIC, LAIC, MNM, PAC, PAC/T, PSC,
SN, SPIM, USDS; Ponca Indian Fair, Ponca City, Okla.; Tulsa Pow Wow
Arts and Crafts Show, and Oil Capitol Art Show. His paintings have hung
at: Brussels' World Fair, Belgium; American Embassy, Paris, France;
Office of the Lord Mayor, Mannheim, Germany; Parkland Hotel, London,
England. *One-man shows*: PAC, SPIM; No Man's Land Museum, Weather-
ford, Okla. *Two-man shows*: GM.
AWARDS: AIE, ITIC, MNM, PAC; (two Grand Awards).
COLLECTIONS: *Public*: BIA, GM, IACB, MAI, MNM, PAC. *Private*: Dock-
stader, Obermire.
ADDRESS: c/o Mrs. Orville Woodring, Gore, Okla.

Woohkinih (*see* Roman Nose)

Wo Peen (*see* Gonzales, Louis)

Wounded Face (Chief)   *Mandan*
COLLECTIONS: *Public*: PU/M (autobiographical drawings on muslin, presented as a gift, 1891).

Wuxpais (*see* Little Chief, Daniel)

Wynne, Bruce   *Spokane* (?)
BORN: *ca.* 1944, near Wellpinit, Wash., on the Spokane Reservation.
EDUCATION: Schools in a "small town near Spokane"; graduated from Mead (Wash.) High School, 1962; graduated Institute, major in sculpture and painting, 1964.
CAREER: Free-lance artist, 1964–.
EXHIBITIONS: FAIEAIP, FANAIAE, ITIC, PAC, SN; "Origin of American Indian Sculpture," Santa Fe, N.M.
ADDRESS: Box 122, Mead, Wash.

Yaka (*see* Moquino, Delfino)

Yates, George   *Nambé*
COLLECTIONS: *Public*: MNM (executed in ninth grade, 1955).

Yazzie, Carl   *Navaho*
COLLECTIONS: *Public*: MNM.

Yazzie, Daniel Wilbur   *Navaho*
BORN: Date unknown. Son of Hosteen Yazzie Bedonie.
EDUCATION: Riverside, 1964.
HONORS: Philomathic Club of Anadarko Scholarship to art school of his choice, 1964.
ADDRESS: Little Water, via Shiprock, N.M.

Yazzie, Deswood H.   *Navaho*
EDUCATION: Ganado (Ariz.) Mission School, (tenth grade, 1961).
COLLECTIONS: *Private*: Wyman.

Yazzie, James Wayne   *Navaho*
BORN: 1943.
EXHIBITIONS: AIAE/WSU, FAIEAIP.
COLLECTIONS: *Public*: AF, MAI. *Private*: Mullan.
ADDRESS: Sheep Springs, N.M.

Yazzie, Merlin   *Navaho*
EDUCATION: Greasewood (Ariz.) Boarding School, fifth grade, 1965.
EXHIBITIONS: Greasewood Boarding School Art Show, 1965.
AWARDS: Greasewood Boarding School Art Show, first award, 1965.

Yazzie, Richard Kee   *Navaho*
BORN: 1944, Crownpoint, N.M.
EDUCATION: Santa Fe; Albuquerque, 1960's; Institute, 1965–66.
EXHIBITIONS: 1960–66: Five, including MNM, PAC, SAIEAIP, SN.
AWARDS: SN student award, 1962.
COLLECTIONS: *Private*: Elkus.
ADDRESS: San Ildefonso Pueblo, via Santa Fe, N.M.

Yazzie, Sybil L.   *Navaho*
The artist received international recognition while a student in Santa Fe. Her
painting of 179 Navahos, in full costume, and 59 horses, was exhibited in London
and Paris in 1937 and brought the comment that"it was not naive and childish,
but a finished work of art, expert in draftmanship, intricate in detail, and uner-
ring in color."
EDUCATION: Santa Fe, 1937.
EXHIBITIONS: AIW, NGA; London, Paris.
COLLECTIONS: *Public*: SM. *Private*: Dietrich, D. Kramer.
ADDRESS: Garcia Store, Chinle, Ariz.

Yazzie, Tom K.   *Navaho*
BORN: 1942.
EDUCATION: Arizona, "Southwest Indian Art Project," summer, 1960.
EXHIBITIONS: 1962–63: PAC, USDS.
COLLECTIONS: *Public*: BIA, IACB; SMNAI (woodcarving).

Yazzie Bahe (*see* Tsinajinnie, Andrew Van)

Yellow Arrow (*see* Shelton, Peter H., Jr.)

Yellow Blanket   *Sioux*
Shinagi, Yellow Blanket (also *Schinagi*)
One of five artists whose works, commissioned and collected by Rudolf Cronau,
1880–83, are now referred to as the Cronau Album (*see* Sinte).
COLLECTIONS: *Public*: AMNH.

Yellow Feather   *Mandan*
Sikchida (or *Sik Chida*)
BORN: Date unknown, near Fort Clark, N. Dak., *ca.* 1833–34. Son of a
prominent Mandan chief.
"During their winter's sojourn at Fort Clark, near the Mandan villages, in 1883–
1834, Prince Maximilian and Karl Bodmer were visited by a number of Indians
who were fascinated by Bodmer's artistic talents. The white artist gave pencils,
watercolors, and paper to some of these Indians and encouraged them to make
pictures for the Prince's collection. These watercolors are the earliest known
examples of paintings executed by Plains Indians in the white man's art medium.
In their striving to portray the details of human and horse anatomy, of costume
and accessories, these Indian artists produced paintings which are quite unlike
the traditional picture-writing of their people. There are nine examples of this
new style of painting in Prince Maximilian's collection. Four of them were
executed by Yellow Feather, of whom the Prince wrote: 'He came almost every
evening, when his favorite employment was drawing, for which he had some
talent, though his figures were no better than those drawn by our children.'"
Catlin, Bodmer, Miller (exhibition catalog).
WORK PUBLISHED: *Catlin, Bodmer, Miller*, Joslyn Art Museum, 1963.
COLLECTIONS: *Public*: BM (unconfirmed), NNGCC.

Yellow Hair (*see* Hood, Rance)

Yellow Hair (*see* Toppah, Herman)

Yellow Horse   *Arapaho* (?)
BORN: Date unknown; lived at one time in the area of Bozeman, Mont.
Killed possibly in 1869.
In 1933, D. S. Warren of Iowa owned drawings by Yellow Horse that were photo-
graphed by the Smithsonian Institution. Then, the drawings were at the Iowa
Historical Society in Des Moines; their present whereabouts are unknown.

SERVICE: U.S. Army.
COLLECTIONS: *Public*: OAA/SI.

Yellow Lodge   *Santee-Yanktonai Sioux*
BORN: Date unknown; lived at Cannonball, N. Dak.
The Yellow Lodge Winter Count, owned by Eugene Burdick of Williston, N. Dak., and placed on indefinite loan with the North Dakota State Historical Museum in 1932, includes the years 1785–86 to 1930–31. A copy of this count, complete through 1951–52, was kept by Mrs. Teresa Yellow-lodge of Fort Yates, N. Dak. (*See* BAE, *Bull. 173*, pp. 335–416.)
WORK PUBLISHED: BAE, *Bull. 173*.

Yellow Nose   *Ute*
(Also known as Little Robe; Crow Indian.)
BORN: 1850's; when he was about four, he and his mother were captured on the Rio Grande by Cheyennes and Arapahos led by Dive Backwards. His mother escaped, and he was adopted by Spotted Wolf. He was living near Geary, Okla., in 1909.
CAREER: Warrior, took part in many historical battles.
COLLECTIONS: *Public*: JAM, MAI (350 ledger style paintings collected *ca.* 1880 by John Gregory Bourke).
WORK PUBLISHED: *Catlin, Bodmer, Miller*, Joslyn Art Museum (1963); Cohoe (1965).

Yellow Tail   *Plains*
COLLECTIONS: *Public*: SMNAI (buffalo hide painting).

Yellow Wolf (Chief)   *Comanche*
In the collection of RMAS is an oil portrait of Chief Yellow Wolf by Col. Arthur T. Lee, with the Eighth Infantry in Texas, who befriended Yellow Wolf.
COLLECTIONS: *Public*: RMAS (drawing, *ca.* 1859, on blue foolscap painted for, and given to, Col. Lee).

Yepa, Emilina   *Jémez*
BORN: Date unknown. Deceased.
EDUCATION: Santa Fe, *ca.* 1932–37.
EXHIBITIONS: NGA, 1953.
COLLECTIONS: *Private*: M. Kramer.

Yepa, Rita   *Jémez*
BORN: *ca.* 1944.
EDUCATION: Jémez, *ca.* 1960.
EXHIBITIONS: AAIE, AIE, PAC.
AWARDS: 1957: two, including AIE.

Yeppa, Franklin   *Pueblo [Jémez?]*
COLLECTIONS: *Private*: Bush.

Yeppa, Jimmie   *Jémez*
EDUCATION: Santa Fe, *ca.* 1958.
EXHIBITIONS: MNM, 1958.

Yo Sumce Witke   *Sioux*
COLLECTIONS: *Public*: MPM (pictographic style on paper).

Young, Mary Cecilia *Choctaw*
BORN: April 14, 1928, Muskogee, Okla. Daughter of Herman Bresser and Lillie Willis (Choctaw).
MARRIED: Revere A. Young, May 16, 1950. Two children: Lillian Diane, 1951; Robert Mark, 1954.
EDUCATION: Sacred Heart School, Muskogee, Okla., 1934–42; graduated Muskogee Central High School, 1946; St. Mary's of Notre Dame, South Bend, Ind., 1947; Bacone College, art classes, 1960–61; studied under Ruth M. White (*q.v.*), Roger Lee White, John Arthur, John Kennedy, George Calvert, Joan Hill (*q.v.*), Helen Rowland, and Dick West (*q.v.*).
CAREER: Housewife, painter; active in Service League of Muskogee, a civic organization.
HONORS: Chairman, Muskogee Annual Art Show, 1960; Chairman Ways and Means Committee, Decorating Chairman, Service League of Muskogee.
EXHIBITIONS: PAC, MNM, SAIEAIP, SN; Muskogee Annual Art Show; Muskogee Art Students Guild; Oklahoma State Fair, Muskogee, Okla.; Indian City, Anadarko, Okla.
COLLECTIONS: *Private*: G. Carter, W. Fenton, Gulager, Johnet, L. Keene, Nichols.
ADDRESS: 1415 Seventh Street, Apt. D., Riverside, Calif.

Young Deer (*see* Roberts, Frank)

Young Man Afraid of His Horses *Sioux*
BORN: Date unknown; lived in the area of Pine Ridge, S. Dak., in 1880. The artist, a minor chief, opposed Red Cloud on the sale of Sioux land. [*See* Hyde (1956).]
HONORS: Appointed head of the Bear People by Agent McGillicuddy, 1879.
COLLECTIONS: *Public*: MAI.

Yutsuwuna (*see* Eckiwaudah, Tennyson)

Zepko Ettee (*see* Big Bow, Chief)

Zeyouma, Phillip *Hopi*
EDUCATION: Santa Fe, *ca.* 1932–33.
EXHIBITIONS: NGA.
COLLECTIONS: *Public*: DAM. *Private*: M. Kramer.

Zone Keuh *Kiowa* (?)
The artist was among the 72 Plains Indians taken as prisoners from Fort Sill, Okla., to Fort Marion, St. Augustine, Fla., in 1875.
COLLECTIONS: *Public*: YU/BRBML.

Zotigh, Barbara Tallamonts *Kiowa-Arapaho-Isleta*
Acenemah, Always Prepared; Sweet Fruit.
BORN: September 29, 1925, Detroit, Mich. Daughter of Carew H. Tallamonts (Isleta) and Carrie Hunt (Kiowa-Arapaho).
MARRIED: 1947; divorced 1960. Married Ben Shoemake, 1967.
The artist has been painting since about 1961. She has been most encouraged by Mrs. Homer Abbott and Tom Manhart.
EDUCATION: Graduated Haskell, 1942; graduated Haskell, Business College, 1943; Kansas, 1944; St. Anthony's Hospital School, 1947; Tulsa, 1960–.

CAREER: X-ray Technician, 1944–.
EXHIBITIONS: FAIEAIP, PAC, SN.
AWARDS: PAC.
ADDRESS: 3531 South Oswego, Tulsa, Okla.

Zotom   *Kiowa*
(Also known as Zo Tom; Biter.)
MARRIED: Mary Buffalo (Kiowa).
  The artist was among the 72 Plains Indians taken as prisoners from Fort Sill,
  Okla., to Fort Marion, St. Augustine, Fla., in 1875.
COLLECTIONS: *Public*: HI, MAI, YU/BRBML. *Private*: Curtin.

Zshingka Heka (*see* Standingbear, George Eugene)

Zuazua, Michael   *Mescalero Apache*
EXHIBITIONS: MNM, student division, 1963.
ADDRESS: Mescalero, N.M.

Zuyaterila (*see* Tough Soldier)

TRIBAL INDEX

ACOMA
Byrnes, James Michael
Hunt, Clyde "Sunnyskies"
Hunt, Wolf Robe
Paytiamo, James P.
Torivio, Lolita
Vallo, Pedro

ALEUT
Backford, Alexandra

APACHE
Archilta, Clara
Botella, Emmett
Buffalo Meat
Caje, Richard
Chester, Richard
Cosen, Gilbert
Cosen, Lydia M.
Cut Ear
Dewey, Wilson
Enjady, Errol
Gregg, Wilkie
Hosetosavit, Arden
Houser, Allan C.
Hunting Wolf
Little, Bernadette
Loco, Moses
Mana
Martin, Ringlin
Morgan, Robert
Naiche
Nash, Daniel
Nash, Wesley
Nosie, Montie
Palmer, Ignatius
Patterson, Pat
Paz, Carol
Penrod, Michael
Polan Yi Katon
Puerto, Leonard
Sine, David
Smith, Gibson R.
Stevens, Jim
Takzi
Toppah, Herman
Treas, Byron L.
Treas, Rudolph
Venego, Florenzo
Vicenti, Carl A.
Vicenti, Steven

Vigil, Calvin
Vigil, Frank Paul
Whitehead, Ernest
Williams, David Emmett
Wolf Face
Zuazua, Michael

ARAPAHO
Beard, Lorenzo
Bushyhead, Allan
Packer
Shave Head
Sweezy, Carl
White Bear
Whiteman, A.
Yellow Horse
Zotigh, Barbara Tallamonts

ARIKARA
Eagle, Thomas, Jr.
Fox, Elaine
Horn, Miles S.
Plenty Chief, Walter, Sr.
Ripley, David J.
White Bear, Alton

ASSINIBOIN
Boyd, George, Jr.
Emerson, Roberta Joan Boyd
Standing, William
Wilder, Leonard

ATHABASCAN
Blackmore, Bill

BANNOCK
Farmer, Ernie

BLACKFOOT
Big Brave
Big Springs, William, Sr.
Burdeau, George Henry
Clarke, John Louis
Double Runner
Elk Horn
Feathers, Gerald T.
Grass, John
Kuka, King
Parsons, Neil
Pepion, Dan
Pepion, Victor
Racine, Albert Batiste
Red Crane
Ripley, David J.

Sanderville, Richard
Schildt, Gary Joseph
Schultz, Hart Merriam

BRULÉ (*see* Sioux)

CADDO
Armstrong, Tirador
Cannon, Tommy
Martin, Mike

CHEROKEE
Alberty, Dewey
Archuleta, Betty Keener
Ballard, Louis Wayne
Beeler, Joe
Bolin, Floyd
Boswell, Helen
Brave, Franklin P.
Brim, Mary
Burton, Jimalee
Cassady, Ann Virginia
Chisholm, Calvin
Cochran, George McKee
Cochran, J. Woody
Cornine, Barbara
Costilow, Eunice
Damrow, Charles
Davenport, Julia Chisholm
Denton, Coye Elizabeth
Dick, Cecil
Flores, William Vann
Freeman, Brenda
García, Ruth Bussey
Green, Homer
Gritts, Franklin
Hanson, Joan Stone
Hill, Joan
Holton, Anne Tennyson
Johnson, Alfred
Mathews, Fadie Mae
Orr, Howell Sonny
Owen, Narcissa Chisholm
Pahsetopah, Loren Louis
Pahsetopah, Paul
Rogers, Will Paul
Seabourn, Bert D.
Taylor, Virginia
Thornton, Clinton Evan
Tracy, Jo Ellis
Waano-Gano, Joe T. N.
White, Riley

CHEYENNE
Ahsit
Antelope, W.
Armstrong, Tirador
Beard, Lorenzo
Bear's Heart, James

Big Back
Blackowl, Archie
Buffalo Meat
Bushyhead, Allan
Buzzard
Chief Killer
Cohoe, William
Dawes, Ermaleen
Goodbear, Paul J.
Hollowbreast, Donald
Howling Wolf
Left Hand
Little Chief, Daniel
Little Chief, William
Little Finger Nail
Making Medicine
Nick
Packer
Red Bird
Red Cloud
Roman Nose, Henry Caruthers
Shave Head
Soaring Eagle
Squint Eyes
Tichkematse
West, Dick
Whirlwind
White Bird
White Buffalo, Herbert
Whiteman, A.
Wild Hog
Wooden Leg

CHICKASAW
Boyiddle, Parker, Jr.
Colbert, Frank Overton
Collins, Martha Adele
Davenport, Julia Chisholm
Murray, Alice Hearrell
Northcutt, Harrell
Orr, Howell Sonny
Pringle, Wilma Jane Reed
Saul, C. Terry

CHIPPEWA
Boswell, Helen
Brando, Stephen
Des Jarlait, Patrick Robert
Freimark, Robert M.
Kahgegagahbowh
Maulson, Gerald
Moore, Georgianna
Morrison, George
St. Pierre, Rodger
Walz, Peter Frank
Wilkie, Laurence

CHIRICAHUA (*see* Apache)

CHOCTAW
Collins, Martha Adele
Dage, Lynn
Hessing, Valjean McCarty
Ingram, Jerry Cleman
Mauldin, Carol Jane McCarty
Murray, Alice Hearrell
Perry, Angela Lee
Phillips, Dwight E.
Pringle, Wilma Jane Reed
Saul, C. Terry
Wade, Bobby
Young, Mary Cecilia

COCHITÍ
Arqurero, Avelino
Chávez, Manuel "Bob"
Herrera, Delphino
Herrera, Joe Hilario
Herrera, Justino
Herrera, Victor
Melchior, Ray
Ortiz, Louis
Otelaleya
Pecos, Jose D.
Quintana, Ben
Quintana, Joe A.
Quintana, Trinidad
Romero, Cipriana
Romero, Santiago
Suina, Herman
Suina, Theodore
Trujillo, Andy

COLVILLE
Carraher, Ronald G.
Desautel, Ernie
Ingram, Veronica Marie
Leholm, Mary Frances Pichette
Noyes, Phyllis
Orr, Caroline Louise
Palmenteer, Theodore

COMANCHE
Ayawat, William
Bosin, Blackbear
Davis, Jesse Edwin, II
Eckiwaudah, Tennyson
García, María
Geionety, George
Hobah
Hood, Rance
Jones, Laura Asah
Qussay Yah
Riddles, Leonard
Saryerwinnie, Houston
Saupity, Larry
Taulbee, Daniel J.
Terasaz, Marian

Toppah, Herman
Watchetaker, George Smith
Weckeah
Yellow Wolf

CREE
Standing Chief, Robert

CREEK
Anderson, Jimmy
Ball, Lois Harjo
Beaver, Fred
Blue Eagle, Acee
Burton, Jimalee
Crumbo, Woodrow Wilson
Deere, Eli
Deere, Noah
Ducee Blue Buzzard
Fife, Phyllis
Hill, Joan
McCombs, Solomon
Randall, Bunnie
Sampson, William, Jr.
Scott, Johnson Lee
Tiger, Jerome Richard
Wolfe, Edmond Richard

CROW
Bellrock, Buster
Big Man, Max
Biss, Earl
Charges Strong
Cree
Horse Tail
Medicine Crow
Red Star, Kevin
Spotted Tail
Washakie, Charles
White Bear

DELAWARE
Boyiddle, Parker, Jr.
Jones, Ruthe Blalock
Parks

ESKIMO
Ahgupuk, George Aden
Chauncey, Florence Nupok
Gough, Agnes
Immana, Annie Weokluk
Kakarook, Guy
Katexac, Bernard T.
Mayokok, Robert
Minoch, Milo
Monignok, Gabriel
Moses, James Kivetoruk
Naumoff
Norton, Jerry R.
Nutchuck
Octuck, J.

Timeche, Bruce
Timeche, Harold
Tomossee, T.
Tuvahoema, Kyrate
Twoitsie, Hansen
White Bear
Zeyouma, Phillip
HUNKPAPA (*see* Sioux)
HURON
　Le Coeur, Leon
IOWA
　Murray, Daniel M.
IROQUOIS
　Cornplanter, Carrie
　Cornplanter, Jessie
　DeMott, Helen
　Dorsey, Tom
　Leholm, Mary Frances Pichette
　Lyons, Oren R.
　Natatches, James J.
　Patterson, Pat
　Poodry, C. Earl
　Roberts, Frank
　Smith, Ernest
　Thomas, Edson
　Two Arrows, Tom
ISLETA
　Abeita, Tom Diego
　García, Ernest P.
　Jaramillo, Edward Gilbert
　Jojola, E.
　Lente, José Bartolo
　Montoya, José L.
　Zotigh, Barbara Tallamonts
JÉMEZ
　Casiquito, Lucy
　Casiquito, Vidal, Jr.
　Chamon, John A.
　Chinana, Christina
　Chinana, Felipe
　Chinana, Lawrence
　Chinana, Paul
　Chinana, Ricky
　Coloque, Mary Nancy
　Doyce, Clarence
　Fragua, Augustine
　Gachupin, Juan
　Gachupin, Maxine
　Gachupin, Paul
　Gachupin, Rose M.
　Loretto, José Richard
　Loretto, Leonard
　Lucero, Alondo
　Lucero, Guadalupe
　Lucero, Lupita
　Lucero, Mary Rose

Lucero, Nora Alice
Lucero, Victor
Luci
Panana, Gerald
Panana, Sophie
Panana, Veronica
Shendo, Joe Ray
Toledo, José Rey
Toledo, Mike
Tosa, Lawrence
Tosa, Mary
Tosa, Tony
Toya, Johnny
Toya, José María
Toya, Mary Isabel
Toya, Patricio
Toya, Pete
Toya, Rosie
Vigil, Alfred
Vigil, Andrea
Vigil, Priscilla
Vigil, Ralph
Vigil, Tom
Yepa, Emilina
Yepa, Rita
Yeppa, Franklin
Yeppa, Jimmie
JICARILLA (*see* Apache)
KAROK
　Wilder, Leonard
KICKAPOO
　Kishketon, George
　Murdock, Cecil
KIOWA
　Anko
　Anquoe, Evans
　Asah, Spencer
　Auchiah, James
　Bear's Heart, James
　Belindo, Dennis
　Big Bow
　Big Bow, Abel
　Big Bow, "Old Man"
　Big Bow, Woody
　Bosin, Blackbear
　Boyiddle, Parker, Jr.
　Darby, Raymond Lee
　Etahdleuh
　Hanna, R. W.
　Hill, Bobby
　Ho Haw
　Hokeah, Jack
　Horse, Perry
　Hummingbird, Jerome
　Jones, Laura Asah
　Keahbone, George Campbell

Casias, Johnny Gabriel
Chee, Robert
Chester, Eddie
Chetlahe
Choh
Clah, Alfred
Coho, Vernon
Colville, Clyde
Crispin, Sutero
Dahadid, Posey
Davis, Ralph U.
Davis, Truman
De Groat, Jay
Denetdale, Myron
Denetsosie, Hoke
Dodge, Aydee
Draper, Robert D.
Draper, Teddy, Sr.
Ellen, Mary
Franklin, Ernest
Gamble, Thomas J.
Ghost Wind
Gorman, Alfred Kee
Gorman, Carl Nelson
Gorman, R. C.
Gould, Jay
Gruber, Raymond
Hadley, Wade
Hapaha, L.
Harvey, Pete, Jr.
Hastings, Cain
Hicks, Bobby
Holgate, Eugene, Jr.
Hoskie, Larry
Hunter, Elwood
Huskett, John
Jim, Frank
Jim, Wilson
Joe, Ray
John, Angelo Marvin
Johns, David
Kahn, Chester
Kirk, Ernest
Lee, Charlie
Lee, J. S.
Lee, Jerry
Lee, Nancy Isabel
Lee, Nelson
Lee, Paul
Leslie, Ernest
Lewis, Albert Artie
Lewis, Jimmy
Lewis, Roger
Lizer, Vera
Long, Charles Vee
Manuelito, Monte

Martin, Raymond
Martine, Bob
Mitchell, George Charlie
Mitchell, Peter
Mitchell, Stanley C.
Montoya, Sidney, Jr.
Morez, Mary
Morris, Ruth Ella
Nailor, Gerald
Natatches, James J.
Natay, Ed
Nez, Ford
Nilchee, Betty Jean
Nofchissey, Alberta
Notah, Ned
Paddock, Hugh
Paladin, Dave
Paradis, Rena
Peshlakai, Fred
Pilli, Donna
Pinto, Dennis Paul
Platero, Lorenzo
Platero, Raymond
Platero, Tom
Rafael, Donald
Roan
Roanhorse, Ralph
Salt, Freddie
Sandoval, Ronald
Sandoval, Tony
Secatero, McCoy
Shirley, Charles Keetsie
Shirley, Walter
Singer, James
Smith, Gibson R.
Stevens, Leroy
Stewart, Albert
Tahoma, Quincy
Taliwood, Richard
Todacheenie, Barry
Todea, Rocky
Tom, Herbert, Jr.
Tracy, Edmund
Tsina
Tsinajinnie, Andrew Van
Tso, John
Tsosie, George
Tsosie, Paul
Walters, Harry
Wilson, John
Wilson, Lucy
Wood, Harvy
Yazzie, Carl
Yazzie, Daniel Wilbur
Yazzie, Deswood H.
Yazzie, James Wayne

SAN FELIPE
  Aragón, Ralph
  Candelario, James
  Chávez, Calvin Fenley
  Chevarillo, Dario
  Sandoval, Benny
  Townsend, Roger
  Townsend, Roy C.

SAN ILDEFONSO
  Aguilar, Alfred
  Aguilar, José Angela
  Aguilar, José Vicente
  Apomonu
  Atencio, Gilbert Benjamin
  Atencio, Pat
  Atencio, Tony
  Awa Tsireh
  Da, Anthony
  Da, Popovi
  Gonzales, Louis
  Martínez, Crescencio
  Martínez, Daisy
  Martínez, John D.
  Martínez, José Miguel
  Martínez, Julián
  Martínez, Miguel
  Martínez, Philip
  Martínez, Raymond
  Martínez, Richard
  Martínez, Santana R.
  Montoya, Alfredo
  Montoya, Charles
  Montoya, Isabelita
  Oqwa Pi
  Peña, Christino
  Peña, José Encarnación
  Peña, Tonita
  Piño, Barbara
  Ridourt, Lucile
  Roybal, José D.
  Roybal, Juan Cruz
  Roybal, Seferino
  Sánchez, Guadalupito
  Sánchez, Ramos
  Vigil, Albert
  Vigil, Romando

SAN JUAN
  Abeyta, Emiliano
  Aquino, Frank
  Aquino, Juan B.
  Aquino, Robert
  Atencio, John
  Atencio, Lorencita
  Calvert, John
  Casias, Johnny Gabriel
  Cruz, Ramoncita

García, Alexander
García, Carlos
García, Marcelino
García, Peter
Ka Tside
Montoya, Gerónima Cruz
Montoya, Guadalupe
Montoya, Juan B.
Montoya, Ned
Montoya, Nellie
Montoya, Sidney, Jr.
Montoya, Thomas
Ortiz, Joseph
Trujillo, Ascensión
Trujillo, Manuel

SANS ARC (see Sioux)

SANTA CLARA
  Baca, Henry
  Cordova, Louis (or Luis)
  Gutiérrez, Clarence
  Gutiérrez, José la Cruz
  Gutiérrez, José Leandro
  Gutiérrez, Juan B.
  Hardin, Helen
  Leandro, José
  Naranjo, Adolph
  Naranjo, Ben
  Naranjo, José Dolores
  Naranjo, Louis
  Naranjo, Victor
  Padilla, Michael
  Silva, Marcus
  Singer, James
  Sisneros, Marie
  Tafaga, Joseph
  Tafoya, Camilio
  Tafoya, Mary Agnes
  Tafoya, Rosita
  Tafoya, Teofilo
  Velarde, Pablita

SANTEE (see Sioux)

SANTO DOMINGO
  Bird, Larry
  Coriz, Fidel
  García, José J.
  García, Lorenzo
  Herrera, Martin
  Lee, Nancy Isabel
  Lovato, Ambrosio
  Naranjo, Balardo
  Nieto, Balardo
  Steatuma, Tony
  Velarde, Neito

SAUK-FOX
  Duncan, Dallas

Quiver, Robert A.
Rain In The Face
Rave, Austin
Red Bull, Elmer
Red Dog
Red Elk, Herman
Red Fish
Red Hail
Red Hawk
Red Horn Bull Buffalo
Red Horn Elk
Red Horse
Red Living Bear
Roman Nose
Runner, O. B.
Running Antelope
Running Deer
Runs Over
Samuel
Short Bull
Shortbull, Norman
Shows The Feather
Sinte
Sitting Bull
Sitting Crow
Sitting Eagle
Sitting Hawk
Spotted Elk, Leo
Spotted Horse
Standing Bear
Standing Bear, Andrew
Standingbear, George Eugene
Standing Soldier, Andrew
The Swan
Swift Dog
Tahcawin
Tasumke Witka
Tough Soldier
Turning Bear
Two Eagle, Violet
Two Strikes
Tyndall, Calvin T.
Whirlwind Hawk
White Bull
White Cow Killer
White Eagle
Wife Eagle Deer
Wilkinson, Douglas
Yellow Blanket
Yellow Lodge
Yo Sumce Witke
Young Man Afraid Of His Horses

SNOHOMISH
Gobin, Henry
Henry, Woodworth V.

SPOKANE
Wynne, Bruce

TAOS
Archuleta, Antonio
Archuleta, Trinidad
Bernal, Eloisa
Bernal, Pauline
Concha, John
Good Rain
Harvier, Michael
Keahbone, Gordon
Lomayn Do
Luján, Albert
Luján, Alfred
Luján, Gilbert
Luján, James
Luján, Jerry
Luján, Lorenzo A.
Luján, Manuel
Luján, Margaret
Luján, Mike
Luján, Tonita
Luján, Vicente
Luján, Wahleah
Martínez, Albert
Martínez, Jerry
Martínez, José R.
Martínez, Manuel
Martínez, Ralph
Mirabel, Eva
Mirabel, Vicente
Pop Chalee
Pop Wea
Romero, Frankie
Trujillo, Jennie

TESUQUE
Abeyta, Augustine
Coriz, Nat
Durán, Joe Evan
Herrera, Diego
Herrera, Elroy
Herrera, Ernest
Herrera, José
Herrera, Senofre
Hinds, Patrick Swazo
Leno, Marce
Pajoma, Peni
Pin, Pagna
Piño, Juan Isidro
Piño, Lorenzo
Samuel, Tony
Swazo, Juan G.
Vigil, Jo
Vigil, Juanita
Vigil, Lucy
Vigil, Pete

Quetoque, Jefferson
Quetoque, Leo
Rani, Bist
Sandy, Percy Tsisete
Shebola, Dixon
Shebola, Philbert
Shebola, Sullivan
Sheyka, P.
Sterne, Mabel
Telese, Gilbert
Toshewana, Robert Leo
Tsabetsaye, Roger
Tucson, Loren
Twakuku
Vacit, Gary
Vicenti, Charles
Vigil, Marco
Weakee, Teddy

SPECIFIC TRIBES UNKNOWN
Andrews, William A.
Blackbear, Levi
Brunette, J. M.
Cariz, Santiago
Chavarria, Elmer
Chuokaichi, Linland
Cleveland, Frederick
Coffee
Connery, Stanley
Crispin, Santiago
Henry, Gary
Hicks, Al
Hiuwa Tuni
Hoffman, Delores
Holgate, J.
Jaramillo, Joseph Louis
Keevama, David
Lee, Frank
Little Sheep
Louis, James M.

Louis, Julian J.
Martínez, Anecito
Martínez, Dave
Melford, Earl
Miller, Frances
Mirabel, Leon
Mitchell, James
Old Dog
Pa O Kelo
Piño, Kathy
Po Ye Gi
Quintana, Johnnie
Quintana, Marcelino
Red Bird, Robert
Red Robin
Ringo, Good
Romero, Richard
Roybal, Louis
Sánchez, Aresenio
Sánchez, Laura
Saves Life, George
Scott, Duard
Smallcanyon, Evelyn
Spencer, Marlene R.
Standing Leaf
Stone Man
Sturr, Jonathan
Tafoya, Francis
Thompson, Alex
Toledo, Jerome
Tomo
Tracy, E.
Trujillo, Gregory
Valencia, Anna Lou
Walter, Roy M.
Ware, Woodrow
Warner, Fred
Webster, David
Wilson, J.
Yellow Tail

KEY TO ABBREVIATIONS

BAE   Bureau of American Ethnology, Smithsonian Institution, Washington, D.C.
BAE, AR   *Bureau of American Ethnology, Annual Report,* Smithsonian Institution, Washington, D.C.
BAE, B   *Bureau of American Ethnology, Bulletin,* Smithsonian Institution, Washington, D.C.

GA   grandaunt
GF   grandfather
GGF   great-grandfather
GGGF   great-great-grandfather
GGM   great-grandmother
GM   grandmother
GU   granduncle

IT   Indian Territory (now Okla.)

M/GA   maternal grandaunt
M/GF   maternal grandfather
M/GGF   maternal great-grandfather
M/GGGF   maternal great-great-grandfather
M/GGGU   maternal great-great-granduncle
M/GGU   maternal great-granduncle
M/GGM   maternal great-grandmother
M/GM   maternal grandmother
M/GP   maternal grandparents
M/GU   maternal granduncle
M/U   maternal uncle

OU/A   Auditorium, University of Oklahoma, Norman, Okla.

P/GA   paternal grandaunt
P/GF   paternal grandfather
P/GGF   paternal great-grandfather
P/GGGF   paternal great-great-grandfather
P/GGM   paternal great-grandmother
P/GGP   paternal great-grandparents
P/GM   paternal grandmother
P/GU   paternal granduncle
P/U   paternal uncle

USDS   U.S. Department of State, Washington, D.C.

WPA   Works Progress Administration
WWI   World War I
WWII   World War II

SCHOOLS

ALBUQUERQUE   U.S. Albuquerque Indian School, Albuquerque, N.M.
ALFRED   Alfred University, Alfred, N.Y.
AMERICAN   American Indian Institute, Wichita, Kan.
ARIZONA   University of Arizona, Tucson, Ariz.
ARIZONA S.C./F.   Arizona State College, Flagstaff, Ariz.
ARIZONA S.C./T.   Arizona State College, Tempe, Ariz.

ARKANSAS F.   University of Arkansas, Fayetteville, Ark.
ARKANSAS L.R.   University of Arkansas, Little Rock, Ark.
ART   Art Students League, New York, N.Y.

BACONE   Bacone College and/or High School, Bacone, Okla.
BENEDICTINE   Benedictine Heights College, Tulsa, Okla.
BLACK MT.   Black Mountain College, near Black Mountain, N.C.

CALIFORNIA   University of California, Berkeley, Calif.
CALIFORNIA C.   California College of Arts and Crafts, Oakland, Calif.
CARLISLE   U.S. Carlisle Indian School, Carlisle, Pa.
CARNEGIE   Carnegie Institute, Pittsburgh, Pa.
CARSON   U.S. Carson Indian School, Carson, Nev.
CENTRAL   Central State College, Edmond, Okla.
CHICAGO   Chicago Art Institute, Chicago, Ill.
CHILOCCO   U.S. Chilocco Indian School, Chilocco, Okla.
CHINLE   U.S. Chinle Boarding and/or Indian School, Chinle, Ariz.
CLAREMONT   Claremont College, Claremont, Calif.
COCHITI   U.S. Cochiti Pueblo Indian School, Cochiti Pueblo, N.M.
CONCHO   U.S. Concho Indian School, Concho, Okla.
CONNORS   Connors State College, Warner, Okla.
CORNELL   Cornell University, Ithaca, N.Y.

EAST   East Central State College, Ada, Okla.
ESPAÑOLA   Española High School, Española, N.M.

FLAGSTAFF   Flagstaff High School, Flagstaff, Ariz.
FLORIDA   University of Florida, Gainesville, Fla.
FORT SILL   U.S. Fort Sill Indian School, Lawton, Okla.
FORT WINGATE   Fort Wingate Indian School, Fort Wingate, N.M.

GALLUP   Gallup High School, Gallup, N.M.
GEORGIA   University of Georgia, Athens, Ga.

HAMPTON   Hampton Institute, Hampton, Va.
HASKELL   U.S. Haskell Institute, Lawrence, Kan.
HILER   Hiler College, Santa Fe, N.M.
HILL   Hill and Canyon School of Art, Santa Fe, N.M.
HOPI   Hopi High School, Oraibi, Ariz.
HOTEVILLA   U.S. Hotevilla Day School, Hotevilla, Ariz.

INSTITUTE   Institute of American Indian Arts, Santa Fe, N.M.
INTER-MT.   U.S. Inter-Mountain Indian School, Brigham City, Utah
IOWA   State College of Iowa, Cedar Falls, Iowa

JÉMEZ   U.S. Jémez Pueblo Day School, Jémez Pueblo, N.M.
JICARILLA   U.S. Jicarilla Indian School, Dulce, N.M.

KANSAS   University of Kansas, Lawrence, Kan.
KANSAS CITY   Kansas City Art Institute, Kansas City, Mo.
KANSAS S.   Kansas State College of Pittsburgh, Pittsburgh, Kan.

LOS ANGELES   Los Angeles Art Center School, Los Angeles, Calif.
LOYOLA   Loyola University, New Orleans, La.

MEXICO   University of Mexico, Mexico City, D. F., Mexico
MEXICO C. C.   Mexico City College, Mexico City, D. F., Mexico
MILLS   Mills College, Oakland, Calif.
MUSKOGEE   Muskogee Junior College, Muskogee, Okla.

NEW MEXICO   New Mexico Highlands University, Las Vegas, N.M.
NEW MEXICO U.   University of New Mexico, Albuquerque, N.M.
N. DAKOTA   University of North Dakota, Grand Forks, N.Dak.
NORTHEASTERN   Northeastern State College, Tahlequah, Okla.
NORTHEASTERN A.M.   Northeastern Oklahoma A. & M. College, Miami, Okla.
NORTHERN   Northern State Teachers College, Aberdeen, S.Dak.

OAKLAND   Oakland College of Arts and Crafts, Oakland, Calif.
OKLAHOMA   University of Oklahoma, Norman, Okla.
OKLAHOMA C.U.   Oklahoma City University, Oklahoma City, Okla.
OKLAHOMA S.U.   Oklahoma State University, Stillwater, Okla.
OKLAHOMA S.U./S.T.   Oklahoma State University, School of Technology, Okmulgee, Okla.
OREGON   University of Oregon, Eugene, Oreg.
OTIS   Otis Art Institute, Los Angeles, Calif.

PHILANDER   Philander Smith College, Little Rock, Ark.
PHOENIX   U.S. Phoenix Indian School, Phoenix, Ariz.
PHOENIX J.C.   Phoenix Junior College Phoenix, Ariz.

REDLANDS   University of Redlands, Redlands, Calif.
RHODE ISLAND   Rhode Island School of Design, Providence, R.I.
RIVERSIDE   U.S. Riverside Indian School, Anadarko, Okla.
ROCHESTER   Rochester School of American Craftsmen, Rochester, N.Y.
ROCHESTER S.T.   Rochester School of Technology, Rochester, N.Y.

SAN CARLOS   U.S. San Carlos Day School and/or Indian School, San Carlos, Ariz.
SAN FRANCISCO   San Francisco State College, San Francisco, Calif.
SAN ILDEFONSO   U.S. San Ildefonso Pueblo Day School, San Ildefonso Pueblo, N.M.
SAN JOSE   San Jose State College, San Jose, Calif.
SAN JUAN   U.S. San Juan Pueblo Day School, San Juan Pueblo, N.M.
SANTA CLARA   U.S. Santa Clara Pueblo Day School, Santa Clara Pueblo, N.M.
SANTA CRUZ   Santa Cruz High School, Santa Cruz, N.M.
SANTA FE   U.S. Santa Fe Indian School, Santa Fe, N.M.
SCHOOL   School of American Research, Santa Fe, N.M.
SECOND MESA   U.S. Second Mesa Day School, Second Mesa, Ariz.
SENECA   U.S. Seneca Indian School, Wyandotte, Okla.
SEQUOYAH   U.S. Sequoyah Indian School, Tahlequah, Okla.
SHERMAN   U.S. Sherman Institute, Riverside, Calif.
SHIPROCK   U.S. Shiprock Indian Schools, Shiprock, N.M.
SHUNGOPOVI   U.S. Shungopovi Day School, Shungopovi, Ariz.
SOUTH DAKOTA   University of South Dakota, Vermillion, S.Dak.
STANFORD   Stanford University, Stanford, Calif.
STEWART   U.S. Stewart Indian School, Stewart, Nev.
ST. CATHERINE'S   St. Catherine's Indian School, Santa Fe, N.M.
ST. JOSEPH'S   St. Joseph's College, Albuquerque, N.M.
ST. MICHAELS   St. Michaels Indian School, St. Michaels, Ariz.
ST. PATRICK'S   St. Patrick's Mission School, Anadarko, Okla.

TAOS   Taos Valley Art School, Taos, N.M.
TESUQUE   U.S. Tesuque Pueblo Day School, Tesuque Pueblo, N.M.
TULSA   University of Tulsa, Tulsa, Okla.

UTAH   University of Utah, Salt Lake City, Utah
UTAH S.   Utah State University, Logan, Utah

WASHINGTON   University of Washington, Seattle, Wash.
WASHINGTON S.C.   Washington State College, Ellensburg, Wash.
WHITE CONE   U.S. White Cone Day School, White Cone, Ariz.
WICHITA   University of Wichita, Wichita, Kan.

YALE   Yale University, New Haven, Conn.

ZIA   U.S. Zia Pueblo Day School, Zia Pueblo, N.M.
ZUNI   Zuni High School, Zuni Pueblo, N.M.

COLLECTIONS

Public

ACM   Anadarko City Museum, Anadarko, Okla.
AF   The Amerind Foundation, Dragoon, Ariz.
AH   Atlantic House, Inc., Provincetown, Mass.
AHM   Atlanta High Museum, Atlanta Art Association, Atlanta, Ga.
AIHA   Albany Institute of History and Art, Albany, N.Y.
AK   Abbott Kimball, Inc., New York, N.Y.
AMNH   The American Museum of Natural History, New York, N.Y.
ASU   Arizona State University, Tempe, Ariz.
AU/ASM   University of Arizona, Arizona State Museum, Tucson, Ariz.
BAM   Baltimore Museum of Art, Baltimore, Md.
BC   Bacone College, Bacone, Okla.
BIA   Bureau of Indian Affairs, U.S. Department of Interior, Washington, D.C.
BIA/A   Bureau of Indian Affairs, Aberdeen, S. Dak.
BIA/B   Bureau of Indian Affairs, Billings, Mont.
BIA/D   Bureau of Indian Affairs, Anadarko, Okla.
BIA/M   Bureau of Indian Affairs, Muskogee, Okla.
BIA/P   Bureau of Indian Affairs, Portland, Oreg.
BIA/R   Bureau of Indian Affairs, Rosebud, S. Dak.
BM   Berne Museum, Berne, Switzerland
BM/B   Brooklyn Museum, Brooklyn, N.Y.
BMFA   Boston Museum of Fine Arts, Boston, Mass.
BMJ   Bezalel Museum of Jerusalem, Jerusalem, Israel
CAM   Cincinnati Art Museum, Cincinnati, Ohio
CAM/M   Chrysler Art Museum of Provincetown, Provincetown, Mass.
CAMSL   City Art Museum of St. Louis, St. Louis, Mo.
CBC   Colville Tribal Business Council, Nespelem, Wash.
CC   Claremont College, Claremont, Calif.
CCH   Cook County Hospital, Grand Marais, Minn.
CCHM   Creek Indian Council House and Museum, Okmulgee, Okla.
CCHS   Cook County High School, Grand Marais, Minn.
CGA   The Corcoran Gallery of Art, Washington, D.C.
CGFA   Columbus Gallery of Fine Arts, Columbus, Ohio
CHS/FG   The State Historical Society of Colorado, Fort Garland Museum, Fort Garland, Colo.
CIS   Cranbrook Institute of Science, Bloomfield Hills, Mich.
CMA   Cleveland Museum of Art, Cleveland, Ohio
CM/C   Willis Carey Historical Museum, Cashmere, Wash.
CMNH   Chicago Natural History Museum, Chicago, Ill.
CU/LMA   University of California, The Robert H. Lowie Museum of Anthropology, Berkeley, Calif.
CWC   Curtiss-Wright Corporation, Dayton, Ohio
DAI   Dayton Art Institute, Dayton, Ohio
DAM   Denver Art Museum, Chappell House, Denver, Colo.
DCC   Dartmouth College Collection, Dartmouth College, Hanover, N.H.
DFNB   Dewitt First National Bank, Dewitt, Iowa
DMFA   Dallas Museum of Fine Arts, Dallas, Tex.
EB   Encyclopedia Britannica Collection (This collection was broken up and sold.)
EOC   East Oregon College, Walter Pierce Museum, La Grande, Oreg.
FCTM   Five Civilized Tribes Museum, Muskogee, Okla.
FOM   Fort Okanogan Historical Museum, Brewster, Wash.
FSM   U.S. Army Artillery and Missile Center Museum, Fort Sill, Okla.
GCD   Grand Coulee Dam, Spokane, Wash.

GCG   Grand Central Art Galleries, New York, N.Y.
GM   Gilcrease Institute of American History and Art, Tulsa, Okla.
GO   Gilbert Originals, Chicago, Ill.
GWS   Gates Western Store, Stillwater, Okla.
HI   Hampton Institute, College Museum and Huntington Library, Hampton, Va.
HM   The Heard Museum of Anthropology and Primitive Art, Phoenix, Ariz.
HMFA   Museum of Fine Arts of Houston, Houston, Tex.
HSMC   Historical Society of Marshall County, Marshalltown, Iowa.
HSP/L   The Historical Society of Pennsylvania, Library, Philadelphia, Pa.
HU/PM   Harvard University, Peabody Museum of Archaeology and Ethnology, Cam-
    bridge, Mass.
IACB   Indian Arts and Crafts Board, U.S. Department of Interior, Washington, D.C.
IAIA   Institute of American Indian Arts, Santa Fe, N.M.
IBM   International Business Machines Corp., Gallery of Arts and Sciences, New York,
    N.Y.
JAM   Joslyn Art Museum, Omaha, Nebr.
KM   The Kiva Museum of the Koshare Indian, Boy Scouts of America, La Junta, Colo.
KSHS   Kansas State Historical Society Museum, Topeka, Kan.
LJMA   La Jolla Museum of Art, La Jolla, Calif.
LMA/BC   Logan Museum of Anthropology, Beloit, Wisc.
LNBTC   Liberty National Bank and Trust Co., Oklahoma City, Okla.
LS   Litho Studios, Inc., New York, N.Y.
MAI   Museum of the American Indian, Heye Foundation, New York, N.Y.
MAM   The Montclair Art Museum, Montclair, N.J.
MHDYMM   M.H. De Young Memorial Museum, San Francisco, Calif.
MHS   Missouri Historical Society, Pictorial History Dept., St. Louis, Mo.
MHS/B   Massachusetts Historical Society, Boston, Mass.
MHS/H   Montana Historical Society, Helena, Mont.
MIA   Minneapolis Institute of Arts, Minneapolis, Minn.
MKMcNAI   Marion Koogler McNay Art Institute, San Antonio, Tex.
MM   Mattatuck Museum, Waterbury, Conn.
MMA   Museum of Modern Art, New York, N.Y.
MMFA   Montgomery Museum of Fine Arts, Montgomery, Ala.
MNA   Museum of Northern Arizona, Flagstaff, Ariz.
MNA/KHC   Museum of Northern Arizona, Katherine Harvey Collection, Flagstaff, Ariz.
MNCA   Museum of Navajo Ceremonial Art, Santa Fe, N.M.
MNM   Museum of New Mexico, Fine Arts Museum, Santa Fe, N.M.
MPI   Museum of the Plains Indian, Browning, Mont.
MPM   Milwaukee Public Museum, Milwaukee, Wisc.
MRFM   Millicent Rogers Foundation Museum, Taos, N.M.
MSIC   Mutual Service Insurance Co., St. Paul, Minn.
MWPI   Munson-Williams-Proctor Institute, Utica, N.Y.
NCHF   National Cowboy Hall of Fame, Oklahoma City, Okla.
NL   Newberry Library, Chicago, Ill.
NMAS   Norfolk Museum of Arts and Sciences, Norfolk, Va.
NMSF   New Mexico State Fair, Albuquerque, N.M.
NNGCC   Northern Natural Gas Company of Omaha Collection, Joslyn Art Museum,
    Omaha, Nebr.
NU   The University of Nebraska Art Galleries, F.M. Hall Bequest, Lincoln, Nebr.
NYU   The New York University, Art Gallery, New York, N.Y.
OAA/SI   Office of Anthropology Archives, Smithsonian Institution, Washington, D.C.
OAC   Oklahoma Art Center, Oklahoma City, Okla.
OA/USNM   Office of Anthropology, U.S. National Museum, Washington, D.C.
OHSM   Oklahoma Historical Society Museum, Oklahoma City, Okla.
OL   Okanogan Library, Okanogan, Wash.
OPS   Omak Public Schools, Omak, Wash.

OSAF/GC   Oklahoma Science and Art Foundation, Inc., Gerrer Collection, Oklahoma City, Okla.
OSU/TL   Oklahoma State University, School of Technology, Library, Okmulgee, Okla.
OU   University of Oklahoma, Norman, Okla.
OU/L   University of Oklahoma, Library, Norman, Okla.
OU/MA   University of Oklahoma, Museum of Art, Norman, Okla.
OU/SM   University of Oklahoma, Willis Stovall Museum of Science and History, Norman, Okla.

PAC   Philbrook Art Center, Tulsa, Okla.
PAM   Portland Art Museum, Portland, Oreg.
PMA   Philadelphia Museum of Art, Philadelphia, Pa.
PSU   Pennsylvania State University, Altoona, Pa.
PU/M   University of Pennsylvania, University Museum, Philadelphia, Pa.

RM   Riverside Museum, New York, N.Y.
RMAS   Rochester Museum of Arts and Sciences, Rochester, N.Y.

SAHSL   St. Augustine Historical Society Library, St. Augustine, Fla.
SCI   State College of Iowa, Cedar Falls, Iowa
SC/MA   Smith College Museum of Art, Northampton, Mass.
SDMM   San Diego Museum of Man, San Diego, Calif.
SFRR   Santa Fe Railroad, Chicago, Ill.
SHSND   State Historical Society of North Dakota, Bismarck, N. Dak.
SHSW   The State Historical Society of Wisconsin, Madison, Wisc.
SI   Smithsonian Institution, Washington, D.C.
SIECC   Sioux Indian Exhibit and Craft Center, Rapid City, S. Dak.
SI/MNH   Smithsonian Institution, Museum of Natural History, Washington, D.C.
SLAC   Salt Lake Art Center, Salt Lake City, Utah
SM   Southwest Museum, Los Angeles, Calif.
SMNAI   The Southeast Museum of the North American Indian, Marathon, Fla.
SPIM   Southern Plains Indians Museum, Anadarko, Okla.
SPL   Seminole Public Library, Seminole, Okla.
SU   Stanford University, Stanford, Calif.

TM   Colorado Springs Fine Arts Center and Taylor Museum, Colorado Springs, Colo.
TWA   Trans-World Airways, Inc., Collection, Executive Offices, New York, N.Y.
TWS   Teal Wing Scouts, Dallas, Tex.

UBC   University of British Columbia, Vancouver, B.C., Canada
UM   University of Minnesota, Tweed Gallery, Duluth, Minn.
UM/LG   University of Miami, The Joe and Emily Lowe Art Gallery, Coral Gables, Fla.
UPA   United Pueblo Agency, Albuquerque, N.M.
USDI   U.S. Department of Interior, Washington, D.C.

VMA   Virginia Museum of Fine Arts, Richmond, Va.

W   Whitney Museum of American Art, New York, N.Y.
WA   Wadsworth Antheneum, Hartford, Conn.
WAAG   Wichita Art Association, Inc., Gallery, Wichita, Kan.
WAC   Walker Art Center, Minneapolis, Minn.
WAM   Wichita Art Museum, Wichita, Kan.
WHCO   Walt Horan Congressional Office, Washington, D.C.
W/JSC   The Wilmington Society of the Fine Arts, Delaware Art Center, John Sloan Collection, Wilmington, Del.
WLU   Washington and Lee University, Lee Chapel Museum, Lexington, Va.
WM   *Western Magazine*, Colorado Springs, Colo.
WM/CU   Cornell University, Andrew Dickson White Museum of Art, Ithaca, N.Y.
WRNGA   William Rockhill Nelson Gallery of Art, Kansas City, Mo.
WU/S   Wisconsin State University, Superior, Wisc.

YU/BRBML   Yale University, Beinecke Rare Book and Manuscript Library, New Haven, Conn.

PRIVATE

AARON Mae Todd Aaron (*deceased*)

ABE K. Margaret Abe, Kobe, Japan

ABBOTT Mrs. Homer Abbott, Tulsa, Okla.

H. ADAMS Mrs. Hall Adams, Santa Fe, N.M.

K. ADAMS Mrs. Kenneth Adams, Santa Fe, N.M.

ADDINGTON Carl Addington, Yukon, Okla.

E. ADKINS Eugene Adkins, Tulsa, Okla.

R. ADKINS Richard Adkins, Muskogee, Okla.

ADLERBLUM Clara Adlerblum, New York, N.Y.

AGOOS Herbert Agoos, Cambridge, Mass.

ALBERT Carl Albert, McAlester, Okla.

ALDRIDGE C. Clay Aldridge, Miami, Fla.

G. ALEXANDER Geronimo Alexander, Albuquerque, N.M.

T. ALEXANDER T. C. Alexander, Okmulgee, Okla.

ALFONSO King Alfonso XIII of Spain

ALFORD Kenneth Alford, Austin, Tex.

L. ALLEN Mrs. Lee Allen, Tulsa, Okla.

L. D. ALLEN L. D. Allen, Tulsa, Okla.

P. ALLEN Perry Allen, Window Rock, Ariz.

AMBRISTER Mrs. H. Ambrister, Tulsa, Okla.

ANDELMAN S. Y. Andelman, Tulsa, Okla.

ANN. ANDERSON Annette Anderson, Muskogee, Okla.

ART ANDERSON Art Anderson, Springfield, Oreg.

J. ANDERSON Jean Anderson, New York, N.Y.

J. A. ANDERSON J. A. Anderson, Rapid City, S.Dak.

J. W. ANDERSON John W. Anderson, Williston, N.Dak.

O. ANDERSON Mrs. O. R. Anderson, Aberdeen, S.Dak.

R. ANDERSON Raymond Anderson, Rolling Hills, Calif.

ANDREWS Richard Andrews, Lancaster, Calif.

ANSARA Michael Ansara, Hollywood, Calif.

ARBOUCHON John Arbouchon, Pasa Robles, Calif.

ARKEKETA Ben Arkeketa, Sand Springs, Okla.

ARNOLD Margerie Arnold, Washington, D.C.

ARROW Jenny Lane Arrow, Watford City, N.Dak.

ASIP Mark Asip, Lampe, Mo.

ASKEW Patsy Askew, Muskogee, Okla.

ATTRIDGE Clarence Attridge, Rochester, N.Y.

AUSTIN Gene Austin, Las Vegas, Calif.

BAILEY Archie Bailey, Morris, Okla.

A. BAKER Amos Baker, Park Hill, Okla.

C. BAKER Claudia Baker, Tulsa, Okla.

T. BAKER Thornton Baker, Houston, Tex.

BALCOMB Pete Balcomb, Chambers, Ariz.

BALLENGER Irby Ballenger, Albuquerque N.M.

BALPH Mrs. Charles F. Balph, Shawnee, Okla.

BAMROOK Walter Bamrook, Albuquerque N.M.

BARTLESON Georgia Bartleson, Muskogee, Okla.

BARTLETT Mrs. C. M. Bartlett, Miami, Okla.

BASEHART Richard Basehart, San Francisco, Calif.

BASORE Robert Basore, Tulsa, Okla.

BASS Henry Bass, Enid, Okla.

BATES C. F. R. Bates, Santa Fe, N.M.

BAYNE Robert Bayne, Lawton, Okla.

BEACH Mrs. O. A. Beach, Wichita, Kan.

BEAVER Scotty Beaver, Pawhuska, Okla.

BEDLAENDER H. Bedlaender, Montvale, N.J.

BEEBE Lee Beebe, Anadarko, Okla.

BELFORD Roy C. Belford, Tulsa, Okla.

BELL H. P. Bell, Sapupla, Okla.

BELLMON Henry Bellmon, Oklahoma City, Okla.

BENACERRAF B. Benacerraf, New York, N.Y.

BENAMI Henri BenAmi, New York, N.Y.

BENNETT Susan Bennett, Washington, D.C.

BENSON Charles Benson, Omak, Wash.

BERG Duane O. Berg, Gallup, N.M.

BERKELEY David S. Berkeley, Stillwater, Okla.

BETTS Virginia Betts, Arlington, Tex.

BIALAC James T. Bialac, Phoenix, Ariz.

BIGGERS Hope Biggers, Oklahoma City, Okla.

BILLINGSLEA Frank R. Billingslea, Tulsa, Okla.

BIMSON Walter Bimson, Phoenix, Ariz.

BING Alexander Bing, New York, N.Y.

BINNICI Joseph Binnici, Tacoma, Wash.

BIRCHMORE H. A. Birchmore, Athens, Ga.

BISHOP Mrs. R. H. Bishop, Sault Sainte Marie, Mich.

BIXBY Tams Bixby, Muskogee, Okla.

BLACKLEY Glenn E. Blackley, Cardiff, Calif.

BLAKE Marion J. Blake, Tulsa, Okla.

BLUE EAGLE   Acee Blue Eagle (*deceased*)
BLUMENSCHEIN   Helen Blumenschein, Taos, N.M.
BOCK   Royal Bock, Muskogee, Okla.
BOLES   Linn Boles, Hobart, Okla.
BOND   Lt. Gregg Bond, U.S. Army.
BOSHELL   Edward Boshell, New York, N.Y.
BOTT   Mrs. Pat Bott, New York, N.Y.
BOULDIN   Raymond Bouldin, Oklahoma City, Okla.
BOYNOFF   Irma Boynoff, Berkeley, Calif.
BRAWNER   Donald L. Brawner, Tulsa, Okla.
BRENNAN   John Brennan, Providence, R.I.
BRENNER   Alice Brenner, Scottsdale, Ariz.
BRIGGS   Al Briggs, Denver, Colo.
BRITTON   Mrs. T. M. Britton, Hemet, Calif.
D. BROCK   Dan Brock, Norwalk, Calif.
L. BROCK   L. E. Brock, Tulsa, Okla.
BROWGH   Tom Browgh, Mexico City.
BRITT BROWN   Britt Brown, Wichita, Kans.
BARB. BROWN   Barbara Brown, Nespelem, Wash.
BARC. BROWN   Barceley Brown, Wenatchee, Wash.
C. BROWN   C. Brown, San Francisco, Calif.
D. BROWN   David Brown, Berkeley, Calif.
E. BROWN   Edward Brown, Omak, Wash.
I. BROWN   Ivan Brown, Broken Arrow, Okla.
JEAN BROWN   Jean Brown, Tulsa, Okla.
JOHN BROWN   John Brown, Bixby, Okla.
W. BROWN   Winey Brown, Atoka, Okla.
BROWNSTONE   W. J. Brownstone, New York, N.Y.
BRUESTLE   Beaumont Bruestle, Tulsa, Okla.
BRUNER   Paul Bruner, Muskogee, Okla.
BRYANT   Art Bryant, Seattle, Wash.
BUCK   Clifton L. Buck, Seattle, Wash.
BUDDRUS   Mrs. Kirk Buddrus, Muskogee, Okla.
BULLARD   Trudy Bullard, Grand Forks, N.Dak.
BURDICK   D. L. Burdick, Newington, Conn.
BURDOCK   Zona Burdock, Las Vegas, Nev.
BURGESS   Mrs. C. T. Burgess, Rapid City, S.Dak.
BURKS   Alice Burks, Chattanooga, Tenn.
BURRIDGE   Gaston Burridge, Sevierville, Tenn.
BURSHEARS   Buck Burshears, La Junta, Colo.
BUSH   Mitchell L. Bush, Jr., Anadarko, Okla.
C. BUSSEY   Chief D. Bussey, Hulbert, Okla.
J. BUSSEY   John Bussey, Claremore, Okla.
W. BUSSEY   Wauhillan Bussey, Albuquerque, N.M.

W. W. BUSSEY   W. W. Bussey, Oklahoma City, Okla.
BUTLER   Lowell Butler, Los Angeles, Calif.
BYNUM   William Bynum, Reno, Nev.

CADENHEAD   Joy E. Cadenhead, Tulsa, Okla.
CALDWELL   Mel M. Caldwell, Miami, Okla.
CALLAWAY   Jack Callaway, Tulsa, Okla.
H. CAMPBELL   Harry M. Campbell, Stillwater, Okla.
JA. CAMPBELL   James Campbell, Jackson, Mich.
JU. CAMPBELL   Justin Campbell, Muskogee, Okla.
CANAVAN   Carol Canavan, Mill Valley, Calif.
CAPPS   J. L. Capps, Oklahoma City, Okla.
CARLSON   Mrs. Paul J. Carlson, Atlanta, Ga.
CARROLL   Norman Carroll, Los Angeles, Calif.
C. CARTER   C. A. Carter, Los Angeles, Calif.
E. CARTER   Ernest S. Carter, Mountain View, Calif.
G. CARTER   George Carter, Tulsa, Okla.
H. CARTER   Harland Carter, Okmulgee, Okla.
J. CARTER   John Ed Carter, Columbia, S.C.
M. CARTER   Martha Carter, Muskogee, Okla.
S. CARTER   Shirley Carter, Oklahoma City, Okla.
M. CASEY   M. Casey, Spokane, Wash.
T. CASEY   T. Casey, Buffalo, N.Y.
CHAMBERLIN   Gene Chamberlin, Pawhuska, Okla.
CHAMBERS   R. T. Chambers, Creswell, Oreg.
K. CHANDLER   Mrs. Kathryn Chandler, Okmulgee, Okla.
M. CHANDLER   Mrs. Maxine Chandler, Okmulgee, Okla.
CHASE   Frank Chase, New Town, N.Dak.
CHÁVEZ   Clemente Chávez, Vista, Calif.
CHESHEWALLA   Andrew Cheshewalla, Fort Worth, Tex.
CHOTEAU   William Choteau, Tulsa, Okla.
CHRISTENSEN   Jack R. Christensen, Bismarck, N.Dak.
CHRYSLER   Walter P. Chrysler, Jr., Provincetown, Mass.
G. CLARK   Gordon Clark, New York, N.Y.
R. CLARK   R. L. Clark, Morgan City, La.
CLAY   G. W. Clay, Ardmore, Okla.
CLEARMAN   Hank Clearman, Denton, Tex.
COCHORAN   Giff Cochoran, Oviedo, Fla.
COCHRAN   Abel Cochran, Wheatridge, Colo.
COCKE   Mrs. A. L. Cocke, Temple, Tex.
COFFEY   Raymond Coffey, Albuquerque, N.M.

COKE   Cecil Coke, Macon, Ga.

COLBERT   Marion Colbert, Las Cruces, N.M.

COLBY   Louis Colby, Johnston, R.I.

COLEMAN   Marvin Coleman, Okmulgee, Okla.

COLLINS   Ray Collins, Cleveland, Okla.

COLT   Thomas C. Colt, Dayton, Ohio

COMBS   Marv Combs, Tulsa, Okla.

CONE   Laurance Cone, Sacramento, Calif.

CONNELL   Kathleen Connell, Pawhuska, Okla.

CONNELLY   Harry S. Connelly, Tulsa, Okla.

CONNERS   Bill Conners, Bapchule, Ariz.

CONROTH   Ann Conroth, Mandan, N.Dak.

CONRY   W. F. Conry, Tulsa, Okla.

COOK   Nadine Cook, Tulsa, Okla.

COOLIDGE   Calvin Coolidge (deceased)

CORKILLE   Ralph R. Corkille, Jr., Tulsa, Okla.

P. CORWIN   Mrs. Paul Corwin, Aberdeen, S.Dak.

R. CORWIN   Roma Corwin, Northridge, Calif.

COSGROVE   Mae F. Cosgrove, Tulsa, Okla.

COTNER   Richard Cotner, Cleveland, Ohio

COVELLE   L. K. Covelle, Okmulgee, Okla.

COWLING   Peter Cowling, Decauter, Ga.

COX   Ruth Cox, Anadarko, Okla.

CRAIN   Joel W. Crain, Tulsa, Okla.

CRAVENS   Mrs. George Cravens, Ada, Okla.

CRAWFORD   Phillis Crawford, Santa Fe, N.M.

CRICKMER   Charles D. Crickmer, Houston, Tex.

CRISLER   Ruth Crisler, McAlester, Okla.

CROSS   George Cross, Norman, Okla.

CURLECHIEF   Robert Curlechief, Tulsa, Okla.

CURNOW   Dorthea E. Cornow, Stillwater, Okla.

CURRY   Charles Curry, Enid, Okla.

CURTIN   L. S. M. Curtin, Santa Fe, N.M.

H. CUSHMAN   Harriet C. Cushman, Fiskdale, Mass.

W. CUSHMAN   W. Allen Cushman, Tokyo, Japan

DAILEY   Louis Dailey, Hominy, Okla.

DALE   E. B. Dale, Manhattan, Kan.

DALGREN   Ronald Dalgren, Providence, R.I.

DALTON   Karl Dalton, Ganado, Ariz.

DANA   Lester Dana, Boston, Mass.

H. DAVIDSON   H. L. Davidson, Bolivar, Tenn.

M. DAVIDSON   Margaret Davidson, New York, N.Y.

DAVIS   Fred Davis, Anadarko, Okla.

DEANER   Mel Deaner, Oakland, Calif.

DEEL   Julia Deel, Holdenville, Okla.

DEEM   Mrs. Dallas S. Deem, Tulsa, Okla.

C. DEFFER   Catherine M. Deffer, Arlington, Va.

P. DEFFER   Phillip A. Deffer, San Antonio, Tex.

DEIGHTON   Frank Deighton, Durban, Republic of South Africa

DELONG   Bob DeLong, Fort Smith, Ark.

DENMAN   William and Leslie Van Ness Denman (deceased)

C. DENNIS   Chester Dennis, Albuquerque, N.M.

R. DENNIS   Roy G. Dennis, Cushing, Okla.

DENTZEL   Carl Dentzel, Los Angeles, Calif.

DEUPREE   Harry L. Deupree, Oklahoma City, Okla.

DEWEY   Daniel Dewey, Berkeley, Calif.

DICKINSON   J. M. Dickinson, Wichita, Kan.

DICUS   G. P. Dicus, San Diego, Calif.

DIETRICH   Margretta S. Dietrich (Now owned by Dorothy Dunn Kramer)

DiRE   Edith DiRe, San Francisco, Calif.

DITTEMORE   Harold E. Dittemore, Liberal, Kan.

DIXON   James R. Dixon, Louisville, Ky.

DOBSON   Nellie Dobson, Miami, Okla.

DOCKSTADER   Frederick J. Dockstader, New York, N.Y.

DODDS   George Dodds, Beverly Hills, Calif.

DOLAN   Jim Dolan, Harvard City, Ind.

DORFMAN   Julian Dorfman, Los Angeles, Calif.

DOUNEY   Marlan W. Douney, Oklahoma City, Okla.

DOWELL   Dudley Dowell, New York, N.Y.

DOWNING   Mrs. Joseph P. Downing, New York, N.Y.

DOWNS   Booth Downs, Ada, Okla.

DOYLE   William H. Doyle, Muskogee, Okla.

DUNCAN   Bob Duncan, Seattle, Wash.

DUNN   (see D. Kramer)

DUSTIN   Charles Dustin, Albuquerque, N.M.

DUTTON   Margaret Dutton, San Francisco, Calif.

EASTMAN   Gates Eastman, Santa Fe, N.M.

EDER   Earl Eder, Poplar, Mont.

EDMONDSON   Ed Edmondson, Muskogee, Okla. and Washington, D.C.

EDWARDS   Ralph Edwards, Hollywood, Calif.

EGERTSON   Darrell Egertson, Hopkins, Minn.

EGGERT   Justin Eggert, Philadelphia, Pa.

EISENHOWER Dwight D. Eisenhower, Gettysburg, Pa.

EKBERG William Ekberg, Bismarck, N.Dak.

ELKINS Marvin Elkins, Muskogee, Okla.

ELKUS Ruth and Charles DeYoung Elkus, San Francisco, Calif. (*deceased*)

ELSOHN Julie Elsohn, New York, N.Y.

ELWELL Alcott Farrar (*deceased*)

ENLOWS Sharkey Enlows, Corvallis, Oreg.

O. EVANS Orron D. Evans, St. Louis, Mo.

R. EVANS Robert Evans, Monroe, La.

EWING Frances Ewing, Dallas, Tex.

FACTOR Walter Factor, Okmulgee, Okla.

FARMER J. C. Farmer, Tulsa, Okla.

FARWELL Wes Farwell, Torrance, Calif.

FEEMSTER Hal Feemster, Tulsa, Okla.

FEEMSTER III J. H. Feemster, III, Lake Forest, Ill.

FEINWILER Charles Feinwiler, Albuquerque, N.M.

FEIOCK Mrs. Al Feiock, Poplar, Mont.

C. FENTON Carroll Lane Fenton, New Brunswick, N.J.

W. FENTON William N. Fenton, Albany, N.Y.

FIELD Clark Field, Tulsa, Okla.

FIELDS David Fields, Jr., Tulsa, Okla.

FINCHER Jack Fincher, Fort Worth, Tex.

FINLEY David E. Finley, Washington, D.C.

FISHER Fern Fisher, Ponca City, Okla.

FITCHOWAY Cecil Fitchoway, Walters, Okla.

FITE E. H. Fite, Jr., Muskogee, Okla.

F. FLEET Frank Fleet, Ada, Okla.

M. FLEET Martin Fleet, Ada, Okla.

FLEISCHMANN Julius Fleischmann, Chatham, Mass.

FLEISHMAN Alfred Fleishman, Farmington, Mo.

J. FLETCHER Jarvis Fletcher, Muskogee, Okla.

M. FLETCHER Margaret Fletcher, Muskogee, Okla.

FLOOD Richard Flood, Idaho Falls, Idaho

FLORENCE Jack Florence, Toledo, Ohio

FONTAINE Tracy Claire Fontaine, Houston, Tex.

A. FORBES Anne Forbes, Cambridge, Mass.

J. FORBES Jack M. Forbes, Reno, Nev.

FOREMAN Mrs. Grant Foreman, Muskogee, Okla. (*deceased*)

FORKNER Mrs. Richard Forkner, Langden, N.Dak.

D. FOSTER Donald Foster, Seattle, Wash.

W. FOSTER Wayne Foster, Okmulgee, Okla.

FRANKLIN Lorena Franklin, Okmulgee, Okla.

FRANKS Carrol Franks, Ardmore, Okla.

FRASER Le Rox Fraser, Funtridge, Calif.

FRAZIER Bernard Frazier, Lawrence, Kan.

FREEMAN Norman Freeman, Dallas, Tex.

FRITH David H. Frith, Okmulgee, Okla.

FROST Albert Frost, Albernie, B.C., Canada

FROVIS David Frovis, Ruidoso, N.M.

FRUSTI Roy A. J. Frusti, Albuquerque, N.M.

FRY D. A. Fry, Wichita, Kan.

A. GARCIA Arthur Garcia, Albuquerque, N.M.

P. GARCIA Pablo Garcia, Albuquerque, N.M.

T. GARCIA Tony Garcia, San Juan Pueblo, N.M.

GARLAND R. C. Garland, Las Cruces, N.M.

GARRETT Claude Garrett, Fort Gibson, Okla.

GASTON Benjamin Gaston, Muskogee, Okla.

GATLIFF Betty Pat Gatliff, Norman, Okla.

GAY Charles Gay, Las Cruces, N.M.

GEIS Mrs. Frank Geis, San Juan Pueblo, N.M.

GEPHARDT Gordon Gephardt, Muskogee, Okla.

GERASH Gerald Gerash, Oakland, Calif.

GERMESHAUSEN Kenneth Germeshausen, Boston, Mass.

GERMUNDSON Niles G. Germundson, Teterboro, N.J.

GERSHENSON Wilbur Gershenson, New York, N.Y.

GESS Robert Gess, New York, N.Y.

GIANNINI Bernadette Giannini, Berkeley, Calif.

GIERKE Herman Gierke, Watford City, N.Dak.

GILMORE Harry Gilmore, Miami, Okla.

GIRDLER Allan T. Girdler, Tulsa, Okla.

GIRDLEY A. T. Girdley, Tulsa, Okla.

GOFF Bruce Goff, Bartlesville, Okla.

GOMBERG Harold Gomberg, New York, N.Y.

GONZALES Hector Gonzales, Albuquerque, N.M.

GORMAN Steve Gorman, Daggett, Calif.

GOSFELDT Nadine Gosfeldt, Los Angeles, Calif.

GRAMMER Maurine Grammer, Albuquerque, N.M.

C. GRANT Campbell Grant, Santa Barbarra, Calif.

M. GRANT Mrs. Margaret Grant, Bartlesville, Okla.

GRAUBARTH   Harry Graubarth, Dayton, Ohio

GRAWE   Mrs. O. R. Grawe, Rolla, Mo.

GREEN   Harold Green, Valley Forge, Pa.

GREENBERG   Earl Greenberg, Las Vegas, Nev.

GREENBLATT   Gerome Greenblatt, Albuquerque, N.M.

GREENE   Robert Greene, New York, N.Y.

GRENDER   G. C. Grender, Houston, Tex.

D. GRIFFIN   D. E. Griffin, Albany, Calif.

J. GRIFFIN   John Griffin, Muskogee, Okla.

GROSSMANN   Julius Grossmann, Boston, Mass.

GRUBB   Robert Grubb, Tulsa, Okla.

GUILLAUME   Harry Guillaume, Cedar Falls, Iowa

GULAGAR   Clu Gulagar, Hollywood, Calif.

GUNN   Mrs. Raymond Gunn, Tulsa, Okla.

GUTHRIE   J. Guthrie, Detroit, Mich.

A. GUTIÉRREZ   Andres Gutiérrez, Albuquerque, N.M.

J. GUTIÉRREZ   John P. Gutiérrez, Albuquerque, N.M.

HADDOCK   Mrs. Fred Haddock, Tulsa. Okla.

J. HALL   J. Donald Hall, Muskogee, Okla.

R. HALL   Mrs. Ruby Aunko Hall, Lawton, Okla.

HAMILTON   Phil Hamilton, Mexico City, Mexico

HAMMETT   Robert W. Hammett, Tulsa, Okla.

HAMMOND   Marian Hammond, Berkeley, Calif.

HANKS   W. V. Hanks, Tulsa, Okla.

HANSON   S. Hanson, Anaheim, Calif.

HARBOUR   Betty Harbour, Muskogee, Okla.

HARDY   Henry G. Hardy, Oakland, Calif.

HARMON   Rhonda Harmon, Honolulu, Hawaii

C. HARRIS   Mrs. Cecelia Harris, Tulsa, Okla.

CH. HARRIS   Charles Harris, Tulsa, Okla.

D. HARRIS   Mrs. Darcie J. Harris, Berkeley, Calif.

F. HARRIS   Fred Harris, Lawton, Okla. and Washington, D.C.

G. HARRIS   George Harris, Phoenix, Ariz.

J. HARRIS   Mrs. Jack Harris, Konawa, Okla.

HART   William B. Hart, Ansonia, Conn.

HARVEY   Byron Harvey III, Phoenix, Ariz.

HASSRICK   Royal B. Hassrick, Elizabeth, Colo.

HATFIELD   Mark Hatfield, Washington, D.C.

HAUGER   John Hauger, Ada, Okla.

HAWORTH   Fred Haworth, Tulsa, Okla.

HAY   Clarence Hay, New York, N.Y.

HAYDEN   Donald Hayden, Tulsa, Okla.

HAYES   James Hayes, Tulsa, Okla.

HEARNE   Allen Hearne, Richmond, Calif.

HECKSCHER   August Heckscher, New York, N.Y.

HEDGES   Mrs. Harold Hedges, Chevy Chase, Md.

A. HENDERSON   Alice Corbin Henderson

R. HENDERSON   Mrs. R. W. Henderson, Bismarck, N.Dak.

W. HENDERSON   William Penhallow Henderson (*deceased*)

HENNEKE   Ben Henneke, Tulsa, Okla.

HENRY   James R. Henry, Monroe, La.

HENSCHEN   Gustave Henschen, New York, N.Y.

HERTZ   Amelia Hertz, Syracuse, N.Y.

HERWICK   Rudolph Herwick, Berkeley, Calif.

HEUGHLAND   Richard Heughland, Muskogee, Okla.

HEWETT   Edgar Lee Hewett (*deceased*)

D. HILL   Daniel Hill, Tacoma, Wash.

E. HILL   Eleanor Hill, Tulsa, Okla.

L. HILL   Mrs. Lee Hill, Encinitas, Calif.

W. C. HILL   W. C. Hill, Tulsa, Okla.

W. M. HILL   W. M. Hill, Muskogee, Okla.

HILLMAN   John Hillman, Okmulgee, Okla.

HINCHMAN   Margaretta Hinchman, Philadelphia, Pa.

HIVELY   Margaret M. Hively, Muskogee, Okla.

HODGES   Mrs. John Hodges, Minot, N.Dak

HOGUE   Alexandre Hogue, Tulsa, Okla.

HOHN   Thomas Hohn, Muskogee, Okla.

HOLCH   Vagn Holch, Horsens, Denmark

HOLLIS   Pauline Hollis, Tulare, Calif.

HOLLON   Eugene Hollon, Norman, Okla.

HOLMES   Allen Holmes, Okmulgee, Okla.

HOLT   Phillip E. Holt, Anchorage, Alas.

HOLTON   Bob Holton, Okmulgee, Okla.

HOLWAY   Donal K. Holway, Tulsa, Okla.

H. HOOVER   Mrs. Herbert C. Hoover (*deceased*)

HERB. HOOVER   Herbert C. Hoover (*deceased*)

R. HOOVER   Robert Jack Hoover, Ada, Okla.

HOWE   Elliott Howe, Tulsa, Okla.

HOWELLA   Jack Meade Howella, New York, N.Y.

HUCKSTEIN   C. G. Huckstein, Los Angeles, Calif.

HUGHES Mrs. E. A. Hughes, Bismarck, N.Dak.

HULDERMANN Paul Huldermann, Scottsdale, Ariz.

HULS Phil Huls, Eufaula, Okla.

HUMPHREY Donald G. Humphrey, Tulsa, Okla.

HUMPHRIES Henry Humphries, Wichita, Kan.

HUNDLEY Hal Hundley, Tucson, Ariz.

N. HUNT N. B. Hunt, Dallas, Tex.

W. HUNT Wolf Robe Hunt, Tulsa, Okla.

HUNTER Robert Hunter, Riverside, Calif.

HUNTINGTON Anna Hyatt Huntington, Bethel, Conn.

HURLEY Mrs. Patrick Hurley, Santa Fe, N.M.

HURR Louis Hurr, Santa Fe, N.M.

HYAM Earle Hyam, Providence, R.I.

IRBY J. H. Irby, Walnut Creek, Calif.

JACOBS Ben Jacobs, Muskogee, Okla.

E. JACOBSON Edward Jacobson, Phoenix, Ariz.

O. JACOBSON O. B. Jacobson (deceased)

JAMELL O. C. Jamell, Muskogee, Okla.

H. JAMES Harry James, Banning, Calif.

J. JAMES Joe James, Muskogee, Okla.

JAMESON Mrs. Chet H. Jameson, Tulsa, Okla.

N. JARAMILLO Nicholas Jaramillo, Albuquerque, N.M.

R. JARAMILLO Robert Jaramillo, Albuquerque, N.M.

JASINSKY M. Jasinsky, Sequim, Wash.

JEFFERSON Irene Jefferson, Fairfax, Okla.

JOHNET Jacques E. Johnet, Novato ,Calif.

A. JOHNSON Mrs. Arthur Johnson, Muskogee, Okla.

E. JOHNSON E. Johnson, Tulsa, Okla.

F. JOHNSON Felix Johnson, New York, N.Y.

I. JOHNSON Imo Johnson, Tulsa, Okla.

M. JOHNSON Monte Johnson, New York, N.Y.

P. JOHNSON Port Johnson, Muskogee, Okla.

JOHNSTON Donald Johnston, Albuquerque, N.M.

C. JONES Carroll Jones, Okmulgee, Okla.

E. JONES Mrs. Edith Jones, Albuquerque, Okla.

F. JONES Frances M. Jones, Scottsdale, Ariz.

H. JONES Hester Jones, Santa Fe, N.M.

I. JONES Irwin Jones, Okmulgee, Okla.

N. JONES Neil Jones, Tahlequah, Okla.

O. JONES O. C. Jones, Tahlequah, Okla.

S. JONES Sam Jones, Little Rock, Ark.

JORDAHM Inga Jordahm, Nederling, Tex.

JORGENSEN Arlene Jorgensen, Brigham City, Utah

JUDKINS M. O. Judkins, Muskogee, Okla.

JUSTIN John Justin, Jr., Fort Worth, Tex.

KAEL Pauline Kael, Berkeley, Calif.

KAHO Noel Kaho, Tulsa, Okla.

KALISPELL Nelson Kalispell, Kalispell, Mont.

KALLON Eugene Kallon, Norman, Okla.

KAMEN-KAYE Maurice Kamen-Kaye, Boston, Mass.

L. KEENE Lee Keene, Tulsa, Okla.

O. KEENE O. L. Keene, Watford City, N.Dak.

KEITH Lyle Keith, Spokane, Wash.

KELLY Gerald Kelly, Henryetta, Okla.

KEMM James O. Kemm, Tulsa, Okla.

J. KENNEDY John Fitzgerald Kennedy (deceased)

M. KENNEDY Michael Stephen Kennedy, Helena, Mont.

R. KENNEDY Robert S. Kennedy (deceased)

KERSHAW L. R. Kershaw, Muskogee, Okla.

KIDD Phil Kidd, Jr., Norman, Okla.

KILEY Robert Kiley, Falls Church, Va.

KILLEBREW Walter Killebrew, Canadian, Tex.

KIMBALL Yeffe Kimball, New York, N.Y.

KING Zella King, Stillwater, Okla.

KINKADE Claire Kinkade, Barnsdall, Okla.

KIRSHNER Philip Kirshner, Muskogee, Okla.

KLICK J. H. Klick, Lafayette, Calif.

KLOTZ C. J. Klotz, San Francisco, Calif.

KNICKERBOCKER Frank Knickerbocker, Dallas, Tex.

KOCH John Koch, Tulsa, Okla.

KOENIG Peter Koenig, Zurich, Switzerland

A. KRAMER Art Kramer, Tulsa, Okla.

D. KRAMER Dorothy Dunn (Mrs. Max Kramer), Los Altos, Calif.

M. KRAMER Max Kramer, Los Altos, Calif.

S. KRAMER Sam Kramer, New York, N.Y.

KROGH Mrs. O. J. Krogh, Northridge, Calif.

KROLL Daniel R. Kroll, Stillwater, Okla.

B. KRONENBERG Bernard Kronenberg, New York, N.Y.

BOR. KRONENBERG Boris Kronenberg, New York, N.Y.

KRUEGER Mrs. Elsie C. Krueger, Chicago, Ill.

KRUSS Betty Kruss, Indianola, Nebr.

LACY Mrs. Sam Lacy, Tulsa, Okla.

LA FARGE Oliver La Farge (*deceased*)

LAKE Mae Lake, Pawhuska, Okla.

LANG Heinz H. Lang, Seattle, Wash.

LANNON J. Patrick Lannon, Chicago, Ill.

LANTRE Mrs. Norma Lantre, Los Alamos, N.M.

LARSON Guy Larson, Bismarck, N.Dak.

LASLEY Buster Lasley, Fairfax, Okla.

LAUGHLIN Mary Laughlin, Oklahoma City, Okla.

LAURITZEN Jonreed Lauritzen, Thousand Oaks, Calif.

LEAKE James Leake, Muskogee, Okla.

LEATHERS H. Leathers, Muskogee, Okla.

LEE Howard Lee, Denver, Colo.

LEIBENSPERGER R. Leibensperger, Timion, Md.

LENG Loren Leng, Grand Marais, Minn.

LENO Arthur Leno, Bismarck, N.Dak.

LEONARD Mary Leonard, Tulsa, Okla.

A. LEWIS Argie Lewis, Tulsa, Okla.

J. LEWIS Jack Leon Lewis, Oakland, Calif.

LIBHART Myles Libhart, Washington, D.C.

LIGHT Walter Scott Light, San Antonio, Tex.

LINCOLN John W. Lincoln, Providence, R.I.

LINDSEY Father Lucien Lindsey, Chicago, Ill.

LINDSTROM R. C. Lindstrom, Santa Monica, Calif.

LINK Martin Link, Gallup, N.M.

LIPELT Janice Lipelt, Napa, Calif.

LITTLE George Little, Berkeley, Calif.

LIVINGSTON Kathie Livingston, Tulsa, Okla.

LOCKETT Clay Lockett, Tucson, Ariz.

LOCKWOOD Mrs. John Lockwood, New York, N.Y.

LOHMAN Mrs. H. R. Lohman, Tulsa, Okla.

LOHR Edison P. Lohr, Eastham, Mass.

LONG Cindy Long, Oklahoma City, Okla.

LOO Orin Loo, Colorado Springs, Colo.

LOVE Mrs. Pauline Love, Konawa, Okla.

LOWEIRO Ruby Loweiro, San Francisco, Calif.

LOWRY George W. Lowry, Clinton, Okla.

LUTON John Luton, Muskogee, Okla.

LYNDE George Lynde, Muskogee, Okla.

MACKAY Condon MacKay, Tulsa, Okla.

MADDY K. Maddy, Tulsa, Okla.

MAGEE W. E. Magee, St. Louis, Mo.

MANCHESTER John Manchester, Taos, N.M.

MARKEN Harry Marken, Woodward, Okla.

MARKS Jerry Marks, Bristow, Okla.

MARRIOTT Alice Marriott, Oklahoma City, Okla.

MARSHALL Ben Marshall, Muskogee, Okla.

MARTIN Mrs. Betty Martin, Okmulgee, Okla.

M. MARTÍNEZ Mescal Martínez, New York N.Y.

T. MARTÍNEZ Tony Martínez, San Ildefonso Pueblo, N.M.

D. MASON Drew Mason, Oklahoma City, Okla.

T. MASON Tom Mason, Muskogee, Okla.

J. MAULDIN Jane Mauldin, Tulsa, Okla.

JER. MAULDIN Jerry Mauldin, Tulsa, Okla.

D. MAXWELL Dorothy Field Maxwell, Farmington, N.M.

G. MAXWELL Gil Maxwell, Farmington, N.M.

R. MAXWELL Roy Maxwell, Las Vegas, Nev.

MAYER-OAKES William Mayer-Oakes, Winnipeg, Manitoba, Canada

MAYHUE C. C. Mayhue, Ada, Okla.

MAYTUBBY E. B. Maytubby, Muskogee, Okla.

McALISTER L. S. McAlister, Muskogee, Okla.

J. McALPIN Jeff McAlpin, Bismarck, N.Dak.

R. McALPIN Mrs. R. J. McAlpin, Bismarck, N.Dak.

McCABE Maurice McCabe, Window Rock, Ariz.

McCANN Margaret V. McCann, Oklahoma City, Okla.

McCORD Mrs. Bemeil McCord, Saratoga, Wyo.

B. McCORMICK Bob McCormick, Tulsa, Okla.

F. McCORMICK Mrs. Fowler McCormick, Scottsdale, Ariz.

K. McCORMICK Kate McCormick, Pawhuska, Okla.

McCRACKEN Harold McCracken, Cody, Wyo.

McDONALD O. L. McDonald, Prairie View, Ill.

McELROY J. H. McElroy, Okmulgee, Okla.

McGEE Wm. E. McGee, Ariz.

McGILHRA David McGilhra, Okmulgee, Okla.

McGILLIWAY Don McGilliway, Berkeley, Calif.

McGOVERN George McGovern, Bismarck, N.Dak.

McGRATH James McGrath, Santa Fe, N.M.
McIUNE Thomas McIune, San Francisco, Calif.
McKEE Robert S. McKee, Muskogee, Okla.
McKEEVER Douglas McKeever, Enid, Okla.
McKING Edgar S. McKing, Radnor, Pa.
McKINNEY Mrs. King McKinney, Marietta, Okla.
McLARENS Stanley McLarens, Monterey Park, Calif.
McMAHAN Harold McMahan, Okmulgee, Okla.
McMORRIS Wm. McMorris, Tulsa, Okla.
McNAUGHT James R. McNaught, Tulsa, Okla.
J. McPHERSON J. Havard McPherson, Tucson, Ariz.
R. McPHERSON Ramona McPherson, Peru, Ind.
MEDINA Frank Medina, Austin, Tex.
MELLOR Alvin Mellor, Providence, R.I.
MELVILLE David B. Melville, New York, N.Y.
MENDHALL M. Mendhall, St. Petersburg, Fla.
MERCADO Josie Mercado, Dodge City, Kan.
MERITS Mrs. M. Merits, Fort Wayne, Ind.
MERRICK Ward Merrick, Jr., Ardmore, Okla.
MERTZ Frona Mertz, Deland, Fla.
MEYERS Gary D. Meyers, Okmulgee, Okla.
MICHELS Mrs. E. T. Michels, Vermillion, S.Dak.
MICHENER M. Lee Michener, Arlington, Tex.
MIDDLETON William S. Middleton, Madison, Wisc.
MIGLIACCIO Mrs. C. A. Migliaccio, Washington, D.C.
MILBERGER Mrs. Doris Milberger, Oklahoma City, Okla.
G. MILBURN Glen Milburn, Wichita, Kan.
J. MILBURN Joe Milburn, Tulsa, Okla.
MILEHAM Jack C. Mileham, Chandler, Okla.
F. MILLER Fred Miller, Oklahoma City, Okla.
K. MILLER Kate E. Miller, Louisville, Ky.
R. MILLER Robert Miller, Morris, Okla.
MILLS George A. Mills, Jr., Oakland, Calif.
MILNER Mrs. John Milner, Okmulgee, Okla.
MINER Claire E. Miner, Berkeley, Calif.
MISHLER Donald L. Mishler, Morris, Okla.
MONROE Angus Monroe, Browning, Mont.
M. MOORE Mrs. Marguerite Moore, Tulsa, Okla.

R. MOORE Robb W. Moore, Oklahoma City, Okla.
MORELAND James W. Moreland, San Bernardino, Calif.
MORFORD R. Morford, Edmonton, Alberta, Canada
MORRIS Virginia Morris, Tulsa, Okla.
MORRISON Mrs. Peggy Morrison, Encinitas, Calif.
MORRISSETTE Raymond Morrissette, Stillwater, Okla.
MORROW Gladys Morrow, Walters, Okla.
MOUNT Houston Mount, Tulsa, Okla.
MULLAN Reed Mullan, Phoenix, Ariz.
MURPHEY Pamela Murphey, Hollywood, Calif.
MYERS Roy Myers, Muskogee, Okla.
MYLE Herbert Myle, Chantilly, Va.

NASH Philleo Nash, Washington, D.C.
NEEDHAM Belle Needham, Red Lake, Minn.
NEELY Mrs. Chris F. Neely, Middletown, Ohio
NEILSON Margaret Neilson, New York, N.Y.
NELSON Hardin Nelson, Muskogee, Okla.
NEUMANN Mrs. L. Murray Neumann, Tulsa, Okla.
NEVELSON Louise Nevelson, New York, N.Y.
NEW Lloyd Kiva New, Santa Fe, N.M.
NEWCOMB Franc Newcomb, Nava, N.M.
NEWELL Charles Newell, Gallup, N.M.
NICHOLS Dudley Nichols, Washington, D.C.
NOBLE C. E. Noble, Las Vegas, Nev.
NORDLING Joan Nordling, Denver, Colo.
NORTNER John Nortner, Berkeley, Calif.
NYKOLAYOW Andrew Nykolayow, Robinson, N.Dak.

OBERMIRE Art Obermire, Tulsa, Okla.
O'BRIEN Joseph T. O'Brien, Phoenix, Ariz.
B. OLDHAM Brown Oldham, Muskogee, Okla.
I. OLDHAM I. B. Oldham, Jr., Muskogee, Okla.
OLIPHANT George Oliphant, Rialto, Calif.
OLSON Ray Olson, Grand Marais, Minn.
ORDON Von Ordon, Berkeley, Calif.
ORR Herbert Orr, Tulsa, Okla.
OWENS Chester A. Owens, Muskogee, Okla.

PABST John F. Pabst, San Antonio, Tex.
PACE Clark Pace, Oklahoma City, Okla.
PACKER James Packer, Philadelphia, Pa.
PAHSETOPAH Louis Pahsetopah, Pawhuska, Okla.

PALMER Gordon Palmer, Los Angeles, Calif.

PAPPIO Joe Pappio, Midwest City, Okla.

PATANIA Frank Patania, Santa Fe, N.M.

PATMAN Julie Patman, Tulsa, Okla.

PATTON Mrs. Mark Patton, Tulsa, Okla.

PAYNE Hugh Payne, Oklahoma City, Okla.

PEDERSON Margaret Pederson, Sioux City, Iowa

PELLER Mrs. Richard Peller, Winston-Salem, N.C.

PERDUE Winnie Guess Perdue, Muskogee, Okla.

C. PEREYMA Constantine Pereyma, Troy, Ohio

E. PEREYMA Eugene Pereyma, Detroit, Mich.

PERLMAN Mrs. W. Perlman, New Rochelle, N.Y.

D. PERRY Doyle Perry, Muskogee, Okla.

O. PERRY Oseph Perry, Ganado, Ariz.

R. PERRY Roger Perry, Phoenix, Ariz.

PETERS Mrs. Susie Peters (deceased)

PETERSEN Karen Daniels Petersen, St. Paul, Minn.

B. PETERSON Bill Peterson, Okmulgee, Okla.

I. PETERSON Irene Peterson, San Francisco, Calif.

L. PETERSON Lynn Peterson, Jr., Washington, D.C.

M. PETERSON Mrs. Mollie Peterson, Bismarck, N.Dak.

PETTINGER Gordon Pettinger, Vallejo, Calif.

PHERIGO Mrs. Bobbie J. Pherigo, Rosewell, N.M.

PHILLIPS Philip Phillips, Bartlesville, Okla.

PHILLIPS II Mrs. John A. Phillips, II, Durant, Okla.

PICKART Walter Pickart, Gary, Ind.

PICKETT Marie Pickett, Muskogee, Okla.

PIERCE Earl Boyd Pierce, Muskogee, Okla.

PIÑA Trina Piña, Berkeley, Calif.

PITTS Donald S. Pitts, Sacramento, Calif.

PLACE Bradley Place, Tulsa, Okla.

PLUMMER Ed Plummer, Window Rock, Ariz.

POLAND Scott B. Poland, San Francisco, Calif.

POSER Lillian Poser, Dallas, Tex.

H. POTTER H. Vinton Potter, Tulsa, Okla.

R. POTTER R. W. Potter, Carmel, Calif.

POWELL Father Peter Powell, Chicago, Ill.

POWERS Anna Powers, Alexandria, Va.

POWHATAN C. A. Powhatan, Muskogee, Okla.

PRATT John N. Pratt, Sacramento, Calif.

H. PRICE Hollis Price, Muskogee, Okla.

V. PRICE Vincent Price, Beverly Hills, Calif.

W. PRICE William Price, Oakland, Calif.

W. S. PRICE William S. Price, Tulsa, Okla.

PRIETO Mrs. Pat Prieto, Leucadia, Calif.

PRIMROSE W. Alek Primrose, New York, N.Y.

PRITZLAFF Richard Pritzlaff, Sapello, N.M.

PRITZLOFF Mrs. John Pritzloff, Phoenix, Ariz.

PROCTOR Charles Proctor, Santa Fe, N.M.

PUTNAM L. H. Putnam, Bismarck, N.Dak

RACHLIN Carol Rachlin, Oklahoma City, Okla.

D. RAMSEY Dick Ramsey, Rialto, Calif.

S. RAMSEY Mrs. Sylvia Ramsey, Frankfort, Ky.

RANDOLPH Robert Randolph, Tulsa, Okla.

REAGAN Roberta Reagan, Midland, Tex.

REED Paul Reed, Denton, Tex.

REGAN Amelia M. Regan, Oakland, Calif.

RENA Tony Rena, Taos, N.M.

RENNER Autro Renner, Austrian Embassy, U.S.A.

REXROTH Frank Rexroth, Indianapolis, Ind.

REYNOLDS J. P. Reynolds, Walters, Okla.

RHODD Jean Rhodd, Tulsa, Okla.

RICE Eugene Rice, Muskogee, Okla.

RIED Edward Ried, New York, N.Y.

RIGGERT Wilbur Riggert, Wounded Knee, S.Dak.

RILEY Jim Riley, Santa Fe, N.M.

ROACH James Roach, Plainfield, Iowa

E. ROBERTS Mrs. E. M. Roberts, Midwest City, Okla.

H. ROBRTS Holly Roberts, Woodward, Okla.

J. ROBERTS J. B. Roberts, Oklahoma City, Okla.

ROBINETT Mrs. Walter Robinett, Visalia, Calif.

H. ROBINSON Hugh Robinson, Okmulgee, Okla.

R. ROBINSON Roy Robinson, Chicago, Ill.

ROCKEFELLER Mrs. John D. Rockefeller (deceased)

RODEE Howard D. Rodee, Columbus, Ohio

B. ROGERS Bolles Rogers, Minneapolis, Minn.

R. ROGERS Roy Rogers, Hollywood, Calif.

W. ROGERS Will Rogers, Jr., Tubac, Ariz.

ROOSEVELT Eleanor Roosevelt (*deceased*)

ROSALLINI Albert Rosallini, Olympia, Wash.

ROSENWALD Janet Rosenwald, Santa Fe, N.M.

J. ROSS Joe Ross, Dallas, Tex.

L. ROSS Larry Ross, Bolivar, Tenn.

ROULLION M. Roullion, French Embassy, Ottawa, Canada.

ROUNDTREE George D. Roundtree, Houston, Tex.

ROUSCH Robert W. Rousch, Tulsa, Okla.

ROUSE Louis Rouse, Riverton, R.I.

ROWLAND Mrs. Lloyd Rowland, New Orleans, La.

ROWSEY Paul Rowsey, Muskogee, Okla.

RUBIN H. J. Rubin, Tulsa, Okla.

RUBY Russell Ruby, Muskogee, Okla.

RUCINSKI Kenneth Rucinski, Corpus Christi, Tex.

RUE Melton Rue, Sr., Bismarck, N.Dak.

RUEDIN Edgar Ruedin, Cressirr-Neuchâtel, Switzerland

RUGGLES Roy Ruggles, Escondido, Calif.

RUSSELL John Russell, Leupp, Ariz.

RUST Mrs. Fifer Rust, Normal, Kan.

RYAN William Ryan, Tulsa, Okla.

SALAZAR Frank A. Salazar, Albuquerque, N.M.

SALTONSTALL Nathan Saltonstall, Boston Mass.

B. SANDERS Mrs. Bob Sanders, Fort Smith, Ark.

H. SANDERS Harold R. Sanders, Stillwater, Okla.

SANGSTER Raymond C. Sangster, Glen Head, L.I., N.Y.

SATTERWHITE Sylvia Satterwhite, Wagoner, Okla.

SCHAEFER Doris Schaefer, Baltimore, Md.

W. SCHOFIELD William Schofield, Rancho Santa Fe, N.M.

WM. SCHOFIELD William Schofield, Orange, Calif.

SCHONWALD Mrs. Fred P. Schonwald, Oklahoma City, Okla.

SCHREIBER Allen Schreiber, St. Joseph, Mo.

SCHROEDER Florence Schroeder, Albuquerque, N.M.

SCHWARZ C. A. Schwarz, Aberdeen, S.Dak.

A. SCOTT Andrew Scott, St. Paul, Minn.

L. SCOTT Les Scott, Chinle, Ariz.

O. SCOTT O. Scott, Sioux Falls, S.Dak.

SELASSIE H. M. Hailie Selassie, Ethiopia

SELIGMAN Thornton Seligman, Albuquerque, N.M.

SEWELL Brice Sewell, Taos, N.M.

SHACKELFORD Helen Shackelford, Phoenix, Ariz.

SHAEBER Anna Shaeber, Pawhuska, Okla.

SHAW Edmund C. Shaw, Villanova, Pa.

SHEETS Millard Sheets, Padua Hills, Calif.

SHELTON Ted Shelton, Okmulgee, Okla.

SHEPARD Herb Shepard, Scottsdale, Ariz.

SHILLIN Allen Shillin, New York, N.Y.

SHIPLEY Jack Shipley, Morris, Okla.

SHIPPY Homer Shippy, Gallup, N.M.

SHOEMAKER Stanley Shoemaker, East Providence, R.I.

SILBERMAN Arthur Silberman, Oklahoma City, Okla.

SILVA Angelo Silva, San Francisco, Calif.

SIMANK William L. Simank, Stillwater, Okla.

SIMONTON Reverend Simonton, Santa Fe, N.M.

SIMPSON Mrs. H. G. Simpson, Memphis, Tenn.

SLACK Rex Slack, Muskogee, Okla.

SLOBODKIN Martin Slobodkin, Cambridge, Mass.

B. SMITH Mrs. Boyd Smith, Winfield, Kan.

H. SMITH Herbert Smith, Del Mar, Calif.

L. SMITH Leonard Smith, Crystal City, U.

M. SMITH Mary Smith, Vernon, Tex.

R. SMITH Roger G. Smith, Dallas, Tex.

V. SMITH Vivian Smith, Tulsa, Okla.

W. SMITH Waits Smith, Sedona, Ariz.

SMITHSON John Smithson, Las Cruces, N.M.

SMOKER John Smoker, Raton, N.M.

SMYTH Ed Smyth, St. Louis, Mo.

SNEIDER Barbara Sneider, New York, N.Y.

SNELL Frank Snell, Phoenix, Ariz.

C. SNODGRASS Charles Snodgrass, Muskogee, Okla.

H. SNODGRASS Howard Snodgrass, Las Vegas, Nev.

J. SNODGRASS Jeanne O. Snodgrass, Shaker Heights, Ohio

SOLBERG I. E. Solberg, Bismarck, N.Dak.

SOLOW Anthony Solow, Tulsa, Okla.

SPELL Faralee Spell, Brigham City, Utah

SPENCER Dick Spencer, Colorado Springs, Colo.

SPIELMAN Henry William Spielman, Washington, D.C.

SPILLERS G. C. Spillers, Jr., Tulsa, Okla.

SPRAKER Bonnie Spraker, Muskogee, Okla.

SPRINGER Neilson Springer, Colorado Springs, Colo.

SPURLOCK Doyle Spurlock, Alexandria, Va.

STALCUP William J. Stalcup, Oklahoma City, Okla.

STALLMAN William Stallman, Wise River, Mont.

STANLEY Prina Stanley, Sausalito, Calif.

STEED Mrs. John Steed, Ardmore, Okla.

STEFFENS Carsten Steffens, Menlo Park, Calif.

STEPHENSON Wendell Scott Stephenson, West Hartford, Conn.

G. STEVENS George Stevens, Tulsa, Okla.

J. STEVENS Mrs. John Stevens, Albuquerque, N.M.

L. STEWART Mrs. L. D. Stewart, Tulsa, Okla.

S. STEWART Spencer Stewart, Phoenix, Ariz.

STIEFEL Kenneth Stiefel, Tulsa, Okla.

STIGLETS Melvin Stiglets, Muskogee, Okla.

STILES William Stiles, New York, N.Y.

STINSON David Stinson, Falls Church, Va.

STINSON, JR. David Stinson, Jr., Springfield, Va.

STOKES Quincy Stokes, Flagstaff, Ariz.

J. STONE John Stone, Muskogee, Okla.

W. STONE Willard Stone, Locust Grove, Okla.

STORY Mrs. Lorenzo Story, San Miguel de Allende, Mexico

STOUT Cephas Stout, Tulsa, Okla.

STRICKLAND Renard Strickland, Muskogee, Okla.

STRYKER Phillip Stryker, Stillwater, Okla.

STUELAND Marie Stueland, Duluth, Minn.

SUKMAN Robert Sukman, Oklahoma City, Okla.

SUMMERS R. L. Summers, Tulsa, Okla.

SUNDET N. J. Sundet, Kadoka, S.Dak.

SUTTON Carol Daube Sutton, Ardmore, Okla.

SUZUKI Pat Suzuki, Hollywood, Calif.

SWARD Paul Sward, Brigham City, Utah

SWIFT EAGLE Lavonne Swift Eagle, Watford City, N.Dak.

SWINCHATT Jonathan P. Swinchatt, Tulsa, Okla.

SWINDLER James Swindler, Muskogee, Okla.

SYRIER A. J. Syrier, Netherlands

TALLEY Frank Talley, Preston, Okla.

TARNASKY Ralph E. Tarnasky, Bismarck, N.Dak.

TARPLEY Tom Tarpley, Muskogee, Okla.

TARRANT Samuel Tarrant, Newark, N.J.

TATGENHORST George Tatgenhorst, Burbank, Calif.

TAYLOR Louise Colbert Taylor, Oklahoma City, Okla.

TEAGUE Charles Teague, Albuquerque, N.M.

TENNYSON William David Tennyson, Little Rock, Ark.

B. TERRY Boyd Terry, Fort Sill, Okla.

P. TERRY Porter Terry, Santa Fe, N.M.

THOENY Oscar W. Thoeny, Phoenix, Ariz.

R. THOMAS Ray Thomas, Corpus Christi, Tex.

R.M. THOMAS R.M. Thomas, Muncie, Ind.

THOMPSON Francis W. Thompson, San Francisco, Calif.

H. THORNE Mrs. Harold Thorne, Corpus Christi, Tex.

N. THORNE Niblack Thorne, Paradise Valley, Ariz.

THURTON Ed Thurton, Tacoma, Wash.

TIFFANY Jerry Tiffany, Sioux Falls, S.Dak.

TIKKER Joanne Tikker, San Rafael, Calif.

TISHMAN Jack Tishman, New York, N.Y.

TISSERANT Eugene Cardinal Tisserant, Vatican, Rome, Italy

TODD F. C. Todd, Stillwater, Okla.

TOLLER Bill Toller, Morris, Okla.

TRUEX A. F. Truex, Tulsa, Okla.

TSO Etta Tso, San Francisco, Calif.

TSOSY Marietta Tsosy, Phoenix, Ariz.

TUCKER Paul W. Tucker, London, England

TURNER Kay Turner, Covina, Calif.

TWINS Clinton Twins, Okla.

UNDERWOOD Don Underwood, Tulsa, Okla.

UPTON Howard Upton, Tulsa, Okla.

D. VANCE Dave Vance, Los Angeles, Calif.

E. VANCE Earl Vance, Gallup, N.M.

VANCLEVE Frank VanCleve, Tahlequah, Okla.

VANDIVORT W. C. VanDivort, Wenatchee, Wash.

D. VANN Dorothy Vann, Saint Michaels, Ariz.

M. VANN Mark Vann, West Englewood, N.J.

VANVOORHUYSEN H. W. VanVoorhuysen, Houston, Tex.

VENTURA Marco Julio Ventura, Mexico, D.F., Mexico

VERNON Mrs. W. C. Vernon, Norman, Okla.

VERRYDEN Jerome Verryden, Detroit, Mich.

VICKERY Ward Vickery, Wichita, Kan.

VINSON   B. W. Vinson, Tulsa, Okla.

B. C. VON ASPE   B. C. Von Aspe, San Pedro, Calif.

B. W. VON ASPE   B. W. Von Aspe, Tulsa, Okla.

WADLEY   Ellen Wadley, Washington, D.C.

WALCH   Father John L. Walch, Oklahoma City, Okla.

J. WALKER   James A. Walker, Muskogee, Okla.

R. WALKER   Richard Walker, Oklahoma City, Okla.

C. WALKINGSTICK   Charles Walkingstick, Oklahoma City, Okla.

H. WALKINGSTICK   Howard Walkingstick, Oklahoma City, Okla.

WALLER   Julian A. Waller, El Cerrito, Calif.

WALLOP   Malcolm Wallop, Sheridan, Wyo.

WALSH   Anthony Walsh, Montreal, Quebec, Canada

E. WALTERS   Elizabeth Walters, Muskogee, Okla.

H. WALTERS   Hettie O. Walters, Stewart, Nev.

WALTON   Thomas Walton, Radnor, Pa.

R. WARD   Rose Ward, Bismarck, N.Dak.

S. WARD   Mrs. Sam Ward, Miami, Okla.

WASHBURN   Eddie Washburn, Fort Sill, Okla.

WATERHOUSE   Anne Waterhouse, Tulsa, Okla.

WATERS   Frank Waters, Taos, N.M.

WATKINS   Barbara K. Watkins, Alexandria, Va.

WAYMAN   Jim Wayman, Fallbrook, Calif.

WEARIN   Otha Wearin, Hastings, Iowa

WEAVER   William N. Weaver, Muskogee, Okla.

J. WEBER   John Weber, Los Angeles, Calif.

W. WEBER   Wally Weber, Muskogee, Okla.

WEBSTER   James E. Webster, Stillwater, Okla.

WEINBERG   Michael Weinberg, New York, N.Y.

WEINICKE   E. A. Weinicke, Tulsa, Okla.

WELBORN   Orange Welborn, Ada, Okla.

WELCH   E. P. Welch, Los Angeles, Calif.

WELLER   Louis Weller, Albuquerque, N.M.

WENGARD   Sherman Wengard, Albuquerque, N.M.

WERMY   Cynthia Wermy, Anadarko, Okla.

C. WEST   Carl West, Anadarko, Okla.

E. WEST   El Reno West, Hominy, Okla.

H. WEST   Howard West, Tulsa, Okla.

R. WEST   Raymond L. West, Orinda, Calif.

WEYR   George Weyr, New York, N.Y.

N. WHEELER   Nettie Wheeler, Muskogee, Okla.

R. WHEELER   Roger Wheeler, Tulsa, Okla.

WHEELRIGHT   Mary Cabot Wheelright (*deceased*)

A. WHITE   Amelia Elizabeth White, Santa Fe, N.M.

E. WHITE   Ed White, Denver, Colo.

I. WHITE   Ira White, Weatherford, Okla.

M. WHITE   Marie White, Muskogee, Okla.

WHITEFORD   Patricia Whiteford, New York, N.Y.

WHITEMAN   Jack Whiteman, Colorado Springs, Colo.

WHITNEY   Mrs. C. V. Whitney, New York, N.Y.

WHITRIDGE   William C. Whitridge, Baltimore, Md.

WIESENDANGER   Martin Wiesendanger, Tulsa, Okla.

WIESS   John Wiess, Las Vegas, Nev.

WILF   Al Wilf, Okmulgee, Okla.

WILKINS   Doris Wilkins, Walters, Okla.

A. WILLIAMS   Al Williams, Leupp, Ariz.

G. WILLIAMS   Glyn Williams, Troy, N.Y.

I. WILLIAMS   Irvin A. Williams, Weleetka, Okla.

L. WILLIAMS   Lonnie Williams, Gallup, N.M.

M. WILLIAMS   Mary T. Williams, Tulsa, Okla.

WILLIAMSON   Susan Williamson, Aspen, Colo.

C. WILSON   Charles Banks Wilson, Miami, Okla.

E. WILSON   E. M. Wilson, Anadarko, Okla.

M. WILSON   Mrs. Charles M. Wilson, Anadarko, Okla.

WISNER   J. E. Wisner, Albuquerque, N.M.

H. WISTER   Herbert Wister, Hominy, Okla.

O. WISTER   Owen Wister (*deceased*)

WITKAMP   Georgia Witkamp, Scottsdale, Ariz.

WIXMAN   M. Wixman, Berkeley, Calif.

WOFFARD   Mrs. Keith Woffard, Santa Fe, N.M.

WOLAVER   Bill Wolaver, Tulsa, Okla.

WOOD   Nancy Wood, Philadelphia, Pa.

J. WOODARD   John Woodard, Sedona, Ariz.

M. WOODARD   M. L. Woodard, Gallup, N.M. (*deceased*)

WOODBURN   J. T. Woodburn, Muskogee, Okla.

WOODRING Carl Woodring, Charlotte, N.C.
WOODRUFF William Woodruff, Richland, Wash.
WOODWARD Dorothy Woodward, Albuquerque, N.M.
WOOLLEY Judy Woolley, Rialto, Calif.
WORTH James Worth, Scottsdale, Ariz.
WRAY Jeanne Adams Wray, Ada, Okla.
WRIGHT Richard Wright, Odessa, Tex.
WURLITZER Helene Wurlitzer, Taos, N.M.
WYMAN Leland C. Wyman, Jamaica Plain, Mass.
YAGOL Ben Yagol, Ada, Okla.
YARBOROUGH Kenneth Yarborough, Amarillo, Tex.

YDENS Jan Ydens, Albuquerque, N.M.
YELLOWHORSE Juan Yellowhorse, Scottsdale, Ariz.
D. YOUNG Daniel Young, Washington, D.C.
J. YOUNG Mrs. J. K. Young, Glenshaw, Pa.
R. YOUNG Revere Young, Riverside, Calif.
YULKE I. G. Yulke, New York, N.Y.

ZAVATSKY J. B. Zavatsky, Wichita, Kan.
ZEFF Leo Zeff, Berkeley, Calif.
ZELLEHOFER Howard Zellehofer, Las Vegas, Nev.
ZELONIS E. J. Zelonis, Berkeley, Calif.

EXHIBITIONS

AAA/T Avenue of American Art Tour of U.S. Conducted by Winifred Scott, 1951–53. Sponsored by the Artists of the Southwest.
AAID All-American Indian Days, Sheridan, Wyo. Annually in Aug.
AAIE Annual American Indian Exposition, Chicago, Ill. (since 1953). Sponsored by the American Indian Center. (No longer held.)
AAIEAE Second Annual American Indian and Eskimo Art Exhibition and Stage Pageant, Mar. 2–14, 1964, Washington, D.C. Sponsored by the American Indian and Eskimo Cultural Foundation, Inc.
AAUW American Association of University Women.
ACC Arts Club of Chicago, Chicago, Ill. "An Exhibition of American Indian Paintings and Applied Arts," Oct. 23–Nov. 12, 1925.
AEOP/T Aquachromatic Exhibit, 1955–, and Original Palette Permanent Collection, 1957–. Tour of the U.S. Sponsored by M. Grumbacher, Inc., New York, N.Y.
AFA Two-Arrows Exhibition-Tour of the U.S. Sponsored by the American Federation of Arts with paintings from the collection of the AIHA.
AGAA Addison Gallery of American Art, Phillips Academy, Andover, Mass.
AHNHG Aiea Heights Naval Hospital Gallery, Honolulu, Hawaii.
AIAE/WSU First Annual American Indian Art Exhibition, May 6–14, 1964, Wayne State University, Detroit, Mich.
AIE The American Indian Exposition, Anadarko, Okla. Annually, one week in July.
AIEC American Indian Exposition and Congress, Oct. 21–23, 1937, Tulsa, Okla.
AIE/T First American Indian Exposition, 1936, Tulsa, Okla.
AIHA Albany Institute of History and Art, Albany, N.Y.
AIM Annual Indian Market, the Governor's Palace, Santa Fe, N.M. Annually in Aug. since 1922. Sponsored by the Southwest Association on Indian Affairs, Inc.
AIW Third Annual American Indian Week, Oct. 18–22, 1938, Tulsa Fairgrounds, Tulsa, Okla.
AMNH The American Museum of Natural History, New York, N.Y.
ASC Arizona State College, Flagstaff, Ariz.
ASF Arizona State Fair, Phoenix, Ariz.
ASPS Annual Southwest Print and Drawing Exhibition, 1964, Dallas Museum of Fine Arts, Dallas, Tex.
AU University of Arizona, Tucson, Ariz.
AU/ASM University of Arizona, Arizona State Museum, Tucson, Ariz.

BA Bank of America, Studio City, Calif.
BAA Bloomington Normal Art Association, Bloomington, Ill.
BAC Boston Art Club Exhibition, 1932, Boston, Mass.

BC　Bacone College, Bacone, Okla.
BG　Botts Gallery, Albuquerque, N.M.
BHH　Beverly Hills Hotel *and* Beverly Hilton Hotel, Beverly Hills, Calif.
BI　Butler Institute of American Art, Youngstown, Ohio
BIA　Bureau of Indian Affairs, U.S. Department of Interior, Washington, D.C.
BIA/A　Bureau of Indian Affairs, Aberdeen, S. Dak.
BMA　Birmingham Museum of Art, Birmingham, Ala.
BM/B　Brooklyn Museum, Brooklyn, N.Y.
BMFA　Boston Museum of Fine Arts, Boston, Mass.
BNIAS　Bismarck National Indian Art Show, 1963, Bismarck, N.Dak. Sponsored by
　　the Chamber of Commerce and Bismarck Art Association.

CAA　Concord Art Association Gallery, Concord, Mass.
CAC　California Art Club, Los Angeles, Calif.
CAG　E. B. Crocker Art Gallery, Sacramento, Calif.
CAI　The Art Institute of Chicago, Chicago, Ill.
CAM　Cincinnati Art Museum, Cincinnati, Ohio.
CBMM　Charles W. Bowers Memorial Museum, Santa Ana, Calif.
CCHM　Creek Indian Council House and Museum, Okmulgee, Okla.
CCP　Chicago Century of Progress, 1934, Chicago, Ill.
CFS　Central Federal Savings, Santa Monica, Calif.
CG　Campbell Galleries, Los Angeles, Calif.
CGA　The Corcoran Gallery of Art, Washington, D.C.
CI　Colonial Inn, Los Angeles, Calif.
CIFA　Carnegie Institute, Museum of Fine Art, Pittsburgh, Pa.
CIFS　California International Flower Show, Los Angeles, Calif.
CPLH　California Palace of the Legion of Honor, San Francisco, Calif.
CSF　California State Fair, Sacramento, Calif.
CU　University of Chicago, Chicago, Ill.
CWC/I　Chicago Women's Club, Chicago, Ill.

DAI　Dayton Art Institute, Dayton, Ohio
DAM　Denver Art Museum, Chappell House, Denver, Colo. "Annual Indian Artists'
　　Exhibition," since *ca.* 1951 (exhibit no longer being held).
DAM/I　Denver Art Museum, "Own Your Own Invitational," 1964.
DAR　Daughters of the American Revolution, Washington, D.C.
DG　The Dulin Gallery of Art, Knoxville, Tenn.
DMFA　Dallas Museum of Fine Arts, Dallas, Tex.
DMG　Davenport Municipal Art Gallery, Davenport, Iowa.
DSG　Walt Disney Studio Gallery, Burbank, Calif.

EITA　Exposition of Indian Tribal Arts, Inc. Sponsored by, and circulated through,
　　the College Art Association. This major exhibit included 600 examples of art by 21
　　tribes. First shown in New York City at the Grand Central Galleries for a period of
　　three months beginning in Dec. 1931, it subsequently toured the U.S. until 1933.
　　Organized by American painter John Sloan, nearly 40 museums and private collec-
　　tors contributed to the exhibit. *See* Sloan and La Farge (1931).

FAG/S　The Fine Arts Gallery of San Diego, San Diego, Calif.
FAIEAIP　"First Annual Invitational Exhibition of American Indian Paintings," Nov.
　　24, 1964–Jan. 29, 1965, USDI.
FANAIAE　First Annual, National American Indian Art Exposition of Charlotte,
　　N.C., 1964. Annually one week in Oct. Sponsored by the American Indian College
　　Foundation at Charlottetown Mall, Charlotte, N.C. (No longer held).
FANEA　First Annual National Exhibition of Art, New York, N.Y.
FCTM　Five Civilized Tribes Museum, Muskogee, Okla.
FMC　Friday Morning Club, Los Angeles, Calif.

FNAIC   International Indian Art Show and Handicraft Trade Fair, Aug. 3–11, 1964, Bismarck, N.Dak. Sponsored by the Foundation of North American Indian Culture.
FWAC   Fort Worth Art Center, Fort Worth, Tex.
FWG   Fred Wilson Gallery and Trading Post, Phoenix, Ariz.

GAG   Carolina Art Association, Gibbs Art Gallery, Charleston, S.C.
GCG   Grand Central Art Galleries, New York, N.Y.
GCIC   Gallup Community Indian Center, Gallup, N.M.
GG   Galerie Giroux, Brussels, Belgium.
GM   Gilcrease Institute of American History and Art, Tulsa, Okla.
GPL   Glendale Public Library, Glendale, Calif.
GTA   Greek Theatre Annual, Los Angeles, Calif.

HAU   Hellenic American Union, Athens, Greece.
HB   Havenstrite Building, Los Angeles, Calif.
HBBA   Hermosa Beach Biltmore Annual, Hermosa Beach, Calif.
HFA   Hollywood Festival of Arts, Hollywood, Calif.
HM   The Heard Museum of Anthropology and Primitive Art, Phoenix, Ariz.
HMFA   Museum of Fine Arts of Houston, Houston, Tex.

IAESS   International Art Exhibition of Sport Subjects. Held in connection with the 1922 Olympics, Los Angeles, Calif.
IDM   Isaac Delgado Museum of Art, New Orleans, La.
IPSE   Intermountain Painting and Sculpture Exhibition, 1964, Salt Lake Art Center, Salt Lake City, Utah.
ITIC   Inter-Tribal Indian Ceremonials. Gallup, N.M. Annually five days in Aug.

JAM   Joslyn Art Museum, Omaha, Nebr.
JGS   An Exhibition of American Indian Painters, Oct. 15–Nov. 15, 1955. James Graham and Sons, New York, N.Y.
JKA   John F. Kennedy International Airport, New York, N.Y.

KCF   Kern County Fair, Bakersfield, Calif.
KM   The Kiva Museum of the Koshare Indians, Boy Scouts of America, La Junta, Colo.
KU   University of Kansas, Lawrence, Kan.

LACC   Los Angeles City College, Los Angeles, Calif.
LACF   Los Angeles County Fair, Pomona, Calif.
LACM   Los Angeles County Museum of Art, Los Angeles, Calif.
LAIC   Los Angeles Indian Center, Los Angeles, Calif.
LBAG   Laguna Beach Art Association Gallery, Laguna Beach, Calif.
LH   Lever House, New York, N.Y.

MA   La Jolla Museum of Art, La Jolla, Calif.
MAF   Madonna Art Festival, Los Angeles, Calif.
MAG   Municipal Art Gallery, Los Angeles, Calif.
MAG/H   Metcalf's Art Gallery, North Hollywood, Calif.
MAI   Museum of the American Indian, Heye Foundation, New York, N.Y.
MAM   The Montclair Art Museum, Montclair, N.J.
MCA   Museum of Contemporary Art, Dallas, Tex.
MG   Martínez Gallery, North Hollywood, Calif.
MHDYMM   M. H. De Young Memorial Museum, San Francisco, Calif. "American Indian Painting Competition." (Exhibit no longer held.)
MHS/H   Montana Historical Society, Helena, Mont.
MHS/W   Mattatuck Historical Society, Waterbury, Conn.
MJG   Martha Jackson Gallery, New York, N.Y.
MMA   Museum of Modern Art, New York, N.Y. "Exhibit of Indian Art," 1941.
MNA   Museum of Northern Arizona, Flagstaff, Ariz.

MNM   Museum of New Mexico, Fine Arts Museum, Santa Fe, N.M. In most instances, "Contemporary Indian Artists Annual Exhibition," formerly held annually during the summer.

MNM/T   Museum of New Mexico, Fine Arts Gallery Tour of the U.S., 1956–64. Selections made from the museum's "Contemporary Indian Artists Annual Exhibition."

MPI   Museum of the Plains Indian, Browning, Mont.

MSAC   Mt. Santanio College, Pomona, Calif.

MVAG   Mountain View Art Gallery, Altadena, Calif.

NACG   Navaho Arts and Crafts Guild, Window Rock, Ariz.

NAMC   Northeastern Oklahoma A. & M. College, Miami, Okla.

NAWA/T   National Association of Women Artists Tour of the U.S. and Japan, 1958–59.

NCHF   National Cowboy Hall of Fame, Oklahoma City, Okla.

NDU   University of North Dakota, Grand Forks, N. Dak.

NGA   National Gallery of Art, Washington, D.C. "Contemporary American Indian Painting," Oct. 1953.

NJSM   New Jersey State Museum, Trenton, N.J. "Contemporary American Indian Paintings," Nov. 8, 1959–Feb. 29, 1960.

NMSF   New Mexico State Fair, Albuquerque, N.M. Annually, 11 days in Sept.

NTF   Navaho Tribal Fair and Rodeo, Window Rock, Ariz. Annually, since 1946.

NYWF   New York World's Fair, 1964–65, New York, N.Y.

OAC   Oklahoma Art Center, Oklahoma City, Okla.

OHSM   Oklahoma Historical Society Museum, Oklahoma City, Okla.

OTP   Old Town Plaza, Albuquerque, N.M.

OU   University of Oklahoma, Norman, Okla.

OU/ET   University of Oklahoma European Tours; 60 paintings assembled by the University's College of Fine Arts for the U.S. Information Service in Rome and shown in nearly one dozen European cities. About half the exhibit was from the university collection, the remaining works were lent from the H. Adams, Denman, and Dietrich collections, June 1955–May 1956. Forty-seven paintings from the university collection toured Austria and Germany, from 1958 to 1961.

OU/MA   University of Oklahoma, Museum of Art, Norman, Okla.

PAC   Philbrook Art Center, Tulsa, Okla. In most instances, "Annual American Indian Artists Exhibition," held since 1946, generally in May.

PAC/T   American Indian Paintings from the permanent collection of Philbrook Art Center, tour of the U.S., Colombia, Guatemala, and Mexico City, 1947–1965.

PAM   Portland Art Museum, Portland, Oreg.

PAM/C   The Pasadena Art Museum, Pasadena, Calif.

PSC   Philander Smith College, Little Rock, Ark. "Exhibition of American Indian Paintings," 1961.

RAC   Roswell Museum and Art Center, Roswell, N.M.

RAC/M   Rochester Art Center, Rochester, Minn.

RG   Rehn Gallery, New York, N.Y.

RM   Riverside Museum, New York, N.Y.

RMAS   Rochester Museum of Arts and Sciences, Rochester, N.Y.

RRG   Raymond and Raymond Galleries, Los Angeles, Calif.

SAIEAIP   "Second Annual Invitational Exhibition of American Indian Paintings," 1965, USDI.

SAM   Seattle Art Museum, Seattle, Wash.

SAM/S   Springfield Art Museum, Springfield, Mo.

SBM   Santa Barbara Museum of Art, Santa Barbara, Calif.

SDU   University of South Dakota, Vermillion, S.Dak.

SFMA   San Francisco Museum of Art, San Francisco, Calif.

SFNB   Security First National Bank, Reseda, Calif.

SFWF   San Francisco World's Fair, San Francisco, Calif. 1939–40. (Includes Golden Gate International Exposition, Feb. 18–Oct. 29, 1939.)

SGAG   San Gabriel Artist's Guild, San Gabriel, Calif.

SI   Smithsonian Institution, Washington, D.C.

SIAE   "Society of Independent Artists Exhibition," *ca.* 1918–19, New York, N.Y.

SIECC   Sioux Indian Exhibit and Craft Center, Rapid City, S.Dak.

SI/T   Paintings from the collection of the Riverside Museum, New York, N.Y., circulated by the Smithsonian Institution, Oct. 1964–Mar. 1966.

SLAC   Salt Lake Art Center, Salt Lake City, Utah.

SM   Southwest Museum, Los Angeles, Calif.

SMM   The Norwich Free Academy, Slater Memorial Museum, Norwich, Conn.

SN   Scottsdale National Indian Art Exhibition. Annually in Feb. since 1962. Scottsdale, Ariz.

SPIM   Southern Plains Indians Museum, Anadarko, Okla.

SU   Stanford University, Stanford, Calif.

SUAG   Stanford University Art Gallery, Stanford, Calif.

TAC   Tuesday Afternoon Club, Glendale, Calif.

TAI   Terry Art Institute, Miami, Fla.

TKG   Tirca Karlis Gallery, Provincetown, Mass.

TM   Colorado Springs Fine Arts Center *and* Taylor Museum, Colorado Springs, Colo.

TMA   Toledo Museum of Art, Toledo, Ohio.

UC   University Club, Los Angeles, Calif.

UG   University of Georgia, Museum of Art, Athens, Ga.

UNM   University of New Mexico, Albuquerque, N.M.

UO   University of Ohio, Athens, Ohio.

USDI   U.S. Department of Interior, Washington, D.C. In most instances, The Art Gallery which opened in 1964; in a few instances, the Indian Arts and Crafts Board Offices and the Denman Collection Exhibit, May 12–Oct. 2, 1964.

USDS   "Contemporary American Indian Art," March 4–9, 1963, U.S. Department of State, Washington, D.C. Co–sponsored by U.S.I.A. Recreation Association.

UVM   University of Virginia, Museum of Fine Arts, Charlottesville, Va.

UWC   University Women's Club, Los Angeles, Calif.

UW/G   University of Washington, Henry Art Gallery, Seattle, Wash.

W   Whitney Museum of American Art, New York, N.Y.

WA   Wadsworth Atheneum, Hartford, Conn.

WAA   Westwood Art Association, West Los Angeles, Calif.

WAAG   Wichita Art Association, Inc., Gallery, Wichita, Kans.

WAM   Wichita Art Museum, Wichita, Kans.

WCH   Woman's Club of Hollywood, Hollywood, California.

WFS   Wilshire Federal Savings Art Salon, Los Angeles, Calif.

WM/T   Witte Memorial Art Museum Painting Exhibition. Regularly tours Texas, Louisiana and Oklahoma.

WMWA   Whitney Museum of Western Art, Cody, Wyo.

WRNGA   William Rockhill Nelson Gallery of Art *and* Atkins Museum of Fine Arts, Kansas City, Mo.

WU   Wichita University, Wichita, Kans.

WU/S   Wisconsin State College, Superior, Wisc.

YAIA   "Young American Indian Artists," Nov. 14, 1965–Jan. 16, 1966, at Riverside Museum, New York, N.Y.

YK/T   "Yeffe Kimball, a Retrospective Exhibition." A selection of her work exhibited and placed on tour of the U.S. by Philbrook Art Center, 1966–67.

YMCA   Young Men's Christian Association.

YWCA   Young Women's Christian Association.

BIBLIOGRAPHY

ABEITA, LOUISE [E-yeh-shure]
    1939   *I Am a Pueblo Girl*. New York: William Morrow & Co., 25 pp.
ALEXANDER, HARTLEY BURR
    1932   *Pueblo Indian Painting*. Nice, France: C. Szwedzicki, 18 pp. + 50 plates.
    1938   *Sioux Indian Painting*. Nice, France: C. Szwedzicki, 2 vols., portfolio.
ANONYMOUS
    1965   "The Ancient, New Talent of Jerome Tiger, Indian Artist." *Checkerboard Service
        Magazine* (March).
ARNOLD, ELLIOTT
    1947   *Blood Brother*. New York: Duell, Sloan & Pearce, 558 pp.

BAHTI, TOM
    1966   *Southwestern Indian Arts and Crafts*. Flagstaff, Ariz.: KC Publications, 34 pp.
BARRETT, STEPHEN M.
    1906   *Geronimo's Story of His Life*. New York: Duffield & Co., 216 pp.
BASS, ALTHA
    1950   *The Thankful People*. Caldwell, Idaho: Caxton Printers, 135 pp.
BERTHRONG, DONALD J.
    1963   *The Southern Cheyennes*. Norman: University of Oklahoma Press, 446 pp.
BIRNEY, HOFFMAN
    1935   *Ay-Chee, Son of the Desert*. Philadelphia: Penn Publishing Co., 112 pp.
BLEEKER, SONIA
    1963   *Indians*. New York: Golden Press.
BLISH, HELEN H.
    1967   *A Pictographic History of the Oglala Sioux*. Lincoln: University of Nebraska
        Press, 530 pp.
BLUE EAGLE, ACEE (ed.)
    1959   *Oklahoma Indian Painting—Poetry*. Tulsa, Okla.: Acorn Publishing Company.
BRINDZE, RUTH
    1951   *The Story of the Totem Pole*. New York: The Vanguard Press, 62 pp.
BROWN, WILLIAM COMPTON
    1961   *The Indian Side of the Story*. Spokane, Wash.: C. W. Hill Printing Co., 469 pp.

CARTER, E. RUSSELL
    1955   *The Gift is Rich*. New York: Friendship Press, 117 pp.
CATLIN, GEORGE
    1832   *Letters and Notes of the North American Indian*. New York: Wiley & Putnam,
        2 vols.
CLARK, ANN NOLAN
    1940– *Little Herder Series*. Washington: Office of Education, Bureau of Indian Affairs,
    1942   4 vols.
    1940a *Who Wants to be a Prairie Dog?* Washington: Office of Education, Bureau of
        Indian Affairs, 72 pp.
    1940b *Little Boy With Three Names*. Washington: Office of Education, Bureau of
        Indian Affairs, 55 pp.
    1941   *In My Mother's House*. New York: Viking Press, 56 pp.
    1942   *There Still Are Buffalo*. Washington: Office of Education, Bureau of Indian
        Affairs, 86 pp.
    1943   *Young Hunter of Picuris*. Washington: Office of Education, Bureau of Indian
        Affairs, 56 pp.

1944   *Bringer of the Mystery Dog.* Washington: Office of Education, Bureau of Indian
       Affairs, 84 pp.
1945   *Sun Journey.* Washington: Office of Education, Bureau of Indian Affairs, 122 pp.
1947   *Singing Sioux Cowboy.* Washington: Office of Education, Bureau of Indian
       Affairs, 114 pp.
1954   *Blue Canyon Horse.*
1957   *Little Indian Basket Maker.* Los Angeles: The Melmont Publishers, 31 pp.
1960   *Putie the Pack Rat and Other Desert Stories.*
1962   *The Desert People.* New York: Viking Press, 59 pp.

COCHRAN, GEORGE MCKEE
1939   *Indian Portraits of the Pacific Northwest.*

COHOE (Karen Petersen, ed.)
1964   *A Cheyenne Sketchbook.* Norman: University of Oklahoma Press, 96 pp.

CORNPLANTER, JESSE
1938   *Legends of the Longhouse.* Philadelphia: J. B. Lippincott, 216 pp.
1903   *Iroquois Indian Games and Dances.* 15 pp.

CURTIS, EDWARD S.,
1907– *The North American Indian.* Cambridge, Mass.: Harvard University Press,
1930   20 vols.

CUSICK, DAVID
1827   *Sketches of Ancient History of the Six Nations.* Lewiston, Maine: the Author, 28 pp.

DECAMP, L. SPRAGUE
1960   *Man and Power.* New York: Golden Press, 189 pp.

DEHUFF, ELIZABETH WILLIS
1922   *Taytay's Tales.* New York: Harcourt Brace & Co., 213 pp.
1924   *Taytay's Memories.* New York: Harcourt Brace & Co., 255 pp.
1926   *Swift Eagle of the Rio Grande.* Chicago: Rand McNally Co., 186 pp.
1930   *Five Little Katchinas.* Boston: Houghton Mifflin, 86 pp.

DEL MONTE, H. D.
n.d.   *Life of Chief Washakie and the Shoshone Indians.* Lander, Wyo.: Noble Hotel.

DINES, GLEN and RAYMOND PRICE
1961   *Dog Soldiers: the Famous Warrior Society of the Cheyenne Indians.* New York:
       Macmillan, n.p.

DOCKSTADER, FREDERICK J.
1954   *The Kachina and the White Man; the Influence of the White Man on the Hopi
       Indian Kachina Religion.* Bloomfield Hills, Mich.: Cranbrook Institute of
       Science, 202 pp.
1961   *Indian Art in America.* Greenwich, Conn.: New York Graphic Society, 224 pp.
       + 250 plates.

DODGE, RICHARD IRVING
1882   *Our Wild Indians: Thirty-three Years' Personal Experience Among the Red Men
       of the Great West.* Hartford, Conn.: A. D. Worthington & Co., 650 pp.

DOUGLAS, FREDERIC and RENÉ D'HARNONCOURT
1941   *Indian Art of the United States.* New York: Museum of Modern Art, 219 pp.

DUNN, JACOB PIATT, JR.
1886   *Massacres of the Mountains.* New York: Harper & Bro., 784 pp.

EWERS, JOHN CANFIELD
1939   *Plains Indian Painting.* Stanford, Calif: Stanford University Press, 84 pp.
1965   *Artists of the Old West.* New York: Doubleday & Co., 240 pp.

GIBBONS, LULU (comp.)
n.d.   *Indian Recipes from Cherokee Indians of Eastern Oklahoma.* Muskogee, Okla.:
       Hoffman Printing Co.

GLUBOK, SHIRLEY
1964   *The Art of the North American Indian.* New York: Harper & Row, n.p.

GOLDFRANK, ESTHER S.
  1962   *Isleta Paintings.* Washington: Bureau of American Ethnology, Bulletin 181. 299pp.
  1967   *The Artist of "Isleta Paintings."* Washington: Smithsonian Contributions to Anthropology, V., 227pp.
GREGORY, JACK and RENNARD STRICKLAND
  1967   *Sam Houston With the Cherokees, 1829–1833.* Austin: University of Texas Press, 206pp.
GRINNELL, GEORGE BIRD
  1895   *Story of the Indian.* New York: D. Appleton & Co., 270pp.
  1915   *The Fighting Cheyennes.* New York: C. Scribner's Sons, 431pp.
  1923   *The Cheyenne Indians.* New Haven, Conn.: Yale University Press, 2 vols.

HAMILTON, CHARLES (ed.)
  1950   *Cry of the Thunderbird; the American Indian's Own Story.* New York: Macmillan, 283pp.
HAMM, MARY ALICE and WILLIAM S. INGLISH
  1960   *A History of the Baird-Scales Family.* Tahlequah, Okla.: Go-Ye Mission.
HANNUM, ALBERTA
  1945   *Spin a Silver Dollar.* New York: Viking Press, 173pp.
  1958   *Paint the Wind.* New York: Viking Press, 206pp.
HARRINGTON, MARK RAYMOND
  1921   *Religion and Ceremonies of the Lenape.* New York: Museum of the American Indian, 249pp.
HASKELL. ARNOLD L.
  1960   *The Story of Dance.* London: Rathbone Books, Ltd., 93pp.
HASSRICK, ROYAL B.
  1964   *The Sioux; Life and Customs of a Warrior Society.* Norman: University of Oklahoma Press, 337pp.
HEBARD, GRACE RAYMOND
  1930   *Washakie: an Account of Indian Resistance of the Covered Wagon and Union Pacific Railroad Invasions of Their Territory.* Cleveland: Arthur H. Clark, 337pp.
HOLTON, ANNE TENNYSON
  1964   *Song of the Cherokees.* Privately published.
HOWARD, JAMES H.
  1960   "Butterfly's Mandan Winter Count: 1833–1876." *Ethnohistory*, VII #1 (January–March), pp. 28–43.
HYDE, GEORGE E.
  1937   *Red Cloud's Folk; a History of the Oglala Sioux Indians.* Norman: University of Oklahoma Press, 331pp.
  1956   *A Sioux Chronicle.* Norman: University of Oklahoma Press, 334pp.
  1961   *Spotted Tail's Folk: A History of the Brulé Sioux.* Norman: University of Oklahoma Press, 330pp.

JACOBSON, OSCAR B.
  1929   *Kiowa Indian Art.* Nice, France: C. Szwedzicki, 11pp. + 30 plates.
  1952   *North American Indian Costumes, 1564–1960.* Nice, France: C. Szwedzicki, 50 plates.
  1964   *Indian Artists from Oklahoma.* Norman: University of Oklahoma.
JACOBSON, OSCAR B. and JEANNE D'UCEL
  1950   *American Indian Painters.* Nice, France: C. Szwedzicki, portfolio.
JAMES, AHLEE
  1927   *Tewa Firelight Tales.* New York: Longmans, Green, 248pp.
JOHNSON, W. FLETCHER
  1891   *The Red Record of the Sioux; Life of Sitting Bull and History of the Indian War of 1890–91.* Philadelphia: Edgewood Publishing Co., 606pp.

JOSEPHY, ALVIN M., Jr. (ed.)
  1961a *The American Heritage Book of Indians*. New York: American Heritage Publishing Co., 424 pp.
  1961b *The Patriot Chiefs; a Chronicle of American Indian Leadership*. New York: Viking Press, 364 pp.
JUDD, MARY CATHERINE
  1902 *Wigwam Stories Told by American Indians*. Boston: Ginn & Co., 276 pp.

KABOTIE, FRED
  1949 *Designs From the Ancient Mimbreños, With a Hopi Interpretation*. San Francisco: Grabhorn Press, 80 pp.
KEECH, ROY A.
  1940 *Pagans Praying*. Clarendon, Tex.: Clarendon Press, 94 pp.
KEIM, RANDOLPH
  1885 *Sheridan's Troopers on the Borders*. Philadelphia: David McKay, 308 pp.
KELLY, LUTHER S.
  1926 *Yellowstone Kelly: the Memoirs of Luther S. Kelly*. New Haven, Conn.: Yale University Press, 268 pp.
KE MOTTA
  1952 *Sally of Woolaroc*. Bartlesville, Okla.: Frank Phillips Foundation, Inc.
KENNARD, EDWARD A.
  1944 *Field Mouse Goes to War*. Washington: Office of Education, Bureau of Indian Affairs, 76 pp.
  1948 *Little Hopi Hopihoya*. Washington: Office of Education, Bureau of Indian Affairs, 201 pp.
KENNEDY, MICHAEL STEPHEN (ed.)
  1961 *The Assiniboines; From the Accounts of the Old Ones Told to First Boy (James Larpenteur Long)*. Norman: University of Oklahoma Press, 209 pp.
KIMBALL, YEFFE and JEAN ANDERSON
  1965 *The Art of American Indian Cooking*. Garden City, N.Y.: Doubleday & Co., 215 pp.

LAFARGE, OLIVER
  1956 *A Pictorial History of the American Indian*. New York: Crown Publishers, 272 pp.
  1960 *The American Indian*. New York: Golden Press, 213 pp.
LAFLESCHE, FRANCIS
  1900 *The Middle Five; Indian Boys at School*. Boston: Small, Maynard & Co., 227 pp.
LEEKLEY, THOMAS B.
  1965 *The World of Manabozho; Tales of the Chippewa Indians*. New York: Vanguard Press.
LLEWELLYN, KARL N. and E. ADAMSON HOEBEL
  1941 *The Cheyenne Way*. Norman: University of Oklahoma Press, 360 pp.
LYBACK, JOHANNA R. M.
  1963 *Indian Legends of Eastern America;* and *Indian Legends of the Great West*. Chicago: Lyons and Carnahan, Inc., 2 vols.

MADRANO, DAN M.
  1955 *Heap Big Laugh*. Tulsa, Okla.: no publisher.
MANNING, PHYLLIS A.
       Spirit Rocks and Silver Magic. Caldwell, Idaho: Caxton Printers.
MARQUIS, THOMAS B.
  1931 *A Warrior Who Fought Custer*. Minneapolis: The Midwest Co., 384 pp.
MARRIOTT, ALICE
  1952 *Winter-telling Stories*. New York: Thomas Y. Crowell, 84 pp.
MAYHALL, MILDRED P.
  1962 *The Kiowas*. Norman: University of Oklahoma Press, 315 pp.
MOYER, JOHN W.
  1957 *Famous Indian Chiefs*. Chicago: M. A. Donohue & Co., 86 pp.

NEIHARDT, JOHN G.
1932 *Black Elk Speaks.* New York: W. Morrow & Co., 280pp.
NELSON, JOHN LOUW
1937 *Rhythm for Rain.* Boston: Houghton Mifflin, 271pp.
NEWELL, CICERO
1912 *Indian Stories.* Boston: Silver, Burdett & Co., 191pp.
NUTCHUCK
Back to the Smoky Sea. New York: Julian Messner.
Son of the Smoky Sea. New York: Julian Messner.
NYE, WILBUR STURTEVANT
1962 *Bad Medicine and Good; Tales of the Kiowas.* Norman: University of Oklahoma Press, 291pp.

PARKER, ARTHUR C.
1910 *Iroquois Uses of Maize and Other Food Plants.* Albany: New York State Museum, Bulletin 44, 119pp.
1913 *The Code of Handsome Lake, the Seneca Prophet.* Albany: New York State Museum, Bulletin 163, 148pp.
1923 *Seneca Myths and Folk-Tales.* Buffalo, N.Y.: Buffalo Historical Society, 465pp.
PAYTIAMO, JAMES P.
1932 *Flaming Arrow's People.* New York: Duffield & Green, 157pp.
PENNINGTON, ROBERT
1961 *Oscar Howe, Artist of the Sioux.* Sioux Falls, So. Dak.: Dakota Territorial Centennial Commission, 61pp.
PENNEY, GRACE JACKSON
1953 *Tales of the Cheyennes.* Boston: Houghton Mifflin, 117pp.
PETERSEN, KAREN D.
1968 *Howling Wolf; a Pictorial History of the Cheyenne Indians.* Palo Alto, Calif.: American West Publishing Co., 64pp.
PETERSON, HAROLD L.
1965 *American Indian Tomahawks.* New York: Museum of the American Indian, 142pp. + 314 plates.
PIERSON, WILLIAM H., JR., and MARTHA DAVIDSON
1960 *Arts of the United States.* New York: McGraw-Hill, 452pp.
PRAUS, ALEXIS
1962 *The Sioux, 1798–1922; a Dakota Winter Count.* Bloomfield Hills, Mich.: Cranbrook Institute of Science, 32pp.

RAABE, MARTHA
1942 *The Little Lost Sioux.* Chicago: A. Whitman & Co., 30pp.
ROOSEVELT, THEODORE
1899 *The Rough Riders.* New York: Charles Scribner's Sons, 298pp.
RUSHMORE, HELEN and WOLF ROBE HUNT
1963 *The Dancing Horses of Acoma; and Other Acoma Indian Stories.* Cleveland: World Publishing Co., 164pp.

SANDOZ, MARI
1953 *Cheyenne Autumn.* New York: McGraw-Hill, 282pp.
1961 *These Were the Sioux.* New York: Hastings House, 118pp.
SCHEVILL, MARGARET [LINK]
1956 *The Pollen Path; a Collection of Navajo Myths Retold.* Stanford, Calif.: Stanford University Press, 205pp.
SCHMITT, MARTIN F., and DEE BROWN
1948 *Fighting Indians of the West.* New York: Charles Scribner's Sons, 362pp.
SHUFELDT, ROBERT WILSON
1889 *A Navajo Artist and his Notions of Mechanical Drawing.* Washington: Smithsonian Institution, Annual Report for 1886, pp. 240–244.

SLOAN, JOHN and OLIVER LAFARGE
  1931 *Introduction to American Indian Art.* New York: The Exposition of Indian Tribal Arts, Inc., 2 Vols.
SMITH, DECOST
  1943 *Indian Experiences.* Caldwell, Idaho: Caxton Printers, 387 pp.
SMYTH, ED
  1965 "Meet the Great Talent of Jerome Tiger." *Checker Links* (January–February).
SONNICHSEN, CHARLES LELAND
  1958 *The Mescalero Apaches.* Norman: University of Oklahoma Press, 315 pp.
STANDING BEAR, LUTHER
  1928 *My People, the Sioux.* Boston: Houghton Mifflin, 288 pp.
STEINER, STAN
  1961 *The Last Horse.* New York: Macmillan, 71 pp.
STIRLING, MATTHEW W. (ed.)
  1938 *Three Pictographic Autobiographies of Sitting Bull.* Washington: Smithsonian Miscellaneous Contributions, No. 97. 57 pp. + 46 plates.
  1955 *Indians of the Americas.* Washington: National Geographic Society, 431 pp.
STREET, ELOISE (comp.)
  1963 *Sepass Poems: the Songs of Y-Ail-Mihth.* New York: Vantage Press, 110 pp.

TANNER, CLARA LEE
  1957 *Southwest Indian Painting.* Tucson: University of Arizona Press, 157 pp.
TSATOKE, MONROE
  1957 *The Peyote Ritual; Visions and Descriptions.* San Francisco: Grabhorn Press, 66 pp.

UNDERHILL, RUTH M.
  1938 *Singing for Power; the Song Magic of the Papago Indians of Southern Arizona.* Berkeley: University of California Press, 158 pp.
  1940 *The Papago Indians of Arizona, and their Relatives the Pima.* Washington: Office of Education, Bureau of Indian Affairs, 68 pp.
  1944 *Pueblo Crafts.* Washington: Office of Education, Bureau of Indian Affairs, 147 pp.
  1946 *Workaday Life of the Pueblos.* Washington: Office of Education, Bureau of Indian Affairs, 174 pp.
  1951 *People of the Crimson Evening.* Washington: Office of Education, Bureau of Indian Affairs, 127 pp.
  1965 *Red Man's Religion; Beliefs and Practices of the Indians North of Mexico.* Chicago: University of Chicago Press, 301 pp.

VELARDE, PABLITA
  1960 *Old Father, the Story Teller.* Globe, Ariz.: Dale Stuart King, 66 pp.
VESTAL, STANLEY
  1932 *Sitting Bull, Champion of the Sioux.* Boston: Houghton Mifflin, 350 pp.
  1934 *Warpath: the True Story of the Fighting Sioux Told in a Biography of Chief White Bull.* Boston: Houghton Mifflin, 291 pp.

WATERS, FRANK
  1963 *The Book of the Hopi.* New York: Viking Press, 347 pp.
WILLOYA, WILLIAM and VINSON BROWN
  1962 *Warriors of the Rainbow.* Healdsburg, Calif: The Naturegraph Co., 94 pp.
WYMAN, LELAND C.
  1965 *Big Lefthanded, Pioneer Navajo Artist.* Flagstaff, Ariz.: Museum of No. Arizona, *Plateau.*
  1966 *Snake Skins and Hoops.* Flagstaff, Ariz.: Museum of No. Arizona, *Plateau.*
  1967 *The Sacred Mountains of the Navaho—Four Paintings by Harrison Begay.* Flagstaff, Ariz.: Museum of No. Ariz., *Plateau.*